EU Enlargement

Current Challenges and Strategic Choices

P.I.E. Peter Lang

Bruxelles · Bern · Berlin · Frankfurt am Main · New York · Oxford · Wien

Finn LAURSEN (ed.)

EU Enlargement

Current Challenges and Strategic Choices

Multiple Europes
No.50

The book is published under the auspices of the EU Centre of Excellence at Dalhousie University with financial support from the European Commission

Éditions scientifiques internationales
Brussels, 2013
1 avenue Maurice, B-1050 Brussels, Belgium
www.peterlang.com; info@peterlang.com

Printed in Germany

ISSN 1376-0904
ISBN 978-2-87574-067-0
D/2013/5678/59

CIP also available from the British Library, GB and Library of Congress Cataloging-in-Publication Data

Bibliographic information published by "Die Deutsche Nationalbibliothek"
"Die Deutsche Nationalbibliothek" lists this publication in the "Deutsche Nationalbibliografie"; detailed bibliographic data is available on the Internet at <http://dnb.d-nb.de>.

Contents

Preface

Historically enlargements of the European Union (EU) have often been linked with deepening of integration. It could be argued that there is enlargement fatigue at the moment. Some may see it is linked with the eurozone crisis, which takes up much of the time and energy of EU leaders. Still, the next enlargement, with Croatia set to join the EU in 2013, is just around the corner, and there are a number of candidate countries that have expectations to the EU and hope to join in the future. This raises questions about the necessary preparations both in the EU and in the applicant countries.

This book deals with some of these issues. It is among of the outcomes of a project entitled "Widening and Deepening of European Integration: Challenges and Strategic Choices Facing the European Union." A call for papers went out in November 2011 and a number of papers were selected and subsequently presented at a conference organized by the EU Centre of Excellence (EUCE) at Dalhousie University, Halifax, NS, Canada, in April 2012. The chapters in this book are based on a set of papers dealing with enlargement issues, which were revised after the conference. Papers focusing on the eurozone crisis and other internal policy challenges will be published in a separate volume.

In the call for papers we asked, *inter alia*:

"What are the prospects for future enlargements? [...] What obstacles have to be overcome in the Western Balkan countries which want to become EU members? Will the membership perspective be a stimulus for reforms? What are the lessons from Bulgarian and Romanian accession in 2007? Were they insufficiently prepared? And, in the longer term, may some countries now offered Eastern Partnerships become candidates for EU accession?" The chapters in the book shed light on these and connected questions, many written by scholars that have deep knowledge about many of the applicant states as well as the EU. Hopefully the book will stimulate renewed thinking about enlargement, a topic that has been somewhat neglected lately.

Finn Laursen

Halifax, September 2012

Acknowledgements

This book is published under the auspices of the EU Centre of Excellence (EUCE) at Dalhousie University, Halifax, Nova Scotia, Canada. The EUCE is currently financed by a second three-year grant by the European Commission, now administered by the Service for Foreign Policy Instruments. Without the support from the Commission, the production of this book would not have been possible. The current grant period expires on 4 December 2012.

The editor, who has directed the EUCE at Dalhousie since the beginning in 2006, also wants to acknowledge the contributions of Danijela Juric, the Administrative Secretary of EUCE. She assisted with the logistics in connection with the research project, including the 6th annual EUCE conference, 11-13 April 2012, where early versions of the chapters were first presented and discussed. Also thanks to Karen Snaterse, Faton Tony Bislimi and Carolyn Ferguson with practical assistance during the conference.

I want to thank Dr. Robert Summerby-Murray, Dean, Faculty of Arts and Social Sciences, Dalhousie University for welcoming the participants on the 11th of April and Dr. Donna Rogers, Associate Dean Academic, Faculty of Arts and Social Sciences, for addressing the opening session on the 12th April. Special thanks go to His Excellency Ambassador Matthias Brinkmann, Head of the European Delegation to Canada, for coming to Halifax on this occasion and giving a very substantial and informative opening address. I further want to thank Kasper Gimsing, Policy Advisor, the Danish Embassy, Ottawa, for presenting the programme of the Danish Presidency. The recognition given by the Dalhousie and EU leaderships was much appreciated.

Jenn Harris, Phyllis Singer and Carolyn Ferguson are thanked for their diligent work as language checkers and copy editors. Carolyn is also thanked for helping with typesetting and preparation of the index.

Finally I want to thank PIE Peter Lang, Brussels, for agreeing to publish this book. In particular I thank the director, Emilie Menz, and the editor of the "Multiple Europes" series, Hagen Schulz-Forberg, for excellent and efficient cooperation, which is much appreciated.

Finn Laursen

Halifax, December 2012

List of Abbreviations

AFSJ	Area of Freedom, Security and Justice
AKEL	Progressive Party of the Working Peoples
AKP	Justice and Development Party
AWS	Solidarity Electoral Action
CAP	Common Agricultural Program
CAPPD	Croatian Agency for Protection of Personal Data
CARDS	Community Assistance for Reconstruction, Development and Stabilization
CC	Candidate Countries
CC	Control of Corruption Index
CDU	Christian Democratic Union
CEE	Central and Eastern Europe
CEECs	Central and Eastern European Countries
CFSP	Common Foreign and Security Policy
CHP	Republican People's Party
CSU	Christian Social Union
CVM	Cooperation and Verification Mechanism
DISY	*Dimokratikós Sinayermós*
EA	Europe Agreements
EC	European Communities
ECB	European Central Bank
ECJ	European Court of Justice
ECR	European Conservatives and Reformists Group
ECSC	European Coal and Steel Community
EEC	European Economic Community
EEZ	Exclusive Economic Zone
EFA	European Free Alliance
EFTA	European Free Trade Association
ELDR	European Liberal Democrat and Reform party
EMU	Economic and Monetary Union
ENP	European Neighbourhood Policy

EP	European Parliament
EPC	European Political Cooperation
EPP	European People's Party
EU	European Union
EULEX	European Union Rule of Law Mission in Kosovo
EUL-NGL	European United Left – Nordic Green Left
EUROTOM	European Atomic Energy Community
EUSR	European Union Special Representative
FE	Fixed Effects Regression Model
FIC	Flight Information Region
FRY	Former Republic of Yugoslavia
FYROM	Former Yugoslav Republic of Macedonia
GAL	Green/alternative/libertarian
GDP	Gross domestic product
GONG	Građani organizirano nadgledaju glasanje
HDI	Human Development Index
ICO	International Civilian Office
ICR	International Civilian Representative
ICTY	International Criminal Tribunal for Yugoslavia
IGC	Intergovernmental conference
IPA	Instrument for Pre-Accession Assistance
ISPA	Instrument for Structural Policies for Pre-Accession
ITA	Interim Trade Agreement
JHA	Justice and Home Affairs
KHD	Christian Democratic Movement
KKM	Kaufmann, Kraay, and Mastruzzi
KSCM	Communist Party of Bohemia and Moravia
LPR	League of Polish Families
MEP	Member of the European Parliament
MHP	National Movement Party
MLP	Malta Labour Party
MS	Member states
NAO	National Authorizing Officer
NATO	North Atlantic Treaty Organization
NGO	Non-Government Organizations

ODS	Czech Civic Democrats
ÖVP	Die Österreichische Volkspartei (Austrian People's Party)
PES	Party of European Socialists
PHARE	Poland and Hungary: Assistance for Restructuring their Economies
PiS	Law and Justice Party
PO	Civic Platform
PSL	Polish Peasant Party
QMV	Qualified Majority Voting
RoC	Republic of Cyprus
SAA	Stabilisation and Association Agreement
SAP	Stabilisation and Association Process
SAPARD	Special Accession Programme for Agriculture and Rural Development
SEA	Single European Act
SEIO	Serbian European Integration Office
SFRY	Socialist Federal Republic of Yugoslavia
SLD	Democratic Left Alliance
TAN	Traditionalism/authority/nationalism
TEA	Treaty of European Union
TFEU	Treaty on the Function of European Union
TRNC	Turkish Republic of Northern Cyprus
UBP	National Unity Party
UMP	Union for a Popular Movement
UN	United Nations
UNMIK	United Nations Mission in Kosovo
UP	Labour Union
USSR	Union of the Soviet Socialist Republics
US	United States
UWWT	Urban Waste Water Treatment
VMRO-DPMNE	Internal Macedonian Revolutionary Organization – Democratic Party for Macedonian National Unity
WB	Western Balkan
WGI	World Governance Indicators

PART I

ISSUES IN ENLARGEMENT POLICY

EU Enlargement

Issues and Policy Developments

Finn LAURSEN

Introduction

On 1 May 2004, the European Union (EU) became a Union of 25 Member States (EU-25). Eight Central and Eastern European Countries (CEECs) as well as Cyprus and Malta joined the EU in its largest enlargement. Before this widening of the Union could take place, both sides, the ten newcomers and the EU itself, had to go through various reforms in the hope that the new much larger Union would be able to function in a satisfactory way. The next enlargement followed in 2007, when Bulgaria and Romania joined. Croatia is set to join in 2013. The current candidates include Iceland, Turkey, and eventually the remaining countries in the Western Balkans. Macedonia – or the Former Yugoslav Republic of Macedonia as we are supposed to say – is an official candidate, but because of the name dispute with Greece accession, negotiations have not started. Serbia and Montenegro are now also official candidates.

During time the EU, starting with the six original Member States of the European Communities (EC) in the 1950s, has kept enlarging. Where will it end? When will the remaining eligible countries join? What are the membership conditions? Have they changed over time?

In connection with EU enlargements in the past, the debate was often defined as "Deepening versus Widening" (Wallace 1989; De la Serre 1991; Wessels 1996). Widening, or enlargement, was linked with deepening because decision-making in a wider union was expected to become more difficult.

The first enlargement agreed at the summit in The Hague in 1969 was, for instance, linked with the creation of European Political Cooperation (EPC), the foreign policy cooperation among the Member States, which started in 1970, as well as Economic and Monetary Union (EMU). The latter did not materialise at the time, but EPC was in place when the UK, Ireland and Denmark joined the then existing Communities in 1973 (Preston 1997, pp. 23-45).

Greek membership followed in 1981 without similar EC reforms, but Spanish and Portuguese membership in 1986 came in parallel with the Single European Act (SEA), which was the first major reform of the EC (*ibid.*, pp. 46-86). In order to complete the internal market, qualified majority voting (QMV) was introduced for harmonisation of national legislation necessary to complete the single internal market. The SEA thereby contributed to giving the process of European integration a new momentum in the mid-1980s.

The enlargement that brought Austria, Finland and Sweden into the EU on 1 January 1995 was made on the basis of the Maastricht Treaty, which had created the EU in 1993 (*ibid.*, 87-109). It deepened integration in various ways, *inter alia* by more concretely outlining three phases towards EMU. It also gave the European Parliament (EP) the right of co-decision in a number of areas, and it added several new policy chapters, even including education and culture, and by upgrading EPC to become Common Foreign and Security Policy (CFSP), which for the first time also included defence policy. Maastricht further started a more formalised Justice and Home Affairs (JHA) cooperation (Laursen & Vanhoonacker 1992).

The Maastricht Treaty foresaw an intergovernmental conference (IGC) to review the treaty in 1996. This conference, which produced the Amsterdam Treaty, was seen as the conference that would make the next big enlargement possible, allowing for the accession of the CEECs, which had now applied for membership. Cyprus and Malta applied for membership in 1990. Ten CEECs applied during the mid-1990s in the following order: Hungary, 31 March 1994; Poland, 5 April 1994; Romania, 22 June 1995; Slovakia, 27 June 1995; Latvia, 13 October 1995; Estonia, 24 November 1995; Lithuania, 8 December 1995; Bulgaria, 14 December 1995; the Czech Republic, 17 January 1996; and Slovenia, 10 June 1996 (Friis 1999, Appendix A).

All these applications came after the EU decided at its summit in Copenhagen in June 1993 that the CEECs would be able to join in the future once certain specified conditions were fulfilled.

Prior to the applications from the CEECs, Turkey had applied in 1987. However, the Commission had concluded in its opinion in 1989 that Turkey, although in principle eligible, was not ready for membership (European Commission 1989). Only in 1999 was Turkey officially recognized as a candidate, after a lot of political pressure.

Most enlargements have been controversial. French President de Gaulle twice vetoed British membership, in 1963 and 1967 respectively. Among the reasons: The UK was considered too Atlantic/US-oriented. Greek membership in 1981 was also controversial. The European

Commission actually advised against Greek membership, finding the country insufficiently prepared. But the Council of Ministers overrode the Commission for political reasons, in recognition of introduction of democracy in the country after the dictatorial rule of the colonels. The main problems with the Iberian enlargement in 1986 were agricultural – and fisheries – policy and contributions from the Structural Funds. The former European Free Trade Association (EFTA) countries that joined in 1995 did not pose serious economic problems. However, there were doubts about their foreign policy orientations (Preston 1997).

Why Enlargement?

To put the current situation into context, we need to dwell a little on the big Eastern enlargement in 2004. It was a gradual and rather long process. It took time partly because it was a group of countries that needed to go through economic and political transitions from Communist rule and central economic planning to democracy and market economy. At the same time, however, it is fair to say that a number of Member States of EU-15 were not excited about the Eastern enlargement. Any change of this *ampleur* affects vested interests. If we use rational models to explain enlargement, we will face a puzzle (Sedelmeier 2000). Countries depending on the Common Agricultural Policy (CAP) had no interests in the accession of the competitors from the East. The hesitant countries included France, which has benefitted a lot from the CAP. Nor did countries receiving substantial amounts of money from the Structural Funds have an interest in getting in the competitors from the East. Even if it can be argued that all EU-15 had in interest in stability in Europe, the EU could try to contribute to stability in other ways, such as the financial aid which was given to the CEECs anyway from early on after the end of the Cold War.

For some of the EU-15 Member States there was a rational argument in favour, namely a larger market. Freer trade and investment flows would contribute to economic growth, but again these effects could largely be realized through free trade agreements.

In the end, enlargement was a political choice taken by EU-15, much aided by the European Commission, which played the role of a supranational leader or policy entrepreneur. The decisive decisions taken along the way by the European Council from the Copenhagen meeting in June 1993, when the CEECs were promised membership, to the Copenhagen meeting in December 2002, when eight CEECs as well as Cyprus and Malta concluded their accession negotiations, were largely based on recommendations from the Commission.

The many statements in favour of assisting the CEECs after the end of the Cold War – indeed, during the Cold War, too – gradually added up to a discourse that implied a moral commitment to accept these states as members. Much of this discourse was based on a certain idea of a collective European identity. It focused upon democracy and human rights. A leading scholar talked about "rhetorical entrapment" (Schimmelfennig 2003). These normative aspects dealing with democracy and individual rights were reinforced within the EU by successive treaty reforms, from the Maastricht Treaty in 1993 to the Lisbon Treaty in 2009

Seen from the perspectives of the applicant countries, the EU was a success story. Integration started with six countries in the early 1950s. At that time, the UK and the Scandinavian countries did not join. But the alternative organisation, the EFTA, which they created in 1960 together with Switzerland and Portugal, turned out to be a disappointing organisation. Eventually most EFTA countries concluded that the costs of exclusion from the EC were too great (Mattli 1999). They joined a club whose rules some of them did not fully support. This included the UK and Denmark, which joined in the first enlargement in 1973, and which arguably have been foot-dragging members since. The last EFTA countries to join in 1995, Austria, Sweden and Finland, were those who, for geopolitical reasons, had concluded that they could not join during the Cold War. Similarly the CEECs could only contemplate joining after the end of the Cold War. In between, Greece, Spain and Portugal could only join after they had shed authoritarian regimes.

So the EC/EU has been an expanding club of democratic European states. In parallel with this geographical expansion, the process of European integration has also gradually expanded the functional scope of integration, from limited sector integration in the 1950s to become a full-fledged internal market with a number of common policies by the early 1990s. The Maastricht Treaty set out to crown economic integration with an EMU but also take some, albeit modest, steps towards political union.

This process has contributed to creating what Karl Deutsch called a "security community" in Europe (Deutsch *et al.* 1957). This community is now gradually been expanded to include the whole of Europe. That in the end arguably can be seen as the most important achievement of European integration.

However, EMU, which created the single currency, the euro, in 1999, had structural defects, which contributed to the current economic crisis in the eurozone, the group of 17 countries that have introduced the euro. In connection with this current crisis, there is renewed talk of deepening of integration, by moving towards a fiscal union and improved possibilities of adopting growth policies. The crisis has clearly demonstrated the asymmetry between a centralised monetary union and decentralized fiscal policy and the need for further integration, including possibilities of mutualising debt, for instance, by allowing the European Central Bank (ECB) to issue eurobonds.

The Development of EU Enlargement Policy

From the start of the European integration process, from the Schuman Plan in 1950 and the creation of the European Coal and Steel Community (ECSC) in 1952, with six Member States, viz., France, West Germany, Italy, the Netherlands, Belgium and Luxembourg, the idea was that other European states that so wished could join, and after the creation of the two other Communities, the European Economic Community (EEC) and the European Atomic Energy Community (EURATOM) in 1958, these Communities went through three enlargements before the Maastricht Treaty created the EU, in 1993.

The Maastricht Treaty in Article O stipulated:

> Any European State may apply to become a Member of the Union. It shall address its application to the Council, which shall act unanimously after consulting the Commission and after receiving the assent of the European Parliament, which shall act by an absolute majority of its component members.
>
> The conditions of admission and the adjustments to the Treaties on which the Union is founded which such admission entails shall be the subject of an agreement between the Member States and the applicant State. This agreement shall be submitted for ratification by all the contracting States in accordance with their respective constitutional requirements.

Article O was procedure oriented. The basic procedure has not really changed since then. The EP must give its "assent" – now called "consent" since the Lisbon Treaty. The EP has had this power since the SEA in 1987. It means that the EP has a veto on enlargement. Given the fact that unanimity is required in the Council, each Member State also has a veto. A new member must be European, which has never been well defined. But Morocco, which applied in 1987, was told that it cannot join because it is not European. Although the Commission opinion on Turkish membership in 1989 was negative, the question of eligibility was answered in the affirmative. So Turkey can hope eventually to join, once certain political and economic obstacles have been removed. At the moment it does not look so good for Turkey, though. Negotiations have largely ground to a halt.

The European Council meeting in Maastricht in December 1991 issued a short statement on enlargement, saying "any European State whose system of Government is founded on the principle of democracy may apply to become a member of the Union." In reality, democracy has been an implied principle from the beginning, which partly explains the delayed memberships of Greece, Spain and Portugal. This condition was confirmed by the Amsterdam Treaty, which added a reference to a new Article 6 that states: "The Union is founded on the principles of liberty, democracy, respect for human rights and fundamental freedoms and the rule of law".

In December 1991, the European Council had invited the Commission to prepare a report on enlargement for the Lisbon summit in June 1992. The Commission presented this report on "Europe and the challenge of enlargement" to the meeting in Lisbon. It referred to a new context, partly because of the completion of the internal market and the signing of the Maastricht Treaty, and partly because of the end of the Cold War. The integration of the CEECs was now seen as "a historic opportunity". It could contribute to the "unification of the whole of Europe" (European Commission 1992).

The Lisbon Report suggested the following conditions of membership:

1. Democracy and the respect of fundamental human rights;

2. Acceptance of the Community system and capacity to implement it, including a functioning and competitive market economy, and an adequate legal and administrative framework;

3. Acceptance and capacity to implement the Common Foreign and Security Policy "as it evolves over the coming years".

The concern at this time was still mainly with the applicants that subsequently joined in 1995, then all members of EFTA. That Austria, Sweden and Finland had been neutral or non-aligned during the Cold War explains the explicit reference to CFSP. At the time of the Lisbon summit in 1992, none of the CEECs had applied for membership, but it was known that they wanted to join. Association agreements, called "Europe Agreements", had been negotiated with Poland, Hungary and Czechoslovakia – later renegotiated with the Czech Republic and Slovakia after the country split up in 1993 –, and negotiations on similar agreements were taking place with Bulgaria and Romania. Trade and cooperation agreements had been signed with the three Baltic States, Estonia, Latvia and Lithuania, as well as Albania.

The Europe Agreements acknowledged that membership was the goal of the CEECs, but the EC side did not offer such membership at the time. The subtle language used, for instance, in the Hungarian agreement, was that "the final objective of Hungary is to become a member of the Community and that this association, in the view of the

Parties, will help to achieve this objective" (OJ L 347, 31 December 1993).

A breakthrough concerning membership for the CEECs came at the Copenhagen meeting of the European Council, 21-22 June 1993, where the heads of state or government agreed that "the associated countries in Central and Eastern Europe that so desire shall become members of the European Union". The economic and political conditions were listed in the following way:

> Membership requires that the candidate country has achieved stability of institutions guaranteeing democracy, the rule of law, human rights and respect for and protection of minorities, the existence of a functioning market economy as well as the capacity to cope with competitive pressure and market forces within the Union. Membership presupposes the candidate's ability to take on the obligations of membership including adherence to the aims of political, economic and monetary union (quoted from Laursen & Vanhoonacker 1994, p. 458).

The presidency conclusions then went on: "The Union's capacity to absorb new members, while maintaining the momentum of European integration, is also an important consideration in the general interest of both the Union and the candidate countries".

Put differently, both the EU and the candidate countries had to be ready. Widening was linked with the EU's capacity to continue the process of integration, although different Member States had different ideas of what that meant, making the Member States decisive actors in the process.

Agenda 2000[1]

Agenda 2000 was the name given to the opinions and composite documents on enlargement published as a series of communications from the Commission on 15 July 1997, after the negotiation of the Amsterdam Treaty (European Commission 1997).

Concerning the applicants, the Commission concluded that Poland, the Czech Republic, Hungary, Estonia and Slovenia were closest to meeting the membership criteria set up at the European Council meeting in Copenhagen in June 1993. It was therefore recommended to start accession negotiations with these five CEECs. The remaining five should receive further assistance through a reinforced pre-accession strategy.

---

1 The author followed the Eastern enlargements and their preparation in earlier publications; see Laursen 1996, 2001, 2005 and 2006a. Subsequent sections partly rely on these publications.

Basically, politics put one country into the second group of countries not yet ready to start accession negotiations, and economics put four countries, Latvia, Lithuania, Bulgaria and Romania, into the second group, leaving five CEECs plus Cyprus (5+1) in the group that should start negotiations first.

The differentiation proposed by the Commission between the five front runners and the remaining five in a second group led to a fair amount of discussion during the fall of 1997. (At this point in time, Malta had withdrawn its application). The European Council decided in Luxembourg in December 1997 "to launch an accession process comprising the ten Central and East European applicant States and Cyprus". The accession process would be launched on 30 March 1998 by a meeting of the foreign ministers of the fifteen Member States and eleven applicant countries. There would be an enhanced pre-accession strategy including accession partnerships and increased pre-accession aid. Bilateral intergovernmental conferences would be convened in the spring of 1998 to begin negotiations with Cyprus, Hungary, Poland, Estonia, the Czech Republic and Slovenia (5+1). At the same time, "the preparation of negotiations with Romania, Slovakia, Latvia, Lithuania and Bulgaria will be speeded up in particular through an analytical examination of the Union acquis". There would be a review procedure. "From the end of 1998, the Commission will make regular reports to the Council, together with any necessary recommendations for opening bilateral intergovernmental conferences, reviewing the progress of each Central and East European applicant State towards accession in the light of the Copenhagen criteria, in particular the rate at which it is adopting the Union acquis" (European Council 1997; Friis 2003).

The Helsinki Summit 1999

In 1999, the EU finally agreed on some reforms of the CAP as well as the new financial framework for 2000-2006. This happened during the German presidency in the first part of the year.

Prior to the Helsinki summit in December 1999, the Commission had published the second reports on the applicants. This time the Commission recommended that "negotiations should be opened in 2000 with all candidate countries which meet the political criteria for membership and have proved to be ready to take the necessary measures to comply with the economic criteria, i.e. Bulgaria, Latvia, Lithuania, Malta, Romania and Slovakia" (European Commission 1999, p. 31). On Turkey, the Commission remarked: "Turkey has expressed the wish to be a candidate country and should be considered as such" (*ibid.*, p. 11).

The meeting of the European Council in Helsinki followed the recommendation from the Commission: "Determined to lend a positive contribution to security and stability on the European continent and in the light of recent developments as well as the Commission's reports, the European Council has decided to convene bilateral intergovernmental conferences in February 2000 to begin negotiations with Romania, Slovakia, Latvia, Lithuania, Bulgaria and Malta on the conditions for their entry into the Union and the ensuing Treaty adjustments" (European Council 1999). The Kosovo war had now created a sense of urgency about enlargement.

The Helsinki summit also welcomed the launch of talks aiming at a comprehensive settlement of the Cyprus problem. A political settlement would facilitate the accession of Cyprus to the EU. However, the European Council said, "If no settlement has been reached by the completion of accession negotiations, the Council's decision on accession will be made without the above being a precondition. In this the Council will take account of all relevant factors".[2]

Helsinki also decided to make Turkey a formal candidate. The European Council welcomed "recent positive developments in Turkey," and went on to say: "Turkey is a candidate State destined to join the Union on the basis of the same criteria as applied to the other candidate States". Turkey would from now on "benefit from a pre-accession strategy to stimulate and support its reforms".

The Copenhagen Summit 2002: The End Game of the Negotiations

In its Strategy Paper put out on 9 October 2002, the Commission concluded that ten countries, Cyprus, the Czech Republic, Estonia, Hungary, Latvia, Lithuania, Malta, Poland, Slovakia and Slovenia, fulfilled the political criteria for membership. Further, "Bearing in mind the progress achieved by these countries, the track record in implementing their commitments, and taking into account their preparatory work in progress, the Commission considers that these countries will have fulfilled the economic and *acquis* criteria and will be ready for membership from the beginning of 2004" (European Commission 2002).

A meeting of the European Council in Brussels 24-25 October 2002 endorsed the recommendation from the Commission that the ten candidate countries already singled out for membership fulfilled the Copen-

---

[2] In retrospect it could be argued that this decision was a mistake. The EU lost bargaining power with the Greek Cypriots that eventually turned down a reunification plan that was accepted by the Turkish Cypriots in April 2004.

hagen criteria and would be able to "assume the obligations of membership from the beginning of 2004". The Union further reiterated "its preference for a reunited Cyprus to join the European Union on the basis of a comprehensive settlement" and urged "the leaders of the Greek Cypriot and Turkish Cypriot communities to seize the opportunity and reach an agreement before the end of the accession negotiations". Concerning Bulgaria and Romania, the European Council expressed its support for the two countries' "efforts to achieve the objective of membership in 2007". And concerning Turkey, the Union welcomed "the important steps taken by Turkey towards meeting the Copenhagen political criteria" which had "brought forward the opening of accession negotiations with Turkey" (European Council 2002a).

After the Brussels meeting of the European Council, intense individual negotiations with the ten candidate countries took place up to the meeting of the European Council in Copenhagen in December, where the final agreement was reached about enlargement.

The Danish presidency worked out its "final packages" during November. The presidency's proposals were criticized by both the current members and the future members. The presidency admitted, "It was a rough reception on both sides, Member States and candidates. Reactions were more negative than expected". Since the net cost of enlargement for the period 2004-2006, according to the Danish compromise proposal, would be 1.3 billion euro higher than calculated on the basis of the financial package agreed in Brussels, the main "net contributors" (Germany, United Kingdom, Sweden, Netherlands and France) found the presidency's offer too generous, while most candidates considered it largely inadequate (Laursen & Lara Laursen 2003).

At the summit, intense negotiations took place, especially with Poland about money, and with Turkey about a date for the start of negotiations about membership. It was agreed that Cyprus, the Czech Republic, Estonia, Hungary, Latvia, Lithuania, Malta, Poland, Slovakia and Slovenia would be able to join from 1 May 2004. For Bulgaria and Romania, the EU set 2007 as the target date for accession (Denmark 2002, p. 9).

Turkey was pressing for a date. In the end, Copenhagen at least offered a date for a decision. The Commission would present a report to the European Council in the autumn of 2004 and make a recommendation concerning Turkey's fulfilment of the political Copenhagen criteria. If the European Council decided then, on the basis of the Commission report, that Turkey fulfilled the criteria, the EU would initiate accession negotiation with Turkey "without delay" (Denmark 2002, p. 10; European Council 2002b).

The Turkish leaders present in Copenhagen were not satisfied. Their United States (US) ally had also put pressure on the EU leaders, with President George W. Bush personally calling some of them, including Danish Prime Minister Anders Fogh Rasmussen.

At the start of the summit, the presidency tried to get a final agreement with the other Member States about the final financial offers to the candidates. The fifteen approved various "packages" proposed by the presidency while insisting that the financial offer was "at the limit of budgetary resources", as Anders Fogh Rasmussen expressed it in a press briefing (Laursen & Lara Laursen 2003).

Institutional Issues

In parallel with preparations for and actual negotiations with the CEECs, there was an effort to adapt the EU institutions for the expected big enlargement. The first effort was the Amsterdam Treaty in 1997, but it largely failed to solve these issues (Laursen 2002). The Nice Treaty negotiations, which followed in 2000, succeeded partly, especially by changing the weights of votes in the Council of Ministers (Laursen 2006b).

But as the heads of state or government left Nice, some of them had their doubts. They decided to have yet another Intergovernmental Conference (IGC) in 2004 in order to make the EU more efficient and legitimate. The Laeken summit in December 2001 decided that this IGC should be prepared by a convention, with relatively large representation by the EP and national parliaments. By July 2003, this convention produced a draft so-called constitutional treaty, which was then sent to an IGC that started on 4 October, 2004. A meeting of the European Council in Brussels in December 2003 failed to reach a final agreement on the constitutional treaty. Especially the question of voting in the Council was still controversial. The convention had proposed a simple double majority; a majority of states that should also represent at least 60 per cent of the EU's population would constitute a QMV. But Spain and Poland defended the more cumbersome system of weights agreed in Nice because Nice gave them a relatively high number of votes. In the end, an agreement was found during the Irish presidency by June 2004. The double majority system was accepted, but the thresholds were increased to at least 55 per cent of the states representing at least 65 per cent of the EU population. This system would have started in 2009 if the constitutional treaty had been ratified by all 25 Member States. But it was rejected by voters in referendums in France and the Netherlands in 2005 (Laursen 2008).

Eventually in June 2007, during the German presidency, the EU members agreed on a detailed mandate for an IGC that would adopt a so-called reform treaty. This treaty was signed in Lisbon toward the end of the year and became known as the Lisbon Treaty. Methodology and terminology changed, but the content on institutions did not change much. The new treaty entered into force in December 2009 (Laursen 2012a and 2012b). The expectation was that the EU now should be ready for further enlargements from an institutional point of view. But the debacle concerning the constitutional treaty had a negative effect on the pro-integration and enlargement attitudes in some Member States.

Overview of Book Chapters

The development of the EU's enlargement policy after the 2004/07 enlargements is covered in the following chapters, especially the chapter by Eli Gateva, which follows. She argues that there was a renewed consensus in 2006. It included additional conditions in a time of declining enthusiasm for enlargements. She focuses on inter-institutional dynamics, the interplay between the Commission and the Member States. Focusing in particular on Croatia, Turkey and Macedonia, she finds that bilateral relations between these applicants and some Member States have been particularly important. They have had, and still have, a detrimental effect on the accession process.

In Chapter 3, Tanel Kerikmäe and Lehte Roots also focus on recent changes, the Lisbon Treaty and the eurozone crisis, and ask whether a new theoretical paradigm is needed. The chapter is partly informed by the Estonian experience. Estonia joined in 2004, joined the Schengen area, the EU's cooperation to abolish internal border controls, in 2007 and the eurozone in 2011. But not all CEECs have been equally successful. Bulgaria and Romania still have problems joining Schengen and many CEECs have not joined the euro. Arguably the euro crisis calls for further integration which could make future enlargements more difficult.

In Chapter 4, Federiga Bindi and Irina Angelescu also take a critical look at the current situation. The focus here is very much on the EU's international roles. Basically the question is whether the EU's postmodernist foreign policy is being replaced by a more pragmatic one that may confuse neighbours and other international actors, including the United States. The current lack of commitment to enlargement is explained by an absence of a sense of historical legacy, justification based on the economic crisis, lack of popular support and a sense of "enlargement fatigue". Political leaders are blamed for the current deadlock.

After these introductory chapters, the next section focuses on the process of preparing for membership, going through the required economic and political adaptations. In Chapter 5, Heather Mbaye looks at compliance. She develops a conceptual framework and discusses cases in some of the existing Member States. She then uses the insights gained to discuss what kind of compliance can be expected in Turkey, Iceland and the Balkan countries.

In Chapter 6, Svet Derderyan takes on the issue of corruption. Although not explicitly mentioned in the Copenhagen criteria in 1993, this issue has become important and is covered in detail in the annual Commission reports on the candidates. The chapter finds that corruption decreased in the CEECs prior to membership, but also that there was no backsliding after membership. Thanks partly to money transfers from the Structural Funds, the EU has retained leverage. In the cases of Bulgaria and Romania, a Cooperation and Verification Mechanism has been introduced, and in one case, funding was cut for Bulgaria. There has also been a diffusion of democratic norms and values.

In Chapter 7, Graeme Crouch discusses the concept of Europeanisation, arguing that existing top-down and bottom-up approaches must be supplemented by a middle-level approach where the role of transnational actors must be studied. Using the case of Croatia, the next country to join, he finds that these actors were important in Croatia's preparations, for instance, through twinning projects that brought in actors from the existing Member States. Aid in the environmental area, for instance, brought in representatives from environmental organisations.

In Chapter 8, Milos Milenkovic and Marko Milenkovic look at "culturalisation" of accession criteria in Serbia. It is argued that accession criteria have been altered to enhance rebuilding and reconciliation in the Western Balkans. This has provoked reactions about the "loss of identity" in Serbia. The country has been divided into what resembles "culture wars". The narratives of "regional singularity", "facing the recent past", and "moral purification" have had a negative effect on support for membership. It is suggested that reconciliation and tolerance can better be achieved in the EU after membership than before. The chapter gives an interesting anthropological perspective that challenges some established positions.

The next section deals with political parties. How do we explain the different attitudes to European integration of various political parties? Is it ideology or strategy? How do parties adapt to membership and, in the case of candidates, the prospect of membership.

Alan Siaroff starts with a chapter on the impact of expansion on the party system institutionalisation in the EP. Comparing party systems in

Western and Eastern Europe, he is interested in how the new Member States fit in. Many of these fit in quite well with the Western patterns of dominating Christian democratic or conservative parties, socialists and liberals. Since membership, there has been a greater degree of volatility in the party politics of the CEECs. Recently, because of the economic crisis, Western Europe has also experienced volatility. Some of the candidate countries, including Serbia and Turkey, have relatively low "fit".

In Chapter 10, Seçkîn Bariş Gülmez studies the accession countries. Instead of euroscepticism, the concept used to study certain parties in the Member States, he prefers to talk about EU-scepticism in the candidate countries, because the focus is on EU membership, not the wider questions of European integration after membership. Facing membership conditions, certain parties are reluctant or opposed to membership. He finds that this opposition is not ideological but strategic. It is also reversible. Parties basically are rationally calculating, but the EU's legitimacy also plays a role. The moment EU membership becomes a credible option, some sceptical parties have become more supporting.

In Chapter 11, Marko Stojic focuses on Serbia and Croatia. He too finds that party attitudes are not correlated with ideology. Parties are seen as strategic actors that maximize their changes of coming to power. History and political circumstances determine the strategic situations. In the two countries in question, growing nationalism and war contributed to the situations. He divides the parties into six groups: socialist/social-democratic, conservative, Christian-democrat, agrarian, liberal and radical right. Socialist parties have tended to pro-European, including the Socialist Party of Serbia since 2008. Christian-democratic and agrarian parties, which only exist in Croatia, have also been pro-European. There are three conservative parties in Serbia. Two have tended to be pro-European, but the Democratic Party of Serbia has been eurosceptic since 2008. The liberal parties have been pro-European. The radical right parties have been eurosceptic.

The next section of three chapters engages the issues in the Western Balkan countries and their prospects of membership. In Chapter 12, Gentian Elezi gives some specific background of particular importance to these countries, the conclusions from the Thessaloniki summit in 2003 and the Stabilisation and Association process that should speed up the pre-accession process. Nevertheless, a decade after Thessaloniki most of these countries are not making progress towards membership. This raises questions about the conditionality part of the process, which arguably worked for the CEECs, but seemingly not for some of the Western Balkan countries. There is a clear implementation deficit, and support for membership has declined. Even if there have been economic reforms, democratic consolidation appears more difficult. Lack of administrative capacity remains a serious problem.

Shirley Cloyes DioGuardi continues in Chapter 13 with a very critical analysis on the situation in the Western Balkans as well as some of the policies of the EU – and the United States. Inter-ethnic conflicts are rampant. Serbia continues not to accept the independence of Kosovo. The Dayton Peace Accord has produced a de facto division of Bosnia. Ethnic majorities discriminate against ethnic minorities in Macedonia and Montenegro. Five EU countries have not recognized the independence of Kosovo, and Greece will not allow Macedonia to call itself Macedonia. The EU divisions on these points seriously affect the EU's possibility of leverage in the region.

In Chapter 14, Faton Bislimi deals with the rather unique case of Kosovo. He finds that the continued presence of foreign actors – the UN, NATO and the EU – is now making it more difficult for the country to establish a true representative democracy. The uncertain political status also makes it difficult to attract foreign direct investments. Overall, the country is in a very bad situation.

The final section focuses on Turkey and the risk of the enlargement process grinding to a halt, with the serious implications this may entail. Nanette Neuwahl looks at the institutional implications of Turkish membership. Given Turkey's size, this problem remains relevant in the minds of some decision-makers. The Turkish population is close to that of Germany, and it grows faster. Given the tremendous attention given to the weights of the votes of the Member States in the Council of Ministers during the recent treaty reforms, from Amsterdam via Nice and the Constitutional Treaty to the Lisbon Treaty, the question cannot be ignored.

In Chapter 16, Demetrios Nicolaides looks at implications of non-accession of Turkey. He finds that non-accession is likely to slow down reforms in Turkey and expects the country increasingly to turn to the Middle East and Arab world. Relations with Israel have deteriorated. Turkish accession, on the other hand, could facilitate a reunification of Cyprus and lower tensions in the region. Tensions between Turkey and Cyprus have increased recently after the discovery of oil and natural gas in the Eastern Mediterranean. Implied by the analysis is a European interest in moving forward in membership negotiations with Turkey.

Finally, in the last chapter Boyka Stefanova discusses integration theory as it relates to enlargement, including liberal intergovernmentalism and social constructivism. She sees enlargement as a political process. National preferences are important but not fixed. They depend on both the historic and geopolitical context. Turkey is used as a case to show how conditionality can be strengthened for various political reasons and how veto politics by some Member States has become important, especially after 2005.

The chapters in this book leave a number of important questions for the future: Is enlargement grinding to a halt? Will more leadership eventually become available in favour of enlargement? What kind of events may change the calculations of the Member States and other actors? Will the financial crisis and institutional difficulties of the eurozone further slow down enlargement? Or will the EU muddle through as has usually happened in the past?

References

De la Serre, Françoise. 1991. "The Integration Dilemma: Enlarging and/or Deepening the Community," in *Futures*, Vol. 23, No. 7 (September), pp. 739-746.

Denmark, Ministry of Foreign Affair. 2002. Results of the Danish EU Presidency. One Europe. From Copenhagen to Copenhagen. Originally downloaded from www.eu2002.dk. [Accessed January 2003].

Deutsch, Karl *et al.* 1957. *Political Community and the North Atlantic Area: International Organization in the Light of Historical Experience.* Princeton, NJ: Princeton University Press.

European Commission. 1989. "Commission Opinion on Turkey's Request for Accession to the Community", SEC(89) 2290 final, Brussels, 18 December.

European Commission. 1991. "A Strategy for Enlargement. Preliminary Report of the SG Study Group on Enlargement". Brussels: Commission of the European Communities, 14 November.

European Commission. 1992. "Europe and the Challenge of Enlargement", in *Europe*, Documents No. 1790, 3 July.

European Commission. 1997. "Agenda 2000: For a stronger and wider Union. Document drawn up on the basis of COM(97) 2000 final", in *Bulletin of the European Union*, Supplement 5/97.

European Commission. 1999. "Composite Paper: Reports on Progress Towards Accession by Each of the Candidate Countries. http://www.europa.eu.int/comm/enlargement/report_10_99/pdf/en/composite_en.pdf.

European Commission. 2002. "Towards the Enlarged Union. Strategy Paper and Report of the European Commission on the progress towards accession by each of the candidate countries". http://www.europa.eu.int/comm/enlargement/report2002/strategy_en.pdf.

European Council. 1993. Presidency Conclusions, The European Council, Copenhagen, 21-22 June, *EC Bulletin*, No. 6.

European Council. 1997. Presidency Conclusions, Luxembourg European Council.

European Council. 1999. Presidency Conclusions. Helsinki European Council, 10 and 11 December. http://www.europa.eu.int/council/off/conclu/dec99/dec99_en.htm.

European Council. 2002a. "Brussels European Council 24 and 25 October 2002: Presidency Conclusions", Brussels 26 November. http://www.foreignpolicy.org.tr/eng/eu/presidency_conclusions.pdf.

European Council. 2002b. "Presidency Conclusions: Copenhagen European Council 12 and 13 December 2002". http://www.ecdel.org.au/archive/Laeken%20Presidency%20Conclusions.pdf.

Friis, Lykke. 1999. *An Ever Larger Union? EU Enlargement and European Integration.* Copenhagen: Danish Institute of International Affairs.

Friis, Lykke. 2003. "EU Enlargement … And Then There Were 28?", in Elizabeth Bomberg and Alexander Stubb (eds.), *The European Union: How Does it Work?* Oxford: Oxford University Press, pp. 177-194.

Laursen, Finn. 1996. "Relations between the EU and the Central and Eastern European Countries since 1989: An Overview", in Finn Laursen and Søren Riishøj (eds.), *The EU and Central Europe: Status and Prospects.* Esbjerg: South Jutland University Press, pp. 3-28.

Laursen, Finn. 2001. "EU Enlargement: Interests, Issues and the Need for Institutional Reform", in S.S. Andersen and K.A. Eliassen (eds.), *Making Policy in Europe.* 2nd ed. London: SAGE, pp. 206-228.

Laursen, Finn, ed. 2002. *The Amsterdam Treaty: National Preference Formation, Interstate Bargaining and Outcome.* Odense: Odense University Press.

Laursen, Finn. 2005. "The Eastern Enlargement of the EU: Why, How and Implications", in Zainal Mantaha and Toshiro Tanaka (eds.), *Enlarging European Union and Asia.* Singapore: Asia-Europe Foundation, pp. 19-56.

Laursen, Finn. 2006a. "The EU Enlargement Policy: Can Widening and Deepening Be Combined?" in Joaquín Roy and Roberto Domínguez (eds.), *Towards the Completion of Europe: Analysis and Perspectives of the New European Union Enlargement.* Miami, FL: Miami-Florida European Union Centre of Excellence, pp. 125-135.

Laursen, Finn, ed. 2006b. *The Treaty of Nice: Actor Preferences, Bargaining and Institutional Choice.* Leiden: Martinus Nijhoff Publishers/Academic Publishers Brill.

Laursen, Finn, ed. 2008. *The Rise and Fall of the Constitutional Treaty.* Leiden: Martinus Nijhoff Publishers/Academic Publishers Brill.

Laursen, Finn, ed. 2012a. *The Making of the EU's Lisbon Treaty: the Role of the Member States.* Brussels: PIE Peter Lang.

Laursen, Finn, ed. 2012b. *The Lisbon Treaty Institutional Choices and Implementation.* Farnham: Ashgate.

Laursen, Finn and Berenice Lara Laursen. 2003. "The Danish Presidency 2002: Completing the Circle from Copenhagen to Copenhagen", *ZEI Discussion Paper* (Bonn: Zentrum für Europäische Integrationsforschung) No. C123.

Laursen, Finn and Sophie Vanhoonacker, eds. 1992. *The Intergovernmental Conference on Political Union: Institutional Reforms, New Policies and International Identity of the European Community*. Dordrecht: Martinus Nijhoff Publishers, and Maastricht: European Institute of Public Administration.

Laursen, Finn and Sophie Vanhoonacker, eds. 1994. *The Ratification of the Maastricht Treaty: Issues, Debates and Future Implications*. Dordrecht: Martinus Nijhoff Publishers, and Maastricht: European Institute of Public Administration.

Mattli, Walter. 1999. *The Logic of Regional Integration: Europe and Beyond.* Cambridge: Cambridge University Press.

Preston, Christopher. 1997. *Enlargement and Integration in the European Union.* London: Routledge.

Schimmelfennig, Frank. 2003. *The EU, NATO and the Integration of Europe: Rules and Rhetoric.* Cambridge: Cambridge University Press.

Sedelmeier, Ulrich. 2000. "Eastern Enlargement: Risk, Rationality, and Role-Compliance", in Maria Green Cowles and Michael Smith (eds.), *The State of the European Union: Risks, Reform, Resistance, and Revival.* Oxford: Oxford University Press, pp. 164-185.

Wallace, Helen. 1989. Widening and Deepening the European Community and the New European Agenda", *RIIA Discussion Paper* No. 23. London: The Royal Institute of International Affairs.

Wessels, Wolfgang. 1996. "Evolutions possible de l'Union européenne. Scénarios et stratégies pour sortir d'un cercle vicieux", *Politique Étrangère*, 61(1), 139-50.

EU Enlargement Policy and Institutional Battles

Can the Commission's Entrepreneurship Make Up for the Lack of Strong Political Will in the Council?

Eli GATEVA

Introduction*

In December 2006, two weeks before the accession of Bulgaria and Romania (which marked the completion of the historical fifth enlargement of the European Union), the European Council approved a renewed consensus on enlargement that significantly shaped the development of EU enlargement policy. On the basis of the lessons learnt from the previous enlargement rounds, the Commission outlined a set of concrete measures aimed at improving the quality of the accession process, which highlighted the growing relevance of EU's integration capacity, the need for a systematic use of benchmarks and the relevance of the early stages of the accession process for tackling challenging issues such as judicial reform and the fight against corruption (European Commission 2006).

Despite the growing body of literature on the mechanisms and the effectiveness of EU enlargement policy and the continual engagement of the Union with Turkey and the Western Balkan countries, the impact of the revised enlargement strategy remains under-researched. The evolution of EU enlargement conditionality, which is characterised by the establishment of additional membership conditions (such as the Stabilisation and Association Process (SAP) conditionalities); the increasing application of differentiation through individual country specific benchmarks; the gradual introduction of new landmarks in the early pre-accession stage, and also the declining enthusiasm and ques-

* I would like to thank University Association for Contemporary European Studies for their generous support of my field trip to Brussels. I would also like to express my gratitude to all the interviewees for allowing me to take of their time.

tionable political commitment of the Member States, offers exciting new avenues for research.

In order to analyse the evolution of EU enlargement policy and its potential to overcome the growing anti-enlargement sentiment in EU Member States, the chapter discusses the implications of the renewed consensus for the inter-institutional dynamics between the Commission and the Council and the advancement of the ongoing accession process. The study, which draws on more than eighty extensive interviews with senior EU and national officials and examination of key EU documents, proceeds in four steps. First, it highlights the main fields of research in the academic literature on EU enlargement. Second, it reflects on the key new developments of EU enlargement policy, introduced on the basis of the renewed consensus on enlargement. Third, the chapter discusses the impact of EU Member States on the development of EU enlargement policy towards Croatia, Turkey and the Former Yugoslav Republic of Macedonia (FYROM). The analysis focuses on three key aspects: (1) bilateral issues between candidate countries and Member States; (2) shifts in Member States' attitudes towards enlargement and (3) Member States' impact on opening and closing benchmarks. The fourth step looks into the role of the Commission in keeping enlargement firmly on the EU agenda. The study concludes with a reflection on the significance of the renewed consensus on enlargement and the future of the accession process with the countries of South-eastern Europe.

Reviewing the Existing Literature on EU Enlargement

The numerous challenges and the great political significance of the unique historical enlargement of the Union to the East lent speed to the emergence and development of the study of EU enlargement as a key research area. Although the majority of the early studies investigated the puzzle of the EU's decision to enlarge with the Central and Eastern European Countries (CEECs) (Baldwin 1995; Schimmelfennig 1998; Fierke and Wiener 1999; Sjursen 2002; Sedelmeier 2005), the research focus expanded quickly to include other dimensions. The impact of the EU enlargement, with reference to both the impact of the EU on the applicant countries and the impact of the Eastern enlargement on EU policies, is one of the areas that has blossomed and accumulated a growing body of literature during the last decade (Zielonka 2001; Schimmelfennig and Sedelmeier 2004; Vachudová 2005; Grabbe 2006; Sedelmeier 2011). Although the influence of the Union varies across different policy areas and issues, most of the studies identify the credibility of the membership perspective as a key explanatory factor for the transformative power of EU enlargement policy. However, the theoretical literature focuses predominantly on the Eastern enlargement and the applicants' compliance with the membership conditions. In recent years, research has gradually shifted to studying the impact of EU conditionality after accession by looking into new members' compliance with EU rules (Toshkov 2007, 2008; Sedelmeier 2008; Dimitrova & Toshkov 2009; Schimmelfennig & Trauner 2009). The effectiveness of the EU's neighbourhood policy (Lavenex, 2008; Schimmelfennig & Scholtz 2008) and the diffusion of the EU's impact beyond candidate and potential candidates and neighbouring countries (Börzel & Risse 2012a; 2012b) have also shaped and expanded the debate on the mechanisms and effectiveness of the EU's influence.

Despite the growing body of literature and the EU's continual engagement with Turkey and the candidate and potential candidate countries of the Western Balkans, research has largely neglected two important questions:

– what factors shape the development of the enlargement policy (and respectively enlargement conditionality);

– how to explain change and continuity across the recent enlargement rounds.

Although some studies examine the role of the Member States' preferences (Tewes 1998; Hyde-Price 2000; Piedrafita 2007; Schukkink & Niemann 2010) and the European Commission (Bellier 2004; Avery 2009; Lass-Lennecke & Werner 2009) for the development of the fifth enlargement round, multi-dimensional comparative investigations remain scarce (but see İçener, Phinnemore & Papadimitriou, 2010). The literature concerned with the "supply side" of enlargement focuses predominantly on the EU's decision to embark on enlargement with the CEECs. Mattli and Plumper (2002) summarise the "supply-side" arguments into three categories: negative externalities; economic gains and norms. The negative externalities argument suggests that the exclusion of "poor and commercially unattractive countries" is costlier than their integration into the Union and links the EU's decision to enlarge with "outsiders" to "the extent of actual or potential crisis spill-over" from the applicant states (Mattli & Plumper 2002, pp. 553-554). The economic gains argument, which focuses on trade and investment, establishes the new opportunities and benefits of extending EU rules and policies to Central and Eastern Europe (CEE) as the reasons for the expansion of the Union. The third category of "supply-side" arguments draws heavily on Schimmelfennig's work on "rhetorical action" (Mattli & Plumper 2002). He emphasises the strategic use of norm-based argumentation and claims that pro-enlargement Member States rhetorically entrapped their opponents into a firm commitment to the Eastern enlargement by grounding their support in the constitutive values and norms of the EU (Schimmelfennig 2001). Although the supply-side arguments are very helpful in illuminating the motivations of the key actors involved in the accession process, they focus exclusively on significant historical decisions regarding the Eastern expansion of the Union rather than on enlargement at large.

In order to examine change and continuity, the chapter develops a multi-dimensional approach and specifies that the *EU enlargement policy is a function of differentiated influences from multiple actors and external pressures.* The definition highlights the complex constellations of actors involved in the accession process and emphasises their relevance by focusing on the influence that they can exert rather than on their competences. As it is virtually impossible to account for all the groups of actors and external shocks that affect the development of EU enlargement policy, the scope of the study is limited to analysing the impact of the EU's inter-institutional dynamics between the EU Council and the Commission. Instead of looking into the role of the Council, undoubtedly the most powerful non-unitary actor in the accession process, the chapter analyses the influence of individual Member States on the development of EU enlargement policy. The examination of Member States' preferences is not limited to the impact of their attitudes towards enlargement (in general) or the accession of a/group of candidate country/ies (in particular). It also investigates the relevance of bilateral relations between Member States and candidate countries by focusing on the implications of bilateral issues for the advancement of the accession process. The analysis discusses the impact of the Commission by reflecting on the scope and significance of the new developments incorporated in the Union's enlargement strategy towards Southeastern Europe.

Key Elements of the Renewed Consensus on Enlargement

In 2005, the enlargement of the EU entered a new historic phase with the opening of the accession negotiations with Turkey and Croatia and the recognition of FYROM as a candidate country. Although the enlargement strategy of the Union towards Southeastern Europe was modelled on the experience from the previous enlargement, the failure of the ratification of the constitutional treaty had significant implications for the development of the policy. The Commissioner for Enlargement Olli Rehn warned that "We face a serious situation. The EU's enlargement fatigue started and became a scapegoat in June 2005, after the two failed referenda on the Constitutional Treaty" (Rehn, 2006b). He also pointed out that "the climate at the time was marked by uncertainty about the EU's commitment to the Balkans. France and the Netherlands had voted 'no' in the referenda in 2005, and 'absorption capacity' was top of the agenda" (Rehn, 2008a).

Following an in-depth debate on enlargement, the European Council in December 2006 enhanced the rules of the accession process by defining a renewed consensus on enlargement. The consensus, which is based on the three principles of the Commission's approach towards enlargement – consolidation, conditionality and communication – and the EU's capacity to integrate new members, has become a fundamental part of the EU's enlargement policy.

The new approach of the Commission has had important implications for the development of the range and scope of the conditions with which candidate and potential candidate countries need to comply. The Amsterdam Treaty expanded the *conditions for applying for membership* by specifying that any European state "which respects the principles set out in Article 6(1) may apply" (*Official Journal* 1997). However, the Lisbon Treaty amended them further by confirming that any European state "which respects the values referred to in Article 1a *and is committed to promoting them may apply*" [emphasis added], the treaty also expanded the range of prerequisites (previously referred to in Article 6(1) by including human dignity and equality and specifically emphasising the significance of the rights of persons belonging to minorities[1] (*Official Journal* 2007). Nevertheless, the EU has stringently avoided defining one of most essential but also controversial requirements – the "Europeanness" of the applicants – while the Commissioner for Enlargement Olli Rehn dismissed the debate on the geographical borders of the EU by insisting, "Geography sets the frame, but fundamentally it is values that make the borders of Europe" (Rehn 2005).

The 2005 enlargement strategy strengthened the link between the SAP and the integration of the Western Balkans into the Union by outlining the stages leading to and the conditions for the conclusion of the Stabilisation and Association Agreements (SAAs). Furthermore, the Commission confirmed that "A country's satisfactory track-record in implementing its SAA obligations (including the trade-related provisions) will therefore be *an essential element for the EU to consider any membership application*" [emphasis added] (European Commission 2006).

In addition to establishing a firm set of conditions with which the potential candidate countries need to comply in order to advance their relationship with the Union, the Commission elaborated on the scope and range of the *conditions for opening accession negotiations*. It

1 Furthermore, Article 1a specified that the societies of EU Member States are characterised by "pluralism, non-discrimination, tolerance, justice, solidarity and equality between women and men" (*Official Journal* 2007).

incorporated full compliance with the ICTY into the Copenhagen political criteria by stating:

> Before accession negotiations can be opened, the country needs to reach a sufficient degree of general compliance with the Copenhagen criteria. The political criteria must be met,[2] including full cooperation with the International Criminal Tribunal for the Former Yugoslavia (ICTY) where relevant. (European Commission, 2005a)

The increasing differentiation and specification of the EU conditions are further evidenced by the Union's approach to Skopje. The Commission elaborated on the *conditions for opening of accession negotiations* with FYROM by noting: "The Accession Partnership identifies eight key priorities for progress in the accession process by the former Yugoslav Republic of Macedonia. The Commission assesses these key priorities as benchmarks in this Progress Report. A recommendation on the start of accession negotiations will depend on the results achieved" (European Commission 2009a).

The EU also modified the scope of the conditions with which the candidate countries need to comply during the negotiation stage by increasing the number of negotiations chapters from 31 to 35 and introducing opening benchmarks. The change in the negotiation chapters should not be treated as a pure organisational matter or a mere reflection of the expansion of the EU legislation. The Commission remarked on the significance of one of the new chapters by stressing that "the current negotiating framework provides for a chapter on Judiciary and Fundamental Rights, under which the political issues are to be addressed. This permits progress in crucial areas to be kept under close scrutiny" (European Commission 2006), whereas, some of the big chapters such as Energy and Agriculture were split into two smaller chapters[3] for more practical reasons. The urgency of addressing the issues related to the areas of Judiciary and Fundamental rights (Chapter 23) and Justice and Home Affairs (Chapter 24) was also flagged by the Commission in the latest enlargement strategy, published on 12 October 2011 (European Commission 2011). Some reports suggest that the EU is to highlight further their importance and revolutionise the conduct of the negotiations by making the opening of chapters conditional on progress in Chapters 23 and 24 (Euractiv 2011b).

The introduction of opening benchmarks is another novel development, which reflects the growing application of differentiated and targeted conditionality.

---

2 As specified by the European Council at Helsinki in December 1999.

3 Trans-European Networks and Energy; Agriculture and Rural Development and FoodSafety, Veterinary and Phytosanitary Policy.

The EU confirmed that:

> Benchmarks are measurable and linked to key elements of the acquis chapter. In general, opening benchmarks concern key preparatory steps for future alignment (such as strategies or action plans), and the fulfilment of contractual obligations that mirror acquis requirements. Closing benchmarks primarily concern legislative measures, administrative or judicial bodies, and a track record of implementation of the acquis. For chapters in the economic field, they also include the criterion of being a functioning market economy. (European Commission 2006)

This change has also influenced significantly the dynamics of the accession negotiations by establishing a two-step negotiations process, which requires the unanimous decision from the Member States on: (1) the conditions for opening a chapter[4] and (2) the conditions for the provisional closure of a chapter. In the accession negotiations with Zagreb, the EU laid down opening benchmarks for 11 chapters and closing benchmarks for all the chapters with the exception of Science and Research; Education and Culture and the two non-acquis chapters: Institutions and Other Issues (Government of Croatia 2011). One senior Croatian contextualised the extensive benchmarking by noting that "Croatia had 134 benchmarks for opening chapters, and around 400 measures that are parts of benchmarks" (*Kujundžić* 2011).

Furthermore, the ongoing accession process with Turkey and the Western Balkan countries rekindled the debate on the relevance and the definition of the EU absorption capacity. Although the Commission renamed it to "integration capacity" and specified (for the first time) that "it is first and foremost a functional concept", it followed a differentiating approach by noting that it would be "a condition to be observed" in the case of Turkey, but not Croatia (European Commission 2006).

The new developments of the scope and range of conditions and the structure of the accession negotiations show that the Commission's approach towards the candidate and potential candidate countries of South-eastern Europe has become much more stringent compared to the fifth enlargement. The expansion of the conditions for applying for membership and opening accession negotiations highlight the importance of the early stages of the enlargement process and the need for a tailor-made approach. The introduction of the new chapter on Judiciary and Fundamental Rights illustrates the growing significance of compliance with the political criteria for the advancement of the accession negotiations. The extensive use of opening and closing benchmarks reflects the increasing application of targeted conditionality and the high level of specification of the EU conditions. If we are to summarise the

4 If applicable.

combined impact of the main novelties of the new enlargement strategy, we can conclude that the Commission has a firmly cemented track record of implementation as the key condition for the advancement of the accession process (in contrast to credible promises in the case of the CEE countries).

EU Member States' Preferences and Impact

Despite the rigorous approach of the Commission, the advancement of the accession process with the candidates from South Eastern Europe has become a challenging feat. The aim of this section is to examine the impact of the relations between the Member States and Croatia, Turkey and FYROM on the development of EU enlargement policy. The analysis focuses on three key aspects: (1) bilateral issues between candidate countries and Member States; (2) shifts in Member States' attitudes towards enlargement and (3) Member States' impact on opening and closing benchmarks.

The first part examines the implications of bilateral problems for the advancement of the accession process by looking at the border dispute between Croatia and Slovenia; the issues between Turkey and Cyprus and Greece; and the name issue between FYROM and Greece. The second part reflects on Member States' preferences, focusing particularly on France's and Germany's attitudes towards Turkey and the divisions among Member States regarding the Union's enlargement policy. The third part analyses the increasing application of opening and closing benchmarks and their impact on Member States' veto powers in the accession negotiations.

Although bilateral issues were present in the fifth round of enlargement, none of them had such a detrimental effect on the accession process, as in the case of Croatia, Turkey and FYROM. One senior official commented that: "Bilateral issues between current Member States and candidate countries or bilateral issues between candidate countries, these have now become the biggest obstacles for progress in enlargement and I don't think this was really the case with the previous rounds" (Interview 5, 2009).

The Commissioner for Enlargement Olli Rehn noted, "Each of the problems has its own historical and contextual background. We cannot put them all into the same basket; they have different characteristics" (*Agence Europe* 2009). However, the aim of the chapter is not to examine in detail the nature of disputes but to analyse their impact on EU enlargement conditionality, particularly with reference to the incentive structure and the range and the scope of the conditions set out by the EU.

Shortly after the Commission presented an indicative roadmap for the completion of the technical part of the accession negotiations with Croatia, a long-standing border dispute between Croatia and Slovenia put the accession negotiations on hold for almost a year. The dispute, which had persisted since the breakup of the former Yugoslavia, escalated in December 2008 when Slovenia decided to effectively block the accession negotiations with Croatia "on the grounds that some of the material that Croatia has submitted to the EU, including documents on fisheries, prejudged the resolution of the dispute over their border in the Bay of Piran" (*European Voice* 2009). The Commission consistently maintained the view that "the border issue is a bilateral issue that should not be brought to the table of the accession negotiations" and encouraged both states to solve the open border dispute "in the spirit of good neighbourly relations" (European Commission 2009c). Furthermore, it actively participated in intense consultations.

Following the escalation of the border dispute between Slovenia and Croatia, the Slovenian Foreign Affairs Minister Samuel Zbogar announced that Croatia's accession to the EU may be put to a referendum (Euractiv 2009). Although both countries managed to reach an agreement on a settlement mechanism, Slovenia decided to call a referendum on the border arbitration deal (Euractiv 2010). It was narrowly approved by Slovenians, with 51.5 per cent in favour, but a No vote could have had a detrimental impact on Zagreb's membership talks (*Financial Times* 2010).

The advancement of the accession process with another candidate country has also been put on hold because of a long-running bilateral dispute. The name issue between FYROM and Greece has prevented FYROM from opening accession negotiations and moving to the second phase of the SAA implementation. Despite the Commission recommendations (European Commission 2009b, 2010a, 2011), the Council has not yet reached a unanimous decision. In December 2010, the Greek Foreign Minister Droutsas reiterated the Greek stance:

> Our position on Skopje's accession perspective is clear and well known to everyone. We sincerely want the opening of FYROM's accession negotiations with the EU. We support the accession of this country, but with full respect for the rules and obligations FYROM has undertaken to the EU and all of its member states. One basic rule is respect for good neighbourly relations. This is stressed once again. And a basic demand for our being able to talk about the opening of accession negotiations with FYROM is the resolution of the name issue. Like last year, all of this is reiterated in a clear manner, in clear language. (Droutsas 2010)

Although the resolution of the bilateral problem between FYROM and Greece was not included as a formal condition for the start of the accession negotiations, the Commission confirmed that it was "essential" (European Commission 2010a, 2011). However, the name issue is not the only bilateral issue between a candidate country and Greece. The Aegean Sea Continental Shelf dispute has strained the relations between Turkey and Greece and the EU. The high degree of importance attached to the enlargement process by Greece was confirmed by Droutsas who stressed that "the enlargement process is interwoven with Greece's foreign policy. This enlargement policy is very important to us, and it is obvious that we want to have – and do have – a strong voice in the development of the discussion in the EU on this subject" (Droutsas 2010).

One senior Commission official pointed out that although the dispute between Greece and Turkey "is a very old and difficult bilateral problem", the issue between Cyprus and Turkey "is quite [an] unusual bilateral problem, I mean, there are Turkish tanks and Turkish soldiers in Cyprus" (Interview 4, 2009). Turkey's failure to extend the implementation of the Ankara Protocol to Cyprus virtually brought the accession negotiations to a halt as the General Affairs Council agreed not to open eight chapters and decided not to provisionally close any chapters "until the Commission verifies that Turkey has fulfilled its commitments related to the Additional Protocol" (Council of the European Union 2006).

The impact of individual Member States on the ongoing enlargement process has not been limited to blockages related to bilateral issues. Some Member States have shaped significantly the EU enlargement policy. The negotiating frameworks with Turkey and Croatia introduced a new development by declaring that "the accession negotiations are an open-ended process, the outcome of which cannot be guaranteed" (European Commission 2005b, 2005c). One senior official confirmed that "this was a hook given to Schüssel to convince him to start the accession negotiations, and, in 2005, when they discussed the negotiating framework with Turkey, Plassnik, the Austrian foreign Minister, she fought for having mentioned the privileged partnership also as a possibility, but she did not manage" (Interview 4, 2009).

However, in the case of Turkey, controversy and disagreement between Member States have not been limited to the start of the accession negations, as a Turkish national official confirmed:

> In total there are 18 chapters blocked, 8 are the additional protocol chapters, 5 of them are blocked by France and one of them is overlapping, which is the agriculture chapter, in total 12 chapters by France and the additional protocol issue; and in addition to these 12 chapters we have 6 other chapters blocked by individual member states. (Interview 2, 2009)

A senior EU official summarised the French position on Turkey's bid for membership by saying:

> What France does, the French approach to the negotiations with Turkey is that: we want a privileged partnership and all the chapters which can be compatible with a possible future privileged partnership, we open them, not a problem, but block those chapters which prejudge accession, so those chapters are budget, because only EU members can benefit from the EU budget, we block regional policy, the chapter on regional policy because it is about central funds and only members can get central funds, we block agriculture because it's the CAP remains the first budgetary post in the EU budget and only members get it, we block institutions because only members can participate in EU institutions, as members of Parliament, etc., etc. and we block EMU because it prejudges membership to the Euro (Interview 4, 2009).

However, France is not the only Member State opposed to Turkey's accession. The Commissioner for Enlargement remarked:

> Many European politicians have advocated the idea of a privileged partnership for Turkey rather than full membership. This takes place despite the fact that the EU and its leaders in the European Council unanimously decided to open accession negotiations, while underlining that the negotiations are by their very nature an open-ended process with no predetermined outcome (Rehn 2006b).

Furthermore, the outcome of the accession negotiations with Turkey is expected to be dependent on public support. In this respect, the strong opposition to Turkish membership in France and Austria, where about 60 per cent of the citizens have been consistently against it (Eurobarometer, 2005a; 2005b; 2006; 2008; 2010) is a serious concern as both countries are committed to holding referendums. France amended its constitution to impose "an automatic referendum for ratification of any new accession, after that of Croatia", whereas Austria has promised to hold a referendum on Turkey's accession, but its commitment is not yet legally binding (*Agence Europe* 2008; Euractiv 2011a).

However, Turkey has also received a lot of support from some Member States. In December 2010, the foreign ministers of Britain, Sweden, Finland and Italy published a joint letter in the *International Herald Tribune* and warned Europe against "turning its back on Turkey" (EU Observer 2010).

One senior EU official reflected on the shifts in the Member States' preferences regarding the on-going enlargement by stating:

> The political situation is different, we can see in some Member States vis-à-vis enlargement, let me say, should I use the word reluctance or for example, if we take Germany, there is clearly in the programme of the governing Christian-democrats "you need a phase of consolidation" evident in the pro-

> gramme and of course they have this in the programme and now of course you have to read between the lines: what could it mean? What does it mean? Of course, they are very interested in getting Croatia on board, but not necessarily Turkey (Interview 5, 2009).

The EU official pointed out that, "Out of the original EU six, Italy is a strong enlargement supporter, but the five other are not that strong in supporting enlargement as they were until 2004" (Interview 5, 2009).

Against the background of divisions among Member States, the growing application of closing benchmarks and the introduction of opening benchmarks have significant implications not only for the veto power of individual Member States, but also for the scope and range of EU conditions. As the Greek foreign minister pointed out following the start of the accession negotiations with Turkey, "We have passed from the time when we did not set conditions to a time when we set conditions, a great many conditions, that Turkey is obliged to accept" (Agence Europe 2009).

Following the completion of the accession negotiations with Croatia, Commissioner for Enlargement Füle emphasised the fact that benchmarks multiply the veto power of Member States by noting that the 138 benchmarks that Croatia had had to meet represented "138 possibilities for any member state to veto" (European Voice 2011).

The analysis shows that the lack of strong consensus among Member States and growing divisions regarding both the scope and the speed of the EU enlargement process have strongly influenced the relationships between the Union and Croatia, Turkey and FYROM. The research also highlights the growing relevance of outstanding bilateral issues between Member States and candidate countries for EU enlargement. The recent developments during the on-going enlargement round illustrate their full potential to severely disrupt the dynamics of the accession process by blocking partially or completely its advancement. The examination illustrates how the growing application of opening and closing benchmarks multiplies not only the veto power of Member States, but also allows them to influence the scope and the range of the conditions that candidate countries need to satisfy. Furthermore, the strong comparative dimension of the study shows that most Member States have proactively shaped the development of the enlargement policy; therefore, we can confirm that the policy is not under the control of a few.

Commission: Dominant Driving Force for Enlargement

As the previous section noted the emergence of growing divisions among the Member States about the direction and the speed of the enlargement process, this section examines the influence of the inter-institutional dynamics of the Union by focusing on the role of the Commission in keeping enlargement firmly on the EU agenda. It reflects on the growing entrepreneurship of the Commission by looking into its impact on: the opening of the accession negotiations with Ankara and Zagreb; the establishment of renewed consensus on enlargement and the mediation of bilateral disputes between candidate countries and Member States.

Although the Union recognised Turkey as a candidate country in 1999, the advancement of the accession process with Ankara proved to be highly controversial. In the midst of growing opposition to Turkey's application, the Commission actively pursued a viable solution. Although the negotiating framework confirmed that "the shared objective of these negotiations is accession", it also for the first time specified that "these negotiations are an open-ended process the outcome of which cannot be guaranteed beforehand" (European Commission 2005c). One senior EU official confirmed that new development was the result of a negotiated compromise and highlighted the Commission's role by noting:

> We had to find a formula accepted by all member states, so we had to find a text which was acceptable to those countries which were not happy about it. Austria was until the very end blocking the opening of the accession negotiations with Turkey. Austria was very negative on Turkey, but Austria was not the only one, you can imagine other countries: Cyprus, France, so we had to find a text that the countries being negative on Turkey can live with – one aim and the second was we did not want the mandates [for negotiations] between Croatia and Turkey to be very different. They had to be somewhat similar and that was the end result, but it was proposed by the Commission. (Interview 3, 2009)

It should be noted that the reference to the accession negotiations as an open-ended process has become a characteristic feature of the ongoing enlargement of the Union as it was also included in the negotiating frameworks with Croatia and Iceland (European Commission 2005b; 2010b). However, a senior EU official highlighted another new development that was engineered in order to launch negotiations with Ankara by pointing out that the Commission included only for Turkey the possibility of applying permanent safeguard clauses (Interview 7, 2009; European Commission 2005c).

The role of the Commission for the development of the EU enlargement policy was not limited to facilitating the agreement on the start of the membership talks with Ankara and Zagreb. It also reaffirmed the political significance of the ongoing accession process by establishing the key principles of the EU's enlargement policy towards Turkey and the Western Balkans and reorganising the structure of the accession negotiations. One senior EU official reflected on the link between the declining enthusiasm for further enlargement and the growing entrepreneurship of the Commission and commented that: "The situation for Verheugen was a lot easier because everybody supported it [enlargement], now Olli Rehn invented the sense of the carefully managed enlargement policy" (Interview 3, 2009).

Commissioner Rehn justified the new approach of the Commission by pointing out that: "The virtue of the renewed consensus on enlargement is that it both emphasises the strategic value of enlargement, i.e. the EU's soft power and, at the same time, identifies the ways and means to ensure our capacity to function, while gradually integrating new members" (Rehn 2008b).

The reaffirmed commitment of the Union towards Southeastern Europe was accompanied by practical measures aimed at improving the quality of the accession process. Olli Rehn highlighted one of the key aspects of the new approach by noting that "we now use benchmarks more systematically" (Rehn, 2008b). Although there is a virtual agreement among EU officials that the systematic use of benchmarks has significantly improved the accession negotiations, it is difficult to establish whether the new approach has strengthened the position of the Commission vis-à-vis the Council. A senior member of the Council Secretariat reflected on the new inter-institutional dynamics by noting:

> At the beginning I thought that this [benchmarking] gives an enormous power to the Commission but then I noticed that at least some members look very carefully, of course, it depends on the strength of your administration, your administrative capacity. If you take France, we all know, they have a very efficient public administration they look very carefully; they come regularly with questions, comments, proposals. (Interview 8, 2009)

However, a senior official from one of the candidate countries insisted that the extensive use of benchmarks has shifted the inter-institutional balance and commented:

> Now when they [the conditions] are spelled out you cannot do anything, now you cannot lobby [member states] to close a chapter if you don't fulfil the benchmarks, previously, chapters were closed based on some political decisions […] Now because it is less political, more technical and the Commission has more power in a way to decide. If it is more technical, they [Commission officials] tend to be more objective than the member states. (Interview 1, 2009)

Although it is difficult to argue that the Commission has become more influential than the Council, as the Council is the institution that decides unanimously on the opening and closing of the negotiation chapters, most interviewees highlighted the Commission's potential to influence the development of the accession process. One national official reflected on the reorganisation of the accession negotiations and stressed: 'This time around, deliberately, I think the concentration, the discussion is now in the Commission and then [the] Commission suggests to the Council" (Interview 1, 2009). The comments were echoed by an EU official who noted that "the debate is structured by what the Commission proposes and it is a way of having the debate in a certain direction" (Interview 9, 2009).

The Commission's commitment to strengthening the credibility of the accession process is also reflected by its involvement in mediating bilateral issues between candidate countries and Member States. Following the escalation of the Croatia-Slovenia border dispute, Olli Rehn actively sought to facilitate the dialogue between the two countries and help them find a solution (*EU Observer* 2009).

A national official acknowledged the complexity of the situation and insisted that "in a sense the Commissioner is the only one who can do that [mediate] because no member state can take it up" (Interview 6, 2009). Although the Commission has not intervened in the name dispute between Greece and FYROM, it has tried to mitigate its impact. In March 2012, with a view to lending a new momentum to the accession process with FYROM, the Commission launched a High Level Accession Dialogue with Skopje (European Commission 2012). The Commissioner for Enlargement pointed out that the new initiative "is by no means a substitute for actual negotiations" and commented that the "aim is to support the reform process, to inject new dynamism into it and to boost the European perspective for the country" (Füle 2012).

The analysis shows that against the background of declining enthusiasm for further enlargement, the Commission's activism has intensified significantly. In addition to steering the accession negotiations into a more technical direction, the Commission has pursued a very active role in counteracting the damaging effects of bilateral disputes between candidate countries and Member States. The growing influence of the Commission on shaping the parameters of the accession process highlights its crucial role as a driving force for the development of EU enlargement policy.

Conclusion

The comparative analysis of the impact of the inter-institutional dynamics on the evolution of EU enlargement policy towards Turkey, Croatia and FYROM shows that the influence of the Council of the EU and the Commission is not a direct function of their competences and responsibilities. The study acknowledges the leading role of the Council in decision-making; however, it also illustrates the increasing relevance and growing influence of the Commission. Despite the growing application of detailed differentiated and targeted conditionality and the restructuring of the accession negotiations, the on-going enlargement process with the countries of South-eastern Europe has faced a number of serious challenges. Although the Commission envisaged the completion of the technical negotiation with Zagreb by end of 2009, it was only after the Slovene-Croat border issue was resolved that the EU managed to conclude the accession negotiations successfully in June 2011 (European Commission 2008; 2011). Unlike Croatia, FYROM and Turkey are yet to find a resolution to their bilateral issues with EU Member States. The long-standing name dispute between Greece and FYROM has had a detrimental impact on the advancement of the accession process with Skopje. Although the Commission first issued a positive recommendation for the start of the accession negotiations with FYROM in 2009, the Council has failed to reach a unanimous decision. The advancement of the accession process with another candidate country – Turkey – has also been significantly damaged by bilateral issues and growing opposition towards the prospect of its membership. Since the opening of the chapter on Food Safety, Veterinary and Phytosanitary in June 2010, the accession negotiations with Ankara have stalled. In addition to the restrictions introduced because of Turkey's failure to fully implement the Ankara Protocol, individual Member States have blocked the opening of eighteen chapters; and thus only '3 chapters remain that can be open in case the technical opening criteria are satisfied" (Government of Turkey 2011).

The renewed consensus on enlargement has improved the quality of the accession process and confirmed the EU's commitment to countries of South Eastern Europe. However, the very slow pace of advancement of the relations between the Union and Turkey and FYROM illustrate the damaging impact of bilateral issues on the EU's most successful foreign policy. Furthermore, the current financial crisis has not only endangered the survival of the single currency and made saving the eurozone the Union's highest priority, but also has fuelled strong anti-enlargement sentiments. The drastic changes in the political climate in Europe have significantly weakened the credibility of the EU's commitment to further enlargement. Although the lack of strong supporters for the ongoing accession process has limited the Commission's scope for manoeuvring, it is evident that Directorate General Enlargement should actively seek a new direction aimed at reinvigorating the momentum of the enlargement project

References

Agence Europe. 2008. "EU/Enlargement: Referendum Remains Compulsory in France for All New EU Accessions, after that of Croatia". 5 July.

Agence Europe. 2009. "EU/Enlargement: Accession of Balkan Countries and Turkey Will Not Necessarily Prevent Deepening of EU, states Rehn". 30 April.

Avery, G. 2009. "Uses of Time in the EU's Enlargement Process". *Journal of European Public Policy* 16 (2): 256-269.

Baldwin, R. 1995. "The Eastern Enlargement of the European Union". *European Economic Review*, 39 (3-4): 474-481.

Bellier, I. 2004. "The European Commission between the Acquis Communautaire and Enlargement". In *The Changing European Commission*, ed., D. Dimitrakopoulos. Manchester: Manchester University Press, 138-152.

Börzel, T. and T. Risse. 2012a. "From Europeanisation to Diffusion: Introduction." *West European Politics* 35 (1): 1-19.

Börzel, T. and T. Risse. 2012b. "When Europeanisation Meets Diffusion: Exploring New Territory". *West European Politics* 35 (1): 192-207.

Council of the European Union. 2006. 2770th Council Meeting, General Affairs and External Relations, General Affairs, C/06/352, Brussels, 11 December.

Dimitrova, A. and D. Toshkov. 2009. "Post-Accession Compliance between Administrative Co-Ordination and Political Bargaining". European Integration Online Papers 13(2), 19. http://eiop.or.at/eiop/texte/2009-019a.htm (Last accessed 1 May 2012).

Droutsas, D. 2010. "Foreign Minister Droutsas's Press Conference at the General Affairs and Foreign Affairs Councils", Brussels, 14 December 2010. http://www2.mfa.gr/www.mfa.gr/GoToPrintable.aspx?UICulture=en-US& GUID={A5B5D35D-35C7-41AD-BF4E-EC35F2BA2CE2} (Last accessed: 1 May 2012).

EU Observer. 2009. "Slovenia Wants Changes to Croatia Border Resolution Plan". 19 May. http://euobserver.com/15/28153 (Last accessed 1 May 2012).

EU Observer. 2010. "Turkey Allies Speak Out after EU Accession Talks Stall". 15 December. http://euobserver.com/15/31507 (Last accessed 1 May 2012).

Euractiv. 2009. "Slovenia Waves Referendum Card at Croatia". 8 January. http://www.euractiv.com/enlargement/slovenia-waves-referendum-card-croatia/article-178349 (Last accessed 1 May 2012).

Euractiv. 2010. "Slovenian Vote Clears Main Obstacle to EU Accession". 7 June. http://www.euractiv.com/enlargement/slovenian-vote-clears-croatia-s-main-obstacle-eu-accession-news-494916 (Last accessed 1 May 2012).

Euractiv. 2011a. "Austria Mulls Turkey Referendum, Ankara Unimpressed". 6 May. http://www.euractiv.com/enlargement/austria-mulls-turkey-referendum-ankara-unimpressed-news-504579 (Last accessed 1 May 2012).

Euractiv. 2011b. "EU Bets on Montenegro Keep Enlargement Alive". 12 October. http://www.euractiv.com/enlargement/eu-bets-montenegro-keep-enlargement-alive-news-508306 (Last accessed 1 May 2012).

Eurobarometer. 2005a. Eurobarometer 63 – Public Opinion in the European Union. Brussels: European Commission.

Eurobarometer. 2005b. Eurobarometer 64 – Public Opinion in the European Union. Brussels: European Commission.

Eurobarometer. 2006. Eurobarometer 66 – Public Opinion in the European Union. Brussels: European Commission.

Eurobarometer. 2008. Eurobarometer 70 – Public Opinion in the European Union. Brussels: European Commission.

Eurobarometer. 2010. Eurobarometer 74, Autumn 2010 – Public Opinion in the European Union. Brussels: European Commission.

European Commission. 2005a. Communication from the Commission – 2005 Enlargement Strategy Paper. COM (2005) 561 final. Brussels: European Commission.

European Commission. 2005b. Negotiating Framework for Croatia, Brussels: European Commission.

European Commission. 2005c. Negotiating Framework for Turkey. Brussels: European Commission.

European Commission. 2006. Communication from the Commission to the European Parliament and the Council – Enlargement Strategy and Main Challenges 2006-2007, Including Annexed Special Reports on EU's Capacity to Integrate New Members. COM (2006) 649 final. Brussels: European Commission.

European Commission. 2008. Communication from the Commission to the Council and to the European Parliament – Enlargement Strategy and Main Challenges 2008-2009. COM (2008) 674 final. Brussels: European Commission.

European Commission. 2009. Commission Staff Working Document – The Former Yugoslav Republic of Macedonia 2009 Progress Report, SEC (2009) 1335 final. Brussels: European Commission.

European Commission. 2009b. Communication from the Commission to the European Parliament and the Council – Enlargement Strategy and Main Challenges 2009-2010, COM (2009) 533 final. Brussels: European Commission.

European Commission. 2009c. *Enlargement Newsletter, 13 January 2009.* http://ec.europa.eu/enlargement/press_corner/newsletter/130109_en.htm (Last accessed 1 May 2012).

European Commission. 2010a. *Communication from the Commission to the European Parliament and the Council – Enlargement Strategy and Main Challenges 2010-2011*, COM (2010) 660 final. Brussels: European Commission.

European Commission. 2010b. *Negotiating Framework for Iceland.* Brussels: European Commission.

European Commission. 2011. *Communication from the Commission to the European Parliament and the Council – Enlargement Strategy and Main Challenges 2011-2012*, COM (2011) 666 final. Brussels: European Commission.

European Commission. 2012. In "Skopje to Launch High Level Accession Dialogue".http://ec.europa.eu/commission_2010-2014/fule/headlines/news/2012/03/20120314_en.htm (Last accessed: 1 May 2012).

European Voice. 2009. "Slovenia Ready to Lift Veto on Croatia's EU Bid". 11 September.

European Voice. 2011. "Croatia Completes EU Talks". 30 June.

Fierke, K. and A. Wiener. 1999. "Constructing Institutional Interests: EU and NATO Enlargement". Journal of European Public Policy, 6 (3): 727-742.

Financial Times. 2010. "Slovenians Approve Border Deal with Croatia". 6 June. http://www.ft.com/cms/s/0/18cf2722-7163-11df-8eec-00144feabdc0.html#axzz1uqdJV5ia (Last accessed 1 May 2012).

Füle, Š. 2012. "Policy Address at the Plenary Debate on the Former Yugoslav Republic of Macedonia". Speech 12/186 European Parliament. Strasbourg, 14 March.

Grabbe, H. 2006. *The EU's Transformative Power. Europeanization through Conditionality in Central and Eastern Europe*. Basingstoke: Palgrave Macmillan.

Government of Croatia. 2011. "Progress at EU-Croatia Negotiations at a Glance".http://www.eu-pregovori.hr/DOWNLOAD/2011/09/14/Progress_in_EU-Croatia_accession_negotiations-2011-06-16-M.pdf (Last accessed 1 May 2012).

Government of Turkey. 2011. "Turkey-EU Relations". http://www.mfa.gov.tr/relations-between-turkey-and-the-european-union.en.mfa (Last accessed 1 May 2012).

Hyde-Price, A. 2000. *Germany and European Order: Enlarging NATO and the EU.* Manchester: Manchester University Press.

İçener, E., D. Phinnemore, and D. Papadimitriou. 2010. "Continuity and Change in the European Union's Approach to Enlargement: Turkey and Central and Eastern Europe Compared". *Southeast European and Black Sea Studies*, 10 (2): 207-223.

Interview 1. 2009. Official, Mission of Croatia. Brussels. July.

Interview 2. 2009. Official, Mission of Turkey. Brussels. July.

Interview 3. 2009. Official, European Commission, DG I. Brussels. July.

Interview 4. 2009. Official, European Commission, DG I. Brussels. July.

Interview 5. 2009. Official, European Commission, DG I. Brussels. June.

Interview 6. 2009. Official, Permanent Representation (New Member State). Brussels. June.

Interview 7. 2009. Official, European Commission, DG I. Brussels. June.

Interview 8. 2009. Official, General Secretariat of the Council of the European Union. Brussels. July.

Interview 9. 2009. Official, European Commission, DG II. Brussels. July.

Kujundžić, M. 2011. Relations with the EU: Experience of a Candidate Country, CDL-UDT (2011) 018. http://www.venice.coe.int/docs/2011/CDL-UDT%282011%29018-e.pdf (Last accessed, 1 May 2012).

Lass-Lennecke, K., and A. Werner. 2009. "Policies, Institutions and Time: How the European Commission Managed the Temporal Challenge of Eastern Enlargement". *Journal of European Public Policy* 16 (2): 270-285.

Lavenex, S. 2008. "A Governance Perspective on the European Neighbourhood Policy: Integration Beyond Conditionality?" *Journal of European Public Policy* 15 (6): 938-955.

Mattli, W., and T. Plumper. 2002. "The Demand-Side Politics of EU Enlargement: Democracy and the Application for EU Membership". *Journal of European Public Policy*, 9 (4): 550-574.

Official Journal. 1997. Treaty of Amsterdam, C 340. 10 November.

Official Journal. 2007. Treaty of Lisbon Amending the Treaty on European Union and the Treaty Establishing the European Community, signed at Lisbon, 13 December 2007, C306. 17 December.

Piedrafita, S. 2007. "Setting EU Eastern Enlargement Policy: Spain's Preferences for an Inclusive Process". *South European Society and Politics*, 12 (2): 203-220.

Pridham, G. 2007. "Change and Continuity in the European Union's Political Conditionality: Aims, Approach, and Priorities". *Democratization*, 14 (3): 446-471.

Rehn, O. 2005. "Values Define Europe, not Borders". 4 January. http://www.ft.com/cms/s/0/26bde788-5df5-11d9-ac01-00000e2511c8.html#axzz1uwuEWpbb (Last accessed 1 May 2012).

Rehn, O. 2006a. "Europe's Next Frontiers". Speech 06/561. Lecture at Bilkent University, Ankara. 4 October.

Rehn, O. 2006b. "Enlargement Package". Speech 06/727. European Parliament, Foreign Affairs Committee. Brussels, 21 November.

Rehn, O. 2008a. "Communication on the Western Balkans: Enhancing the European Perspective". Speech 08/140. Western Balkans, Workshop. Brussels. 11 March.

Rehn, O. 2008b. "A Stronger Union through Deeping and Widening". Speech 08/184. EPP Conference on Enlargement and Consolidation of the European Union. Brussels. 8 April.

Schimmelfennig, F. 1998. "Liberal Norms and the Eastern Enlargement of the European Union: A Case for Sociological Institutionalism", *Österreichische Zeitschrift für Politikwissenschaft*, 27 (4): 459-472.

Schimmelfennig, F. 2001. "The Community Trap: Liberal Norms, Rhetorical Action and the Eastern Enlargement of the European Union". *International Organization*, 55 (1): 47-80.

Schimmelfennig, F., and H. Scholtz. 2008. "EU Democracy Promotion in the European Neighbourhood: Political Conditionality, Economic Development and Transnational Exchange". *European Union Politics*, 9(2): 187-215.

Schimmelfennig, F., and U. Sedelmeier. 2004. "Governance by Conditionality: EU Rule Transfer to the Candidate Countries of Central and Eastern Europe", *Journal of European Public Policy*, 11 (4): 661-679.

Schimmelfennig, F., and F. Trauner, eds. 2009. "Post-Accession Compliance in the EU's New Member States". *European Integration Online Papers (EIoP)*, Special Issue 2 (13).

Schukkink, M., and A. Niemann. 2010. "Portugal and the EU's Eastern Enlargement: A Logic of Identity Endorsement". European Foreign Policy Unit (EFPU) Working Paper 2010/1. http://www2.lse.ac.uk/international Relations/centresandunits/EFPU/EFPUpdfs/EFPUworkingpaper2010-1.pdf (Last accessed 1 May 2012).

Sedelmeier, U. 2005. *Constructing the Path to Eastern Enlargement: The Uneven Policy Impact of EU Identity*. Manchester: Manchester University Press.

Sedelmeier, U. 2008. "After Conditionality: Post-Accession Compliance with EU Law in East Central Europe". *Journal of European Public Policy*, 15 (6): 806-825.

Sedelmeier, U. 2011. "Europeanisation in New Member and Candidate States". *Living Reviews in European Governance*, 6 (1).

Sjursen, (2002) "Why Expand? The Question of Legitimacy and Justification in the EU's Enlargement Policy?" *Journal of Common Market Studies*, 40 (3): 491-513.

Tewes, H. 1998. "Between Deepening and Widening: Role Conflict in Germany's Enlargement Policy". *West European Politics*, 21 (2): 117-133.

Toshkov, D. 2007. "In Search of the Worlds of Compliance: Culture and Transposition Performance in the European Union". *Journal of European Public Policy*, 14 (6): 933-959.

Toshkov, D. 2008. "Embracing European Law: Compliance with EU Directives in Central and Eastern Europe". *European Union Politics*, 9 (3): 379-402.

Vachudová, M. 2005. *Europe Undivided: Democracy, Leverage and Integration after Communism*. Oxford: Oxford University Press.

Zielonka, J. 2001. *Democratic Consolidation in Eastern Europe*. Oxford: Oxford University Press.

Changing Theoretical Paradigm of EU Enlargement

Tanel KERIKMÄE and Lehte ROOTS

Introduction

Today's Europe is not the same as it was 50 or even 20 years ago. The continent's aims, influence and cooperation – as well as globalisation in general – have changed our view of the way the region operates today; it has survived many enlargements, and each of these enlargements has brought its own changes to the Union itself.

There have been varying goals and different emphases throughout the EU enlargement process. Enlargement has been seen as a positive political obligation, not only for the EU but also for candidate countries, which assume that EU membership will bring more prosperity (Staszczak, 2011). However, such a statement may not be as valid for some states as it seemed only a few years ago. Leaving aside the history (Lightfoot, 2008; Pusca, 2008), our main question is: Can all the canons and requirements for the candidate states be the same as they were before the Lisbon Treaty? It is dubious to believe so for the following reasons:

1. the changing balance in competences between member states and the EU (losing sovereignty);
2. the European crisis and the formation of a 'new Europe' that may be more fragmented on the basis of belonging to the euro zone, Schengen area and other regional arrangements;
3. changes in global political agendas (Archick and Mix, 2010).

The first aspect can be analysed broadly. It is fact that in becoming a legal person, the EU has gained more power, but also responsibility. At the same time, the balance of powers seems far from clear. Every treaty that has been adopted has changed somehow the competence and powers of the EU. Therefore, the question of whether the Lisbon Treaty would soften any remaining obstacles to further EU enlargement should be taken seriously.

As De Witte (2003) explains, previous enlargements have also acted as catalysts for constitutional change, or at least for rethinking the political and institutional course of the European integration process. Previously there had been few substantial changes to the treaties, but the Lisbon Treaty managed to introduce several changes. It seems that the *acquis communautaire* transition that was used in previous enlargements constituted an insufficient response, not so much for the candidate countries as for the European Union itself. The Lisbon Treaty was developed from the need to change the current treaties in light of the enlargements.

The EU itself has changed dramatically. For example, the competence of the EU was extended by the Lisbon Treaty in the area of freedom, security and justice (European Union, 2007). Lisbon merged the first and third pillars of the EU, and made co-decision the standard legislative procedure for the whole area of freedom, security and justice (further called AFSJ), consequently completing the process of the communitarisation of competences in AFSJ (Roots, 2009). Previously it was referred to as the legislative competence in the area of justice and home affairs.

Legislative authority in immigration and asylum lies now partly in the hands of the EU. It is important in the AFSJ that the new candidate states consider not only that the decision-making power has shifted, but also that the European Court of Justice (ECJ) has rights to judicial decision-making and interpretation in immigration and asylum matters. The UK, Ireland and Denmark nevertheless concluded special arrangements to legalise their special positions in the new situation. The political agendas for the potential member states thus may be more challenging than before. However, new accession states like Croatia cannot change EU policies or legislation adopted before their accession, like the 'old' EU states (Denmark, the UK or Ireland) can do. Those challenges have directly affected the changes that have emerged at the EU level. The candidate countries must essentially think about 'which' European Union they want to join, since there are different stages of accession; for example, the one having the Schengen system or the one using the euro as a means of payment.

One of the key tools in regulating relations between member states and the EU is certainly the principle of subsidiarity (Art. 5 of the Treaty on European Union). As stated by Simona Constantin (2008, p. 165):

> [T]he novelty brought by Lisbon is the Protocol on the application of the principles of subsidiarity and proportionality, which contains a legal framework for a reinforced control of subsidiarity. This protocol opens up access to the European law-making process for national parliaments, which are given the role of controlling the compliance of legislative proposals with the principle of subsidiarity. Until now the *ex ante* protection of subsidiarity was left to the governments and their ability to defend the national regulato-

ry competences. The new framework provides for an *ex ante* role for national parliaments.

At the same time, the post-Lisbon era and euro crisis have both shown that national parliaments play very different roles in decision-making. The Lisbon Treaty has changed the role of the national parliaments and has brought their role and competence into the decision-making processes of the European Union. Article 12 of the TEU states that national parliaments contribute actively to the proper functioning of the Union and that they should be notified of any application for accession to the EU.

The most powerful example of the role of a country's national parliament and courts would be the German constitutional court's decision of 2009 about the Lisbon Treaty's compatibility with the German constitution. It has created new perspectives – not so much about the future of the treaty itself, but precisely from the viewpoint of the EU's internal operating mechanisms on several levels. The Karlsruhe court's decision could be compared against the concepts outlined above. The German constitutional court asserted that the Lisbon Treaty is not, in principle, contrary to the state's constitution. Nevertheless, the ratification process was stopped until the German parliament adopted a law that substantiated its role in determining the EU's integration process and the application of EU norms. Thus, there has been a turn back to a highly normative approach and withdrawal from generalisations that would deny the supremacy of EU law as such. The decision may be seen as a sign of a new relationship between the EU and its member states, which is characterised by what can be called *deliberative supranationalism* (Kerikmäe and Nyman-Metcalf, 2011). The *Lisbon* judgment in that sense forms a continuation of the Maastricht doctrine, as the principle of conferred powers is affirmed. The court again denied the EU a *Kompetenz-Kompetenz* – that is, the power to determine its own powers (Kiiver, 2010). It is a clear example of how the member states are shaping the development of EU law and how new member states might bring to the EU their administrative or legislative culture. The new mechanism provided by the Lisbon Treaty seems to intend an increased scrutiny of this principle. The weak *ex post* control of subsidiarity has been reinforced with an *ex ante* one (Constantin, 2008).

The fact that the differentiation of the competence areas is 'under construction' also needs to be taken into account by both the EU and candidate states in the process of ongoing and possible future enlargements. At the very least, there seems to be a need to give a new margin of appreciation of member states in light of the euro crisis – which, on the contrary, has required stronger EU involvement in decision-making processes.

The post-Lisbon situation supports that member states constitute an even more integral part of the sophisticated European decision-making body. As Voermans explains, the member states may have become full legislative partners in two ways: in contributing to the preparation and adoption of European legislation and in being responsible for perfecting European legislation once adopted (Voermans, 2011). The implementation process (by member states) goes together with interpretation and policy setting and cannot be, therefore, underestimated.

It must be recognised that even if objective planning, collection of information, decision-making, coordination and control are executed at the EU level, by the institutions of the EU, the implementation of the decisions is put into practice on the member state level by the institutions of the member states (Torma, 2008).

Hard cases deriving from the EU judicial system constitute a good basis of analysis for the EU and potential member states in preparing for the accession. Even if the new states can be considered weaker and the founding members still play a leading role (the phenomenon called 'Merkozy'), the leaders of the EU members are themselves aiming to create a more unified and politically stronger Union (the latest example would be the pressure from Germany to have more EU level control over Greek budgetary mechanisms). If we think of the EU as an organisation, we can apply some organisational theories in order to facilitate the enlargement and integration of the newcomers.

"Those are my principles, and if you don't like them...well, I have others" (Groucho Marx)

Joining the EU does not bring only benefits. Accession to the EU includes a significant loss of sovereignty for a state. Nevertheless, the EU is growing. Estonia joined the EU in 2004 before the Lisbon Treaty changes emerged, and it can be said that it was a success for Estonia. As Professor Kerikmäe (2001, p. 291) states, "the new enlargement process has raised the question of the legal and ethical bases of delegating sovereignty". For many states, sovereignty is something that is going to be diminished by joining every new organisation or structure that has its own rules.

Every country that wants to join the EU has to fulfil the Copenhagen criteria that were agreed upon in 1993 during the Council meeting in that city. The criteria are also relevant now as they focus on essential issues – for example, democratic state order, respect of human and minority rights, following the rule of law. The state must have a functioning market economy and be able to cope with the EU's competition conditions. In 1995, the European Council in Madrid clarified that the candidate country has to have the ability to implement the EU's rules and procedures. For accession, the country must create the conditions for its integration by adapting its administrative and judicial structures. It seems, however, that the requirements of accession must be reviewed again in light of the financial crisis of the euro zone.

Nevertheless, the EU's ability to integrate new members must be evaluated as well, since it needs to ensure that its institutions and decision-making processes remain effective and accountable. The aim of the EU is to remain as it is even after the enlargement. It is an impossible task, since all new states bring in their wishes, cultures, and ideas of cooperation, legislation or policymaking.

The concern about enlargement is that it should not influence the EU's ability to develop and implement common policies in all areas. The EU also needs to be in a position to continue financing its policies in a sustainable manner (Official website of the European Union, n.d.).

The procedures and speed of accession depend not only on the amount of the legislation to be reviewed and the states' own capacity to reorganise, but also on the capacity, current issues and willingness of other member states. The EU committed itself to an eastern enlargement at the Edinburgh summit in December 1992. After that, it started to develop the tools to interact purposefully with the eastern candidates. At the Copenhagen summit in June 1993, it set out the general political and economic conditions of membership in the Copenhagen criteria – but it did not evaluate the candidates in terms of these requirements.

Before Estonia could join the EU, there was a need to change the Estonian constitution. Because of the country's oppressive history, it protects its sovereignty exceptionally strictly through several safeguards. The European Commission reached a conclusion that, based on the current constitution, Estonia would not be able to become a full member of the European Union nor did it fulfil the requirements of the Union's legislation (Constitution of the Republic of Estonia, 1996, Chapter IX).

According to Article 1 of its constitution, Estonia is an independent and sovereign democratic republic, wherein the supreme power of the state is vested in the people. The independence and sovereignty of Estonia are timeless and inalienable (Constitution of the Republic of Estonia, 1996). Exactly because of this provision, Estonia needed to pass a referendum in order to give powers to the EU. As Albi (2001) argues, harmonisation under the European Association Agreements as well as other European adaptations, such as institutional reorganisations, accession negotiations and expenditure of state budget for this end do signify a fundamental subordination of a state's independent decision-making powers to the EU and should therefore require either an authorising constitutional amendment or a rather modern, open approach to sovereignty. Under the old treaties, it used to be problematic that the re-delegation of sovereignty was not clear. It was not evident how the member states could step out from under the European Union. It is stated in Article 50(2) of the TEU, however, that every member state has a right to withdraw from Union membership:

> A Member State which decides to withdraw shall notify the European Council of its intention. In the light of the guidelines provided by the European Council, the Union shall negotiate and conclude an agreement with that State, setting out the arrangements for its withdrawal, taking account of the framework for its future relationship with the Union. That agreement shall be negotiated in accordance with Article 218(3) of the Treaty on the Functioning of the European Union. It shall be concluded on behalf of the Union by the Council, acting by a qualified majority, after obtaining the consent of the European Parliament.

By this provision, the problem of losing sovereignty to an indefinite extent is abolished. If the member state feels that participation in the Union is a threat to its sovereignty, it can withdraw from the Union.

The obligation of harmonisation is difficult to reconcile with sovereignty requirements, considering that an acceding state has had no participation in the formation of the *acquis*. Nevertheless, the new member state has to take it on until its membership has been approved, which can take an indefinite amount of time. Moreover, the *acquis* has to be taken over with a minimum of bargaining and with minimum consideration of, for example, Estonia's (and other Central and Eastern European countries') special circumstances. Current accession states are not to be participating, even regarding new draft legislations.

For earlier accession countries – Greece, Spain and Portugal – the EU made considerable compromises. The consolidation of democracy in these countries was expected to take place after EU membership, and long transition periods were allowed to aid economic development: more than a decade for some trade policy issues, agriculture, five to seven years for the abolition of customs duties, and the adjustment of monopolies, among many other things (Grabbe, 1999).

From a political perspective, the Copenhagen criteria (conclusions of the European Council, 1993) are formulated rather broadly and allow a considerable degree of subjectivity. The example of the accession of Greece shows that a country may achieve membership for political reasons: in economic terms, Greece, with its backbone of agriculture and a weak industrial base, was hardly ready for accession. We've seen that Europe needed to help Greece out from its recession and it was not able to effectively control the development of the country. This case shows the importance of a country's readiness to deal with the EU's standards, and it might influence further accessions, where more control over the capacity of the country should be maintained.

During the eastern enlargement in 2004, specific political, economic and legal conditions were applied. For the first time, regular progress reports were produced and a pre-accession strategy was developed, which was founded on bilateral treaty commitments, incorporating 'Accession Partnerships', technical assistance and participation by the candidate states in Community programmes (Cremona, 2003; see also European Union, 2003).

In September 2006, a report was issued where the European Commission found serious problems in the readiness of two new accession countries, Bulgaria and Romania (European Commission, 2005). Nevertheless, it did not stop either the European Parliament or the member states in the Council from proceeding with the sixth enlargement on 1 January 2007, and did not revert to the postponement clause. It is further evidence of the EU's political commitment to enlargement. As these countries are not yet members of the euro zone, the monetary crisis is not so easily evidenced in those states. Instead of postponing their entry or making use of the safeguard clauses,[1] the Cooperation and Verification Mechanism was devised to support ongoing reforms in Bulgaria and Romania.

Romania's most serious weaknesses were identified in the state aid and competition chapters of the *acquis* as well as in the Schengen *acquis.* Moreover, control of external borders, corruption, cooperation between the gendarmerie and police as well as the struggle against organised crime were recognised as issues in that country. This might lead to a suggestion that maybe it is not even advisable to give some countries the possibility of joining all possible agreements. Without the safeguard clauses, Article 258 of the TFEU is applicable and the member state can be brought to the European Court of Justice for non-compliance. However, even when the Romania and Bulgaria have fulfilled all conditions to sign the Schengen Agreement, for political reasons they are still outside of the Schengen area.

On the other hand, it is rather difficult to foresee the problems of every accessing country. For example, Ireland joined the European Union in a weak economic position but it flourished as a member of the euro zone (Taylor, 2011). The 'Celtic Tiger' was a European economic star, a shining example of how to do business. Yet like any engine that burns too hot, the situation quickly deteriorated after the construction industry ran out of steam; it was an industry that Ireland relied on

1 The safeguard clause is a tool of prevention, designed to anticipate compliance, implementation and enforcement inadequacies, and non-compliance.

disproportionately compared to other states. Unfortunately for Ireland's major banks, massive loans, speculative ventures and inflated pricing tied in with the construction industry left the banks desperate for recapitalisation (Taylor, 2011).

The problems in the Union forced the EU and its member states to take measures, described as follows by Piris (2011), which can also be recognised as potential sources for new enlargement criteria for prospective member states:

- increasing complexity;
- the creation of an inner group that imposes its political will on the others;
- the division of eastern and western countries;
- difficulty agreeing on a common list of domains that potential participating states would accept in order to cooperate together.

All of this creates an atmosphere of losing the exact framing of expectations for the accession states.

A Knock on the Door of the Dim Room

There is some evidence from the past that countries joining EU do not join other instruments created by EU at the same time they join the Union. Estonia joined the EU in 2004, the Schengen area only in 2007, and finally the euro zone in 2011. What can we say? The country was ready to join step by step to each of the possible cooperative relationships that were offered. However, the euro zone started to face its crisis, which was induced not by the new member states but by the old ones, which initially were not even ready to join the EU and euro zone. It might thus be very relevant to assess whether all the countries (new and 'old') should join all three levels of cooperation.

The Schengen Agreement is primarily concerned about the free movement and security of the EU. The euro zone is focused mostly on fiscal, economic and monetary security. We should not forget the importance of the institutional capacity of accession states as well as the capacity of the European Union itself.

Institutional capacity is important, not only for accession states' ability to manage the demands of membership but also for the Union itself, as the new members begin to play a part in policy – and decision-making at the Union level.

From the Union side, it was acknowledged already in 1993 by the European Council that the Union's capacity to absorb new members while maintaining the momentum of European integration is an important consideration in the general interests of both the Union and the candidate countries. The threat to the Union's decisional capacity posed by the dramatic expansion of the Union and the cumulative effects of several enlargements has been recognised but not defused.

Why would the Balkan states want to join? Vachudova (2003) argues that the EU is widely recognised as the international actor with the most influence in promoting ethnic reconciliation, shoring up democracy and supporting the economic revitalisation of the Balkans. She also highlights that "the EU policies toward the Balkans have become embedded in the much broader process of EU enlargement that has followed the collapse of communism in Europe's eastern half" (Vachudova, 2003, p. 143).

It was 1999 when the EU-led Stability and Growth Pact promised candidate status to the states of the Western Balkans – Croatia, Macedonia, Albania, the Federal Republic of Yugoslavia and Bosnia-Herzegovina – as soon as democratic standards were maintained and economic requests met. The Balkans, unfortunately, were clearly not ready to join in 2004 as there was a definite lack of some of the apparent prerequisites of successful democratisation.

Alongside the little economic wealth, feeble state institutions and weak civil societies, some Balkan states have had problematic relationships between ethnic minorities and majorities, and with cycles of political extremism brought on by ethnic cleansing and war. EU accession has always been an issue to be deliberated by the elite. The same was true in the Balkans: There was a need to pursue strategies of regional peace building, ethnic tolerance and economic reform. The prospect of EU membership could thus have been foreclosed to Albania and Macedonia but not to the Former Republic of Yugoslavia (FRY) or Croatia.

Vachudova (2003) opines that for Croatia and the FRY, the roadblock was the nationalism and the opportunism of certain political elites in conditions of state creation, economic insecurity and intermingled ethnic geography. While the EU developed some tools to dampen ethnic tensions in east central Europe in the 1990s, it was unable to prevent, contain or stop ethnic conflict in the disintegrating Yugoslavia. The most effective of the tools was based on the conditionality of EU membership.

In central east Europe, changes were peaceful – and the EU had time to adapt itself with the desire of these states to join the EU and to plot a strategy for their association to the Union. After war broke out in Yugoslavia in 1991, the EU government was determined to change the behaviour of post-communist governments elsewhere, particularly those that were using nationalism to threaten the rights of ethnic minorities and peaceful relations with neighbouring states. The EU's first attempt was the Balladur Plan of 1993, which was designed as to use the 'carrot' of future EU membership to encourage candidate states to settle national disputes, to pledge their acceptance of existing boundaries and their protection of the rights of national minorities. The Balladur Plan exhibited the powerlessness of the EU to influence nationalist-pattern governments with the threat of exclusion from a distant first wave of EU expansion.

Other countries, like Romania in 1996 or Slovakia in 1998, elected governments of moderate reformers that worked towards the goal to satisfy the requirements of the EU membership, including promotion of ethnic tolerance. In nationalist states, there was a gap between the 'formal commitment' to fulfilling the requirements of EU membership and their actual implementation by the government. International assistance is only effective where it supports credible domestic reform efforts emerging from the local political process (report by the EastWest Institute and the European Stability Initiative, 2001).

According to Vachudova (2003, p. 160):

> [T]he most powerful and successful aspect of EU foreign policy turned out to be the incentive of EU enlargement – and the Western Balkans are the region where EU enlargement can be used to make the CFSP a success. The success of the CFSP will be measured by its ability to apply the instruments available to the EU – trade agreements, economic aid, investment, technical assistance, visa requirements, and the incentives of EU membership – to fulfilling its declared foreign-policy goals, even if this entails overruling the short-term interests of some Member States and incurring substantial economic costs.

However, there are still some unresolved questions: Will the accession of the Balkan countries be the last accession before the collapse of the Union? Should the European Union enlarge to the African continent in order to spread democracy, human rights and peace? At the moment, we are far from these ideals and it seems that currently it is feasible to have close cooperation agreements under the neighbourhood policy. A good demonstration of such an agreement is the EU's relationship with Turkey, which has been an accession country for a long time but it is probably better that it stays on its own. By having a state with different norms, and religious and cultural values within the EU, it might change the EU and lead it to unwanted developments for old member states.

As some organisational theorists highlight, organisational agents should help newcomers to adjust by providing information, feedback, role models, social relationships and support, as well as access to broader networks (Major *et al.* 1995; Morrison 2002). It could be extremely helpful if older EU countries could provide peer supervision to the newcomers in all necessary fields by focusing on individual differences among the accession countries. Accession of new members should become even more *à la carte* and look at both the needs of the EU and the accession state. We should also not forget that accession of a new country is a learning process for the country – but also for the EU, in how to manage different administrative cultures and so on. The adaptation capacity of the EU towards newcomers and the newcomers' socialisation are both important for the common goal of the EU and maintaining stability in the Union. The EU's organisational role to facilitate these relationships between states is ever strongly needed.

Conclusion

Europe has to learn from its mistakes. Enlargement and accession decisions should not be based only on political will and readiness, but also on the set-up criteria and the economic interests of the Union. We should not forget that one of the primary goals of the European Union was economic cooperation. It is restated in the Lisbon Treaty and should remain as one of the fundamental cornerstones of the Union.

The Copenhagen conclusions helped to stimulate debate on whether the European Union itself should take these basic constitutional values more seriously by entrenching them more firmly in its own legal order. Enlargements have always brought in debates about the values and aims of the Union; for example, democracy and fundamental rights were part of the agenda in 1996 when the Amsterdam Treaty was discussed.

The European Union is very much a social club where members should speak the same language in order to understand each other and to develop the Union. A shared language means similar values, minimal cultural differences and like-minded political and economic goals.

For further enlargements, the EU should ask itself if there are any other states in the world that fulfil the criteria that has been desired by the EU. Different patterns of enlargement have also brought up various issues of political and social culture, and economic thinking. It is like in a big family where not all the members of the family want to support the one who is only spending and does not manage to gain anything for the group. This is said in light of the current right-wing political decision-making, and it might change when the European Union countries become more socially oriented. New enlargements need more screening of potential states as well as reflections on the core reasons of the EU's problems. Some problems might be resolved by financing the accession states, but some cannot be resolved in this way. Nevertheless, the core reasons still should be identified first. Enlargement should take into account the Lisbon Treaty changes and also the EU Charter of Fundamental Rights, and there might also be reason to review the basic criteria for accession to the EU. When the EU is in a crisis, it is clear that the first thing to do is to solve its own problems before expansion.

A new model for enlargement strategy should be elaborated. The new model would take into account the research on organisational socialisation, as the problems in the EU are deriving not so much from its existing formalistic rules but instead from the social cohesion between stakeholders in the EU's economic and legal systems.

The EU should commence in framing the criteria of accession from the principles of the rule of law. The accession criteria should be revised, taking into account the Lisbon Treaty changes and the current situation of the euro crisis in order to avoid the materialisation in new member states of problems such as those experienced by Greece. Moreover, there is a need for a different type of cooperation, based on more control by the other member states if the EU wants to maintain a strong unity. For the sake of objectivity and effectiveness, the authors of this chapter suggest having a clearly formulated enlargement model that recognises the EU as a learning organisation.

The new model for enlargement can be built with the help of research conducted in the field of organisational socialisation. According to Cooper-Thomas and Anderson (2006, p. 492), "organizational socialization is the process through which a new organizational employee adapts from outsider to integrated and effective insider". It is important that the organisation (the EU) and the newcomer (the accession state) share the same expectations, values and ability to adapt. As there are different tactics in organisational socialisation, the most suitable should be taken into account or analysed. The EU should take a position on whether to use collective strategy (for example, a state adapts to the EU on the basis of the principle of equilibrium) or individual strategy (adapted to the group – that is, the EU member states) taking into account the different political and economic categories of existing member states. The EU should be strong and unified enough to use a strategy of investiture, which means that the newcomers receive positive social support from insiders, rather than to continue the divestiture approach on the basis of subjective criteria (old and new, west and east). In this context, the innovative "multi-level learning focused model" (Cooper-Thomas and Anderson, 2006, p. 499) that analyses the process on the basis of Learning Domains (politics, history, future prospects); Success Indicators (performance, social cohesion, internal stability); and Learning Sources (EU law, principles, best practices of member states) would be a new way of thinking about enlargement. The research-based model that is not focused only on rigid and formalistic rules would help to avoid loyalty and identity crises in the future. This research-based model can also help to identify crucial problems in advance and find solutions before crises emerge.

The process of enlargement and accession is a two-way system, and it operates on multiple levels that reveal many objective distribution mechanisms. There should thus be an attempt both to categorise the EU and to give a prospective member state an opportunity to join the type of EU to which the state is suited.

References

Albi, A. 2001. "Europe Agreements in Light of Sovereignty and Legitimacy: Case of Estonia." In *EU Enlargement: The Constitutional Impact at EU and National Level*, eds. A. Kellerman, J.W. de Zwaan and J. Czuczai. Hague: T.M.S. Asser Institute, 195-214.

Archick, K. and D.E. Mix. 2010. "The European Union's Reform Process: The Lisbon Treaty." *Current Politics and Economics of Europe* 21(4): 209-18.

Constantin, S. 2008. "Rethinking Subsidiarity and the Balance of Powers in the EU in the Light of the Lisbon Treaty and Beyond." *Croatian Yearbook on European Law & Policy* 4: 151-77.

Constitution of the Republic of Estonia. 1996. Estonian Translation and Legislative Support Center, 2006.

Cooper-Thomas, H. and N. Anderson. 2006. "Organizational socialization: A new theoretical model and recommendations for future research and HRM practices in organizations." *Journal of Managerial Psychology* 21(5): 492-516.

Cremona, M. 2003. *The Enlargement of the European Union*. Oxford: Oxford University Press.

De Witte, B. 2003. "The Impact of Enlargement on the Constitution of the European Union." In *The Enlargement of the European Union*, ed. M. Cremona. Oxford: Oxford University Press, 209-51.

EastWest Institute and European Stability Initiative. 2001. *Democracy, Security and the Future of the Stability Pact for South Eastern Europe: A Framework for Debate*. Brussels: EastWest Institute and European Stability Initiative.

European Commission. 2005. *Comprehensive Monitoring Report on Bulgaria's and Romania's preparations for EU accession, COM*, 534 Final. Brussels.

European Council. 1993. *Conclusions of the presidency*. Copenhagen, 21-22 June. Brussels: General Secretariat of the Council.

European Union. 2003. "Notice concerning the entry into force of the Treaty of Accession." *Official Journal of the European Union* L 236.

European Union. 2007. "Treaty of Lisbon amending the Treaty on European Union and the Treaty establishing the European Community." *Official Journal of the European Union* C 306.

European Union. 2010. "Consolidated versions of the Treaty on European Union and the Treaty on the functioning of the European Union." *Official Journal of the European Union* C 83.

Grabbe, H. 1999. *Partnership for Accession? The Implications of EU Conditionality for the Central and East European Applicants*. EUI: Robert Schuman Centre, Working Paper No. 99/12.20.

Kellerman, A., J.W. de Zwaan and J. Czuczai. 2001. *EU Enlargement: The Constitutional Impact at EU and National Level*. The Hague: T.M.S. Asser Institute.

Kerikmäe, T. 2001. "Estonian Constitutional Problems in Accession to the EU." In *EU Enlargement: The Constitutional Impact at EU and National Level*, eds. A. Kellerman, J.W. de Zwaan and J. Czuczai. The Hague: T.M.S. Asser Institute, 291-300.

Kerikmäe, T. and K. Nyman-Metcalf. 2011. "Karlsruhe vs. Lisbon: an Overture to a Constitutional Dialogue?" *European Journal of Law Reform* 12: 373-87.

Kiiver, P. 2010. "The Lisbon Judgment of the German Constitutional Court: A Court-Ordered Strengthening of the National Legislature." *EU European Law Journal* 16(5): 578-88.

Lightfoot, S. 2008. "Enlargement and the Challenge of EU Development Policy." *Perspectives on European Politics and Society* 9(2): 128-42.

Major, D.A., S.W.J. Kozlowski, G.T. Chao and P.D. Gardner. 1995. "A longitudinal investigation of newcomer expectations, early socialization outcomes, and the moderating effect of role development factors." *Journal of Applied Psychology* 80(3): 418-31.

Morrison, E.W. 2002. "Newcomers' relationships: the role of social network ties during socialization." *Academy of Management Journal* 45(6): 1149-60.

Official website of the European Union. n.d. http://ec.europa.eu/enlargement/index_en.htm (3 November 2012).

Piris, J.C. 2011. "It is Time for the Euro Area to Develop Further Closer Cooperation Among its Members." *Jean Monnet Working Paper 05/11*. New York: NYU School of Law, 56-7.

Pusca, A. 2008. "Visualising the EU: the Central and East European Enlargement Experience. Perspectives." *Central European Review of International Affairs* 16(1): 5-21.

Roots, L. 2009. "The Impact of the Lisbon Treaty on the Development of EU Immigration Legislation." *Croatian Yearbook of European Law & Policy* 5: 261-81.

Staszczak, D.E. 2011. "Theoretical Interpretations of the European Union Enlargement: Perspectives from a New Global Paradigm." *Journal of Knowledge Globalization* 4(1): 71-92.

Torma, A. 2008. "The Public Administration of the European Union." *Juridical Current* 46: 23-37.

Taylor, S.F. 2011. "Financial Crisis in the European Union: The Cases of Greece and Ireland." Master's thesis, 7 September, Virginia Polytechnic Institute and State University. Blacksburg, Virginia. http://scholar.lib.vt.edu/theses/available/etd-09202011-160932/unrestricted/Taylor_SF_T_2011.pdf (21 October 2012).

Vachudova, M.A. 2003. "Strategies for Democratization and European Integration in the Balkans." In *The Enlargement of the European Union*, ed. M. Cremona. Oxford: Oxford University Press, 141-60.

Voermans, W.J.M. 2011. "The Birth of a Legislature: The EU Parliament after the Lisbon Treaty." *Brown Journal of World Affairs* Spring/Summer, 17(2): 163-80.

The Geopolitical Implications of Future EU Enlargements

Federiga BINDI and Irina ANGELESCU

Introduction

The 'Big Bang' enlargement of 2004-2007 was portrayed as a 'reunification of Europe', but in its aftermath the question of where Europe's frontiers end (and, hence, so does enlargement) was left open. This is most evident in the 2004 European Neighbourhood Policy (ENP) and 2009 Eastern Partnership (EaP) political frameworks, where the promise of membership was purposely avoided. The euro zone crisis, growing xenophobia among the societies of the EU member states and an overall deficient sense of historical legacy all partly explain the lack of enthusiasm for future enlargement. This chapter argues that should the EU continue its wishy-washy approach towards its neighbourhood, the EU's geopolitical weight in its immediate neighbourhood and with the wider world will be dramatically affected.[1]

This chapter adopts a policy perspective and analyses the ways in which the dramatic events of the past two years (from the Arab Spring and the nuclear disaster at Fukushima to the sanctions imposed on Iran) have turned energy security into a major issue in the EU's interaction with its neighbourhood. In this sense, it cautions that the EU's (previously) post-modernist foreign policy language may be replaced by a more pragmatic one, thus confusing its neighbours, the US and other international actors.

Looking into the Past: Putting Enlargement into Historical Perspective

The starting point for any analysis of the geopolitical implications of the EU enlargement – and the EU's relations with its neighbourhood – should be the observation that this process has never been an issue of

---

1 This chapter is based on the conclusions of our co-edited volume, *The Frontiers of Europe: A Transatlantic Problem?*, edited by Federiga Bindi and Irina Angelescu (Washington, DC: Brookings Institution Press in 2011).

European concern exclusively. The history of European integration shows that the very creation of the European institutions and the EU's successive waves of enlargement have been an indirect result of post-World War II transatlantic relations, because the United States has always viewed enlargement as a stabilisation tool in Europe and therefore a matter of national interest. The US has often expressed frustration with the slow rhythm of enlargement (and particularly with regard to Turkey's accession).

The EU's expansion to the countries of the Western Balkans would align both the EU's and the US's geopolitical interests for peace, stability and prosperity in the region. Beyond this geographical area, the situation may change depending on the EU's approach. If the EU adopts a unified voice and acts as a counterbalancing force to US (and Russian) influence in the neighbourhood, the United States would most likely reconsider its priorities – and, indeed, its attitude towards Europe, which could be perceived as a rival or an impediment to US interests. However, if the EU continues to behave like a weak international actor, with its position and actions diminished or divided by the intervention of its individual member states, the Union is likely to continue to benefit from US support.

While the EU's enlargement has so far served well the US interests, the same cannot be said for the reverse of the situation. In the late 1990s and early 2000s, for example, the United States pushed for NATO enlargement to the east in a way that was at least partially counterproductive for the EU enlargement process – as well as for relations with third countries (most notably Russia). The post-Cold War NATO enlargement challenged the EU because the Central and Eastern European countries (CEECs) seemed to favour accession to NATO over the more burdensome EU accession process. Indeed, the CEECs appear to attach more political importance on NATO than do some of the older member states. The shadow of Russia as a military and energetic threat appears to be of more concern to them than debates on the future of the EU's (economic and internal security) governance, still largely dominated by western European – that is, 'old' – member states.

As mentioned above, the EU's enlargements have affected its relations with third countries, most notably its relationship with Russia. During the Cold War, relations with the European Communities (EC) were mostly an afterthought for Russian policymakers. It was only in 1988, toward the end of the Cold War, that the USSR recognised the EC's existence as a legal international entity – and even then out of the need for financial assistance. Despite the fact that the USSR initially viewed the EC as a US Trojan horse in Europe, the EU's 2004-

07 eastern enlargement was of less concern to Russia than NATO expansion. This latter growth has been interpreted in Russia as a shift of the Cold War division to the east. Therefore, although NATO's enlargement challenged that of the EU to the east, it also facilitated the Union's expansion because NATO was the focus of Russian attention and fear (read: opposition), which otherwise would have been directed at the EU.

The tenets and stereotypes of the Cold War have been slow to die and they are still alive in the political leaders' minds. However, they do not occupy the minds of the younger generations, those who are challenging regimes in the Middle East in a way that would have been unthinkable before 1989. In a way, the remaining legacies of the Cold War are being challenged in the Middle East as we write, though it is still unclear what will replace them when today's protesters assume and consolidate their leadership.

Looking Forward: Scenarios for Future EU Enlargements

What is the foreseeable direction of EU enlargement? On 1 July 2013, Croatia is set to become the EU's twenty-eighth member state. On 1 March 2012, Serbia acquired official candidate status. It is possible that Macedonia and Montenegro will follow by 2020. It may be easy to overlook the EU's 'soft power' success in these cases, but the promise of EU accession has gone a long way to convince these countries of the importance of 'getting their act together' not only with regard to domestic reforms, but also in their relations with their neighbours. Consequently, the 'carrot' of membership has convinced Croatia to settle disputes over its borders with Slovenia, although Macedonia has encountered new obstacles in normalising its relations with Greece over the country's name dispute. Similarly, united EU pressure has determined Serbia to enhance efforts for the successful arrest of Ratko Mladić and to slowly engage in the normalisation of its relations with Kosovo.

The other countries in the Western Balkans (Albania, Bosnia and Herzegovina, and Kosovo) face greater domestic and international challenges (for example, five EU member states have not yet recognised Kosovo's independence) and are unlikely to join before the next decade. Iceland initially had the best prospects for accession, but despite progress in negotiations, several challenges remain ahead. In response to the Icelandic population's refusal in a second referendum in April 2011 to pay back the UK and the Netherlands for their assistance during the economic crisis that began in 2008, those countries made it clear that they would take Iceland to court and oppose the country's membership. In addition, there are standing differences over fisheries and whaling policies, and it is unclear whether the citizens of Iceland will support membership (the spectre of Norway's double rejection in popular referenda on membership looms large).

The prospects for Turkey's membership are more complex. Among the contributors to the *Frontiers of Europe* project, there was general consensus that Turkey's EU membership would be in the EU's interest. As a EU member state, Turkey would give added value to the Union as a whole in both energy and geopolitical terms. Unfortunately, the EU appears to have chosen a short-sighted view in its approach to the Turkish case, putting subjective cultural and value-related issues ahead of a pragmatic analysis of its own interests. As a result, the EU may have lost a historic opportunity. Instead of drawing Turkey closer, the EU has been pushing it away. The refusal to offer the prospect of visa liberalisation to its citizens is just a recent example of the tensions between the two actors. Paradoxically, after decades of eagerly seeking and preparing for EU membership and fulfilling many of the conditions to join, Turkey may decide not to continue its pursuit of membership in the Union.

Over the past few years, Turkey has progressively affirmed itself as a broker in the Middle East and on the international scene. As mentioned above, its role in the EU's energy security should not be underestimated, with many of the new pipeline projects meant to cross its territory. The unrest in the Arab world has confirmed the unique role Turkey can play in stabilising the larger neighbourhood. The country is now expanding its economic and diplomatic influence not only in the Middle East, but also in the Balkans. Should the Western Balkan states reject the EU, they may well turn to Turkey as an alternative. Should Turkey decide to unilaterally halt or even break off the negotiations, the cost to the EU in political, economic and, most of all, credibility terms would be enormous. There are signals that Turkey is already considering this scenario, as reflected in Prime Minister Recep Tayyip Erdoğan's speech at the Council of Europe in April 2011, in which he asserted that the EU needs Turkey as a member perhaps more than Turkey needs the EU (Euractiv 2011b).

Why is the EU (Not) Committed to Enlargement?

One reason for the EU's lack of commitment to enlargement is the absence of the sense of historical legacy and obligation that characterised past expansions to the south in 1986 and to the east in 2004-07. It is unclear why this feeling is not present with regard to the (Western) Balkans, which, for better or worse, remain the heart of European history. The EU's 'feelings' toward Turkey seem to be constantly growing colder, yet Franco Frattini emphasised the symbolic significance of

Turkey's accession to the EU by comparing it to two crucial moments in Europe's recent history: the French-German reconciliation and the fall of the Berlin Wall (Frattini 2011).

European politicians have also been using the economic crisis as a justification for not enlarging further. In reality, this is an excuse not supported by historical evidence: there is no correlation between the two. Past enlargements have taken place both in periods of stagnation (1973) and in periods of economic growth (1986). Joining the EU does not automatically mean joining the euro zone, a process that is governed by its own rules and criteria in order to guarantee the stability of the area. For instance, of the 12 countries that acceded to the EU in 2004-07, only five joined the euro zone (Cyprus, Estonia, Malta, Slovenia and Slovakia) – and, despite recent problems with the euro, there is evidence that the other CEECs would like to join the euro and to embark on a series of costly measures to fulfil the conditions for accession.

A bigger EU also means a larger market. External trade by the European Union rose 20 per cent after the EU enlarged to 27 members and, from 2000 to 2006, intra-EU trade rose by 33 per cent (Eurostat 2008). Although the consequences of the economic crisis that began in 2008 are not yet clear, it is certain – if, for instance, we compare this crisis with the one at the beginning of the 1990s – that the existence of the euro partially buffeted the impact of the crisis, especially with regard to financial speculation. Despite the challenges faced in the past few years, the euro is unlikely to be abandoned. In this sense, an expanding EU would contribute to projecting a perception of dynamism and thus make its economy more attractive for investors. This is what happened before the most recent wave of enlargement, when investors turned to the CEECs not only for the cheaper prices, but also for the prospect of becoming part of the single market.

A third reason for the lack of enlargement enthusiasm in the EU is the lack of popular support and a sense of 'enlargement fatigue'. A number of contributing authors to our *Frontiers of Europe* project concluded that there is a growing xenophobia among European citizens and politicians, who perceive immigrants as a threat to the social and economic order and their 'way of life'. The events in the Arab world have unleashed a series of negative reactions from the EU and its member states. Instead of providing a humanitarian response to the growing number of refugees and migrants from north Africa and the Middle East, individual member states engaged in incendiary discourses meant to create panic among their citizens and adopted measures that threatened the very existence of a core EU project: the Schengen space. Italy and France openly called for a reform of Schengen, whereas countries such as Denmark and the Netherlands unilaterally resorted to measures meant to (in)directly 'close' their borders and labour markets. Finally, instead of focusing its efforts on dealing with its economic and financial problems, Greece is increasing its efforts toward building an 'anti-immigrant' wall meant to block a strip of land between its territory and that of Turkey.

All in all, the official European discourse, which is supportive of enlargement, often does not seem to be complemented by the same message from the narratives and practices of its member states. As these conflicting messages reach countries outside the EU's borders (among them aspiring candidate countries and neighbours), they affect perceptions of the EU's commitment to enlargement and to close relations with its neighbours – consequently influence countries' willingness to undertake costly reform. This may result in a catch-22 situation, in which neighbours are not willing to engage in costly reform until they have a firm commitment (to enlargement) from the EU, while the EU is not willing to offer that commitment in the absence of thorough reform.

Prospects for the Future: Forming a EU 'National' Interest?

What are the consequences of the EU's inability to think strategically about enlargement? We argue that this inability is likely to affect the EU's relations in two directions: first, with its neighbourhood, and second, with the wider world. The first consequence, as mentioned already in the case of Turkey, is the possible disenchantment with the EU in the candidate and prospective member countries. The EU's inactivity and Turkey's increasingly proactive stance in foreign affairs could cause the countries of the Western Balkans to gravitate toward the latter. Should this happen, it would deprive the EU of its historical backyard and of a major geopolitical and energy asset (the pipelines planned in that area). Similarly, the countries in the east, driven by the EU's unwillingness to give them a concrete membership perspective, are likely to gravitate toward Russia.

Russia occupies a preeminent role in ensuring Europe's energy supply and, with the unrest in the Arab world, the EU is even more dependent on Russian energy. Although Russia's role in ensuring Europe's energy needs has been a matter of contention between the United States and Europe, and in Europe itself, the unrest in the Middle East will make Russia's contribution far more appealing. US arguments against Europe's energy dependence on Russia will find Europeans less receptive than in the past. With its southern shore becoming increasingly problematic, Europe will need a stable eastern neighbourhood, and it will be less opposed to Russia extending its influence to its former Soviet republics. The consequences for the 'frozen conflicts' in the Caucasus would be substantial. Even the former USSR satellites – now EU members – that joined the United States in vocal protest against Russia in the past may reconsider their position because of their domestic energy demand. The tragic events at Japan's Fukushima nuclear power plant are likely to contribute to this trend if nuclear power is no longer regarded as a secure energy alternative.

The EU will have a big opportunity to contribute to institution-building in the post-Arab Spring, given its record of excellence in creating institutions and its support of democracy. It is hoped that the EU will be able to apply lessons from the past in this part of the world. Stable and well-functioning democratic institutions are of direct interest to the EU, as the waves of immigrants and the energy shortages following the Arab crisis have clearly shown. Likewise, cooperation on development has been one positive example of the EU's transformative power. The EU now has the choice to build on this success. Should it fail to do so, the attractiveness of its soft power will decrease substantially.

The second consequence of the EU's inability to think strategically about enlargement and its neighbourhood concerns the EU's role in the world. The United States has become disenchanted with the EU. There were enormous expectations placed on the post-Lisbon Treaty Europe. For the first time ever, in 2010 the US Department of State created a new position with responsibility for managing relations with the European Union and Western Europe. However, the inability of the EU to speak with one voice because of the desire of its member states to achieve 'privileged' status in Washington has, for the most part, voided the potentiality offered by the Lisbon Treaty in the field of foreign policy.

A similar pattern can be found in other parts of the world. Latin America, for example, has long felt the attraction of EU influence. Institutional frameworks such Mercosur have facilitated the dialogue. More recently, however, emerging economies have pushed for their own place in the sun within Mercosur, just as they have within the EU. In this sense, an eventual Turkish EU membership would have a positive impact on trade and political relations with the EU.

China continues to not place the EU at the top of its political or foreign policy priorities – and, as illustrated by its reaction to the euro zone crisis, appears to be somehow annoyed by the added level of complications. The EU and China speak different foreign policy languages, the former driven by the post-modernist logic of enlargement, the latter guided by pragmatism. Eventual enlargements of the EU would only consolidate this divide. The lack of a proper EU strategy toward China based on a pragmatic analysis of the European 'national' interest is striking. A willingness to meet halfway between the post-modern and pragmatic approaches could translate into greater cooperation and mutual benefits for the two actors.

The EU's apparent incapacity to pragmatically determine what best constitutes its 'national' interest appears to be linked to the fact that it was unable to understand the radical paradigm shift in international relations after the end of the Cold War. The language of diplomacy in the twenty-first century has changed, moving from Cold War diplomacy to geo-economics. Ironically, the European project itself has been built on geo-economic considerations. The inability of the Europeans to understand the vastness of the change and how to cope with it is even more surprising since it is the second time in less than 60 years that they are facing a paradigm shift in international relations and in their role on the world stage.

A similar change occurred in the 1950s and 1960s, during the decolonisation process. This failure to grasp the new reality may be linked to an inward-looking attitude that has characterised the EU since the 1990s. After 1996, the EU appeared obsessed by its need for institutional reform, which it was unable to properly achieve, while the 9/11 terrorist attacks provided new impetus for the European interior ministers to attempt to 'seal the borders' of the EU and to 'export' unwanted immigrants to third countries.

Enlargement remains a measure of success and a test of the EU's credibility in the world and at home – and, as recognised many times by the European Commission itself, it is the EU's greatest foreign policy success. The EU's 'soft power' is likely to become less effective if the EU continues to avoid defining its relations with its neighbourhood and providing a vision for its foreign policy at large. Furthermore, the more self-centered and inward-looking the EU becomes, the more difficult it is to 'sell itself' and its enlargement to the media. The less the media sources write about the EU, the less informed the EU citizens are. This translates into less support for the European project as a whole and into lower turnouts for the elections of the European Parliament (for example, turnout declined from 61.99 per cent in 1979 to 43 per cent in 2009) (*Eurobarometer* 2011). The result is a vicious circle in which elected politicians are unwilling to back further enlargement because of the lack of support and approval of their national constituencies.

However, the main responsibility for the current deadlock seems to lie with the European political leaders. As the former president of the European Commission, Jacques Delors, underlined in 2011, past leaders such as François Mitterrand, Helmut Kohl, Valéry Giscard-d'Estaing, Konrad Adenauer and Charles de Gaulle "have left their mark on the history of Europe because at a given moment they overcame their preconceptions towards the other for a European vision" (Euractiv 2011a). Without a European vision, it is impossible to define where the European interest lies and therefore to pragmatically determine what best to do about enlargement and relations with both the neighbourhood and the world.

It should never be forgotten that are actually three main beneficiaries of enlargement: the candidate countries, which gain in economic, political, financial and security terms; the existing member states, for which enlargement preserves stability and fosters prosperity in the neighbourhood and their own national economies; and the EU project itself because enlargements have historically led to more integration and a more active foreign policy. The EU should include, and prioritise, stability in all its considerations about enlargement and its relations with the neighbourhood. This is not to say that the EU should enlarge tomorrow and at all costs (a mistake that has been made in the past), but that it should continue to engage in the process of enlargement in a dynamic and proactive way. It should also engage its larger neighbourhood more consistently and be clear about putting the prospects for membership on the table. In other words, the EU should demonstrate no prejudices on enlargement and send a message to the neighbourhood that the EU is (yet again) 'open for business'.

References

Euractiv. 2011a. "Delors: 'Superficial' Franco-German Engine Needs Kick-Start." 11 April. www.euractiv.com/en/future-eu/delors-superficial-franco-german-engine-needs-kick-start-news-503853 (22 October 2012).

Euractiv. 2011b. "From Strasbourg, Erdoğan Blasts France over Burqa Ban." 14 April. www.euractiv.com/en/enlargement/strasbourg-erdo-blasts-france-burqa-ban-news-504068 (22 October 2012).

Eurobarometer 74. 2011. "Public Opinion in the European Union." Autumn. Luxembourg: European Commission.

European Parliament. 2009. "Turnout at the European Elections (1979-2009)." www.europarl.europa.eu/parliament/archive/elections2009/en/turnout_en.html (22 October 2012).

Eurostat. 2008. *Internal and Intra-European Union Trade. Statistical Yearbook-Data 1958-2006* (2008 edition available online).

Frattini, F. 2011. "Foreword." In *The Frontiers of Europe: A Transatlantic Problem?*, eds. F. Bindi and I. Angelescu. Washington, DC: Brookings Institution Press, ix-xiii.

PART II

CONDITIONALITY, COMPLIANCE, EUROPEANISATION

The Multiple Dimensions of Compliance in the European Union

Lessons for Applicant States

Heather A. D. MBAYE

Introduction

The European Union has neither the budgetary nor the bureaucratic capability to directly implement its own laws; it must depend on member states. Officials within the member states often take (or fail to take) actions that cause the member state to fail to comply with EU policy. This paper seeks to identify the causes of non-compliance and examine applicant states' potential ability to comply. First, I examine compliance theory and the goodness of fit ideas that arise from Europeanisation.[1] Then, I review several case studies of compliance, discussing how each fits into the theoretical framework. I present quantitative tests of non-compliance and, in light of the political and economic realities of Turkey, Iceland, and Balkan applicant states I use the results to predict compliance viability.

Compliance in International Regulatory Regimes

A theory of EU compliance can begin in international regulatory regimes literature. Here, authors debate the extent to which characteristics of international structures affect compliance. Much of this debate pits the enforcement approach against the management approach (see Chayes and Chayes 1995 and Downs, Rocke and Barsoom 1996).

---

1 This paper uses the concepts of compliance and implementation almost interchangeably, due to the sources of theory I use. Treib (2008, 4) suggests that implementation has grown out of domestic politics, and "…refers to 'what happens after a bill becomes a law.'" Compliance, on the other hand, is a concept that "…refers to 'a state of conformity or identity between actors' behaviour and a specified rule'" (Treib 2008, 4). He further argues that "[i]rrespective of these semantic differences, most compliance and implementation research is interested in both the process of how a given norm is being put in practice and in the outcome in terms of rule conformity" (Treib 2008, 4). This definition for both concepts is the one used herein.

The Political Enforcement Approach

Proponents of this approach suggest that the best method of ensuring compliance is to implement coercive procedures that limit state choice and make compliance an attractive option. International regimes must increase the likelihood that states will make a political choice to comply (for examples see Olson 1965; Axelrod and Keohane 1986; Yarbrough and Yarbrough 1992; and Downs, Rocke, and Barsoom 1996). States are 'rational actors' that weigh the costs and benefits of compliance (including the risk of being caught shirking). Non-compliance is a product of poor incentive structures.

State officials have a choice: to comply or to not comply with an international law. Though they have signed on to an agreement, states may choose not to comply because the costs are great and the risks of discovery are low. According to Haas, "[e]ven if a state may believe that signing a treaty is in its best interest, the political calculations associated with the subsequent decision actually to comply with international agreements are distinct and quite different" (1998, 19). The decision is either based on state priorities and limited resources, otherwise states may disagree with the rules with which they are asked to comply.

Enforcement theory is concerned with regime type. In a cooperative regime, states are more likely to comply because the regime is structured against a common foe. Even if other states do not, the state is motivated to comply. However, in mixed motive situations, or collaborative agreements, states are less likely to comply. Here, states are better off if they all comply, but individual states can gain more from the regime if they can collect the benefits of other states' compliance without outlaying the cost of compliance themselves (Young 1999). According to enforcement proponents, collaborative or mixed motive arrangements dominate the international regulatory regime landscape; thus, the problem of free riding is central to this theory.

In order to generate the benefits states expect when they sign on to an accord, enforcement must deter shirking behaviour. Monitoring regimes, transparency rules, and sanctioning tools increase the cost of shirking to a point at which it ceases to be an attractive option for states. Compliance problems, then, are best solved by increasing both the likelihood of detecting shirking states and by increasing the costs of defection. The secret to improving compliance lies in changing the regulatory regime itself.

The Management Approach

On the other hand, management theorists see non-compliance as a problem of limited state capacity and ambiguity rather than deliberate choice. States comply because it is the norm to do so. When compliance fails it is not a deliberate state choice; rather, it is because the state lacks the capacity to conform. States are not able to force actors within their borders – firms, regional governments, and others – to comply with international law.

Further, ambiguity in policy design may lead to divergent interpretations among local implementers. Compliance might be limited by budgetary and other economic constraints, such as recession. Finally, bureaucracies might simply be too small to effectively implement and monitor international agreements. Management proponents contend that coercion is not necessary – that compliance can be better achieved through cooperative problem solving and capacity-building (for examples see Young 1992, Mitchell 1994, Chayes and Chayes 1995, and Keohane and Levy 1996). Finally, another source of non-compliance is the decentralisation of implementation authority.

Unlike the enforcement approach, the management approach recognises that states are not unitary actors. If local officials choose not to comply and the central government lacks the power to force those actors to act in accordance with international agreements, then we cannot conceive of the 'state' making decisions. As Tallberg notes, "[t]he government may be unable to secure ratification [from the legislature], command compliance from subnational entities, or muster the necessary administrative capacity to comply" (2002 613).

Management theorists see the problem as one of capacity and policy ambiguity. The best method for ensuring compliance is to build the capacity to comply – to aid local officials in interpreting policy, to aid states with small economies or poor economies, and to help build cooperation between firms, the public, and all levels of government within state borders. The Commission has accepted and acted on these ideas, encouraging a variety of cross-border cooperative agreements and mentoring activities both pre- and post-accession.

However, even if one accepts these management ideas, political considerations remain important. While the two approaches are considered to be theoretically at odds, in practical applications, they are typically used in combination (Tallberg 2002). In fact, the EU's compliance regime is an effective, realistic combination of the two theoretic approaches. First, the Commission seeks to build capacity through economic aid, cooperative administration, and policy clarification. At the same time, it punishes those who defect through the threat and employment of treaty-based economic sanctions. In addition, central verification and monitoring by the Commission has increased the relative number of 'own initiative' cases of non-compliance. The Commission has also begun a series of 'know your rights' campaigns designed in part to shift monitoring onto consumers and citizens (Kelemen 2011).

The Commission and others use both management and enforcement approaches (the carrot and the stick), and the combination has ensured that EU compliance is relatively high. Yet non-compliance still exists, suggesting the need to look at additional explanations.

Public Policy Implementation: Top-Down and Bottom-Up Theories

American domestic implementation approaches help us to pinpoint some key differences between political enforcement and management. Concurrently, they provide a pathway that enables the incorporation of various EU theoretical debates into a more well-rounded theory of EU compliance. One can organise the theoretical discussion of compliance in a domestic setting along two dimensions: top-down/bottom-up and politics/management. Almost all authors pursue approaches than can be classified in terms of these two dimensions; these cleavages can be seen as orthogonal (Figure 1).

Figure 1: Dimensions of Approaches to EU Compliance

Politics vs. Management

Top-down Political Enforcement	*Top-down Management*	
Enforcement Limiting shirking State preferences Bargaining power in the Council	Management factors for state elites Commission management	**Top-down**
		vs.
Bottom-up Political enforcement	*Bottom-up Management*	
Horizontally fragmented authority Regional political decisions Bureaucratic choices Veto players Coalitional politics Public opinion	Local elite socialisation Regional autonomous management State capacity Poor communication Bureaucratic inefficiency	**Bottom-up**

The Top-Down and Bottom-up Approach to Compliance

Implementation problems can be viewed from the top-down and from the bottom-up, just as the EU can be seen from 'state-centric' and 'policy networks' perspectives. The classic of top-down literature is Pressman and Wildavsky's *Implementation* (1973, 1984). Essentially, they argue that if the degree of cooperation between relevant agencies and actors is high, then implementation will be achieved effectively. Van Meter and Van Horn (1975) offer a more precise implementation model, focusing on the existence and quality of linkages between policy standards, objections, resources, and organisations, the characteristics of the implementing agencies, the economic, political, and social environment, and the implementers on the ground (in particular their comprehension of policy, their stance on it, and the intensity of that stance).

Consistent with intergovernmental approaches to the EU, the implication of this model is that a high degree of centralised control results in quality implementation. However, in the real world, implementation is far more complex than even Van Meter and Van Horn's model suggests. Several authors have criticised the approach for failing to specify the inherent limits to hierarchical control (Hood 1976; Dunshire 1978).

On the other hand, bottom-up approaches often describe the obstacles to implementation experienced 'on the ground.' In Lipsky's (1971, 1980) account of staff behaviour in policy delivery agencies (his 'street-level bureaucrats'), we find the origin of the bottom-up approach. Lipsky does not argue, however, that these bureaucrats are hard to control, for this would simply reinforce the ideas of the top-down approach. His argument is subtler. People enter the bureaucracy with at least some idea of public service. The nature of bureaucracy, however, is far from ideal. According to Lipsky, "[l]arge classes or huge caseloads and inadequate resources combine with the uncertainties of method and the unpredictability of clients to defeat their aspirations as service workers" (1980, xii). Bureaucrats begin to view themselves as cogs in an oppressive system, and they develop routinised processing techniques in order to cope with the nature of their work. Hill and Hupe state that, "[s]treet-level bureaucrats … find that work situations and outcomes are unpredictable, and they face great pressures of inadequate time in relation to limitless needs. … Control from the top to combat the alleged failures of street-level staff involves the intensification of these pressures" (2002, 53). Lipsky sees policy compliance as coming from Galveston rather than Atlanta or Washington, from Nottingham North rather than from London or, indeed, Brussels. In the EU, we must look at implementation as a problem to be addressed by regional and local officials.

The Politics and Management Debate

The second dimension in the domestic literature mirrors the regulatory regimes debate. On the one hand, the argument that politics structures the choices of policy compliance recognises that problems may be the result of deliberately vague policymaking in which clear communication is sacrificed in the interest of passing a policy, or that non-implementation may be an explicit choice rather than an accident of management. Regimes can be created that do not force cooperation between those who make policy and those who enforce it. Compliance can then become a political game within the government or between governments.

Other theorists conceive of non-implementation as primarily a problem of poor management or poor communication by administrative elites. The management dimension encompasses the communications model appraised by Goggin *et al.* (1990), suggesting that implementation problems result from poor timing and poor choice of implementation tools. In addition, according to Goggin *et al.*, problems are a function of the "nature and direction of change in the program directives" (1990, 48). Poor communication of goals and preferences results in implementation problems. Implementation problems, however, are not a result of politics; rather, they are a result of poor management.

Bringing these Approaches Together

EU literature and international regulatory regimes literature can be combined in a way suggested by the debate in the American politics literature.

Top-Down Political Dimension

Authors in the upper left-hand quadrant of Figure 1 tend to view non-implementation as a problem of elite political choices. The major proponents in this cell are Downs, Rocke, and Barsoom (1996), who argue that enforcement incentives constrain the feasible choices of strategic elite actors in such a way as to control infringements of law. In the context of the EU, enforcement procedures are quite strong, as the final enforcement procedure is taking the case to the Court of Justice and imposing economic sanctions on member states. Member states use the Commission and Court to monitor compliance and enforce EU law. Enforcement is theoretically uniform *yet variation among countries persists*, suggesting this is not a sufficient explanation for non-compliance.

The top-down political approach of the international relations literature formed around Robert Keohane's landmark book *After Hegemony*

(1984). This method theorises implementation without case studies, using formal modelling to homogenise all non-compliance cases. James Fearon (1998, 270) argues that, "conceiving of different issue domains in terms of different strategic structures may be heuristically useful for some purposes, but doing so misunderstands the problem of international cooperation as state leaders typically face it. … [U]nderstanding problems of international cooperation as having a common strategic structure is more accurate and perhaps more theoretically fruitful." This implies that all EU infringement results from the same strategic game. Therefore, understanding one infringement helps in understanding all of them.

In this cell, studies of compliance begin with agreement negotiations. States that are able to bargain an agreement close to their own ideal point will be more likely to implement that agreement, whereas states who fail will not comply as well or as often. Fearon's argument suggests that the ability of state executives to bargain effectively in the Council of Ministers would be reflected in the number of infringements a state incurs. This is bolstered by Aguilar-Fernandez' argument that Spain's position as a peripheral nation is critical to the Spanish inability to comply (1994).

Top-down Management Dimension

The upper-right hand quadrant conceives implementation as an elite management problem. In the EU context, the Commission would be responsible for variation in member state infringements. An activist Commission may bring more cases before the Court, whereas a passive Commission may bring fewer cases. Mendrinou (1996) presents data that suggests that the Commission's role in fact has *not* been related to the nature of the Commission. The number of cases has increased steadily since 1959, suggesting that *as time passes and the acquis grows larger*, more non-compliance is found across member states.

Institutional learning, what we now call 'Europeanisation,' is fundamental to national adaptation to European norms. Paraskevopoulos (1998) argues that elite socialisation to European governance models is a critical factor in the relative success of structural fund programs. Managers at the elite Commission level and managers in both national and subnational governments must learn to work within the EU context. It is not only national institutions that must mesh well with international aims but also elites who must, in essence, learn how to cooperate.

Chayes and Chayes' arguments above suggest that ambiguous international law is less likely to result in infringement than more precisely-worded statutes. However, an alternative view of ambiguous law hints otherwise. Managers in non-elite positions may misinterpret ambiguous law, leading to non-compliance. The Commission has sought to limit this type of non-compliance through clarification.

Bottom-up Management Dimension

Authors in the lower right-hand quadrant focus on national and sub-national management problems that prohibit effective implementation. Problems of state capacity and poor communication between the international regulatory regime and lower government levels create non-compliance with international obligations. Some international organisation approaches that challenge the strategic actor model also fit in this quadrant. Case studies of implementation in the European Union generally support these ideas.

Institutional design matters. Forbes (1989) has demonstrated the impact of institutional design in a study of equal opportunity policies and Weale *et al.* (1996) confirm this finding in a study of environmental policy National administrative structures can cause variation in policy output; corporatism may also be potentially important because it may improve the management problem by reducing the number of 'rogue' actors in a system.

Bottom-up Political Dimension

The final quadrant is probably the least studied of all. Authors here focus on the political decisions made by non-elite actors that influence implementation. Local officials make political choices in an environment that is different from that of the elite officials in that these local and regional officials are constrained by the decisions made by national officials. Political choices made in the bureaucracy and the national administration can affect the implementation of international policy. Coalitional politics, partners, and structural checks and balances can inhibit legislatures from implementing supranational law. More veto points may lead to both lower quality and slower implementation (and therefore higher non-compliance) (Haverland 1999).

Bottom-up approaches include examinations of subnational governments. Levy *et al.* (1995, 289) argue that "hierarchical states in which great authority is vested in the central government will find it easier to translate the provisions of international regimes into national law than decentralised systems in which the central government has limited control over regional and local government." In a decentralised, federal system, the central government may have difficulty in compelling local governments to implement international law simply because they do not have the power to do so.

U.S. federalism literature also points to the effects of decentralisation on implementation. Lowry (1992, 4) states, "[t]he danger of a federal system is that subnational policymakers will... [skew] policies to the extent that outcomes no longer match national outcomes." This is entirely rational: policymakers want to implement laws in the most beneficial (and least painful) way possible. Both political and managerial impulses motivate subnational authorities. In the EU, skewing by subnational actors can have the effect of infringement at the national level; however, states' unitary systems should have greater control of local administrations. No question of ultimate responsibility can exist – the centralised government has both *power and responsibility* within its borders.

Finally, bottom-up political approaches include attention to the public's opinion on integration and the government. Lampinen and Uusikylä (1998) assert that it is easier to implement EU law in countries where public support for the EU is high. They argue that "[s]ince politicians often make policy choices that promote their re-election, it can be assumed that the lower the overall mass support for the country's membership in the EU, the higher the probability that a member-state will face difficulties in implementing European policies" (Lampinen and Uusikylä 1998, 239). In addition, they examine electoral participation, satisfaction with democracy, and political protest.

Case Studies of Compliance

A great many individual cases of compliance exist that can be categorised into one or more quadrants of the theory presented herein. Most involve more than one quadrant, of course, but here I focus on some exemplary cases.

Implementing Directive 91/271/EEC in the Netherlands: Political Issues at the Elite Level

The Urban Waste Water Treatment (UWWT) Directive of 1991 affects the system of wastewater collection (the sewerage system) and describes the guidelines regarding leaks and overflows as well as the guidelines for the treatment of waste so as to limit the pollution entering the surface water in EU countries. The UWWT Directive lays down broad guidelines and leaves it to national authorities to find ways to meet those guidelines.

The Netherlands had a very keen interest in this Directive as water is a critical issue in this low-lying country. Fresh water in the Netherlands comes from rivers: primarily the Rhine, the Meuse, and the Scheldt. These rivers flow first through Germany, Switzerland, Belgium, France,

Luxembourg, and Austria before finally reaching the Netherlands on their way to the sea. The level of pollution in the rivers when they reach the Dutch border is far higher than the level when they leave the Netherlands (Kelder 2000, 27). Wastewater treatment is therefore a very important issue to the Dutch government and it succeeded in getting the subject on the EU agenda. Based on the strength of their preferences on the level of protection and guidelines for water treatment, the Dutch negotiated a policy that was very close to their ideal point. Kelder points out that "[l]ooking back, one can say that the Dutch authorities were quite successful in protecting their approach, which is reflected in the high degree of fit" (2000, 28). This Directive, however, did not aim to change Dutch behaviour, and was therefore implemented cheaply and easily in the Netherlands; the Dutch government intended the Directive to change the behaviour of *other states* in the EU (Kelder 2000, 27-28). Examining the ease of compliance from a top-down perspective with a focus on inter-state bargaining is very fruitful in this case.

The Habitats Directive in the United Kingdom: A Case of Poor Elite-level Management

Council Directive 92/43/EEC of 21 May 1992 on the conservation of natural habitats and of wild fauna and flora (the Habitats Directive) is one of the longest-standing EU directives used for the protection of the environment and particularly endangered species (Ledoux *et al.* 2000, 1). Like the UWWT Directive, the Habitats Directive is a framework policy. Therefore, national and local officials are free to choose whatever implementation methods they see fit.

While the Directive is ostensibly flexible, it designates particular areas as habitats to be protected and specifies that the management of those systems must ensure that there is no net habitat loss. If habitat must be lost, then the same amount of territory on an alternate site with similar ecology must be protected. This has created problems managing dynamic ecosystem transformations (including changes that are not controlled by mankind, like climatic changes) wherein, for example, protected areas are naturally shrinking (Turner *et al.* 1998).

On the northern Norfolk coastline, a natural shingle barrier ridge exists that, in addition to protecting several villages from sea flooding, protects an area of freshwater march from saline water. A number of rare birds live in this unique habitat, protected under the Habitats Directive. However, as a result of storms and other natural occurrences, the natural ridge that protects and creates this marsh is *moving inland* at a rate of one meter per year, reducing the size of the marsh and threatening to block the river Glazen. At the time the Directive was passed, the local authorities had been pushing the ridge back out to sea with construction equipment, which reduced its structural integrity and made it a much less effective protector of the villages and marsh (Ledoux *et al.* 2000, 8-10). These officials called in Cambridge to help. The Coastal Research Unit found that discontinuing management altogether would result in the blockage of drainage from the site, making the marches brackish and dead. A decision was reached to continue to push the natural ridge back out to sea, but also to establish a second flood protection barrier slightly further inland.

While the solution reached was ultimately a sensible one that protected the freshwater marshes from dying altogether, it ultimately fails to comply with the Habitats Directive. The EU has created a Directive that is too narrow and fails to take into account both local preferences and individual cases, despite the nature of the directive as a regulatory framework. The Directive itself is problematic, not the local decision taken in Norfolk. Management at the level of the EU failed to take these issues into account when this law was created.

Local-level Management of Cohesion Policy in EUREGIO

EUREGIO is a cross-border region that encompasses the area of Enschede in the Netherlands and Gronau in Germany. It dates back to the 1950s, has an office in Gronau, and is headed by a Secretariat. The EUREGIO performs functions that are vital to the implementation of many European policies in the area; for example, EUREGIO coordinates the cohesion programs in its area, ensuring that they meet the criteria specified by the EU. The Commission works closely with the Secretariat in coordinating policies locally. The Commission and EUREGIO are similarly problem-driven and outcome-oriented, and they focus on successful spending of cohesion funds for projects in the area (Perkmann 2002, 12).

Through cooperative problem solving and, critically, policy entrepreneurship by the EUREGIO, cohesion funding and other policies can be implemented more effectively in the area. Local administrators have a recognised role and the Commission respects the expertise of the EUREGIO officials. The Commission faces a real problem of motivating actors at various levels to comply reliably and qualitatively. This type of local management can create quality EU compliance and can conversely create infringements if it is ignored or poorly developed.

Political Resistance among Local Officials: Crete's Kouroupitos Landfill

In January 1988, several *local officials* on Crete filed a complaint against the Greek government with the European Commission. The complaint alleged that the government was knowingly operating an illegal and hazardous dump on the island. A gorge at the mouth of the river Kouroupitos in the Chania was being used to dispose of domestic waste, hazardous waste like batteries, and some commercial and industrial waste. By 1989, the Commission had issued a formal letter to the Greek government, informing it that it was in violation of two environmental directives.

When the Greek government failed to move the dump, citing local pressures, the Commission filed suit with the ECJ. The Greek government argued that local officials – the same local officials that filed the original complaint – had blocked the building of alternate waste disposal sites in their jurisdictions and that local populations were opposed to plans to move the site. In a 1992 ruling, the ECJ decreed that, "by failing to take the necessary measures to ensure that in the area of Chania waste and dangerous waste are disposed of without endangering human health and without harming the environment, and by failing to draw up for that area plans for the disposal of waste and of toxic and dangerous waste, Greece has failed to fulfil its obligations..." (ECJ 1992). The Court imposed a daily fine of €20,000 on Greece for non-compliance. This case is quite famous because it was the first time that the Court sanctioned a member with a fine. Interestingly, Greece failed to comply due to local officials' political positions. These local authorities, faced with constituencies intent on avoiding a landfill in their backyards, blocked efforts by the Greek government to make alternative arrangements for waste. This case demonstrates that even in a unitary state like Greece with little subnational autonomy, local political pressure can cause compliance problems.

Compliance Predictors at Multiple Levels

The theory discussed above leads to a multitude of testable hypotheses, many of which have been tested in Mbaye (2010 and 2011). The tests in this chapter begin where those ended. The hypotheses that proved significant in those articles are tested here.

Top-Down Political Hypotheses

Certainly it is the case that policy is easier to implement if it is already very close to national norms; in other words, if states are able to craft favourable policy, they will be more likely to abide by it. We might expect that powerful countries would be more likely to craft such policies.

- H_1: States with more bargaining power in the Council will infringe less often because they are able to negotiate bargains that are close to their own ideal points.

Top-Down Managerial Approaches

Compliance can also be viewed as a problem of management by elites to ensure implementation. In the EU context, it may be that the Commission affects the number of infringements for each member state. An activist Commission may bring more cases before the Court, whereas a passive Commission may bring fewer cases. Additionally, the year variable should capture the effects of Europeanisation among officials: the institutional learning that Paraskevopolous (1998) finds so critical in structural fund policy implementation. This argument suggests a contrary hypothesis: that as time passes, instead of more cases, we should see fewer.

- H_2: As time passes, more noncompliance will be found across all states due to the growing amount of legislation that must be enforced.
- H_3: As time passes, Europeanisation will occur, thus ameliorating the effect of the growing size of the acquis. Fewer cases of non-compliance will be found.

Bottom-Up Political Hypotheses

Political choices made in the bureaucracy and the national administration can affect the implementation of European policy. When political authority is horizontally fragmented, it is harder for governments to ensure that all the actors in the system will comply. Furthermore, it is harder for those governments to transpose law and move it through legislatures, causing transposition non-compliance.

- H_4: States whose governments face many veto players will infringe more often than states whose governments do not.

Authority in many European states is also vertically fragmented. In a decentralised, federal system, the central government may have difficulty in compelling local governments to implement international law simply because they do not have the power to do so. We saw this in the Kouroupitos waste dump case.

- H_5: The greater the autonomy of regions within a state, the greater the level of non-compliance.

It may be easier to implement EU law in countries where public support for the EU is high (Lampinen and Uusikylä 1998). More broadly, implementation may be easier when political culture is stable, democratic, and satisfied.

- H_6: States whose populations approve of EU membership will find compliance easier, and will infringe less often.
- H_7: States whose populations are satisfied with the democracy in their own states will find compliance easier, and will infringe less often.

Bottom-Up Management Hypotheses

Management problems at the national and subnational levels may prohibit effective compliance with EU laws. Problems of state capacity, poor communication between the EU and lower government levels, and administrative neglect can create non-compliance with EU laws. In addition, corporatism reduces the management problem by reducing the number of 'rogue' actors in a system, thus reducing non-compliance. Similarly, one might also expect that corruption may cause management-based compliance problems.

- H_8: States with larger administrative capacities will infringe less often than states with small governments.
- H_9: States with professional bureaucracies will infringe less often than states whose bureaucracies are not merit-based.
- H_{10}: Highly corporatist states will infringe less often than non-corporatist states.
- H_{11}: Countries that face widespread corruption and government inefficiencies will infringe more often than countries that are not corrupt.

All of the data in this chapter comes from Mbaye 2010 and 2011. However, this paper combines the models tested in those two articles. The models demonstrate that hypotheses from all the areas of theory matter.[2] This leads to the conclusion that reliance on any one of these theories, whether international or domestic, elite or local, will lead one to skewed conclusions about the nature of compliance in the EU.

2 I use a negative binomial regression to analyse both dependent variables, as the dependent variables are in count form. Ordinary least squares regression is not appropriate for count data.

Analysis and Results[3]

Table 1: Compliance in the Administrative Phase^{a}

Variables	**Reasoned Opinions**^{b}	*Reasoned Opinions*^{b}	**Reasoned Opinions**^{b}	*Reasoned Opinions*^{c}
Top-Down Political Approach				
Bargaining Power in the Council of Ministers	.033* (.018)	.057*** (.018)	.029** (.013)	.055*** (.020)
Top-Down Managerial Approach				
Year	.066*** (.012)	.081*** (.018)	.062*** (.012)	.069*** (.014)
Bottom-Up Political Approach				
Regional Autonomy	.002 (.022)	.012 (.019)	.015 (.022)	.032 (.031)
Satisfaction with Democracy	.206 (.268)	.408 (.033)		
Satisfaction with EU Membership	-.583*** (.143)		-.636*** (.188)	
Bottom-Up Managerial Approach				
State Capacity	.00008** (.00003)	-.00004 (.00005)	.00009*** (.00003)	-.00002 (.00006)
Bureaucratic Efficiency		-.456*** (.066)		-.455*** (.082)
Corporatism			-.085 (.072)	-.124 (.102)
Control of Corruption	-.066*** (.011)		-.066*** (.007)	
Lagged dependent variable	.002 (.002)	.001 (.003)	.002 (.003)	.003 (.003)
Constant	-122.9*** (23.90)	-158.2*** (21.70)	-112.9*** (24.43)	-134.1*** (28.20)
α^{b}	.239	.250	.237	.289

[3] *Significant at the p<.1 level **Significant at the p<.05 level.
***Significant at the p<.01 level.
[a] The coefficients are negative binomial estimators (not interpreted as in a multiple regression model). The standard errors are in parentheses.
[b] N=227. [c] N=234.
[d] The α statistic suggests that the use of the negative binomial model is correct. If zero, the Poisson model would be the accurate model.

Table 2[4]: Compliance in the Judicial Phase[a]

Variables	**Court Judgments**[b]	*Court Judgments*[b]	**Court Judgments**[c]	*Court Judgments*[c]
		Top-Down Political Approach		
Bargaining Power in the Council of Ministers	.030** (.015)	.030 (.213)	.065*** (.026)	.066*** (.027)
		Top-Down Managerial Approach		
Year	.086*** (.012)	.087*** (.012)	.094*** (.016)	.089*** (.014)
		Bottom-Up Political Approach		
Regional Autonomy	.018 (.016)	.032 (.024)	-.023 (.029)	.004 (.031)
Satisfaction with Democracy	.548* (.307)	.956*** (.303)		
		Bottom-Up Managerial Approach		
Bureaucratic Efficiency		-.238*** (.092)		-.302*** (.142)
Corporatism			.078 (.122)	-.041 (.164)
Control of Corruption	-.066*** (.016)		-.081*** (.015)	
Lagged dependent variable	.087*** (.027)	.105*** (.029)	.103*** (.030)	.140*** (.036)
Constant	-167.1*** (22.61)	-175.9*** (23.13)	-180.6*** (31.63)	-175.63*** (28.31)
α[b]	.408	.467	.433	.539

Bottom-up management variables are the most powerful across the administrative (reasoned opinions) and the judicial (court cases) data, yet the two top-down variables are also very strong. Year, bargaining power, bureaucratic efficiency, public opinion, and control of corruption variables are significant. The two surprises are corporatism and regional autonomy, both of which lose significance when placed in a model with bargaining power. Multicollinearity tests proved negative; however, the

4 *Significant at the $p<.1$ level **Significant at the $p<.05$ level.
***Significant at the $p<.01$ level.
[a] The coefficients are negative binomial estimators (not interpreted as in a multiple regression model). The standard errors are in parentheses.
[b] N=322. [c] N=326.
[d] The α statistic suggests that the use of the negative binomial model is correct.

data on the whole is very volatile and sensitive to shifts in model specifications. I can say here that these variables, while very strong otherwise, are not significant in models that contain bargaining power; therefore, they are dropped from the tables presenting the effects of those models. In both the administrative and judicial data, *ceteris parabis*, the year has the strongest effect on the compliance cases, moving from the minimum on the predictor to the maximum (Table 3). In the administrative phase, going from the minimum to the maximum score yields 25 additional cases. For court cases, year yields four cases (this is setting aside the result presented by the lagged dependent variable). This is astonishingly powerful. The next most influential predictor in the administrative phase is bureaucratic efficiency, which yields a 21-case reduction. Control of corruption reduces administrative compliance problems by about 23, while positive feelings toward the EU reduce cases by 10. Bargaining power and state capacity increase cases by 12 and 9 respectively.

In the judicial phase, the results are a bit different. Year is the most powerful variable, but state capacity is not significant. Satisfaction with EU membership falls away, but satisfaction with democracy is a powerful predictor, increasing court cases by 1.5. Bargaining power increases cases by 1.3, while bureaucratic efficiency reduces cases by .8 and controlling corruption reduces cases by 1.5.

The Applicant States

Turkey, Iceland, and the Balkan applicant states are all as unique as any current member. Beginning with Turkey, this section examines EU applicant states' probable compliance barriers in light of the data presented herein.

Turkey

Most studies of Turkish membership focus on religion and the secular state. Beyond the Muslim question, few studies discuss whether Turkey's democracy, public support for EU membership, state capacity (in terms of revenue and bureaucratic efficiency), control of corruption, and degree of corporatism will enable the country to participate fully in an enlarged EU.

Turkey's ability to comply with EU policies will be governed by its relationship to democracy, the state propensity to use economics as a kind of bribe to insulate social reforms from public pressure, corruption, and state capacity issues.

Table 3[5]: Estimating the Effects of the Predictors[a]

Variable	*Effect on Reasoned Opinions*				*Average Effect*
Bargaining power	9.00	16.41	7.99	15.76	12.29
Year	24.20	30.66	22.27	25.04	25.54
Satisfaction with EU membership	-9.96		-10.73		-10.35
State Capacity	8.68		10.23		9.46
Bureaucratic efficiency		-21.51		-21.27	-21.39
Control of corruption	-22.78		-22.82		-22.80
Variable	*Effect on Court Judgments*				*Average Effect*
Bargaining power	.73	.77	1.79	1.91	1.30
Year	3.65	3.86	4.41	4.23	4.04
Satisfaction with Democracy	1.00	2.07			1.54
Bureaucratic efficiency		-.72		-.90	-.81
Control of Corruption	-1.38		-1.70		-1.54
Lagged dependent variable	3.86	5.69	5.13	11.12	6.45

First, given that most democratic reforms in Turkey have originated from a centre-right religious party, it is somewhat doubtful that Turks will demonstrate much satisfaction with their democracy; however, dissatisfaction leads to more compliance in this case (since Turkish public opinion will be more likely to approve EU policies that change national ones). Turkey also has a history of corporatism and neo-corporatism, which tends to improve compliance. This is changing, though, and economic actors that now find themselves outside of the decision-making nexus may prove to be barriers to compliance with EU policy.

In addition, Yavuz argues that Turkish "...economic policy is partly used to appease potential opposition to the policy areas that the political elite sought to isolate from social pressures" (in Turam 2012). A serious red flag to compliance in economic policy and in other policy areas, economic policy bribery is worrying on several levels. First, Turkish elites will not be able to use economic policy to smooth the way for EU policies, because many EU policies are economic in nature. Secondly, if potential opposition is strong enough to elicit economic 'pork belly' policies, then this opposition represents a problematic veto player in Turkish ability to comply with the EU.

Turkey is more corrupt than most EU members with the exception of Italy (Transparency International 2010). Like Italy, Turkey's inability to

[5] [a] Changes in the predicted number of non-compliance cases for a country and year, when changing the significant independent variable from its minimum value to its maximum value.

address issues of corruption does not bode well for its ability to comply with EU policy.

On the whole, Turkey, should it become an EU member, cannot be expected to be very compliant. The country will probably comply no worse than Italy, but that is not exactly a ringing endorsement of Turkish membership from a compliance perspective.

Iceland

Concerns regarding Icelandic compliance stem from a very different perspective. Iceland has a good bureaucracy, is not corrupt, has a functioning democracy, has no autonomous regions, and possesses few veto players in politics: all indicators of good potential for compliance. However, Iceland has traditionally held itself outside of the EU for several reasons, not the least of which is EU fisheries policy. As in the Netherlands, where water policy is critical, fisheries issues are critical to Iceland.

The Icelandic population seems to feel that EU membership is a sort of last-resort – something they must do to pull themselves out of the hole created by the collapse of the banking industry. For that reason, I question Icelanders' commitment to EU membership. I believe that Iceland will be a very good complier *except where its perceived national interests are challenged* – as with the case of fisheries policy. Some 70 per cent of Icelandic exports are fish and fish products – by far the largest and most important industry in the country (Explore Iceland 2012). Iceland prides itself on its fisheries industry, but it does not follow the same fishing protocols as most European countries. For example, Iceland does not prohibit whaling – a practice found appalling by many Westerners.

Overall, we should expect Iceland to be a very good complier with the exception of fisheries policy. With the national economy so dependent on the fishing industry, and national policy so very un-Europeanised, we should expect clashes between Iceland's preferred policy and EU majority outcomes. Many countries have similar idiosyncrasies (Mbaye 2004). Thus, just as I expect Germany to fail to comply with EU policies on beer, I expect Iceland to fail to comply with EU policies on fisheries.

Croatia, Serbia, Montenegro, and Macedonia

These Balkan states have problems similar to those in Turkey. All but Macedonia essentially dodge the religious questions faced by Turkey; still, fewer than one in three Macedonians is Muslim. Most of the population of these four countries is either Roman Catholic or Orthodox.

However, significant economic difficulties remain. State capacity to comply in these countries will be much lower than in Iceland. With the exception of Croatia, the applicant states have very low GDPs and state capacity cannot be very high in very poor countries. Whether political elites can manage state capacity is an issue; elites and populations may want to comply but be unable to do so. The relatively recent upheavals in and between these countries are also problematic; it is questionable whether these countries will be able to effectively negotiate and compromise with each other. Corruption and the perception of corruption remains very high in these states – all are considered more corrupt than Italy and corruption increases non-compliance. The quasi-liberal economic markets, particularly in Serbia, will make compliance with EU economic policy very difficult. As with other Balkan states that are already EU members, I would expect compliance in these four countries to be mediocre at best.

Conclusion

Policymakers who wish to improve compliance must address the problem from the perspective of international enforcement and management theories. The Commission plays an active role in wielding both the carrot and stick, and in helping state actors in current and prospective member states understand the meaning of a policy and the actions necessary for full compliance. If the Commission is to further improve compliance in the EU, I suggest that it must first take a more active role in discovering shirking rather than waiting for complaints (though the shift to a more adversarial legalism may go far in enforcing policies). The results suggest that compliance is sometimes a political decision; therefore, the Commission should attempt to increase the costs of non-compliance for both state and regional actors. For new applicants in particular, the costs of non-compliance should be high indeed.

However, the Commission is not as able address domestic questions like bureaucracy and corruption as it might like to be. In conjunction with the member states, the Commission would have to change structural factors – like corporatist arrangements and bureaucratic arrangements – and improve communication among regions, between regions and the central government, and between these local officials and the EU more directly. Rather than attempting to make EU elites more 'European,' it may be more necessary to improve communication between elites. The Commission in particular, as guardian of the EU, has an interest in addressing these domestic concerns both in current member states and in assessing the capacity of prospective members to comply.

References

Aguilar-Fernandez, S. 1994. "Spanish Pollution Control Policy and the Challenge of the European Union." *Regional Politics and Policy* 4(1): 102-17.

Axelrod, R. and R. Keohane. 1986. "Achieving Cooperation under Anarchy: Strategies and Institutions." In *Cooperation under Anarchy*, edited by Kenneth Oye. Princeton: Princeton University Press.

Chayes, A. and A. C. Chayes. 1993. "On Compliance." *International Organization* 47:175-205.

Chayes, A. and A. C. Chayes. 1995. *The New Sovereignty: Compliance with International Regulatory Agreements*. Cambridge: Harvard University Press.

Chayes, A., A.C. Chayes, and R. Mitchell. 1998. "Managing Compliance: A Comparative Perspective." In *Engaging Countries: Strengthening Compliance with International Environmental Accords* edited by E Brown Weiss, and H. Jacobson. Cambridge: MIT Press, 39-62.

Court of Justice of the European Communities (ECJ). 1992. *Reports of Cases Before the Court.* Volume 1992. Luxembourg: Office for Official Publications of the European Communities.

Downs, G., D. Rocke and P. Barsoom. 1996. "Is the Good News about Compliance also Good News about Cooperation?" *International Organization* 50(3): 379-406.

Dunshire, A. 1978. *Implementation in a Bureaucracy*. Oxford: Martin Robinson.

Explore Iceland. 2012. "Iceland Fishing – Iceland Fishing Industry." Accessed March 26, 2012. http://www.exploreiceland.is/about_iceland/history_of_iceland/iceland_fishing/.

Fearon, J. 1998. "Bargaining, Enforcement, and International Cooperation." *International Organization* 52(2): 269-305.

Forbes, I. 1989. "Unequal Partners: The Implementation of Equal Opportunities Polcies in Western Europe." *Pubic Administration* 67: 19-38.

Goggin, M., J. Lester, L. O'Toole, and A. Bowman. 1990. *Implementation Theory and Practice: Toward a Third Generation.* Glenwood, Ill.: Scott Foreman/Little Brown.

Haas, P. 1998. "Compliance with EU Directives: Insights from International Relations and Comparative Politics." *Journal of European Public Policy* 5(1): 17-37.

Haverland, M. 1999. "National Adaptation to European Integration: The Importance of Institutional Veto Points." San Domenico. EUI Working Paper RSC No. 99/17.

Hill, M. and P. Hupe. 2002. *Implementing Public Policy: Governance in Theory and Practice.* London: Sage.

Hood, C. 1976. *The Limits of Administration.* London: John Wiley.

Kelder, E. 2000. *National Case Study on Policy Networks and Implementation of the Urban Waste Water Treatment Directive 91/271/EEC in the Nether-*

lands. Final Report for TEP Project, European Commission Framework Programme IV (1994-1998), Environment and Climate Program of DG XII: Brussels.

Kelemen, R.D. 2011. *Eurolegalism: The Transformation of Law and Regulation in the European Union*. Cambridge: Harvard University Press.

Keohane, R. 1984. *After Hegemony: Cooperation and Discord in the World Political Economy*. Princeton: Princeton University Press.

Keohane, R. and M. Levy, eds. 1996. *Institutions for Environmental Aid: Pitfalls and Promise*. Cambridge: MIT Press.

Lampinen, P. and P. Uusikylä. 1998. "Implementation Deficit – Why Member-states do not Comply with EU directives." *Scandinavian Political Studies* 21(3): 231-51.

Ledoux, L., S. Crooks, A. Jordan, and R. Turner. 2000. *Implementing EU Boidiversity: A UK Case Study*. London and East Anglia: CSERGE Working Paper 2000-03.

Levy, M., O. Young, and M. Zürn. 1995. "The Study of International Regimes." *European Journal of International Relations* 1(3): 267-330.

Lipsky, M. 1980. *Street Level Bureaucracy*. New York: Russel-Sage.

Lipsky, M. 1971. "Street Level Bureaucracy and the Analysis of Urban Reform." *Urban Affairs Quarterly* 6: 391-409.

Lowry, W. 1992. *The Dimensions of Federalism*. Durham: Duke University Press.

Mbaye, H. 2004. *Implementation in the European Union: Policy Compliance in the Member-states from Rome to Amsterdam*. PhD diss., University of North Carolina.

Mbaye, H. 2010. "Assessing Competing Explanations for Compliance and Non-Compliance with European Union Policies." *Midsouth Political Science Review* 10(1): 63-82.

Mbaye, H. 2011. "Political Decisions and Management Dilemmas Facing National and Local Officials in Complying with European Union Policies." *Midsouth Political Science Review* 11(1): 59-82.

Mbaye, H. 2001. "Why National States Comply with Supranational Law: Explaining Implementation Infringements in the European Union, 1972-1993." *European Union Politics* 2(3): 259-281.

Mendrinou, M. 1996. "Non-compliance and the European Commission's role in integration." *Journal of European Public Policy* 3(1): 1-22.

Mitchell, R. 1994. *Intentional Oil Pollution at Sea: Environmental Policy and Treaty Compliance*. Cambridge: MIT Press.

Olson, M. 1965. *The Logic of Collective Action: Public Goods and the Theory of Groups*. Cambridge: Harvard University Press.

Paraskevopoulos, C. 1998. "Social Capital, Institutional Learning and European Regional Policy: Evidence from Greece." *Regional and Federal Studies* 8(3):31-64.

Perkmann, M. 2002. "Policy entrepreneurs, multilevel governance and policy networks in the European polity: The case of the EUREGIO." Lancaster: Department of Sociology. http://www.lancs.ac.uk/fss/sociology/papers/perkmann-policy-entrepreneurs.pdf.

Pressman, J., and Wildavsky, A. 1973. *Implementation: How Great Expectations in Washington are Dashed in Oakland.* Berkeley: UC Press.

Tallberg, J. 2002. "Paths to compliance: enforcement, management, and the European Union." *International Organization* 56: 609-43.

Transparency International. 2010. "Corruption Perceptions Index 2010 Results." Accessed March 26, 2012. http://www.transparency.org/policy_research/surveys_indices/cpi/2010/results.

Treib, Oliver. 2008. "Implementing and Complying with EU governance outputs." *Living Reviews in European Governance* 3(5).

Turner, R.K., I. Lorenzoni, N. Beaumont, I. Bateman, I. Langford, A. McDonald. 1998. "Coastal Management for Sustainable Development: Analysing Environmental and Socio-Economic Changes on the UK Coast." *Geographical Journal* 164(3): 269-281.

Van Meter, D. and Van Horn, C.E. 1975. "The policy implementation process: a conceptual framework." *Administration and Society* 6(4): 445-88.

Weale, A., G. Pridham, A. Williams, and M. Porter. 1996. "Environmental Administration in Six European States: Secular Convergence or National Distinctiveness?" *Public Adminstration* 74: 255-74.

Yarbrough, B. and R. Yarbrough. 1992. *Cooperation and Governance in International Trade: The Strategic Organizational Approach.* Princeton: Princeton University Press.

Yavuz, D. 2012. "Conflict, Democratic Reform, and Big Business: Factors Shaping the Economic Elite's Position for Change." In *Secular State and Religious Society*, edited by B. Turam. New York: Palgrave Macmillan.

Young, O. 1992. "The Effectiveness of International Institutions: Hard Cases and Critical Variables." In *Governance without Government: Order and Change in World Politics*, edited by J. Rosenau, and E. Czempiel. Cambridge: Cambridge University Press, 160-194.

Young, O. 1999. *Governance in World Affairs*. Ithaca: Cornell University Press.

The Effectiveness of EU Leverage in Fighting Corruption in Central and Eastern Europe

Svet DERDERYAN

Introduction

The European Union's (EU) eastern enlargement stands as one of the greatest political achievements of the modern era. The two waves of the enlargement in 2004 and 2007 made the Union the world's largest commercial and financial market, with a population exceeding 490 million people and a GDP of more than $13 trillion. The significance of this historic event, however, extends far beyond geography, demography and economics and has deep symbolic implications. As Romano Prodi put it, "Five decades after our great project of European integration began, we are celebrating the fact that Europeans are no longer kept apart by artificial ideological barriers." (Europa 2004) This was a moment when after more than a decade of difficult transitions, 10 post-communist Central and Eastern European (CEE) countries finally broke free from their communist legacies and joined the ranks of the developed world. Authoritarianism and central planning were now buried in the past. Democracy and the free market were 'the only game in town'.

However, institutional developments affected by the accession process have had varying levels of success. Although there have been encouraging results in many areas, there is still ongoing debate about the readiness of some of these newly accepted countries to be full members. The evolution of the fight against corruption in Central and Eastern Europe provides a useful illustration of this concern. This study, however, refutes the scepticism about these countries' success in trying to contain corruption and shows that both before and after membership CEE countries made substantial absolute gains in curbing corruption levels. Although corruption was neither part of the *acquis* nor of the Copenhagen criteria, it was an issue that received tremendous visibility during the accession period through the Commission Regular Reports and the attention of the media in the CEE countries. Taking advantage of its leverage, the EU was able to demand reforms that served to decrease corruption levels during the accession period. After accession, gains in the fight against corruption were not negated as the relative loss of leverage in this time period was compensated by positive pressures coming from continued leverage (Structural and Cohesion Funds and Cooperation and Verification Mechanism reports) and increased linkage (socialisation effects leading to higher demands for accountability of public officials).

Background

The task of reforming the CEE countries during the accession process was a challenging one. Overall, however, the EU's membership conditionality has been widely perceived as a highly effective means of influence. The promise of membership combined with the implementation of the 31 chapters of the *acquis communitaire* during the negotiations phase of the accession period has been credited with the overall alignment of the ten post-communist countries' systems of governance, economies, and legal structures with Western European standards. There is no doubt, therefore, that during the accession period CEE countries received huge incentives to comply and collaborate with EU institutions. As a number of scholars have argued, however, these incentives may have decreased once membership was attained and the EU's leverage correspondingly diminished.

There are some examples of issue areas where compliance has indeed declined after accession, most evidently with respect to party platforms and economic and monetary union (Vachudova 2008; Johnson 2008). At the same time, there is plenty of evidence of continued compliance, such as in the areas of bank privatisation and pension reform (Epstein 2008; Orenstein 2008). It is therefore unclear to what extent the EU has had a system-wide impact and continues to cause political and economic reform in new members after accession. In order to try to shed more light on these ongoing debates I focus on the area of governance that is most likely to engender skepticism: government efforts to fight corruption.

There are many reasons that justify focusing on corruption in particular. Corruption is important because it undermines democratic institutions, reduces economic growth, and challenges liberal democracy, "as political elites violate the legal limits of their power, citizens lose trust in state institutions, and civil society is oppressed and co-opted by powerful networks" (Vachudova 2009). Furthermore, it endangers the cohesion of the Union in a way that few other governance challenges do. First, if the Structural and Cohesion Funds that become available to new members after accession are not fairly allocated, they fail to adequately address the economic and infrastructural challenges these countries face and thus delay their effective integration in the Union. Second, as corruption scandals in CEE countries make more and more headlines, public support for the Union's integration and further enlargement diminishes as both eastern and western European publics become sceptical of the EU. Thus, corruption is an important issue that deserves the attention of both policy-makers and academics.

Many scholars suggest that post-accession compliance would be maintained in cases where dismantling institutions is difficult and domestic costs in general remain high (Epstein and Seledmeier 2008; Vachudova 2005; Kelley 2004). But Epstein and Seledmeier (2008) argue that the power of EU conditionality would be the weakest in areas where the EU never applied specific conditionality, such as rules that are neither part of the *acquis*, nor of the Copenhagen criteria. Such is the case with corruption. Although the membership criteria do call, somewhat broadly, for developing institutional capacities to curb corruption and organised crime, corruption is neither part of the *acquis*, nor of the Copenhagen criteria. Some scholarly evidence suggests that this is not coincidental since there was never a consensus among the older member states to push or emphasise the issue (Vachudova 2009) and some Council members systematically tried to avoid it.

Jacoby (2004) also contributes to the argument that the density of EU rules in each area of reform predetermines their success and longevity. He compares regional and healthcare policy and finds that the sector characterised by more extensive external pressure (stronger EU conditionality), regional policy, made greater progress towards approximating Western European models. The high level of outside incentives and the relative scarcity of domestic actors in the case of regional policy (as opposed to healthcare) compelled and enabled some CEE governments to implement the EU's regional policy rules fairly and faithfully. Thus, Jacoby would also expect to find modest EU-driven progress fighting corruption since the density of EU rules is low.

As stated earlier, if we look at the *acquis* or the Copenhagen criteria, corruption is characterised by a relatively low level of outside incentives. Thus, one can legitimately expect only modest improvements in corruption levels during the candidacy period, and perhaps backsliding after accession when EU leverage diminishes. Yet, as mentioned earlier, I find robust evidence for the positive impact of both EU candidacy and membership on corruption levels in CEE countries.

I will explore the question of how corruption levels were influenced by the EU in several stages. In Part II I will present the theoretical framework that I utilise to formulate my hypotheses. Part III will present the statistical framework of the study including a discussion on the choice and operationalisation of variables and the results from the time series analyses. Part IV will discuss the exact causal mechanisms that may be in play before and after. Finally, the conclusion will summarise the main arguments and findings and discuss their implications for EU policy-making.

Theory and Hypotheses

In this section I outline the theoretical background behind my hypotheses. First, I explain why EU leverage was so powerful during the pre-accession process and why it allowed the EU to push for reforms that went beyond the formal scope of the negotiation chapters. In this context I formulate my first hypothesis about decreasing corruption levels in the pre-accession period. Second, I delineate the alternative mechanisms that have continued the pressure for reform post-accession, when leverage was substantially decreased. These mechanisms serve as the basis of my second hypothesis about the lack of backsliding in corruption levels after accession.

Although many authors have made the case that the power of EU conditionality would be the weakest in areas where the EU never applied specific conditionality (such as rules that are neither part of the *acquis*, nor of the Copenhagen criteria), I argue that the issue of corruption always received a high level of visibility (from the media and from the Regular Reports) and this allowed EU leverage to introduce powerful incentives to try to curb it during the accession period. Furthermore, in the case of the eastern enlargement EU leverage was unprecedented and was thus likely to significantly affect areas, such as corruption, that were not explicitly emphasised.

Pridham (2005) points to four factors that increased the power of EU conditionality. First, he emphasises that as they were shaking off the bonds of communism in the early 1990s, the CEE countries decided to attempt a total overhaul of their political, economic, and social systems. There was hardly an aspect of public or private life that remained untouched. Total overhaul is not easy in an environment of falling incomes, weak institutional capacity, and insufficient familiarity with modern practices. In such a difficult and all-encompassing effort, it was inevitable that the CEE countries would falter in some aspects of reform – and it therefore made sense to seek the expert help of the EU. For example, Bulgaria, which experienced a hyperinflation crisis in 1996-97 decided to implement a currency board and deliberately surrender the conduct of monetary policy to the German and, later, the European Central Bank. The main point here is that countries undergoing complete systemic change are more in need of EU help and are therefore more responsive to EU conditionality than in other circumstances, such as during the southern enlargement in the 1980s.

Second, the onset of conditionality roughly coincided with the collapse of the Soviet Union, and the security imperative was probably high on the minds of CEE elites. In this unstable international environment, EU conditionality may have been more effective, as the perceived geopolitical benefits for candidate states may have been greater.

Third, the EU's fifth enlargement involved a record 12 countries (the ten that joined in 2004 plus Bulgaria and Romania, which joined in 2007). Competition among these applicant countries was fierce, and the media in any given country were reporting on the progress of the rest of the pack. Importantly, corruption was always a salient issue receiving special attention in the Regular Reports of the Commission. Government officials were then under intense pressure from their respective publics to perform, and the public backlash in the countries that were not invited to begin negotiations in late 1997 was severe.

Finally, Pridham argues, most CEE candidates were small states, which wanted to become part of a powerful organisation like the EU. If size and leverage are negatively correlated in international relations, then the domestic environments of the CEE countries were quite conducive to the effects of EU conditionality. Thus, during the entire candidacy period the relationship between CEE countries and the EU was characterised by what Vachudova (2005) has termed *asymmetrical interdependence*: CEE countries needed the EU much more than the EU needed them and this vastly superior bargaining position allowed the EU to influence candidates in ways that went even beyond the *acquis* and the Copenhagen criteria.

Thus, in light of the unprecedented power of EU leverage during the accession period and the high visibility of the issue of corruption, in these countries, I propose the following hypothesis:

H1: *Corruption levels start improving as soon as a country is given the green light to be able to join the EU (credible candidate status) and this trend remains sustainable during the entire candidacy period.*

As stated earlier, many authors have made the case that a slowdown or even backsliding is likely to occur in the post-accession period due to the decrease of leverage after the ultimate reward of membership has been granted. There are three mechanisms, however, which compensate for this loss of leverage in this period and suggest that corruption levels may actually continue to improve. As Levitz and Pop-Eleches (2010) argue, EU leverage, though transformed, remained an important force after membership. Greater dependence on trade and especially the potential threat of freezing the massive Structural and Cohesion funds available to new poorer members acted as a powerful incentive for elites to stay on the reform path. Additionally, greater linkage and exposure to the West for both elites and citizens was associated with higher expectations of government performance and served as an additional pressure to continue compliance. Thus, in light of these arguments I propose the following hypothesis related to the post-accession period:

H2: *Progress in curbing corruption continues after accession, even as EU leverage becomes weaker.*

Methodological Framework

The purpose of this section is two-fold. First, I outline the way the dependent variable, levels of corruption, the independent variables of interest, *EU Candidacy Process and Full Membership, and all the relevant control variables have* been operationalised. Then, I present the findings of the statistical analysis and explain the significance of these results to my hypotheses.

Operationalisation of the Dependent Variable – Corruption

In order to specify the dependent variable, corruption, I refer to the Control of Corruption (CC) index, which is part of the World Bank's World Governance Indicators (WGI). Kaufmann, Kraay, and Mastruzzi (KKM), who have developed the index, define CC as an index "measuring perceptions of the extent to which public power is exercised for private gain, including both petty and grand forms of corruption, as well as 'capture' of the state by elites and private interests." (KKM 2008 p. 8). The index covers 212 countries and territories for the years 1996, 1998, 2000, and 2002-2009. The scores for the years 1997, 1999, and 2001 are manually constructed by averaging the adjoining years.

Operationalisation of the Independent Variables – EU Candidacy Process and Full Membership

The two independent variables of interest in this study are the EU candidacy process and EU membership. The EU candidacy process is defined as the period between the moment when a country has signed an association agreement with the EU (but has not yet entered accession negotiations) and the moment when full membership is achieved. Although the EU candidacy process goes through several stages starting with more general rather than specific conditionality and then moving to actively transposing the full *acquis communautaire* during the negotiations phase, looking at the process as a whole is a sensible approach given that both the softer inactive leverage of the initial phase and the active leverage of the negotiations phase exert powerful influence on acceding members. Per hypothesis 1, I expect to find a strong improvement in corruption levels during the Candidacy Process.

Table 1: Independent Variable – EU Candidacy Process

Status	Country and Period
EU Candidacy Process	Bulgaria 1996-2006, Czech Republic 1996-2003, Estonia 1996-2003, Hungary 1996-2003, Latvia 1996-2003, Lithuania 1996-2003, Poland 1996-2003, Romania 1996-2006, Slovakia 1996-2003, Slovenia 1996-2003

The second independent variable, EU membership, is defined as the moment when all the existing member states have ratified the Treaty of Accession and a country has become a full-fledged member of the Union. Importantly, at that point, the EU can no longer threaten to withhold membership in order to compel a country to comply with its demands, though it can use other types of leverage such as threatening to stop or stopping Structural and Cohesion Funds to new members. This considerable decrease of leverage after full membership is granted is interpreted by many as the main reason why new members may experience backsliding. Therefore, looking at corruption levels post-accession is also extremely important for this study since it will show whether potential gains made during the candidacy process are sustainable. Per hypothesis 2, I expect that the strong improvement in corruption levels achieved during the candidacy period will be sustained in the post-enlargement period.

Table 2: Independent variable – Full Membership

Status	Country and Period
Full Membership	Bulgaria 2007-2009, Czech Republic 2004-2009, Estonia 2004-2009, Hungary 2004-2009, Latvia 2004-2009, Lithuania 2004-2009, Poland 2004-2009, Romania 2007-2009, Slovakia 2004-2009, Slovenia 2004-2009

In the two regressions that follow I am assigning dummies to CEE candidate countries in accordance with the independent variables outlined above. For the first independent variable, the EU accession process, a country receives a 1 if in any given year it is at any stage of the EU candidacy process (if it has signed an association agreement with the EU, is conducting accession negotiations, or has signed a Treaty of Accession). For years that the country is not part of the process it receives a 0. For the second independent variable, full membership, a country receives a 1 for any year in which it is a full member of the Union. Conversely, for years preceding the year of accession it receives a 0. There are no overlapping years and the eight post-communist countries that joined in May 2004 receive a 1 for the entire 2004 period.

Control Variables/Alternative Explanations

In order to isolate the effects of the EU candidacy process and EU membership I refer to the academic literature on corruption to identify factors affecting corruption levels. Thus, the control variables included in the statistical analysis are: size of the public sector (government expenditure), level of economic development (GDP), level of economic competition (ratio of imports to GDP), level of democracy (Freedom in the World – average of political rights and civil liberties scores), freedom of the press, abundance of natural resources, and neighbouring and diffusion effects. The time-sensitive control variables are lagged by one year because corruption perceptions may change slowly rather than immediately in response to these factors.

1. Government Spending (General government final consumption expenditure as a percentage of GDP; United Nations Statistical Division)

Several studies, including LaPalombara (1994), Rijckeghem and Weber (1997), and Elliott (1997), employ this measure and argue that the incidence of corruption may be related to the size of the public sector. Intuitively, a system entailing more frequent and extensive intervention of the state in the economy may sometimes introduce more opportunities for corruption. Such opportunities include, but are not limited to, some of the most obvious forms of corruption, such as nepotism, bribery and extortion.

2. Level of Economic Development (Log of GDP per capita; Economist Intelligence Unit, World Development Indicators)

Studies by Kaufman *et al.* (1999), Poirson (1998) and Leite & Weidmann (1999), Sandholtz and Gray (2003), and Dearden (2000) have all confirmed the significance of economic growth for corruption levels. Although the causal story varies somewhat among low, middle and high-income countries, the effects of economic growth on corruption are unquestionable and it therefore seems appropriate to include the log of GDP per capita as a proxy for level of economic development in a given country.

3. Competition (Imports as a percentage of GDP; United Nations Statistical Division)

The intuition is that opportunities for corruption may increase due to the lack of competition in a national economy. This means that theoretically, more open economies must be less corrupt. Gerring and Thacker (2005) and Ades and Di Tella (1999) prove this correlation empirically by examining the precise relationship between trade openness and levels of political corruption. It is for this reason that using imports as a percentage of GDP (like Ades and Di Tella) to account for the level of competition in a national economy seems like a sensible choice.

4. Level of Democracy (Freedom in the World: average of political rights and civil liberties scores; Freedom House)

Montinola and Jackman (2002) present convincing evidence that democratic practices inhibit corruption especially after a threshold of democratic consolidation is passed. Börzel, Stahn and Pamuk (2010) show that the level of corruption in the Eastern Europe is strongly connected to the success of democratic and economic reforms. Thus, including the Freedom in the World index as a proxy for level of democracy seems appropriate.

5. Freedom of the Press (Freedom House)

Many scholars argue that the media may serve as a powerful check on corruption. Karkins (2005) finds that the media has proven to be one of the most effective promoters of anti-corrupt politics. Freille *et al.* (2007), in a 10-year panel study, find that restrictions on press freedom lead to higher levels of corruption. Holmes (2006) provides survey evidence on the effects of the media on public perceptions of corruption in Bulgaria, Hungary, Poland, Russia, and China and concludes that the media in these countries cover corruption extensively and provide most of the knowledge that the public has of corruption, and therefore it heavily influences the public's perception of corruption in state institutions.

6. Abundance of Natural Resources (Production of minerals and utilities as a percentage of GDP; United Nations Statistical Division)

The logic behind this variable is that abundance of natural resources may create opportunities for rent seeking and thus facilitate corrupt behaviour. Leite and Weidemann (1999), Ades and Di Tella (1999), and Ross (2008) review such arguments and prove their statistical significance. For the purposes of this study I will use production of fuels and minerals as a share of GNP to proxy for abundance of natural resources.

7. Neighbourhood and Diffusion Effects (Average corruption score of neighbouring countries, as calculated from the World Bank's Control of Corruption index).

Controlling for neighbourhood and diffusion effects is also a very good idea. Sandholtz and Gray (2003) argue that international interactions can affect norms and practices that one may think were determined by social and local factors. They focus specifically on corruption and show that corruption tends increase in countries surrounded by corrupt neighbours. Similar regional diffusion effects are also extensively explored in the international political economy literature by Simmons *et al.* (2008).

Statistical Analysis and Results

Table 3 below presents the results of the time-series cross-sectional analyses utilising a Fixed Effects Regression Model (FE). After testing for unit effects and getting a significant F-score, I decided to account for such effects using a FE design. The Hausman test invariably rejected the random effects as an appropriate model, rendering fixed effects the most sensible choice. Fixed effects are particularly appropriate in studies like this, where unobservable country-specific characteristics and historical differences may affect the dependent variable in ways that the control variables by themselves cannot account for.

The table includes three designs (Design 1, Design 2 and Design 3), the difference between which is the choice of the reference group – all countries from around the world in Designs 1, the 27 EU countries in Design 2, and only the post-communist countries in Design 3. All three designs exhibit no autocorrelation. This was illustrated by the application of the Wooldrige test, for which the F-tests in the three designs were insignificant, meaning that we couldn't reject H_0 that there was no autocorrelation.

Table 3: The Effects of EU Candidacy and Membership on Corruption Levels

Drivers	Design 1	Design 2	Design 3
EU Candidacy process	.089** (.056)	.173*** (.052)	.112 *** (.055)
Full Membership	.116** (.064)	.189*** (.063)	.106* (.065)
Level of Economic Development	.156** (.077)	.406* (.248)	.451*** (.137)
Neighbours' corruption	.093*** (.033)	.007 (.101)	.033 (.094)

Size of the Public sector	.438*** (.162)	-1.83*** (.586)	.009** (.004)
Competition	-.062 (.051)	-.126 (.169)	-.000 (.001)
Natural resources	-.421*** (.122)	-.196 (1.66)	-.003 (.003)
Level of democracy ("Freedom in the World" score)	-.068*** (.009)	.015 (.031)	.090*** (.023)
Freedom of the press	-.221*** (.073)	-.439** (.196)	-.002* (.001)
Constant	-.289 (.292)	-.372 (1.03)	-1.71*** (.531)
R-squared	0.63	0.26	0.83
Number of Observations	1898	319	330

Standard errors in parentheses. Significant at: * 10%; ** 5%; *** 1%. One-tailed tests for the independent variables.

In Design 1 the reference group to which post-communist candidate states are compared consists of the entire set of non-candidate countries. Here we test whether a country's inclusion in the EU candidacy process improves corruption levels in any way. Per Hypotheses 1 we expect that corruption would be declining while a country is part of the accession process. Per hypothesis 2 we expect that this trend will remain unchanged after membership is attained.

The results of this analysis confirm both hypotheses. Relative to the base of non-candidate countries from around the world, CEE countries performed strongly, on average, (positive coefficient of .089) and statistically significantly (p-value: 0.05) during the EU candidacy process. After accession, the candidate states did not experience backsliding (positive coefficient of .116) – a result that is statistically significant (p-value: 0.04). Thus, based on this analysis we can infer that the progress made during the accession process led to sound and sustainable results that continued to be present in the post-membership period. Six of the control variables, Level of Economic Development, Neighbouring Corruption, Size of the Public Sector, Natural Resources, Level of Democracy, and Freedom of the Press were also found to be significant drivers of corruption levels. Although they are of no particular interest in the present study, these control variables have signs and levels of statistical significance broadly consistent with theory and prior studies. Incidentally, the negative coefficient on the freedom of the press variable is to be expected, since in this particular Freedom House assessment, higher scores correspond to less freedom. This is important because it also provides some evidence to the claim that the high visibility of the issue of corruption created by the media allowed EU leverage to work even in this area which was not explicitly emphasised in the *acquis* or the Copenhagen criteria. The high R-squared of the design, 63 per cent, further underpins our confidence that these findings confirm the hypotheses that during the accession process corruption levels would be falling and that this process will remain stable even after membership has been obtained and when EU leverage has become weaker.

In Design 2 the reference group to which post-communist candidate states are compared consists of the other EU members. The results of this analysis also confirm both the hypotheses. Relative to the base of old EU members, CEE countries performed strongly (positive coefficient of .173) and statistically significantly (p-value: 0.001) both during the EU candidacy process and after they attained membership (positive coefficient of .189 and p-value: 0.003). However, we have to be rather cautious with the interpretation of these results since old EU members had considerably lower levels of corruption to start with (hence less room and opportunities to improve). That is why it is not surprising that the CEE countries outperformed this base. Nevertheless, the results of this regression are important since they demonstrate that CEE countries are firmly set on a positive trajectory in their fight against corruption and are trying to catch up with their more developed and less corrupt Western European counterparts. Three of the control variables, Level of Economic Development, Size of the Public Sector, and Freedom of the Press were also found to be significant drivers of corruption levels.

Design 3 restricts the sample to the candidate countries plus the non-candidate post-communist states of the former Soviet bloc. The inclusion of this reference group serves a specific methodological goal – to separate the effect of the EU's incentive-based approach from the set of potential domestic issues associated with the post-communist transition period that all these countries were part of. The results of Design 3 are consistent with the results of the previous two designs. Relative to the reference group of post-communist non-candidate states, candidate countries performed better both during the EU candidacy process and after membership, although the positive coefficient for the post-membership dummy is significant only at the 10 per cent level for a one-tailed test (p-value 0.052). Since the coefficient for the full membership period is barely significant, I also ran a joint F-test for the variables indicating the two periods. In this way I was able to test the joint hypothesis that EU leverage, before and after accession, matters and corruption trends do indeed continue to deteriorate after accession. The positive coefficients for the two periods and the significant F-score (p-value: 0.02) confirmed the joint hypothesis. Thus, we can safely say that the overall effect of EU leverage both during and after a country's accession process matters and leads to a decrease in corruption levels. Four of the control variables, Level of Economic Development, Size of the Public Sector, Levels of Democracy and Freedom of the Press were also found to be significant drivers of corruption levels. The R-squared of this design is the highest, 83 per cent, and the findings once again confirm both the hypotheses that before accession corruption would be falling and no backsliding will occur after membership has been obtained and EU leverage diminishes.

Causal Mechanisms

The purpose of this section is to trace the causal mechanisms through which the EU was able to influence the fight against corruption before and after accession. The question of pre-accession leverage is an important one since it both set the tone for the negotiations and delineated the set of expectations after membership was granted. In this period the Commission Regular Reports included detailed demands to fight corruption as well as recommendations on how this should be done. Responsiveness to these demands and recommendations was explicitly tied to a candidate's chances for membership. The more interesting question, however, is what mechanisms have prevented potential backsliding after accession when EU leverage became weaker. I argue that there are two mechanisms in play that compensate for the presumed loss of leverage after membership: continued leverage (Structural and Cohesion Funds and Cooperation and Verification Mechanism (CVM) reports) and increased linkage (socialisation effects).

Focusing first on the period before accession, progress in combating corruption became a recurrent theme in the Commission Regular Reports, which were becoming more detailed and specific as accession was approaching. This was partly due to the candidates' desire for more explicit targets and for assurances that they are meeting all membership criteria (Grabbe 2006). By the early 2000s, specific and detailed recommendations for anti-corruption measures had replaced the vague and formalistic statements of the earliest reports (Hughes, Sasse, Gordon 2004). In fact, corruption had become such a salient issue that the EU built into Bulgaria and Romania's accession treaty a safeguard clause (Article 39) allowing for a delay of accession by one year in the event of insufficient progress in tackling corruption. Importantly, such strictness was not confined only to these presumably more corrupt countries. The EU consistently noted the prevalence of corruption in Hungary as a problem and identified public procurement as an area of concern in both the 1999 and 2000 Regular Reports. The situation was similar in the 1999 Regular Report on Latvia and in the 2002 Regular Report on Poland asserting that corruption "threatens to undermine the functioning of many public spheres" (Regular Reports 1999; 2000; 2002). This is just a sample of a few reports, but corruption is a central issue in many. Furthermore, the issuance of every report was followed by an enormous amount of publicity in the media, thus forging a significant level of domestic pressure for compliance as well. Thus, since corruption was clearly a salient and highly visible issue, EU leverage was substantial. In other words, the incentives for candidates to decrease levels of corruption during the accession period were high since this decrease was directly tied to their prospects of qualifying for membership.

After accession, continued leverage, increased linkage, and spill-over effects, resulting from the implementation of other parts of the *acquis*, compensated for the diminished relative power of the EU. First of all, new members became eligible for significant amounts of Structural and Cohesion Funds (S & C funds) (about 1/3 of the EU budget). These members' dependence on conditional EU funding (which could be cut off in cases of non-compliance as occurred in Bulgaria), therefore, continued to promote governance reforms. Furthermore, in the cases of Bulgaria and Romania a CVM was instituted to ensure that both countries complied with their commitments. Progress in fighting corruption has thus far always been a special focus in these reports. To elaborate a little on how the leverage of S & C funds translates into pressure for reform, I will now turn to a brief case-specific discussion of Bulgaria and Romania.

In response to a corruption scandal in Bulgaria with two officials of the National Road Agency in January 2008, the Commission exercised its leverage by cutting off funding for road construction. Importantly, the investigation was initiated by a scathing article in Bulgaria's leading business newspaper, *Kapital*. In February and March the Commission froze Phare and SAPARD funding in light of more corruption allegations in the ministries of finance and regional development. As a result of its failure to address its looming corruption, Bulgaria ended up with two ministerial resignations, an irreversible loss of 220 million euro and a freezing of 340 million euro. Although the 340 million was later on unfrozen, Bulgarian authorities, and most specifically the new Prime Minister Boiko Borissov realised that the time had come to "wage a full-scale war" on corruption. In early 2010 during operation "Octopus" ("Октопод") the government was able to expose and arrest high-ranking public officials (associated with the State Agency for National Security with jurisdictions to fight corruption) involved in money laundering, tax evasion and siphoning money from a now-defunct steelmaker, among other allegations (Liubomirska 2010). A few months earlier during the operation "Insolent Bastards" ("Наглите") the Borissov government was able to deal a major blow against organised crime by arresting a number of mafia members involved in kidnappings, contract killings, and trafficking.

In 2007 the Commission threatened to freeze agricultural funds to Romania unless the country filled some corruption-inducing gaps in its payments system. Reforms were quickly implemented and allegations of corruption led to the resignation of Tudor Chiuariu, Romania's Justice Minister two months later (Ivanov 2010). All of these developments where closely watched and extensively covered by both the media and a series of EU monitoring reports, which criticized Bulgaria and Romania and called for more intense efforts to curb corruption (CVM Reports June 2007; February 2008; July 2008).

Thus, the EU was clearly able to continue to exert leverage over all its new members through the threat of cutting off conditional funding in cases of non-compliance and through the actual freezing of such funding as in the case of Bulgaria. For Bulgaria and Romania this means of exercising leverage was further supplanted by the implementation of the CVM. CVM reports track and assess progress against corruption (and other commitments), thus establishing a direct monitoring system, which allowed the EU to continue to exert a sustained pressure for reform.

The second mechanism that translates EU influence into domestic changes is the diffusion of democratic norms and values. This includes increasing linkages between new and old EU members, exemplified in more travel and work opportunities in the West for CEE citizens, greater mass media exposure, more joint-business ventures etc., all contributing to greater expectations for good governance (Levitz and Pop-Eleches 2010). In a study focusing specifically on the lack of new EU members' backsliding along an array of indicators Levitz and Pop-Eleches find a strong negative correlation between international travel and share of CEE citizens living in Western Europe and corruption levels. These findings strongly align with the growing literature on socialisation effects (Checkel 2005; Gheciu, 2005; Epstein and Seledmeier 2008).

In explaining the puzzling lack of backsliding in CEE countries, Sedelmeier suggests focusing on the "greater susceptibility of the new member states to shaming" (Sedelmeier 2008, 806). He argues that extended linkages with the West could have made CEE citizens more concerned about public shaming and more demanding as far as compliance goes through a process of socialisation. Levitz and Pop-Eleches add to this argument by empirically showing that East Europeans working and traveling abroad are steadily turning into an electorate with higher expectations about the rule of law and corruption standards, thus exerting an important positive impact on the political culture in their home countries.

To sum up, before accession, CEE leaders had strong incentives to try to curb corruption since it was a highly salient issue specifically emphasised in the Commission Regular Reports. The asymmetric power relationship between the EU and the candidate members allowed the EU to effectively use its leverage to induce change even in areas that were not formally in the *acquis* or the Copenhagen criteria, such as corruption. After accession, the relative loss of leverage was compensated by three mechanisms that sustained the pressure for reform and prevented backsliding: continued leverage (Structural and Cohesion Funds and CVM reports) and increased linkage (socialisation effects).

Conclusion

The ten post-communist countries that joined the EU in 2004 and 2007 constitute a special case in the history of EU enlargement marked by unprecedented EU leverage, which translated into a systemic overhaul of these countries' political, economic, and legal systems. By the end of their long and painful transitions that took most of the 1990s, the majority of CEE states had declared that joining the EU was their top foreign policy goal (Vachudova 2005). There were multiple reasons for this preference, from political and geo-strategic (locking in democracy, guaranteeing national security vis-à-vis Russia, and reducing uncertainty by regulating relations with powerful West European states) to economic (eliminating trade barriers, receiving subsidies, and obtaining a voice in the decision-making process of CEE's most powerful trading partner). Small, economically weak, and politically vulnerable, the CEE countries needed the EU much more than the EU needed them. Thus, this asymmetrical interdependence provided the EU with a solid bargaining position and allowed it to impose comprehensive and intrusive membership conditions that went beyond the scope of the *acquis* and the Copenhagen criteria.

This study makes several important contributions to the leverage and compliance literature. First, although compliance in certain areas did indeed deteriorate in the post-accession period when EU leverage had diminished, I present convincing evidence that this was not the case with corruption. Although it remains a hot topic and an area of continued criticism for many of these countries, absolute gains in progress against corruption have been sustained even after membership. Although corruption was neither part of the *acquis* nor of the Copenhagen criteria, it was an issue that received tremendous visibility during the accession period through the Commission Regular Reports and the attention of the media in the CEE countries. Taking advantage of its leverage, the EU was able to demand reforms that served to curb corruption levels during the candidacy period. Importantly, gains in the fight against corruption were not negated after accession. These findings support the arguments against backsliding (Pop-Eleches and Levitz 2010) and cast doubt on studies suggesting that lack of density of formal rules (Jacoby 2004) or lack of explicit conditionality (Epstein and Sedelmeier 2008) negatively affects the success of reforms.

Second, this study points out two mechanisms that compensated for the relative loss of leverage after membership. First, the EU was able to continue to exert some leverage and thus sustain pressure for reform through the threat of cutting off conditional funding in cases of non-compliance. Having acted on this threat once, in the case of Bulgaria, the EU demonstrated that this was a real and credible punishment mechanism, which it can use if serious violations are uncovered. Secondly, increased linkages between Western and Eastern Europe, exemplified by the number of people travelling and working in the West, led to the gradual emergence of an electorate of more "Europeanised" CEE citizens with higher expectations about the rule of law and corruption. Such socialisation effects serve as the silent underpinnings of a new political culture, one that holds politicians to higher standards and demands good governance at all costs. As opinion polls have indicated, Central and Eastern Europeans are a lot more pro-EU than their Western European counterparts and are therefore unwilling to risk marginalisation with respect to the EU for lack of compliance. Further research is needed to flesh out the exact causality of these two mechanisms.

Nevertheless, absolute improvements in corruption levels in CEE countries do not necessarily mean that a bright future is inevitable. These countries still remain much more corrupt than Western European members and corruption continues to undermine economic progress and the citizens' faith in the democratic system. That is why pressure for reform should persist and perhaps more detailed studies focusing on particular aspects of corruption should be encouraged, so that both the EU and the CEE governments can collectively come up with more targeted and effective strategies to tackle this serious and endemic challenge.

References

Ades, Alberto and Di Tella, Rafael. 1999. "Rents, Competition, and Corruption." *American Economic Review* 89: 982-994.

Börzel, Tanja A., Stahn, Andreas, and Pamuk, Yasemin. 2010. "The European Union and the fight against corruption in its near abroad: can it make a difference?" *Global Crime* 11(2): 122-144.

Checkel, J. 2005. "International Institutions and Socialization in Europe: Introduction and Framework." *International Organization* 59(4): 801-826.

CVM June 2007; February 2008; July 2008.

Dimitrova, A. 2002. "Enlargement, Institution-Building and the EU's Administrative Capacity Requirement." *West European Politics* 25(4): 171-190.

Dearden, S. 2000. "Corruption and Economic Development." DSA European Development Policy Study Group Discussion Paper No. 18.

Epstein, R. and Sedelmeier, U. 2008. "Beyond conditionality: international institutions in postcommunist Europe after enlargement." *Journal of European Public Policy* 15(6): 795-805.

Elliott, Kimberly Ann. 1997. "Corruption as an International Policy Problem: Overview and Recommendations." In *Corruption in the Global Economy*, ed. Kimberly Ann Elliott. Washington, DC: Institute for International Economics, 175-233.

Epstein, R.A. 2008. "Transnational *actors and bank privatization.*" In *Transnational Actors in Central and East European Transitions*. University of Pittsburgh Press.

EU Commission. http://ec.europa.eu/enlargement/enlargement_process/accession_process/how_does_a_country_join_the_eu/negotiations_croatia_turkey/index_en.htm.

Europa. 2004. European Union Enlargement Day Celebrations. Press release. April 29, 2004. http://europa.eu/rapid/press-release_IP-04-559_en.htm?locale=en.

European Commission. *2000 Regular Report from the Commission on Bulgaria's Progress Towards Accession*. Brussels, 2000.

European Commission. *2002 Regular Report from the Commission on Poland's Progress Towards Accession*. Brussels, 2002.

European Commission. *2000 Regular Report from the Commission on Hungary's Progress Towards Accession*. Brussels, 2000.

European Commission. *1999 Regular Report from the Commission on Hungary's Progress Towards Accession*. Brussels, 1999.

European Commission. *1999 Regular Report from the Commission on Latvia's Progress Towards Accession*. Brussels, 1999.

Freille, Sebastian, M., Haque, Emranul, and Richard Kneller. 2007. "A Contribution to the Empirics of Press Freedom and Corruption." E*uropean Journal of Political Economy*. 23(4) 838-862.

Gheciu, Alexandra. 2005. "Security Institutions as Agents of Socialization? NATO and the 'New Europe.'" *International Organization* 59: 973-1012.

Grabbe, H. 2006. *The EU's Transformative Power: Europeanization through Conditionality in Central and Eastern Europe*. New York: Palgrave Macmillan.

Gerring, John and Thacker, Strom. 2005. "Do Neoliberal Policies Deter Political Corruption?" *International Organization* 59: 233-254.

Holmes, L. T. 2006. *Rotten States? Corruption, Post-communism and Neoliberalism*. Durham: Duke University Press.

Hughes, J., Sasse, G., and Gordon, C. 2004. *Europeanization and Regionalization in the EU's Enlargement to Central and Eastern Europe*. New York: Palgrave Macmillan.

Ivanov, Kalin. 2010. "The 2007 accession of Bulgaria and Romania: ritual and reality." *Global Crime Special Issue: Anti-Corruption for Eastern Europe* 11(2).

Jacoby, W. 2004. *The Enlargement of the European Union and NATO: Ordering from the Menu in Central Europe*. Cambridge: Cambridge University Press.

Kelley, J. 2006. *Ethnic Politics in Europe: The Power of Norms and Incentives*. Princeton: Princeton University Press.

Kaufmann, Daniel, Kraay, Aart, and Mastruzzi, Massimo. 2008. "Governance Matters VII: Governance Indicators for 1996-2007." World Bank Policy Research Department Working Paper No. 4654. Washington, DC: The World Bank.

Karklins, R. 2005. *The system made me do it: corruption in post-communist societies*. Armonk: M.E. Sharpe.

LaPalombara, Joseph. 1994. "Structural and Institutional Aspects of Corruption." *Social Research* 61: 325-530.

Lyubomirska, Maia. 2010. "Как държавата затвори кранчето на корупцията" http://www.monitor.bg/article?id=233965.

Leite, C. and Weidmann, J. 1999. "Does Mother Nature Corrupt? Natural Resources, Corruption, and Economic Growth." IMF Working Paper No. 99/85.

Montinola, Gabriella and Robert Jackman. 2002. "Sources of Corruption: A Cross-Country Study." *British Journal of Political Science* 32: 147-170.

Montalvo, J. and Reynal Querol, M. 2004. "Ethnic Polarization, Potential Conflict, and Civil Wars." UPF Economics and Business Working Paper 770.

Orenstein, M. 2008. "Out-liberalizing the EU: pension privatization in Central and Eastern Europe." *JEPP* http://www.informaworld.com/smpp/title~db=all~content=t713685697~tab=issueslist~branches=15 - v1515(6): 899-917.

Pridham, G. 2005. *Designing Democracy: EU Enlargement and Regime Change in Post-Communist Europe*. New York: Palgrave Macmillan.

Pop-Eleches, Grigore and Levitz, Philip. 2010. "Why No Backsliding? The EU's Impact on Democracy and Governance Before and After Accession." *Comparative Political Studies* 43: 457.

Rose, R., and Mishler, W. 2008. "Bridging the gap between the experience and the perception of corruption." *Centre for the Study of Public Policy* 328-332.

Rose, Richard. 2001. "A Diverging Europe" *Journal of Democracy* 12(1): 93-106.

Sasse, G. 2008. "The politics of EU conditionality: the norm of minority protection during and beyond EU accession." *Journal of European Public Policy* 15(6): 899-917.

Sedelmeier, U. 2008. "After conditionality: post-accession compliance with EU law in East Central Europe." *Journal of European Public Policy* 15(6): 806-825.

Schimmelfennig, F., and Sedelmeier, U., eds. 2005. *The Europeanization of Central and Eastern Europe*. Ithaca: Cornell University Press.

Sandholtz, Wayne and Gray, Mark. 2003. "International Integration and National Corruption." *International Organization* 57(4): 761-800.

Sandhotlz, W. and Taagepera, R. 2005. "Corruption, Culture and Communism." *International Review of Sociology* 15(1): 109-31.

Vachudova, M. 2005. *Europe Undivided: Democracy, Leverage, and Integration After Communism*. Oxford: Oxford University Press.

Vachudova, M. 2008. "Tempered by the EU? Political parties and party systems before and after accession." *Journal of European Public Policy 15*(6), 861-879.

Vachudova, Milada Anna. 2009. "Corruption and Compliance in the EU's Post-Communist Members and Candidates." *Journal of Common Market Studies*. Vol. 47: 43-62.

Way, L. and Levitsky, S. 2007. "Linkage, Leverage, and the Post-Communist Divide." *East European Politics and Societies.* 21(1), 48-66.

A Struggle for Influence

A Multi-levelled Appreciation of the Europeanisation Process

Graeme CROUCH

Introduction

The European Union (EU) played a significant role in setting the reform agenda for the candidate states of Central and Eastern Europe (CEE) and, more recently, the Balkans. Domestic change resulted from a process of persuasion, negotiation and coercion referred to as 'Europeanisation'. Unfortunately, the Europeanisation literature has been so infrequently applied to EU-candidate state relations that many contemporary renderings fail to include the intricate and multi-levelled processes crucial to the development and implementation of *acquis*-related reforms. As Heather Grabbe (2003, p. 303) states, "the domestic effects of transferring policies and institutions to them [candidate states] are likely to be comparable" to what is observable in member states, but the political synergy that exists between the EU and the candidate countries certainly "affects how Europeanization occurs".

The scant literature that addresses the Europeanisation of the candidate states relies on the experiences of Central and Eastern European countries (CEECs). These countries offer a wealth of material on the subject because for much of the last 20 years they have been obliged to accept the EU's demands in order to attain EU membership. In some cases, these countries were asked to implement reforms that challenged the very fabric and history of their political arrangements, begging the question: why would the candidate states accept demands that threaten their political status quo? The most common answer is that the candidate countries were/are being 'Europeanised' by an asymmetric process of "downloading", wherein the candidate states are forced to adopt the EU demands as a "package deal" (Grabbe, 2006, p. 2).

Extensive research has been conducted on this 'top-down' rendering of Europeanisation (see Börzel, 1999; Börzel and Risse, 2003; Knill and Lehmkuhl, 1999; Olsen, 1996; Risse *et al.*, 2001). An understanding of the asymmetric processes and manipulative relationships that exist during accession reveals much about the EU's ability to coerce candidate states into limiting their demands and complying with EU initiatives. However, this singular version of events does not take into account the domestic manipulation of the *acquis communautaire* that undoubtedly affects how Europeanisation occurs. Börzel (2002, p. 193) postures that "Europeanization is a two-way process; it entails a 'bottom-up' and a 'top-down' dimension". The bottom-up approach assumes that domestic actors have the ability to 'upload' their preferences to the EU and that subsequently those preferences may be reflected in EU policy. Yet, even a 'two-way' conception of Europeanisation does not recognise the significance of transgovernmental relations and transnational networks.

Using data from Croatia's accession process I argue that Europeanisation theory must integrate a "middle" or horizontal level into its conception (Howell, 2004, p. 2). Contemporary conceptualisations scantily address the role of transnational actors in the development and implementation of *acquis*-related reforms (see Howell, 2004; Radaelli, 2003). As such, I elaborate on the middle level of Europeanisation and integrate it into a multi-levelled conceptualisation of Europeanisation that refutes the two-dimensional process currently advanced by the literature.

This chapter is organised into two distinct sections. The first section introduces the 'top-down' and 'bottom-up' conceptions of Europeanisation and refutes their ability to explain the entirety of the Europeanisation process, demonstrating a need for a "middle" level of influence. The second section illustrates the multi-levelled nature of the Europeanisation process, using specific examples from Croatia's accession to challenge traditional notions of the process. The concluding section amalgamates the three conceptions of Europeanisation into one multi-levelled appreciation and suggests a new research agenda focused on adding more specificity and empirics to the study of Europeanisation.

Conceptualising the Europeanisation Process

Conceptions of the Europeanisation process must define *who* and *what* is being Europeanised (Olsen, 2002). Nearly twenty years of scholarship from leading researchers like Börzel and Risse (2000), Buller and Gamble (2002), Cowles *et al.* (2001), Featherstone (2003), Howell (2004), Knill and Lehmkuhl (1999; 2002), Ladrech (1994), Mörth (2003), Olsen (2002), and Radaelli (2000; 2003; 2004) have approached these questions from either a top-down or bottom-up perspective. However, the field has not remained static; it has continued to integrate new ideas about the structures of influence at play during the

Europeanisation process. As such, a brief overview of the field is necessary before offering a new contribution to the literature.

Widely Accepted: Top-Down and Bottom-Up Europeanisation

Europeanisation has traditionally been conceived as a top-down, or impact-driven process of interaction. Ladrech (1994, p. 69) rendered this approach as:

> ...an incremental process reorienting the direction and shape of politics to the degree that EC political and economic dynamics become part of the organizational logic of national politics and policy-making.

Inherent to this conception is the position of the EU as an influential actor in the policy and institutional development of the Europeanised state. It assumes that domestic actors, structures, institutions, norms and values comply with the EU as a result of some undefined process. In other words, the *who* for this conception is the domestic polity, while the *what* refers to institutional and policymaking systems that differ from EU practice. Yet, this early conception makes several key assumptions that illustrate its inability to rationalise a Europeanisation process that empirical evidence demonstrates is not always dominated by the EU.

First, Ladrech's conception privileges the position of the EU and asserts that its "political and economic dynamics" are exogenous to those of the member and candidate states. The implications of this assumption limit the applicability of the top-down approach when considering the Europeanisation of the candidates. Certainly, the EU utilises the *acquis communautaire* to set the requirements for membership and candidate states must comply with these requirements in order to enter the Union. However, the extent to which these requirements actually become a part of the organisational logic of the candidate states is unclear. The EU possesses but a few institutional and policy models (such as democratic governance, market capitalism) that candidate states can emulate when implementing the *acquis*. For the rest of the *acquis*, the candidate states' compliance is very much an organic process involving domestic, transgovernmental and transnational actors.

Page and Wouters (1995, p. 202) recognised that "there is no clear EC model, distinctive and relevant to the national bureaucracies of nation states, that is likely to find its way through contagion, emulation, the demonstration effect or the natural process of adaptation to an important source of political power". From another perspective, it could be claimed that the EU simply has too many different political and economic examples. As the EU has grown, so too have the number of institutional, legislative and policy arrangements used by the member states to handle the EU's requirements. While many member states share similar monetary policies (Buller and Gamble, 2002), there are, conversely, many different variations of transport and regional policy (Grabbe, 2006; Radaelli, 2000). With so many arrangements, which political and economic model would the EU choose to download to the candidate states?

A normative question that arises from Ladrech's conception is whether it is even appropriate for the EU to download a specific set of requirements to the candidates. I would also ask whether, in its delicate condition, the EU is in a position to Europeanise the candidates using only a top-down approach. As Grabbe (2006) discusses, the EU has been very careful about what it advocates and what it condemns. With such diverse political structures present in its member states, the EU must be politically sensitive when prescribing a certain implementation strategy to the candidates. In many ways, there cannot be an EU model because of concerns that it may reflect an inherent bias. That is why the *acquis* is so broad in nature. The individual chapters are not focused on a universally correct way of reform; rather, they simply present the candidate states with a set of priority areas that the EU believes represent its core values and norms. Thus, it can be deduced that without the presence of a specific implementation plan, the EU cannot be the only actor participating in the Europeanisation process. In order to understand the ways in which the candidate states implement the *acquis*, Europeanisation must be expanded to include a bottom-up and horizontal level.

Demonstrating an evolution of thought, Börzel (2002, p. 193) discussed Europeanisation as a "two-way process". She recognised that which had been lost to many early Europeanisation scholars: the multi-levelled structures of policymaking and governance present in the EU. Based on this expanded understanding, Börzel asserts that states may use formal and informal channels of influence to 'upload' their policy preferences to the EU in hopes that these preferences may translate into new EU norms (Börzel, 2002). Furthermore, states can participate in *pace setting, foot dragging* and *fence sitting* activities that, to varying degrees, enable domestic actors to affect and react to the policymaking environment complicated by a supranational authority (Börzel, 2002). In this regard, Börzel juxtaposes Ladrech's approach by conceiving the *who* as the EU and the *what* as EU legislation. However, even a 'two-way' understanding of the Europeanisation process makes assumptions about the state that overlook the significance of bilateral negotiations and transnational cooperation.

Risse (1996, p. 62) explains that on highly contentious issues – like the adoption of the *acquis communautaire* – state organisations may not act in solidarity. As is the nature of politics, highly politicised issues often lead to conflicting interests among a diverse group of actors. Especially in federal systems or those with coalition or minority governments, sub-units of government may pursue different policy outcomes. When consensus can't be formed, sub-units may look to form 'transgovernmental' relationships in the hope that their preference may influence EU policy.[1] This transgovernmental element has become institutionalised in the accession process, alluding to a middle level of Europeanisation.

The top-down and bottom-up conceptualisations of Europeanisation necessitate a horizontal level not because they are wrong, but rather because they are incomplete. These widely accepted conceptualisations explain a great deal about the Europeanisation process and for this they are not dismissed. Yet, their misgivings imply that there are more complex structures of influence at play during the Europeanisation of the candidate states. As such, it is appropriate to elaborate on this middle level in order for a more complete rendering of the Europeanisation process to emerge.

The Middle Level: Horizontal Europeanisation of the Candidate States

The middle or horizontal level of influence has been largely dismissed when considering the major actors and structures involved in the Europeanisation process. Howell (2004, p. 5) briefly addresses what he calls "horizontal transfer", which, he says, "incorporates learning from, and assimilating other member state policies without EU involvement". Although he goes on to say that Europeanisation is problematised without an inherent EU component, he recognises that change can result from horizontal influence. Even Radaelli (2003, pp. 30-31), who purposely ignores the "transfer of policy between one European country and another", admits that Europeanisation may emanate from something other than a "coherent, rational layer of 'EU decisions'". The fault with only scantily addressing horizontal Europeanisation is that it ignores empirical cases of transgovernmental and transnational influence. In many cases, multilateral partnerships have formed that cross national boundaries, hinting at a transgovernmental dimension. Additionally, sub-state groups often associate with other sub-state and international

1 Transgovernmental refers to "cross-boundary relations among sub-units of national governments in the absence of centralized decisions by state executives" (Risse, 1996, p. 58).

organisations in order to increase their political presence and partake in the decision-making processes occurring during accession.

It is important to clarify that the horizontal level of Europeanisation is no more prominent or effective than either the top or bottom level of influence. Like top-down and bottom-up mechanisms, the horizontal methods also contain deficiencies that candidate states struggle to overcome and their policy outcomes may still fail to properly align a candidate to the *acquis*. Additionally, it is important to differentiate horizontal Europeanisation from convergence or harmonisation because, regardless of their level of cooperation, not all "states will opt for the same types of change" (Montpetit, 2000, p. 590). Regarding the candidate states, the *acquis communautaire* does provide a framework for change but due to the candidate states' diverse "learning capacit[ies]" and "institutional infrastructures", Europeanisation and convergence cannot be equated (Paraskevopoulos, 2001, p. xx). I argue that neither convergence nor harmonisation are goals of horizontal Europeanisation. It is clear from the political and social landscape of the EU that countries rarely implement policies that mirror one another. However, cooperation between states, sub-state actors and representatives of the EU has proven paramount to the success of the EU's past enlargements. Instances of transgovernmental negotiations and transnational networking have shown that while neither harmonisation nor convergence is achieved, horizontal processes exist within the Europeanisation process.

In the context of EU accession, transgovernmental relationships provide member and candidate states the opportunity to learn from similar political situations and provide each other with a diverse set of institutional and policy alternatives (for more, see Radaelli, 2003). Transgovernmental cooperation allows sub-governmental units with similar concerns or interests to mutually develop policy alternatives that may address policy concerns more precisely. The belief is that these sub-governmental units can operate outside of direct state oversight and that operational knowledge and 'best practices' will be exchanged. The EU's twinning programmes have produced one such example of this exchange, where transgovernmental relationships are nurtured and policy alternatives are discussed.

Yet horizontal Europeanisation is not confined to states or state-affiliated organisations. 'Transnational networks' represent the crucial linkages between domestic groups and international interests that facilitate both national and supranational lobbying.[2] Domestic interest groups function as sub-state actors in the policymaking process and transna-

2 Transnational networks refer to "transboundary relations that include at least one non-governmental actor" (Risse, 1996, p. 57).

tional networks arise when these groups form international partnerships to increase their implementation and lobbying capacities. These transnational networks have proven to be influential both in domestic policy negotiations and in supranational policy-setting. The EU's aid programmes have begun to fund more civil society initiatives because of the perception that the participation of these groups increases public consultation. Furthermore, these transnational networks conduct frequent monitoring missions, which provide insights the EU could not otherwise attain. Together with transgovernmental relations, these transnational networks occupy a 'middle level' of influence and thus cannot be ignored when conceptualising the structures of influence at work in Europeanisation and accession processes.

Recognising the "circular, rather than unidirectional, and cyclical rather than one-off" (Goetz, 2002, p. 4) process that Europeanisation so clearly embodies, this middle level will be integrated into a wider appreciation of the Europeanisation process and specific examples of this multi-levelled structure will be presented. By recognising this horizontal level it will become clear that a multi-levelled appreciation of Europeanisation, which marries the top-down, bottom-up and horizontal conceptualisations, is more appropriate.

A Multi-levelled Appreciation of the Europeanisation Process

This section discusses the mechanisms of Europeanisation and aims to demonstrate the various ways actors from domestic, transnational and supranational levels are able to manipulate the Europeanisation of the candidate states. Manipulation in this sense refers to both formal manipulation (such as setting reform agendas and prescribing legislative models) and informal manipulation (through nationalising reform legislation and negotiating compliance) of the Europeanisation and accession processes. This section refutes the notion that Europeanisation occurs as a result of some static and predetermined influence structure (that is, exclusively top-down or bottom-up); it proposes, rather, a combination of these popular conceptions in what is referred to as a multi-levelled structure of influence.

Heather Grabbe (2003, p. 312) classifies the Europeanisation process into five categories: models, financial and technical aid, benchmarking and monitoring, advice and twinning, and gatekeeping. Grabbe reveals that certain mechanisms are dominated by the EU, while others leave much discretion to individual candidate states. Furthermore, some of the mechanisms necessitate the development of relationships between actors from all three levels. Consequently, these mechanisms point to an accession process that is dominated by a multi-levelled system of influence where Europeanisation occurs as the result of windows of opportunity and agency. To demonstrate this multi-levelled structure, three of the mechanisms – benchmarking and monitoring, advice and twinning, and aid – will be analysed.

Benchmarking and Monitoring

Repeatedly mentioned in the 1999 Helsinki European Council conclusions are the words 'progress' and 'assessment', alluding to the fact that candidate states are regularly appraised on how well they meet the *acquis* and other EU requirements (European Council, 1999). As such, benchmarking and monitoring are key functions of the entire Europeanisation procedure. They are processes that occur in nearly every action involved with accession. Benchmarks provide the foundation from which actors align their policy recommendations and implementation strategies. Subsequently, actors must constantly monitor their tasks to make sure that their work is adhering to the appropriate benchmark. However rudimentary it may sound, the ways in which the EU has monitored and assessed its candidate states have not always been so clearly identifiable. Over the past 20 years, the EU has relied on several different documents as the basis for its benchmarking and monitoring abilities.

From 1989-93 the EU relied on the bilaterally agreed-upon Europe Agreements (EA) to govern its relations with Central and Eastern Europe (see Grabbe, 1999; Sedelmeier, 1994; Sedelmeier and Wallace, 1996; Torreblanca Payá, 1997). The EAs were designed to encourage the newly independent former Soviet Republics to reform their command economies and liberalise their political systems. The EAs were based upon a set of five conditions: the rule of law, human rights, a multi-party system, free and fair elections, and a market economy (Grabbe, 1999). The CEECs were expected to show progress in these sensitive policy areas in order to maintain Phare (Poland and Hungary: Assistance for Restructuring their Economies) funding. Failure to comply with the EU recommendations could lead to the suspension of the EAs, although no such suspensions ever occurred (Grabbe, 1999). In terms of the EU's ability to monitor and assess the viability of its eastern neighbours, the EAs represented an initial framework from which the EU was able to conditionally offer support to Central and Eastern Europe in return for compliance with 'European norms'.

In 1993 the Copenhagen Council meeting ushered in a new set of pre-accession conditions called the *acquis communautaire*, which were designed to provide the EU and its candidate states with a guide to the accession process. Unfortunately, in 1993 these demands were still so new to both the EU and its candidate states that it would take nearly 10 years for them to be properly implemented and enforced. In the meantime, the EU chose to pay particular attention to the economic advancement of its eastern neighbours and relied heavily upon the economically charged Single Market White Paper to assess and monitor the preparations of the CEECs. The White Paper emphasised a set of 12 policy areas that the EU believed would help liberalise the CEECs' economies, further preparing them for their 'return' to Europe (see European Commission, 1985; Grabbe, 1999). Although the White Paper was not legally binding, the EU's emphasis on its complete and mandatory acceptance made it resonate in the minds of CEE policymakers (Grabbe, 1999). Moreover, the White Paper represents the EU's first use of specific criteria to reinforce its Europeanisation abilities and judge candidates' preparations for membership.

Since 1997 the EU has used the 'Accession Partnerships' and the annual 'Progress Reports' to assess the readiness of the candidate states. The Accession Partnerships represent a single framework of demands and promises that the EU uses to guide the candidate states through the accession process. Based primarily on the conditionality principle, the Accession Partnerships can be altered and priorities can be reassessed depending on the outcome of the Progress Reports. Depending on the outcome of these yearly assessments, the candidate states can have funding cut or even negotiations suspended. Conversely, a positive assessment may convince the EU to close a chapter, edging the candidate closer to membership. In this way the Accession Partnerships and Progress Reports serve as the key gatekeeping tools from which the EU ultimately decides whether a candidate should pass through to the next level of accession.

Although neither is legally binding, the Accession Partnerships and yearly Progress Reports do represent the "main instrument[s] governing EU-CEE [and Balkan] relations" (Grabbe, 1999, p. 14) and as such must be respected by the candidate states' policymakers. This supposedly top-down mechanism represents the EU's attempt to manipulate the Europeanisation process and ensure that its priorities become the priorities of the candidate states. Yet, although the Accession Partnerships articulate a set of 'key priorities', the importance of each priority is vague, leaving the candidate with the ability to nationalise and prioritise the reform procedures. In some instances the candidate may choose to enlist the help of a member state, introducing a transgovernmental dimension. Depending on the issue, transnational networks may also use their resources to advocate specific policy alternatives. As such, it is unclear whether the Accession Partnerships and subsequent Progress Reports represent exclusive tools of a top-down Europeanisation process or whether there is also an inherent degree of bottom-up and horizontal Europeanisation.

The following discussion of twinning and aid refers to the EU's ability to benchmark and monitor the candidates' progress. It also highlights the integral role played by transgovernmental and transnational relationships in the development, implementation and monitoring of *acquis*-related reforms. Without a horizontal dimension to these Europeanisation processes, neither the EU nor the candidate would be as effective in producing the necessary reforms.

Twinning

It became clear quite early on that the main challenge for the candidate states of Central and Eastern Europe was "adopting their administrative machinery and societies to the conditions necessary to make their legislation work" (European Commission, 1995, sec. 3.25). Benchmarking and monitoring would yield no substantive results if the candidates lacked the capacity to implement *acquis* reforms. As a result, in 1998 (for the fifth enlargement) and 2002 (for the Balkans), the EU implemented twinning as "an instrument for targeted administrative co-operation to assist Candidate Countries (CC) to strengthen their administrative and judicial capacity to implement EU legislation as future Member States (MS) of the European Union" (European Commission, 2009, p. 10). Since 1998, over 1500 twinning projects have been undertaken in the EU's effort to close the administrative gap (European Commission, 2009). Originally designed to develop the candidate's justice and home affairs capacity, the twinning projects have expanded in scope to cover issues ranging from the reform of the Albanian public auction system to more serious issues with road safety in Croatia (Twinning and Sigma Coordination Team, 2009). As the issues facing the CEE and Balkan states have become more diverse, the breadths of the twinning projects have expanded as well.

The development and implementation of a twinning project is "based on a triangular partnership" wherein the European Commission, the twinning member state(s) and the candidate state have varying levels of influence and responsibilities (Papadimitriou, 2002, p. 9). This instrument demonstrates the intentional diffusion of responsibility to various levels of actors. The EU plays a central role in the formation of the twinning project, prioritising projects that will encourage closer cooperation, strengthen the candidate's administrative capacities and prepare them for enlargement (European Commission, 2009). In this way, the EU maintains its ability and right to Europeanise the candidate states' reform priorities. However, the EU has taken a hands-off approach to the selection of twinning partners, simply encouraging "equal opportunity and transparency" (European Commission, 2009, p. 37). As a result, transgovernmental relationships prove crucial in both the development and implementation of *acquis* reforms.

Twinning projects are voluntary: the EU does not force candidate states to form these relationships. Instead they provide a forum for transgovernmental partnerships. The fundamental principle of twinning is recognition from the candidate states that they can benefit from the experiences and knowledge of other state actors and industry experts. In line with the idea of a 'triangle partnership', twinning projects are designed to foster a working relationship between transgovernmental actors, not to supply "one-way technical assistance" (European Commission, 2009, p. 14). The mutual construction of policy solutions is paramount; thus, I refrain from identifying a dominant actor.

That said, detailed plans are necessary to ensure that the relationship between transgovernmental and EU actors remains prosperous. The EU has made it clear that the goal of twinning projects is to "yield mandatory results" and therefore may cut funding if the work plan is insufficiently detailed (European Commission, 2009, p. 14). The EU understands that twinning projects are often "ambitious, large scale and lengthy", and as such may lose track of their ultimate purpose (European Commission, 2009, p. 87). In response, the EU has made it a priority to maintain monitoring mechanisms that ensure each project's compliance with EU demands. The EU requires a National Authorising Officer (NAO) fill out routine Progress Reports, and it reserves the right to conduct on-the-spot checks if necessary (European Commission, 2009). Additionally, the EU's twinning manual (2009) advises that monthly meetings between the NAO and both project countries be held to ensure that their goals and requirements are being met. If these meetings reveal deficiencies in the process, then the implementation of the work plan can be altered to ensure that the "mandatory results" remain the focus.

Twinning projects represent a very systematic way of Europeanising the candidate states. It is clear from the intentional inclusion of actors from multiple political levels that Europeanisation, using this instrument, is not dominated by any one level. As the Croatian example will illustrate, a successful twinning project requires EU influence in goal development and monitoring, as well as transgovernmental influence on target design and implementation. In this way a coordinated effort between multiple actors is needed for Europeanisation to occur.

The Empirics: A Croatian Twinning Project

In 2009, the Croatian delegation to the EU submitted twinning proposal HR/2007/IB/JH/02, entitled "Capacity building of the Croatian

Agency for Protection of Personal Data (CAPPD)" (Republic of Croatia, 2009, p. 2). The project intended to strengthen both the "consultative and supervisory roles of the Croatian Agency for the Protection of Personal Data" by harmonising its policies on the legal protection of personal data and implementing ISO standards on information security systems (Republic of Croatia, 2009, p. 2). In their proposal, Croatia's representatives made clear that "real efforts are needed to bring the legal and technical component of supervisory activities in line with EC requirements" (Republic of Croatia, 2009, p. 5). In order to facilitate this change, the proposal was divided into legal and technical components that structured the project and increased the likelihood that tangible results would be realised. Additionally, the proposal articulated a clear set of objectives to be fulfilled and called upon member states to submit assistance on proposals that would aid Croatia in this transformation. This initial process demonstrates two levels of Europeanisation. On one hand, Croatia recognises that this project must fulfil the "EC requirements" – alluding to the fact that the EU has effectively 'downloaded' their priorities. On the other hand, the fact that Croatia has the ability to develop the objectives and implementation strategies means that there is an opportunity for them to influence the terms of *acquis* compliance. Moreover, Croatia retained the ability to choose from a series of member state proposals, which undoubtedly influenced the orientation of the subsequent reform.

The Croatian government selected Spain over Austria to be their project partner and looked to the Spanish Data Protection Agency to provide the knowledge and technical assistance needed for this administrative overhaul (Croatian Data Protection Agency, 2010). The €1.3 million project, funded through the Instrument for Pre-Accession Assistance (IPA) programme, officially began in August of 2010 under a 22-month mandate to carry out legal and technical activities intended to meet a set of EU benchmarks (Croatian Data Protection Agency, 2010). In order to bring Croatia in line with EU Directive 95/46/EC, one of the key legal benchmarks was the revision and proper implementation of the Act of Personal Information Protection (APIP) (Croatian Data Protection Agency, 2010). Although CAPPD was originally developed in 2003 to oversee Croatia's personal data protection, a recent EU progress report stated that the APIP failed to meet many of the provisions of the EU directive (European Commission, 2008). As a result, the EU concluded that Croatia had to revise its original legislation, paying particular attention to the supervisory role of CAAPD (Republic of Croatia, 2009). Spain's role, therefore, was to aid Croatia in the development of policies and legislation that would improve its oversight abilities and further its capacity to harmonise domestic policies with the *acquis*.

This twinning project also contained a technical component that focused on the development of an information security system based on ISO 27001 standards (Croatian Data Protection Agency, 2010). This component was a highly technical and country-specific task that called on Spain to offer recommendations of 'best practices' and required the development of a multi-levelled security system unique to Croatia's specific accessibility and security needs. By enhancing the effectiveness, reliability and stability of their security system, Croatia hoped to boost the administrative and supervisory capabilities of CAAPD, thus making it "fully operational and completely compliant with relevant EU *acquis*" (Republic of Croatia, 2009, p. 18). Because the technical component aimed to protect Croatian data and citizens, its development and implementation was very much an organic process that relied on the ability of domestic actors to learn from Spanish advisors and implement a hybridised system based on this knowledge. In this way, the Europeanisation of Croatia's data protection system necessitated a transgovernmental partnership between sub-units of governments instead of coercive downloading and infrequent uploading.

Yet the EU ensured that its position of influence was not compromised by the intentional diffusion of influence. Several monitoring provisions were built into the project proposal that enabled the EU to assess the project's viability. These monitoring activities concluded that Croatia and Spain had only partially reached their targets. Croatia's 2011 Progress Report revealed that CAAPD had effectively increased its "supervision and control activities", enabling it to provide citizens with a minimal amount of data protection (European Commission, 2011, p. 53). However, it also warned Croatia that its legislation was not yet in line with Directive 95/46/EC (European Commission, 2011, p. 53). While this reaffirms the popular notion that twinning projects are only minimally effective (see Bartels and Rach, 2009), it also proves that effective Europeanisation necessitates the involvement of multiple actors and a multi-levelled system of influence. Actors from Croatia were needed to provide information about potential deficiencies in the country's previous system of data protection. Sub-governmental units from Croatia and Spain collaborated to develop a clear work plan and address identified deficiencies. EU actors were needed to align domestic and supranational goals and, more importantly, to assess whether these goals were being met. Regardless of the success of this project, it is clear that a multi-levelled structure of influence is fundamental to the twinning mechanism of Europeanisation.

Aid

Twinning is not the only Europeanisation mechanism that possesses a multi-levelled structure of influence. Aid is perhaps the EU's most effective Europeanisation tool and certainly one that, based on conditionality, proves that top-down influence occurs. The EU is the single largest contributor of financial and technical assistance to the candidate countries, providing both directly administered funds as well as facilitating bilateral cooperation that often yields assistance (Grabbe, 2003; 2006). However, the EU's funding packages have been historically disorganised and under-monitored, allowing candidate states and transnational networks to capitalise on various windows of opportunity. To overcome the lack of oversight, the EU has begun involving sub-national and transnational interest groups in their aid schemes in order to: 1. ensure the interaction of public and private interests in the accession process; and 2. overcome the administrative deficiencies of both the EU and the candidates.

In many ways, the effective use of aid has been a learning process. By the time the IPA programme was implemented in 2007, the EU had realised that previous aid packages – Phare, CARDS (Community Assistance for Reconstruction, Development and Stabilisation), ISPA (Instrument for Structural Policies for Pre-Accession), and SAPARD (Special Accession Programme for Agricultural and Rural Development) – had failed to provide the "consistency, complementarity, and concentration of assistance" necessary to be effective Europeanisation tools (European Commission, 2007). The EU's aid packages have been so vaguely designed to encourage "*acquis*-related investment" and "valuable experience" that millions of euros had been spent on questionable projects (European Commission, 2002, pp. 8, 10, 17). In fact, a 2009 evaluation of 25 EU-funded projects conducted from July 2006 to February 2008 revealed that only 52 per cent successfully met the candidates' needs (Bartels and Rach, 2009). Even more alarming is the fact that the same evaluation claimed that only two-thirds of the projects met any of their targets (Bartels and Rach, 2009). One possible explanation for these failures is that although the funding packages offset some of the costs of implementing the *acquis*, they also challenged the candidate states to implement large-scale reform projects without, in many cases, the administrative capacity to effectively do so. Often the candidate states simply did not have the procedural knowledge or capabilities to fulfil the demands of the *acquis*.

The inclusion of transnational networks in recent aid schemes serves two purposes: 1. these networks help candidate states implement policy changes by absorbing the transaction cost; and 2. they advise the Commission on programme needs (Paraskevopoulos, 2001). Depending on the size and aim of the transnational network, their involvement provides the trained and dedicated staff often lacking in the candidates' administrative structure. Furthermore, the resources of these networks offset the EU's monitoring difficulties and produce Progress Reports that enable the EU to better communicate areas that need improvement.

As the following example from Croatia demonstrates, although aid provides the EU with the clearest opportunity to influence the accession process, the complexities of implementing such large aid programmes warranted the involvement of domestic and transnational groups. Thus, a multi-levelled appreciation of the Europeanisation process is once again better at explaining the internal processes that occur during accession.

Aid as a Multi-levelled Process: An Example from the Environment

As the environmental consequences of industrialisation and population growth continue to be discussed, the EU has encouraged its member and candidate states to ratify the Aarhus Convention. The convention broadly aims to increase access to information, public participation and access to justice regarding environmental matters (see United Nations, 1998). In 2008, the EU funded an IPA project that enlisted domestic NGOs from Croatia, Montenegro, and Bosnia and Herzegovina, as well as the European Environmental Bureau – a network of over 140 environmental organisations – to facilitate deeper implementation of the convention throughout the Adriatic region (GONG, n.d.). According to the project's website, the €375,000 project sought to address the "lack of accessible administrative and judicial review procedures" in this region by "strengthening the international CSOs [civil society organisations] network" and implementing a "training program for lawyers, judges, and journalists" (GONG, n.d.). In other words, collaboration between actors from the EU, domestic governments and transnational networks was needed to overcome the EU's monitoring deficiencies and the candidate states' administrative shortcomings.

The project identified a problem with the Croatian government's inconsistent usage of public consultation when developing environmental policy. *Građani organizirano nadgledaju glasanje* (GONG), the organisation in charge of this project, argued that public participation, an integral part of the convention, had been "reduced to bureaucratic exercises" (GONG, n.d.). The failure of the Croatian government in this matter speaks to larger administrative problems found in the Western Balkans and, consequently, the need for transnational partnerships during the aid process. Grabbe (2006, p. 105) argues that the communist legacies of CEECs made them prone to developing institutions that fail to provide the resources and leadership necessary to operate properly. These countries have institutions that are often ill equipped to handle the burdensome tasks necessary for EU membership. In many instances these dysfunctional institutions have been designed purposely to give corrupt political actors the ability to maintain control of the policymaking process (Grabbe, 2006). The institutions are intentionally developed based on the institutional models of the EU, but their operational capacities are deliberately devoid of the manpower and resources to meet the ever-expanding requirements of *acquis* adoption. I do not argue that Croatia is plagued with dysfunctional and corrupt administration. However, its inability to properly implement the Aarhus Convention highlights the need for EU and transnational actors.

This project brought together actors from the EU (funding), transnational organisations (training), and 27 judges, lawyers and journalists from the partner countries (learning) (GONG, n.d.). Through a series of seminars and mock trials, participants from all three levels engaged in discussion and learning in order to better promote the pillars of the Aarhus Convention. The results of this project are still unknown. Yet regardless of success, this project demonstrates the EU's growing reliance on transnational and sub-state actors to implement its initiatives. For the last 10 years, EU aid has involved, to varying degrees, members of sub-national and transnational issue-based networks. For instance, as a part of Phare 2006, over €3 million was allocated to fund Croatian projects designed and implemented by civil society organisations (Republic of Croatia, 2012). Similar to the project I highlighted, these projects called on issue groups to develop and implement programmes that would contribute to Croatia's *acquis*-related reforms. In this way, civil society groups at the domestic and transnational level have actively involved themselves in the Europeanisation process. According to the data on aid implementation, a more appropriate appreciation of Europeanisation is one that accepts a structure of influence composed of supranational, domestic, sub-national and transnational actors.

Conclusion

Traditional conceptualisations of the Europeanisation process – top-down and bottom-up – offer limited insight into the structures of influence and power relationships that affect the accession process. Numerous actors have been shown to participate in the development, implementation and monitoring of *acquis*-related reforms. Consequently, there is little evidence to demonstrate that one jurisdiction dominates the rest. Although the EU has the capacity to set goals and monitor results, candidate states have been able to undermine the EU and implement reforms closely aligned to domestic standards. Furthermore, subnational and transnational actors have actively lobbied domestic and supranational bodies, becoming important actors in both the development and implementation of policy reforms. As such, it is more appropriate to conceptualise the Europeanisation process as a multi-levelled process where legislative, institutional and policy reforms are developed and implemented through a complex process of negotiation, manipulation and coercion involving actors from the EU, transnational and transgovernmental networks, and the candidate states. This definition is supportive of more traditional conceptualisations; however, it more precisely grasps the processes taking place in the EU and its candidates.

I concede that "conceptual stretching looms large" when re-envisioning Europeanisation (Radaelli, 2000, p. 25). However, I would argue that a multi-levelled framework of analysis provides more, not less, clarity to a concept that largely ignores some of the most important processes. Moreover, it would seem that simply adhering to a singular conceptualisation of Europeanisation and using it to explain processes that clearly are not strictly 'top-down' or 'bottom-up' is more of a 'stretch' than the framework I offer. Even the events that the contemporary conceptualisation claims to grasp have been shown to be influenced by numerous additional actors. By including precise examples of this multi-levelled process, I clarify the limits of the concept without excluding the processes it so clearly represents.

In light of the accession processes of the CEECs and Balkan states, a more outcome-oriented path of research is needed to advance this multi-levelled conceptualisation of Europeanisation. For the past 15 years, scholars have concerned themselves with theorising about the processes and interactions inherent in Europeanisation. While these are valuable and necessary endeavours, the discipline must venture away from merely explaining the process and instead must focus on the outcomes of Europeanisation. In this way, the literature will become more action focused. With the EU's reluctance to expand its borders further eastward, membership for the Ukraine, Moldova and the Balkans is becoming less likely. Nevertheless, the EU still wishes to 'Europeanise' these states. A more outcome-oriented approach to Europeanisation research would reveal deficiencies in the Europeanisation process and offer new, more effective ways to encourage reforms that are acceptable to domestic and supranational actors.

While I have admittedly utilised the process-driven research of the past, I have also challenged many of the popular notions concerning the Europeanisation process. By demonstrating that the structures of influence are more elaborate than previously conceptualised, I offer a more thorough appreciation of the Europeanisation process. Further application of this appreciation will garner valuable knowledge about the validity of the Europeanisation process and generate important questions about the prospect of an enlarged European Union.

References

Bartels, M., and Y. Rach. 2009. Twinning projects led by Germany – relevance, effectiveness, impact and sustainability: an evaluation of outcomes by the German National Coordinator for twinning. Berlin: Public Relations Department, Federal Ministry of Economics and Technology. http://ec.europa.eu/enlargement/pdf/financial_assistance/institution_building/german_evaluation_2009_en.pdf (25 May 2011).

Börzel, T. 1999. "Towards convergence in Europe? Institutional adaptation to Europeanization in Germany and Spain." *Journal of Common Market Studies* 39(4): 573-96.

Börzel, T. 2002. "Member state responses to Europeanization." *Journal of Common Market Studies* 40(2): 193-214.

Börzel, T. and T. Risse. 2000. "When Europe hits home: Europeanization and domestic change." *European Integration Online Papers* 4(15): 1-20.

Börzel, T. and T. Risse. 2003. "Conceptualizing the domestic impact of Europe." In *The Politics of Europeanisation*, eds. K. Featherstone and C. Radaelli. Oxford: Oxford University Press, 57-82.

Buller, J., and A. Gamble. 2002. "Conceptualizing Europeanisation." *Public Policy and Administration* 17(4): 4-24.

Cowles, M.G., J.A. Caporaso and T. Risse. 2001. *Transforming Europe: Europeanization and Domestic Change*. Ithaca, NY: Cornell University Press.

Croatian Data Protection Agency. 2010. IPA 2007, Twinning Project HR/2007/IB/JH/02: Capacity Building of the Croatian Agency for Protection of Personal Data azop.hr/download.aspx?f=dokumenti/Razno/IPA_2007_eng.pdf (23 October 2012).

GONG. n.d. Enforcement of the Aarhus Convention in the Adriatic Region Countries, ca. 2008. Project Info: Enforcement of the Aarhus Convention in the Adriatic Region Countries. http://aarhus.zelena-istra.hr/node/1 (10 December 2011).

European Commission. 1985. Completing the Internal Market: White Paper from the Commission to the European Council (Milan, 28-29 June 1985). COM(85) 310 final.

European Commission. 1995. Commission White Paper 1995/163/EC of 5 March 1995 on the preparation of the association countries of Central and Eastern Europe for the integration in the internal market of the Union.

European Commission. 2002. The Enlargement Process and the three pre-accession instruments: Phare, ISPA, and Sapard. Brussels: European Union, Directorate General of Enlargement.

European Commission. 2007. Commission Regulation 2007/718/EC of 12 June 2007 on implementing Council Regulation (EC) No. 1085/2006 establishing an instrument for pre-accession assistance (IPA).

European Commission. 2008. Commission Communication 2008/674/ EC of 5 November 2008 on Croatia 2008 Progress Report.

European Commission. 2009. Institution building in the Framework of European Union Policies Common Twinning Manual. Revised version.

European Commission. 2011. Commission Communication 2011/666/EC of 10 December 2011 on Croatia 2011 Progress Report.

European Commission. 1999. Presidency Conclusions. Helsinki, 10-11 December. http://www.europarl.europa.eu/summits/hel1_en.htm (22 November 2012).

Featherstone, K. 2003. "Introduction: In the name of Europe." In *The Politics of Europeanization*, eds. K. Featherstone and C. Radaelli. Oxford: Oxford University Press, 3-26.

Featherstone, K. and C. Radaelli. 2003. *The Politics of Europeanization.* Oxford: Oxford University Press.

Goetz, K.H. 2002. "Europeanisation in west and east: A challenge to institutional theory." In *First Pan-European Conference on EU Politics*. Bordeaux, France, 26-28 September.

Grabbe, H. 1999. "A partnership for accession? The implications of EU conditionality for the Central and East European applicants." EUI Working Paper 99(12). San Domenico di Fiesole (FI): European University Institute.

Grabbe, H. 2003. "Europeanisation goes east: Power and uncertainty in the EU accession process." In *The Politics of Europeanisation*, eds. K. Featherstone and C. Radaelli. Oxford: Oxford University Press, 303-27.

Grabbe, H. 2006. *The EU's transformative power: Europeanization Through Conditionality in Central and Eastern Europe*. New York: Palgrave Macmillan.

Howell, K.E. 2004. "Developing conceptualisations of Europeanization: Synthesising methodological approaches." *Queen's Papers on Europeanization* No. 3. Belfast: Queen's University.

Knill, C. and D. Lehmkuhl. 1999. "How Europe matters: Different mechanisms of Europeanization." *European Integration Online Papers* 3(7): 1-19.

Knill, C. and D. Lehmkuhl. 2002. "The national impact of European Union regulatory policy: Three Europeanization mechanisms." *European Journal of Political Research* 41(2): 255-80.

Ladrech, R. 1994. "Europeanization of domestic politics and institutions: The case of France." *Journal of Common Market Studies* 32(1): 69-88.

Montpetit, E. 2000. "Europeanization and domestic politics: Europe and the development of a French environmental policy for the agricultural sector." *Journal of European Public Policy* 7(4): 576-92.

Mörth, U. 2003. "Europeanization as interpretation, translation, and editing of public policies." In *The Politics of Europeanisation*, eds. K. Featherstone and C. Radaelli. Oxford: Oxford University Press, 159-78.

Olsen, J.P. 1996. "Europeanization and nation-state dynamics." In *The Future of the Nation-State*, eds. S. Gustavsson and L. Lewin. London: Routledge, 245-85.

Olsen, J.P. 2002. "The many faces of Europeanization." *Journal of Common Market Studies* 40(5): 921-52.

Page, E.C. and L. Wouters. 1995. "The Europeanization of the national bureaucracies?" In *Bureaucracy in the Modern State. An Introduction to Comparative Public Administration*, ed. J. Pierre. Aldershot: Edward Elgar, 185-204.

Papadimitriou, D.G. 2002. "Exporting europeanisation: EU enlargement, the twinning exercise and administrative reform in Eastern Europe." In ECPR [European Consortium for Political Research], Joint Session of Workshops. Turin, Italy, 22-27 March.

Paraskevopoulos, C.J. 2001. *Interpreting Convergence in the European Union: Patterns of Collective Action, Social Learning and Europeanization*. London: Macmillan.

Radaelli, C. 2000. "Whither Europeanization? Concept stretching and substantive change." *European Integration Online Papers* 4(8). http://eiop.or.at/eiop/pdf/2000-008.pdf (21 November 2012).

Radaelli, C. 2003. "The Europeanization of public policy." In *The Politics of Europeanization*, eds. K. Featherstone and C. Radaelli. Oxford: Oxford University Press, 27-56.

Radaelli, C. 2004. "Europeanization: Solution or problem?" *European Integration Online Papers* 8(4): 1-23.

Republic of Croatia. 2009. IPA Project Fiche: Capacity Building of the Croatian Agency for Protection of Personal Data. Croatian Agency for Protection of Personal Data. http://www.euro.lt/documents/es_dokumentai/HR07IBJH02.pdf (23 October 2012).

Republic of Croatia. 2012. EU Programmes. Office for Cooperation with NGOs. http://www.uzuvrh.hr/page.aspx?pageID=71 (29 January 2012).

Risse, T. 1996. "Exploring the nature of the beast: International relations theory and comparative policy analysis meet the European Union." *Journal of Common Market Studies* 34(1): 53-80.

Risse, T., M.G. Cowles and J. Caporaso. 2001. "Europeanization and domestic change: Introduction." In *Transforming Europe: Europeanization and Domestic Change*, eds. M.G. Cowles, J. Caporaso and T. Risse. Ithaca, NY: Cornell University Press, 1-20.

Sedelmeier, U. 1994. "The European Union's association policy towards Central Eastern Europe: Political and economic rationales in conflict." *Sussex European Institute Working Paper* No. 7.

Sedelmeier, U. and H. Wallace. 1996. "Policies towards Central and Eastern Europe." In *Policy Making in the European Union*, third edition, eds. H. Wallace and W. Wallace. Oxford: Oxford University Press, 353-87.

Torreblanca Payá, J.I. 1997. *The European Community and Central Eastern Europe (1989-1993): Foreign policy and decision-making*. Madrid: Centro de Estudios Avanzados en Ciencias Sociales.

Twinning and Sigma Coordination Team. 2009. Notified results for the fiches with deadlines after September 2009. http://ec.europa.eu/enlargement/pdf/financial_assistance/institution_building/results_for_the_fiches_launched_from_mid_2009_05072010.pdf (10 May 2011).

United Nations Economic Commission for Europe. 1998. Convention on Access to Information, Public Participation in Decision-Making and Access to Justice in Environmental Matters. Aarhus: United National Economic Commission for Europe.

Serbia and the European Union

Is the "Culturalisation" of Accession Criteria on the Way?*

Miloš MILENKOVIĆ and Marko MILENKOVIĆ

Introduction

Accession to the European Union is generally conceived as conditional on the fulfilment of the Copenhagen (and Madrid) criteria, which are aimed at profound legal, economic, political and administrative transformation. Those conditions were *prima facie* designed to be culturally neutral, widely acceptable, and objectively verifiable through administrative monitoring and reporting by the European institutions. However, due to the troubled recent history of the Western Balkans, those criteria were altered with an ambition to contribute to and stimulate the rebuilding of the region, while enhancing both 'the European perspectives' and cooperation and reconciliation in the region (European Commission, 2008; 2011). This phenomenon of regional customisation of the accession criteria is provoking reactions both in the media and among informants. It is providing reasons for Eurosceptics, interested opponents of the European Union and Europhobes to spread anti-European narratives about the 'loss of identity'; such narratives are increasing at an unimaginable pace in Serbia. In the same fashion, the Europhile discourse is intensifying to the extent that it begins to resemble an apocalyptic narrative of compulsory transformation in order to 'rescue the nation'. The accession process is becoming overburdened with issues of identity, which in Serbia are generally subject to mythologising that is characterised by talk of fatefulness and coupled with questions of national religion (Nedeljković, 2006). This process is seen as a transformation of "insufficiently European" countries through "Europeanization policy" (Featherstone, 2003; Glenn, 2004), while its critics in Serbia have presented it as a "loss of national identity" (cf.

* This chapter is a result of research projects funded by the Ministry of Education and Science of the Republic of Serbia: "Identity policies of European Union: Adaptation and Application in Republic of Serbia" (177017) and "Perspectives of implementation of European standards in Serbian Legal System" (179059).

Radović, 2007). Given the degree of fragmentation of Serbian society and the long-lasting presence of narratives of national divisions – represented through the opposition of the national and the European, backward and modern, Oriental and Western (Naumović, 2005) – the accession to the EU has turned into an issue of 'fateful' significance. Instead of unifying and directing the nation toward the political stability that is necessary for successful reform, the accession process has begun to intensely divide the population, or to be represented as a reason for division, and in that way it resembles the 'culture wars' characteristic of North American society.

In this chapter we offer a preliminary argument about what we interpret as a partial but significant cause of the current situation: *(exaggerated) regional customisation*, which, through *culturalisation of the criteria* (particularly through their moralisation) is causing the very effects it was meant to prevent. The EU accession criteria used to be, at least in terms of their official interpretation, culturally and historically neutral; they were political and technical criteria aimed at harmonising the legal and political systems ahead of the economic, cultural, security and strategic unification of partners that are, in principle, equal. At the turn of the millennium, and particularly with regard to the forthcoming accession of the Western Balkans, culturalisation of accession criteria, with *historicising* and *moralisation* as its basic elements, has been put on the agenda. We dedicate this chapter, as the first in a series of studies, to the *contraindications of the enlargement customisation*.

Integration of the Western Balkans in the European Union – Setting the Stage

The accession criteria are often referred to as the "EU's most powerful instrument for dealing with the candidate and potential-candidates countries in post-communist Europe" (Anastasakis and Bechev, 2003, p. 3) and even as "external governance" (Schimmelfennig and Sedelmeier, 2004, p. 661). For the Western Balkan countries, and Serbia in particular, 'culturalisation' of the accession criteria, in addition to regular transformative ambitions, has turned the process into an evaluation of the ability of potential candidates to politically, judicially and culturally deal with a legacy of wars that raged in the region during the 1990s. The outcome has been an accession transformed into a process that a growing segment of the population perceives as a forced re-education and enforced re-evaluation of their relation to the recent past. This has the fairly significant potential to provoke new conflicts instead of remaining future-oriented and uniting all regional populations under a framework devised and proven to prevent warfare. When we take a consequentionalist look at the perceptions of the actors in the political system and their effects on the social reality, and not at the projects and the intentions of decision-makers or those who communicate decisions, the discourse that appears dominant is that of 'accession after the change' and *not* 'accession for the sake of change'. The population perceives that it 'must' give up its 'own' view on the recent past and adopt a 'foreign' view instead. Bearing in mind that European integration was induced as a peace project only six years after World War II, we propose that the same recipe be applied to the Western Balkans, with the application of the principle that might go as 'first include, change later', instead of setting the condition that consensus on sensitive questions must be reached before integration.

Regional Approach for the Western Balkans (WBs)

Until the beginning of the 1990s, EU enlargements were carried out *ad hoc* and not against the present criteria. These conditions were clearly, albeit broadly, spelled out only when enlargement to Eastern countries commenced in the 1990s, while EU conditionality has been gradually built up (Anastasakis and Bechev 2003, p. 5). The Copenhagen criteria (1993) were formulated as: 1. stable, democratic institutions, the rule of law, respect for human and minority rights (political criteria); 2. a functioning market economy and the ability to withstand competition from EU companies (economic criteria); 3. the ability to assume the responsibilities of membership (legal harmonisation); and subsequently, 4. institutional capacity was added by the Madrid Council in 1995 (European Council, 1993; 1995).

In 2003, Anastasakis and Bechev distinguished, in addition to Copenhagen criteria, four different types of conditionality for the WBs – regional; country-specific conditions related to individual projects; grants or loans; and those arising from peace agreements and political deals (for example, Resolution 1244 of the UN Security Council) (Anastasakis and Bechev, 2003, p. 7-8).

The Stabilisation and Association Process (SAP) was introduced as a regional approach in 1999 in order to facilitate multiple EU policy goals in addition to integration itself. It is comprised of four components: 1. Political dialogue; 2. pre-accession aid; 3. autonomous trade measures; and 4. Stabilisation and Association agreements. The former Federal Republic of Yugoslavia was not initially included in the process, as the regime of Slobodan Milošević was under sanctions by the international community. As a part of the process, potential candidates can apply for EU membership and be approved as a candidate country by the European Council. Once the negotiations on the accession are opened, candidates are to enter into an accession treaty, which will eventually lead to membership in the stipulated time and upon ratification by all the member states. Each country formally undergoes the same process, but at a different pace of integration that depends on numerous factors, *inter alia*, the political situation in the respective country and relevant 'conditionality'. In this way, the EU has applied the approach of individual association and accession to each country in the region. The progress of neighbouring countries can have a positive effect, to impact the 'competition' race for membership. However, given the traditional rivalry between Balkan societies and elites, the effects of a separate road for each country can be counterproductive, as they support popular perceptions about the unfairness of the 'international community' to one's own entity. Formulation of the attainment of candidate and membership status as a market-like rivalry instigates anti-European forces and incites enviousness that the common European framework should help to overcome.

Stabilisation and Association agreements are international agreements between the EU, EU member states and potential candidates; the agreements focus on trade liberalisation and the gradual creation of a free trade area. They also envisage a set of legal and political reforms with time limits laid down, and monitoring of the attainments by the Commission. However, we observed two types of conditionality to further progress in European integration – one that arose on a contractual basis and another that appeared as a consequence of *ad hoc* political conditioning at a particular moment of integration. Conditions can be set in different periods of integration, but they are most successful in moments when there is a need to make decisions within the integration process; for example, whether or not to open accession negotiations (Haughton, 2007). Taking the example of the Central and Eastern European (CEE) countries, Pridham argued, "Although the European Commission's approach to conditionality is essentially bureaucratic, high politics may occasionally dominate when member states intervene over conditionality matters" (Pridham, 2006, p. 398). We can expect only to have more such cases in the Western Balkans and Serbia in particular. These might come as a consequence of Serbia's unresolved relations with neighbouring new EU member states, through the exercise of political pressure for the fulfilment of additional 'culturalised' conditionality, or as a reflection of enlargement fatigue in a given member state and tendency to postpone the potential enlargement(s) through ever-growing conditionality.

A Retrospective of Serbia's SAP and Emerging Conditionality

The Socialist Federal Republic of Yugoslavia (SFRY) was the first communist country to officially establish diplomatic relations with the

EU, signing the first trade agreement in the early 1970s. Furthermore, SFRY citizens were allowed to freely travel and, under conditions prescribed by respective national regimes, seek employment in the Western European countries (mostly in Germany, Switzerland and Austria). Over a million people from Serbia, during the last 50 years, have spent or still spend a large portion of their lives working in Western European countries (Kovačević and Krstić, 2011). This was all formative for the long-lasting, intergenerational acculturation processes that took place irrespective of cultural policies and programmed Europeanisation.

Dissolution of Yugoslavia (1990-1992) coincided with a deeper integration within countries of the European Economic Community (EEC) and the creation of the European Union. There was no unified political stand of EEC countries (with twelve member states at the time) towards the political crisis in the former Yugoslavia. In June 1999, the EU introduced the SAP for the WBs, but the FRY was not included in the process due to political reasons. In October 2000, with a political change in Serbia, relations with the EU were re-established and the SAP implemented for the FRY. In June 2003, the Thessaloniki European Council reaffirmed the SAP as EU policy for the Western Balkans, with a reconfirmation that there are membership options for WB countries on the basis of individual progress.

In October 2004, the Council concluded the commencement of Stabilisation and Association Agreement (SAA) process with, at that time, the State Union of Serbia and Montenegro. Finally, in May 2006, Montenegro declared independence and SAA negotiations were blocked due to Serbia's lack of cooperation with the International Criminal Tribunal for the former Yugoslavia (ICTY).

In June 2007, SAA negotiations resumed, and in March 2008 the European Partnership for Serbia was adopted. Kosovo declared independence from Serbia on 18 Feb 2008. In April 2008, both the SAA and Interim Trade Agreement (ITA) between Serbia and the EU were signed, but it was envisaged that SAA (Article 135) should not apply in Kosovo under international administration according to United Nations Security Council Resolution 1244 (European Union, 2008a). It was also agreed in the SAA that the given provision is without prejudice to the current status of Kosovo or the determination of its final status under that resolution. In September 2008, the Netherlands froze the SAA and the trade part of the ITA, again due to the unsatisfactory level of cooperation with the ICTY. In December 2009, the Council unblocked the application of the ITA and Serbia applied for EU membership. Finally, in March 2012, candidacy status was granted after several prolongations and significant uncertainty.

Accession Process for the Western Balkan Countries: Impediments and Challenges

Accession to the European Union is set to bring wide political, economic, legal, administrative and cultural change. However, these changes are not without impediments. In our opinion, the major political impediments of the moment are EU enlargement fatigue and consequent lack of incentive to undertake societal change in the WBs. Furthermore, a number of unsolved issues are pressing bilateral relations in the region. These include the Croatian and Serbian genocide actions before the International Court of Justice, continued political tensions over the functioning of federal institutions in Bosnia, and unresolved relations between Montenegro and Serbia that reflect a huge divide in Montenegrin society between ethnic Montenegrins and Serbs. It is important to note that all of this is happening at a time when the EU is undergoing one of its deepest crises and when the enlargement fatigue can easily be equated (and actually is equated, as preliminary results of qualitative ethnographic research show) with the process, whose indications were noted back in 2003 when the term "Balkan fatigue" was coined (Anastasakis and Bechev, 2003, p. 4) The contemporary fatigue has only deepened following the economic and political problems experienced by many societies in the EU following the 2008 financial crisis. Finally, it remains questionable whether cooperation with the ICTY is no longer a condition for the WB countries, particularly for Serbia. However, it is now possible to contemplate whether the war crimes conditionality was a EU success story. On one hand, it has succeeded in bringing the war crimes suspects before the international court and for their prosecution for the war crimes of the 1990s. On the other hand, continuous pressure on several Serbian governments during the past 12 years has led to tensions in the Serbian public sphere and created a popular perception of the EU as 'blackmailing', thus unfortunately contributing to the rise in popularity of war lords and people accused of war crimes.

The above examples show that Serbia is present in each of the remaining regional problems, which may: 1. lead to further destabilisation in the region; 2. give rise to new conditions being continuously set for the countries in the region and for Serbia in particular. The greatest of the challenges to Serbia's Europeanisation, which already serves as a powerful instrument of conditioning at each stage of integration (for example, through providing the Commission's opinion on the application, and the European Council's decision on candidacy) is finding a solution to the complex relations between Serbia and Kosovo. However, this is a topic for a separate study on the customisation of pre-accession criteria, because this type of admission (that is, one entity considers another as part of its territory, while both access the same international integration) is a case unprecedented in modern political history, given the significant differences with the Cyprus case.

There is an obvious usefulness to structured processes with set timelines and deadlines, as there is an incentive effect both for elites and the general population. Given the fact that EU membership is not going to be achieved in the imminent future, Serbia and other WB countries might be faced with a lack of 'EU enthusiasm' and slowing reform processes. However, different kinds of EU incentives, not only limited to financial aid throughout the period of economic hardship, will be beneficial for keeping the transformative momentum. Ultimately, it will be a sign of political transformation and maturity if political elites in Serbia (and other WB societies) fully commit to stable social change and the modernisation of societies irrespective of any given integration process.

Accession as 'Europeanisation': Accession Criteria Culturalised

If we perceive Europeanisation as a socio-cultural phenomenon (and not just as a political-legal and an economic process), we can utilise anthropological analyses of Europeanisation as a corrective or a supplement to legal and political science models of integration of the Western Balkans and Serbia in particular.

The concept of Europeanisation is used to explain the processes of cultural and political changes, the construction of new identities, administrative innovations and even modernisation itself (Radaelli, 2003). In order to understand the process of Europeanisation, we must go back to the 'construction of Europe' in the field of culture and in historical perspective – that is, to the practice of change in national, regional and local awareness for the adoption of a single European consciousness. So understanding the European cultural identity and the notion of 'the idea of Europe' (Amin, 2004; Gačanović, 2009; Shore, 1993 and 2006) requires an inquiry into the cultural and political foundations of the process of Europeanisation.

For the citizens of European countries to become aware that they are Europeans, it was necessary to create common resources, common institutions, common symbols and a common market (Shore and Black, 1992). Hence, the mid-twentieth century saw the repeated "invention" and reactivation of the category "Europe" by employing concepts of "civilization", "law" and "democracy" (McDonald, 1996, pp. 48-50). The European Union as a supracommunity was conceived as 'unity in diversity'. The Declaration on European Identity (European Union, 1973) of Copenhagen and the Maastricht Treaty on European Union aimed to 'create' European citizenship, which ought to 'share' fundamental European values and European cultural heritage (Gačanović, 2009; Shore, 1993). The official documents of the EU state that, in addition to liberalism, social democracy, Renaissance, humanism, Roman law and the Enlightenment, Judeo-Christianity lies at the foundation of the "European civilization" (Shore, 1993, p. 792).

Questions of how Europe was culturally unified and why it is historically important to have a unified Union are also important to understanding Europeanisation. Europe is generally recognised to be a distinctive entity with certain shared values, culture and identity. As stated in the Article 167 of The Treaty on the functioning of the European Union: "The Union shall contribute to the flowering of the cultures of the Member States, while respecting their national and regional diversity and at the same time bringing the common cultural heritage to the fore" (European Union, 2008b). The European Community is likewise committed to support the "improvement of the knowledge and dissemination of the culture and history of the European peoples, as well as conservation and safeguarding of cultural heritage of European significance" (European Union, 2008b). In spite of the fact that the notion of culture understood in this way, as a "static and enclosed entity", had been criticised and rejected by professional anthropologists, this document renewed such a perception and has provided a basis for the construction of group identity (Sassatelli, 2002, p. 440). In addition, Shore (1993) states that the stabilisation of the European cultural identity does away with the influences and contributions of the non-European population in Europe in the shaping of individual European cultures. In other words, Article 128 of the Maastricht Treaty shows that the European Community has a "cultural policy" and not "policies that affect culture" (Shore, 1993, p. 784). Shore cautions that such a policy, which "encourages" and "promotes" the diversity of European cultures is at the same time a form of centralisation (Shore, 1993, p. 794). Likewise, Sassatelli explains that the officials in the European Union, by protecting and promoting common elements of the European culture, assume that a European consciousness will naturally emerge. Although culture is presented as "the highest product of human activities that should be protected", the EU should contribute to the safeguarding of the common European heritage without provoking negative reactions from local cultures (Sassatelli, 2002, p. 440). According to McDonald (1996, p. 47), the construction of 'Europe' is not only a symbolic process, but an active "building" of a new world, which is held to be right and which, in most cases, involves the institutions of the European Union. Yet what does European culture mean in a time when the notion of culture as closed and unchanging, authentic, homogeneous and a static set of cultural traits is rejected for the sake of the perception of culture as a competitive process in which powerful and dominant groups have the right to create and impose meaning (Wright, 1998)?

Schlesinger (1993, p. 14) cautions that the use of the term "culture" as the basis for a supranational identity is dangerous because the same term is used for the construction of nation states. This is of particular importance if we analyse the current Serbian situation. Although collective identities are founded on "assumptions on common origin and development", Schlesinger warns that the construction of Europeanness is very complicated due to different and sometimes conflicting history among European countries, ethnic nationalism, racism and anti-Semitism (Schlesinger, 1993, pp. 7-8). In line with this understanding of Europe and the 'European', a key question is: how are these "European fundamental values" harmonised and spread through Europe in order to create a unique collective identity (Schlesinger, 1993, p. 14)? On the other hand, the notion of culture may involve the existence and acceptance of a multiplicity of cultural identities while at the same time failing to problematise the possibility of their discord (Sassatelli, 2002, p. 440). In addition, the 'unity in diversity' refers to cross-cultural understanding, but it can also serve the legitimisation of xenophobic nationalism, where the unity of Europe consists of classifying people 'in' diverse cultures (Delanty and Rumford, 2005, pp. 65-6).

The notions of 'unity', 'diversity' and 'unity in diversity' are commonly used to stabilise, promote and explain the idea of the 'existence' of the European cultural identity. Authors who believe in the unity of the European culture presuppose federalism based on the belief in a "deep, rooted unity and common destiny", which is a form of cultural globalisation (Sassatelli, 2002, pp. 438-9). Seeing diversity as a matrix for European culture is described by Sassatelli as a neo-functionalist approach because it supports a plurality of European traditions. Conceived in this way, Europe is an "institutional shelter" to protect and safeguard individual European cultures (Sassatelli, 2002, p. 439). Delanty and Rumford idealise that 'being European' should not mean identification with Europe, but "simply to recognize that one lives in a world that does not belong to a specific people" (Delanty and Rumford, 2005, p. 77). However, the world that would "belong" to the Serbian people has, contrary to this concept, dwindled several times. If we accept the interpretation that, up until the mid-1970s, the Serbs felt comfortable in the entire territory of Yugoslavia, the shrinking of the 'Serbian territories' down to the Republic of Serbia and the Republic of Srpska (an entity within Bosnia and Herzegovina predominantly inhabited by ethnic Serbs) after the 1990s may be considered to be an almost threefold shrinking. So, how to 'sell' the European idea that says that to be European means 'to recognise that one lives in a world that does not belong to a specific people' to a population that now sees what was left of Yugoslavia being shrunk even more? When national borders of neighbouring countries, created on the foundations of the previous, shared state, are fortified on a daily basis, how is it possible to sell the idea that state borders are irrelevant to a population that still suffers the consequences of the rise of nation states in the former Yugoslavia?

Pursuant to the national strategy issued by the Serbian government in 2005, "association with and accession to the European Union is a strategic orientation of Serbia...the road towards the EU is seen as a road towards more modern society with stable democracy and developed economy, and political and economic requirements set by the EU, being consistent with prerequisites for successful political and economic transformation, as a means, not an objective of development" (Serbian European Integration Office, 2005, p. 6). Although it is said that Serbia is a European country, "the ultimate goal of integration is to meet the interests of citizens of all Member States, who are gradually becoming the citizens of Europe. On that basis, Europe is gradually taking its historically new internal and external identity" (Serbian European Integration Office, 2005, p. 9). In the Serbian government's discourse, accession to the EU is equated with the 'de-Balkanisation' of Serbia in view of the fact that, in public political (media and literary) discourse, the Balkan countries are perceived as backward, violent and uncivilised, burdened with a dark past and wars (cf. Todorova, 2006). Joining the European Union, however, is equated with "overcoming the past and finding a common future" (Kovačević, 2005, p. 4; International Commission on the Balkans, 2005). The main problem lies in the fact that the process of overcoming the past and creating a common road towards the future for the old member states is largely completed in the European Union, while it is now revived by the enlargement process, with all the risks that can be involved in a painstakingly attained reconciliation.

Serbian accession to the EU is presented, both by public proponents of EU integration and international officials in the region, as a cultural change (Milenković, 2010) that requires a significant transformation of the self-perception of prospective members. This form of European integration discourse has caused a surge of discussion on identity and dignity, while the discourse of freedom and sovereignty has registered unprecedented results in the polls. Given the propensity of the Serbian elite to instrumentalise traditional symbols and values from the very foundation of the modern state to the present day (Naumović, 2009), it is unlikely that the accession to the EU, such as it is currently communicated, is going to be achieved efficiently. Only a small fraction of the population sees accession as an opportunity to modernise the society (Serbian European Integration Office, 2005); the majority generally sees it as an economic project. Motivation, therefore, lies in the private interest – the sense of a better life, increased employment opportunities, improved overall living standards and so on. The majority of people do not believe that joining the EU should also be a cultural transformation (especially regarding sensitive issues of national history and the moral burden of the recent past).

After several decades of trying to create 'unity in diversity' in the EU, it is now the turn of the population of the Western Balkans to take this on – despite its recent experiences of struggling in vain to live together despite differences, which were, during the wars for Yugoslav succession, mostly presented as cultural (ethnic, religious and so on). After decades of failure to turn Croats, Muslims/Bosniaks, Serbs, Macedonians, Albanians from Kosovo, Hungarians from Vojvodina and the Roma, as well as members of at least a dozen underrepresented nations into Yugoslavs, a new project of their conversion to Europeans has started. Instead of fomenting the prospects of complementary affiliations to the European and the national identities, Serbia saw, within the internal dynamics of war, sanctions and pseudo-democratic, 'soft' dictatorship, the dichotomisation of the identity market – in the sense that the 'European' and the 'national' began to exclude each other. The greatest fear of the creators of European identity – what they have sought for decades to avoid or, more precisely, not to provoke in the course of European integration – has already happened in Serbia. The European was equated with the cosmopolitan, sublime and modern, in contrast to the national, which was a synonym for war, looting, primitivism and barbarism. The construction of this internal myth lasted two decades, and now the consequences have come due. Presently, a significant part of the population perceives 'European' as a negation of the 'national'.

Elements of Criteria Culturalisation

Public attitudes towards EU integration have been regularly followed by the Serbian European Integration Office (SEIO) since 2006. In the last three years, their findings have generally correlated the decline in support with the growing economic problems, enlargement fatigue and signs of troubled internal EU relations (Serbian European Integration Office, 2011). Instead of individual interests – economic prosperity, the rule of law, social security, high standards of health care, and wide access to education, to name but a few of the benefits of European civilisation – Western Balkan populations have now returned to collective sources of the self. Quietly and gradually, culturalisation of the aforementioned criteria was occurring, although we noticed it only subsequently. It was taking place through the interweaving of three dominant additional narratives in the European integration discourse: the narrative of *regional singularity*, the narrative of *facing the recent past* and the narrative of *moral purification* (the latter particularly in Serbia).

The narrative of regional singularity, or regional customisation, was established after the wars at the end of the 1990s and reaffirmed through strategic documents from the EU in the period from 1999-2003 and through the SAA process. This process stressed regional cooperation and the rebuilding of relations in the region. Although modified over time, it has remained. Indeed, while it seemed rational that countries in the region, burdened with many problems from the recent past, should approach the EU at their pace, the actual situation has been quite the opposite. Local populations – and Serbians perhaps most of all, since the status of the former regional power is embedded in their national self-understanding – are extremely prone to myths of national peculiarities. Although typical of every modernist constitution of national identity, which requires homogenisation of a society that is in reality a fragmented entity (Gellner, 1983), the myth of regional or national particularity has been triggered in Serbia and the region by the current customisation of accession criteria – while in public, interpretations of the Serbian singularity are on the rise again.

It is a short way from self-ghettoisation to self-marginalisation. Although it underlies every collective identity, 'particularity' is an especially interesting and dangerous issue in the region that is perceived (and self-perceived) as "Europe's frontier" (Delanty, 1995, p. 49). There is a vast range of historical, anthropological and sociological literature that legal and political analyses can rely on with respect to this region. Balkan nations have been fostering the cult of the 'European border guards' way back from the time of wars waged by small Christian states against the growing power of the Ottoman Empire, and it is a narrative that grew stronger through political issues predominantly communicated on the Internet (Bošković, 1999). This motif of frontier heroship has survived into the nineteenth century and has been built into the very core of Western Balkan citizens' modern national identities: many never fail to highlight their role in 'saving Europe' from 'Islam' and 'the Orient' – seen as a negation of everything European (Aleksov, 2005). Being deeply embedded in the national myth, the picture of oneself as the saviour creates shock, resentment, resistance and defiance in a population facing the Europeanisation call. 'Ungrateful Europe' demands its centuries-old watchmen, border guards of civilisation, to 'Europeanise'. She is hence rejecting them, betraying them and redefining them antagonistically. In other words, she 'does not understand' them (the most common response by informants).

The narrative of facing the recent past is the second supplementary narrative of European integration, which weighs on an otherwise complicated situation in the region. The 'facing' calls for the opening and re-problematising of issues that are weighing on the integration. It opens up the space for Eurosceptics, Europessimists and overt opponents of the EU to instrumentalise painful national issues from the recent past to weigh down the process of reforms to the extent that it becomes either thwarted or significantly slowed down. Therefore, in an indirect manner, the accession process itself is dragged down by the input embedded in its own accession criteria by giving rise to the reactions of those who are to be kept away from the accession process. Although the term seems unproblematic, the 'past' itself is a source of problems, too: in the regional ambit, the population has been taught through the educational system and the media to call upon 'national history' as an important source of national identity and the cornerstone of national dignity. When the past is opposed to history, problems multiply, as national pride becomes triggered by the relativising of national history, which also homogenises a population otherwise overly concerned and overwhelmed by economic problems.

The narrative of facing the recent past, summarised, suggests to the population that problems have not been solved yet, and that what they believe on those issues is not true, because there is not one single history, and there are various pasts and hence the past is a matter of interpretation. If the EU has accepted 'someone else's view of the past', which runs counter to versions that are ingrained in the modern national history, it means that the EU is a hostile entity and thus joining it means renouncing one's self-perception. This is a very risky and dangerous narrative, and the results of years of research in the social sciences and humanities testify to its contraindications. Likewise, instead of the EU being a positive entity enjoying economic stability and prosperity, the culturalisation of the accession criteria has contributed to the picture of the EU held as a goal that requires too much sacrifice: it requires renunciation of one's self-perception while, in return, even for those who do not hold the entity as sacred, it doesn't even offer economic stability and long-term prosperity anymore.

The narrative of moral purification, very akin to the previous one, is specific to Serbia. It was introduced in the pre-accession process, in the antagonistic dynamics inherited from the period of pseudo-democratic dictatorship and the war in the 1990s, and acquires its purest form in the radical dichotomisation of the society known as 'the two Serbias': a context in which pro-European civil society confronts ideologically both the illiberal state and illiberal NGOs (Kostovicova, 2006; Naumović, 2005). For two decades now, this narrative has strived for the population to come to terms with the atrocities of the 1990s. Even though all the Balkan nations had their share of those atrocities, according to the narrative, the Serbian nation had a special, principal role, having taken part in all of the conflicts considered. Being most morally debased, it must also undergo the deepest moral purification. It is defiled and self-humiliated, so it must go through catharsis in order to qualify for participation in the civilised world. In the process of preparing for Europe, it must be 'decontaminated' and its future status may be considered only after years of quarantine (see Fridman, 2011). In addition, millenarian fantasies about a prevailing truth (that Europe will realise that the Serbs in Bosnia were 'protecting it' from fundamentalist pan-Islamism) and a Europe that will 'return to itself' (and realise that the Serbs have been 'protecting it' for centuries against 'the Oriental threat') are making their presence felt again, with Bosnian Muslims (later Bosniaks) recontextualised as terrorists after 9/11 (Erjavec and Volčić, 2007). The task for the administration in general, and particularly for the policy-oriented social sciences, is to protect the society from this culture of millenarianism, which mathematised economic models and the Biblical character of the popular perception that legal norms fit into by taking active part in the management of expectations from the past rather than directing responses to the past.

The narrative of moral purification has turned out to be the most dangerous for the process of European integration of Serbia. Insisting on asymmetrical responsibilities for regional populations, after having defined citizens in the region as 'parts' of the people and not individuals, is an automatic trigger for national pride and the discourse of 'injustice' done to the Serbian people by the 'great powers', including the founding countries of the EU; consequent discussions lead to Euroscepticism, Europessimism or overt opposition to the EU. It is indicative that this reaction occurs also with students and young professionals, independent of their educational level. Moreover, preliminary results of qualitative research show that the narrative of moral purification immediately irritates the interviewees regardless of their preferred political opinions and with no correlation in response to the question of whether Serbia should join the EU.[2] Again, as in the previous two narratives of regional particularities and facing the recent past, the narrative of moral purification also poses questions that are not necessarily linked to the issue of European integration and which weigh on this process to congestion. However, unlike the previous two narratives, the narrative of the need for a specific Serbian purification is particularly dangerous.

2 For further details on a series of research projects aimed at tackling political issues as perceived by Serbian youth, see Jarić (2005; 2008).

Whereas the process of European integration could endure perpetuation of the preceding two narratives, we fear that further insistence on Serbia's moral decline and renewal could permanently prevent European integration.

Conclusion

The accession criteria should de-culturalised. Although cultural change is both inevitable and necessary, it need not be kept in the forefront. As discourses of 'development' have been reduced in the Serbian public to economic development solely, opening any other register, especially a moral one, significantly reduces the prospects of successful completion of the European integration. Paradoxically, although the 'parallel track' seemed like a good idea (Thessaloniki Council), in this decade the criteria should be instead de-customised through deculturalisation and refashioned to technical standards. Only in this way will the idea of joining the EU remain protected from further identity manipulations and the burdens of a contested past.

The promotion of the accession of the Western Balkans is based on a conclusion that does not follow, which is that the Balkan peoples are going to live happily in the EU once they become reconciled first, and not after joining the EU. Hence, a happy ending is offered once the actors go through a series of trials, painful sacrifices, reflective pendulums, self-denials and self-flagellation. The EU was created as a future-oriented project so that the spirits of war would not arise independently, but rather within a common framework designed to curb and redirect them. It is suggested that the Western Balkan countries, seemingly at odds with the initial logic of Europeanisation, must, through historicising and moralisation, face skeletons from their closets before they become 'ready' to live together in the EU. This scenario, according to which Europeanisation should precede European integration, has a very slim chance of success. The deeper that moralisation and historicising become, and the longer these last, the more profound will become the already significant differences in a growing number of election cycles and a prolonged economic crisis. Therefore, reconciliation and tolerance need to happen *in* the EU and *not before* integration is completed. That is, among other things, its essential purpose. To expect that 'facing the past' should occur before the future becomes more certain – moreover, in a way that would be internationally acceptable – is a deeply misguided approach, ignorant of the cultural context that it is supposedly customised for. To put it in even simpler terms, the current model of integration for the Western Balkans is contaminated by its many actors, their narratives and local interpretations of EU policies, so it currently seems contraindicated. We suggest that expectations be put under control and overvalued ideas – about reconciliation after moral lustration, and acceptance of a common version of the past – be replaced by the pragmatic narratives on which the EU itself was built. Although economic challenges and impediments are not the core topic of this article, they tend to be interwoven with other obstacles to the integration process. Trade liberalisation and the opening of national markets, improved implementation of competition law and state aid control, reform of public enterprises and market liberalisation of major sectors are all parts of the overall transition to the market economy. It is our opinion that this type of conditionality might be more appropriate for the troubled region with the lowest levels of income in Europe, high unemployment and high migration potential.

Although each of the narratives deserves separate study and each appear in various forms, if we analyse them jointly in the context of accession, we come to the startling conclusion that *it is the very way in which the accession process has been presented to the Western Balkan populations, and to the Serbian population in particular, that has likely caused a drastic reduction in support for accession.* This is evident in all recent opinion polls. From being a tale about peace, political stability and economic prosperity that turned to a dream come true, the fairy tale of joining Europe has been reduced to stories well-known from the 1990s: threats to national identity before the onslaught of alien interests, because of which individuals should place themselves at the service of the collective and ignore their own needs and interests. These culture-related and identity-bound issues have significant power, both together and independently, to destabilise international integration. In local contexts, the vast majority of the actors involved in the war conflicts from the 1990s are alive and still active in the political arena. Instead of consistent insistence on the criminal responsibility of individuals that committed war crimes as an instrument for civilising the post-Yugoslav societies, youth are being taught stories of injustice done to the people who have lost the most but have been proclaimed 'sole culprit'. This has led to young people praising war criminals as heroes and joining the extreme right movements in significant numbers. In such an atmosphere, the requirements to solve the underlying problems before and not after the accession to the EU appear as a plot from a disaster movie and not as responsible policy. There is significant potential for the narrative of moral lustration to destabilise Serbia's political system, at a time in which it seems otherwise almost impossible to form a stable government. Since such a government is considered a guarantee for successful implementation of reformative policies, in this case it appears that it is the narrative that is most dangerous for Serbia's future European integration. And that implies significant security risks.

In place of the narrative of regional particularities with which populations are otherwise self-contaminated, in place of the narrative of the burden of history that they would otherwise normally carry, and in place of the narrative of moral decline and need for purification that annoys the Serbian population on a large scale (provoking it to turn back to the heritage of the 1990s), the accession process should be altered and the populations of the Western Balkans offered a standardised narrative of economic progress and political development with the preservation of cultural particularities, as was likewise offered to other European populations.

References

Aleksov, B. 2005. "Perceptions of Islamization in the Serbian National Discourse." *Southeast European and Black Sea Studies* 5(1): 113-27.

Amin, A. 2004. "Multi-Ethnicity and the Idea of Europe." *Theory, Culture and Society* 21(2): 1-24.

Anastasakis, O. and D. Bechev. 2003. *EU Conditionality in South East Europe: Bringing Commitment to the Process*. South East European Studies Programme, European Studies Centre, St. Antony's College, University of Oxford.

Bošković, A. 1999. "Virtual Balkans: Imagined Boundaries, Hyperreality and Playing Rooms." *Série Antropologia* 262. Brasília: Departamento de Antropologia, Universidade de Brasília.

Delanty, G. 1995. *Inventing Europe: Idea, Identity, Reality*. Basingstoke and New York: Palgrave MacMillan.

Delanty, G. and C. Rumford. 2005. *Rethinking Europe: Social Theory and the Implications of Europeanization*. Abingdon, New York: Routledge.

Erjavec, K. and Z. Volčič. 2007. "'War on Terrorism' as a discursive battleground: Serbian recontextualisation of George W. Bush discourse." *Discourse and Society* 18(2): 123-37.

European Commission. 2008. *Communication From the Commission to the European Parliament and the Council Western Balkans: Enhancing the European perspective*. Brussels. 5.3.2008 COM(2008), 127 Final.

European Commission. 2011. *Communication from the Commission to the European Parliament and the Council: Enlargement Strategy and Main Challenges 2011-2012*. Brussels. 12.10.2011 COM(2011), 666 Final.

European Council. 1993. Conclusions of the presidency. Copenhagen, 21-22 June. Brussels: General Secretariat of the Council. SN 180/1/93 REV 1.

European Council. 1995. Presidency Conclusions. Copenhagen, 15-16 December. Brussels: General Secretariat of the Council. http://www.europarl.europa.eu/summits/mad1_en.htm (24 November 2012).

European Union. 1973. "Declaration on European Identity (Copenhagen, 14 December 1973)." Bulletin of the European Communities. No. 12. Luxembourg: Office for official publications of the European Communities. http://www.cvce.eu/viewer/-/content/02798dc9-9c69-4b7d-b2c9-f03a8db7da32/en;jsessionid=CA3D6310DDE86CF7A8961E32035232D0 (26 October 2012).

European Union. 2008a. *Stabilisation and Association Agreement between the European Communities and their Member States, of the one part, and the Republic of Serbia, of the other part (SAA)*. CE/SE/en 1. http://ec.europa.eu/enlargement/pdf/serbia/key_document/saa_en.pdf (11 November 2012).

European Union. 2008b. "Consolidated version of the Treaty on the functioning of the European Union." *Official Journal of the European Union* C 115/47, 9.5.2008. http://www.ecb.int/ecb/legal/pdf/fxac08115enc_002.pdf (7 November 2012).

Featherstone, K. 2003. "Introduction: In the Name of 'Europe'". In *The Politics of Europeanization*, eds. K. Featherstone and M. Radaelli. Oxford and New York: Oxford University Press, 3-26.

Fridman, O. 2011. "'It was like fighting a war with our own people': anti-war activism in Serbia during the 1990s." *Nationalities Papers* 39(4): 507-22.

Gačanović, I. 2009. "How to invent a European? An anthropological analysis." *Anthropology* 7: 87-104.

Gellner, E. 1983. *Nations and Nationalism*. Cambridge: Cambridge University Press.

Glenn, J.K. 2004. "From nation-states to member states: accession negotiations as an instrument of Europeanization." *Comparative European Politics* 2(1): 3-28.

Haughton, T. 2007. "When does the EU Make a Difference? Conditionality and Accession Process in Central and Eastern Europe." *Political Studies Review* 5(2): 233-46.

International Commission on the Balkans. 2005. *The Balkans in Europe's Future*. Sofia: Secretariat Centre for Liberal Strategies. http://www.emins.org/sr/dokumenti/downloads/2005/050504-balkans.pdf (30 February 2012).

Jarić, I. 2005. "In the grip of betrayed expectations." *Philosophy and Society* 27: 75-87.

Jarić, I. 2008. "Generation W: From the young people's perspective." *Issues in Ethnology and Anthropology* 3(3): 203-21.

Kostovicova, D. 2006. "Civil society and post-communist democratization: Facing a double-challenge in post-Milošević Serbia." *Journal of Civil Society* 2(1): 21-37.

Kovačević, I. and M. Krstić. 2011. "Between History and Modernity: The Anthropological Study of Migrant Workers in the 21st Century." Issues in Ethnology and Anthropology 6(4): 969-82.

Kovačević, Ž. 2005. *Peoples of the Balkans: In Search of Identity*. European Movement in Serbia. http://www.emins.org/sr/dokumenti/downloads/2005/050317-kovacevic-ietm.pdf (30 January 2012).

McDonald, M. 1996. "'Unity in Diversity': Some Tensions in the Construction of Europe." *Social Anthropology* 4(1): 47-60.

Milenković, M. 2010. "The adoption of European standards in the sphere of economic law and (anticipated) cultural change in Serbia." *Issues in Ethnology and Anthropology* 5(1): 111-35.

Naumović, S. 2005. "The social origins and political uses of popular narratives on Serbian disunity." *Philosophy and Society* 26: 65-104.

Naumović, S. 2009. *Uses of tradition in political and public life of Serbia at the end of 20th and the beginning of 21st century*. Belgrade: Filip Višnjić and Institute of Philosophy and Social Theory.

Nedeljković, S. 2006. "Myth, religion, and national identity: Mythologization in Serbia in the period of national crisis." *Issues in Ethnology and Anthropology* 1(1): 155-79.

Pridham, G. 2006. "European Union Accession Dynamics and Democratization on Central and Eastern Europe: Past and Future Perspectives." *Government and Opposition* 41(3): 373-400.

Radaelli, M.C. 2003. "The Europeanization of Public Policy". In *The Politics of Europeanization*, eds. K. Featherstone and M. Radaelli. Oxford and New York: Oxford University Press, 27-56.

Radović, S. 2007. "Globalization of identity in the delayed transition: Notions about Europe and Serbia among students in Belgrade." *Bulletin of the Ethnographic Institute* SASA 55(1): 45-59.

Sassatelli, M. 2002. "Imagined Europe: The Shaping of a European Cultural Identity Through EU Cultural Policy." *European Journal of Social Theory* 5(4): 435-51.

Schimmelfennig, F. and U. Sedelmeier. 2004. "Governance by conditionality: EU rule transfer to the candidate countries of Central and Eastern Europe." *Journal of European Public Policy* 11(4): 661-79.

Schlesinger, P. 1993. "Wishful Thinking: Cultural Politics, Media, and Collective Identities in Europe." *Journal of Communication* 43(2): 6-17.

Serbian European Integration Office. 2005. *National Strategy of Serbia for the Serbia and Montenegro Accession to the European Union*. Belgrade: Serbian European Integration Office.

Serbian European Integration Office. 2011. European Orientation of the Citizens Of The Republic Of Serbia Trends. Presentation of public poll results (January 2012).
http://www.seio.gov.rs/upload/documents/nacionalna_dokumenta/istrazivanja_javnog_mnjenja/opinionpoll_december_2011.pdf (25 Feb 2012).

Shore, C. 1993. "Inventing the 'People's Europe': Critical Approaches to European Community 'Cultural Policy'." *Man* 28(4): 779-800.

Shore, C. 2006. "'In Uno Plures'(?): EU Cultural Policy and the Governance of Europe." *Cultural Analysis* 5: 7-26.

Shore, C. and A. Black. 1992. "The European Communities and the Construction of Europe." *Anthropology Today* 8(3): 10-11.

Todorova, M. 2006. *Imagining the Balkans.* New York: Oxford University Press.

Wright, S. 1998. "The Politiciziation of 'Culture'." *Anthropology Today* 14(1): 7-15.

PART III

POLITICAL PARTIES AND ENLARGEMENT

Party System Institutionalisation in European Parliament and National Elections

The Comparative Impact of Expansion

Alan SIAROFF

Introduction

The one institution of the European Union that directly represents its citizens is the European Parliament (EP). This is also arguably the institution that has changed the most since the original Coal and Steel Community. At first, an appointed body (with members normally seconded by national parliaments), since 1979, the European Parliament has been directly elected. Even the most recent members of the 2004 and 2007 expansions have each voted twice in EP elections. Originally a very weak body with little legislative power, the EP has seen its powers grow treaty by treaty, so that now it has significant legislative power, as well as reactive power, regarding appointment of the European Commission. Elections to the EP do not directly determine the government as in a parliamentary system, but the EP is required to confirm the Commission and its president. (On the EP and its evolution, see Judge and Earnshaw 2008).

However, elections to the European Parliament have always been problematic in two overarching and interrelated ways: the lack of true pan-European parties and campaigns and their "second-order" nature (Reif and Schmitt 1980; Reif 1985). That is, EP elections are largely fought by national parties and are much more about domestic issues in the Member States than pan-European ones. Voters tend to cast protest votes against national governments and for smaller and/or more extremist parties. Voter turnout is lower than at national elections. Once in Brussels, the elected members form party groups that have coherence, especially the long-established ones, and thus provide stability to the European Parliament. However, as Bardi (1996, 2002) has shown, even though in time the party groups have become more cohesive, individual EP elections act as a disruptive force on this cohesion as is bringing in new Member States with new parties that "need" to be fitted into these party groups.

There are two specific institutionalisation problems that I wish to focus on here: (i) "fitting" certain national parties into the various transnational party groups and (ii) a fairly high level of party system volatility in certain Member States. By looking at the parliamentary composition of both the European Parliament and national legislatures, this chapter will assess the extent to which such problems have been and will be worsened by the arrival of the ten new Central and Eastern European members and further ones to follow. Similar but lesser analysis will occur for the new Mediterranean members and other potential new members. The answers vary from country to country and depend on both domestic electoral volatility and the extent to which the principal domestic parties are from the same main "party families" (von Beyme 1985) as those of Western Europe. Overall, the Central and Eastern European members have definitely increased these problems more so than, for example, Malta has.

Party Systems in Eastern and Western Europe

The potential problem is that post-communist party systems have been assumed to be different from those of Western Europe in three ways. First, at least initially, there was a divide between communist successor parties and others, even "others" that were left-leaning. This was a cleavage not present in Western Europe. However, eventually this cleavage effectively disappeared, so that, for example, in Poland the post-communist SLD (Democratic Left Alliance) was able to ally with the post-Solidarity UP (Labour Union) for the 2001 elections – or at least with what remained of the latter (Millard 2010, p. 101).[1] Second and more generally, the meaning of left and right is different, or more specifically the ideological axis is different: Whereas in the West, the economically left-wing parties are also the socially liberal parties, in the East it is the economically right-wing parties that are the socially liberal ones. The axis of party competition is thus rotated ninety degrees from that of the West (Marks *et al.* 2006). Both of these points imply that Eastern parties and party systems will not "match" those of the West. Third and finally, volatility is high and largely "supply-side", that is, reflecting changes in the supply (creation and dissolution) of parties by political elites and more generally, maintaining a high level of multipartism (Rose 2008, Chapter 15; Bielasiak 2002, pp. 206-207). More

[1] Indeed, in Poland this cleavage first started to break down with the presidential election of 1995, wherein the victorious SLD candidate Kwaśniewski was able to attract votes from former Solidarity supporters. Millard 2010: 82.

generally, as newer party systems in the world (since 1978), it is no surprise that post-communist party systems are likely to be less institutionalised.[2] The new European democracies thus have "competition without institutionalisation" (Rose and Munro 2009, Chapter 5).

Transnational Party Groups

The European Parliament (EP) has always been organized in terms of transnational party groups since parties essentially run national campaigns for the EP and then join a party group with like-minded parties once in Strasbourg. The three core groups of the EP have been the Socialists (PES),[3] the Christian Democrats (EPP) and the Liberals (now ELDR). Bardi (1996, p. 110) has concluded that these three groups "can rightfully be considered as the core of the Europarty system". Each of these three groups go back to June 1953 when party groups were first allowed in the Common Assembly of the European Coal and Steel Community. In May 1992, the British and Danish Conservatives affiliated themselves with the EPP, making that group less clearly Christian and certainly less Catholic but quite broad in coverage (until last year when the British Conservatives ended their membership). If one were to pick the fourth most relevant party group, this would be the Greens. This group was founded after the 1999 EP elections and has remained a stable group ever since. In contrast, other groups on the left, the centre-right, or the far right have all shown much less continuity and have often been more confederal, such as the EUL-NGL (Raunio 2001, pp. 231-232).

It is also the case that the three historical EP groups represent – at least for much of continental Europe – the three classic *familles spirituelles* of Socialists, Christian Democrats and Liberals (Lightfoot 2010, p. 31). These three party families have been the traditional core of national parties systems divided by both class and religiosity. Substituting Conservatives for Christian Democrats gives us the traditional party systems of Scandinavia and Great Britain (von Beyme 1985, Chapter 2; also Hix and Lord 1997, pp. 25ff.). Above and beyond these parties, the Greens have become an important part of national party systems in many continental countries. Consequently, we can argue that the most "European" party systems are those that are dominated by Christian

2 On the distinction between post-1978 party systems and advanced industrial party systems in terms of volatility, see Mainwaring and Zoco 2007.

3 Technically, after the 2009 EP elections the PES teamed up with the Italian Democratic Party to form a Socialists and Democrats party group, but we shall treat this as still being effectively the PES.

Democrats or Conservatives, Socialists and Liberals, with perhaps the Greens now a core player as well.

In terms of the European Parliament, I shall assess this tendency by the extent to which the political parties (members) elected in EP elections sit in one of the three core groups broadly defined (EPP, PES/Socialists and Democrats, ALDE), and alternatively in one of these three groups or the Greens/EFA. No distinction is made amongst these specific party groups in terms of national membership, although it should be noted that in EP elections, voters in post-communist countries have been much less leftist than voters in Western Europe (Schmitt and Thomassen 2010, pp. 50-51). Table 1 shows the collective core groups data for the 2009 and 2004 EP elections (2007 for Bulgaria and Romania). One can note the sharp drop-off in "core" support in the United Kingdom in 2009, reflecting the withdrawal of the British Conservatives from the EPP-led group to form its own European Conservatives and Reformists group. Table 2 then averages the values for these two elections and ranks the countries in descending order by the column of percentage of MEPs in the three core groups. One sees in Table 2 that, ironically, the top four places are all occupied by new members of the EU. It is worth noting that three of these four countries have small or very small delegations in the EP, which limits the number of different parties that can win seats and, ultimately, the number of different party groups these can join.

Nevertheless, the post-communist Member States can be divided into three groups based on Table 1: Slovenia, Hungary, Romania and Estonia all "fit" perfectly or nearly so into the three core groups; Bulgaria, Slovakia, Lithuania and the Czech Republic fit well or reasonably well; whereas Poland and Latvia fit poorly. Given its size, Poland is presumably the most problematic here. Thus, there is a wide variation in terms of how these new members fit into the EP. Certainly, though, the new members at the bottom of the list will impede the institutionalisation or at least the coherence of the EP.[4] So too do many established members – and these have generally done so for some time. Specifically, Table 2 shows that several Western European members – not just the United Kingdom but also Ireland, the Netherlands, Austria and Denmark – rank at the bottom in terms of their "fit" into the core three (especially) or core four party groups. Thus, Latvia and Poland are not that unique in terms of members fitting into the core groups. Indeed, overall, the ten post-communist countries have a slightly better fit into the core three groups than the twenty-seven members as a whole (see Table 2). However, this difference vanishes when the Green group is

4 Cyprus is also worth noting here, especially in contrast to Malta.

included, given the very weak support for Green parties in post-communist Europe. Overall, then, the post-communist Member States are certainly not a specific 'problem' in this regard.

Table 1: Delegations in the European Parliament – (Share of) Seats in the Core Party Groups Since 2004

	Total	Core Three Groups		Core Three Plus Greens	
	Seats	Seats	% of Total	Seats	% of Total
2009 elections					
Austria	17	10	58.8	12	70.6
Belgium	22	16	72.7	19	86.4
Bulgaria	17	15	88.2	15	88.2
Cyprus	6	4	66.7	4	66.7
Czech Republic	22	18	81.8	18	81.8
Denmark	13	8	61.5	10	76.9
Estonia	6	5	83.3	5	83.3
Finland	13	9	69.2	11	84.6
France	72	49	68.1	63	87.5
Germany	99	77	77.8	91	91.9
Greece	22	16	72.7	17	77.3
Hungary	22	19	86.4	19	86.4
Ireland	12	7	58.3	7	58.3
Italy	72	63	87.5	63	87.5
Latvia	8	2	25.0	3	37.5
Lithuania	12	9	75.0	9	75.0
Luxembourg	6	5	83.3	6	100.0
Malta	5	5	100.0	5	100.0
Netherlands	25	14	56.0	17	68.0
Poland	50	35	70.0	35	70.0
Portugal	21	17	81.0	17	81.0
Romania	33	29	87.9	29	87.9
Slovakia	13	11	84.6	11	84.6
Slovenia	7	7	100.0	7	100.0
Spain	50	46	92.0	47	94.0
Sweden	18	14	77.8	17	94.4
United Kingdom	72	24	33.3	29	40.3

Table 1 continued

	Total	Core Three Groups		Core Three Plus Greens	
	Seats	Seats % of Total		Seats % of Total	
2004-07 elections					
Austria	18	13	72.2	15	83.3
Belgium	24	19	79.2	21	87.5
Bulgaria	18	15	83.3	15	83.3
Cyprus	6	4	66.7	4	66.7
Czech Republic	24	16	66.7	16	66.7
Denmark	14	10	71.4	11	78.6
Estonia	6	6	100.0	6	100.0
Finland	14	12	85.7	13	92.9
France	78	59	75.6	65	83.3
Germany	99	79	79.8	92	92.9
Greece	24	19	79.2	19	79.2
Hungary	24	24	100.0	24	100.0
Ireland	13	7	53.8	7	53.8
Italy	78	52	66.7	54	69.2
Latvia	9	4	44.4	5	55.6
Lithuania	13	11	84.6	11	84.6
Luxembourg	6	5	83.3	6	100.0
Malta	5	5	100.0	5	100.0
Netherlands	27	19	70.4	23	85.2
Poland	54	31	57.4	31	57.4
Portugal	24	21	87.5	21	87.5
Romania	35	34	97.1	34	97.1
Slovakia	14	11	78.6	11	78.6
Slovenia	7	7	100.0	7	100.0
Spain	54	50	92.6	53	98.1
Sweden	19	13	68.4	14	73.7
United Kingdom	78	59	75.6	64	82.1

Table 2: Delegations in the European Parliament – Mean (share of) Seats in the Core Party Groups (Average of Last two EP Elections)

	Core Three Groups	Core Three plus Greens
	% of total	% of total
Malta	100.00	100.00
Slovenia	100.00	100.00
Hungary	93.18	93.18
Romania	92.51	92.51
Spain	92.30	96.07
Estonia	91.67	91.67
Bulgaria	85.78	85.78
Portugal	84.23	84.23
Luxembourg	83.33	100.00
Slovakia	81.59	81.59
Lithuania	79.81	79.81
Germany	78.79	92.42
Finland	77.47	88.74
Italy	77.08	78.37
Greece	75.95	78.22
Belgium	75.95	86.93
Czech Republic	74.24	74.24
Sweden	73.10	84.06
France	71.85	85.42
Cyprus	66.67	66.67
Denmark	66.48	77.75
Austria	65.52	76.96
Poland	63.70	63.70
Netherlands	63.19	76.59
Ireland	56.09	56.09
United Kingdom	54.49	61.16
Latvia	34.72	46.53
Overall average	**76.28**	**81.43**
Post-communist average	**79.72**	**80.90**

National Party System Institutionalisation and Volatility

In most advanced industrial countries, the patterns of party politics have been stable, involving the *same* specific parties during several elections. However, such stability in parties is not a given in newer democracies, which leads to the concept of party system institutionalisation. This concept was developed by Mainwaring and Scully in their 1995 edited book on Latin America. An updated analysis of Latin America has been done for the Inter-American Development Bank (Payne *et al.* 2002, Chapter 6). With some modifications, the Mainwaring and Scully approach has also been applied to Africa by Kuenzi and Lambright (2001). These studies have largely used the same variables in assessing institutionalisation in a given country: the inter-election volatility in parties' support, summed for all parties (the lower the better); the difference between presidential and legislative election support (the more people who vote for the same party at both levels, the better); the age of all parties with at least 10 per cent of the vote, or alternatively, the top two parties (the older, the better); the dominance of long-established parties; the general legitimacy of parties and elections, including seeing elections as the only legitimate way to gain and hold power; and the acceptance of electoral defeat by losing parties. Institutionalised party systems have low volatility over time, durable parties with clear roots in society (presumably based on relevant social cleavages such as ethnicity, language, religion, religiosity, class, or region), and broad support for parties and elections as legitimate political institutions. These studies ultimately rank the countries concerned on a continuum, or at least suggest multiple broad categories of institutionalisation, with the lowest category called by Mainwaring and Scully (1995, p. 19) "inchoate" party systems.

Unfortunately, what works for other regions becomes problematic when applied to post-communist East-Central Europe. Measuring variations in presidential and legislative voting does not require a full presidential system, but it does assume an elected president – not true everywhere in East-Central Europe. Mainwaring and Scully (1995, pp. 13-14) define a long-established Latin American party as one founded by 1950; Kuenzi and Lambright (2001, p. 446) note that since most African countries did not become independent until around 1960, they find 1970 to be the relevant cut-off date for Africa. However, for East-Central Europe, many new parties arose after the transition to democracy circa 1990. The issue is thus more the stability of these parties than their longstanding duration, for as Rose and Munro (2009, pp. 47-48) note, only a tiny number of parties in post-communist EU states have competed in every election since democratisation.

Consequently, rather than developing a multi-dimensional measure of party system institutionalisation, we shall settle for a basic ranking of more institutionalised party systems versus less institutionalised ones, as determined by inter-election volatility (using the Pedersen index). This is shown in Table 3, with data through June 2012. This averages the volatility between two elections, with a cut-off date of 1990 for the first election in a pair since, as noted, that was when democratisation occurred in most of post-communist Europe. To clarify, a country that, for example, has had six elections in 1990, 1994, 1998, 2002, 2007 and 2011 has thus had five pairs of consecutive elections: 1990-1994, 1994-1998, 1998-2002, 2002-2007 and 2007-2011. Table 3 shows that the most stable national party system is, in fact, that of the new Mediterranean member Malta, with Cyprus in second place since 1990. In contrast, the new post-communist party systems are quite volatile, and, indeed, ten of the eleven current EU members with above average volatility are all post-communist members. We can also simplify this table into four categories based on the values since 1990: low volatility (<10 per cent), medium-low volatility (from 10 to 20 per cent), medium-high volatility (from 20 to 30 per cent), and high volatility (>30 per cent). Consequently, there are *no* post-communist countries with low volatility; only the Czech Republic – barely – has had medium-low volatility; Romania, Hungary, Estonia and Slovakia have had medium-high volatility; and half of the post-communist countries – Slovenia, Bulgaria, Poland, Latvia and Lithuania – have had high volatility. Thus, in summary, the post-communist current members clearly have volatile party systems, often highly so, and, consequently, this makes it unwise to assume that the parties themselves, and their resulting fit into the EP, will continue – a cautionary point most crucial for those countries that do have a good or indeed perfect fit as of today.

Nevertheless, it may be "unfair" to measure volatility since 1990 across European countries, since for post-communist countries, this covers the entire period of contemporary democracy, and volatility may well be higher in the initial years of a democracy. Indeed, Tavits (2005, p. 293) has argued that "in the beginning of transition the [electoral] volatility increases over time, but starts to decrease once democracies have had time to mature ... it takes about 11 years of democratic experience before the electoral arena starts to move toward stabilization". She thus cautions against earlier assessments of electoral instability in post-communist Europe. We can certainly assess Tavits' point by noting the volatility after this initial time period, that is, since 2000 to pick a round year. Table 3 also provides this data, which is more tentative since it usually involves only two election pairs and sometimes just one. As Table 3 shows, post-communist countries generally have had lower volatility in this shorter time period, with their overall average volatility dropping from 29.8 to 26.8, although the Czech Republic and Bulgaria have each gone in the opposite direction, and Lithuania has had no real change. Still, only Estonia, Hungary and Romania now have medium-low volatility (and Romania barely). Perhaps the only real sign of stabilisation is Poland, where volatility fell to 10.0 in its last election pair (2007 to 2011). Overall, though, even for this more recent time period (since 2000) the modal category for post-communist EU states is medium-high volatility: still higher than average and still indicating a lack of party system institutionalisation.

Ultimately, there can be no assumption that volatility in post-communist Europe and Western Europe will even out. On this point, one can note Lane and Ersson's (2007) finding that there is a strong relationship between (higher) level of socioeconomic development (which they measure via the UN Human Development Index) and (lower) electoral volatility across Europe, and generally, the gap in HDI values is still significant between Eastern and Western Europe. The one, hardly positive, way in which a partial evening out of volatility has occurred is in those Western European countries where the party system has recently imploded – and thus volatility has spiked – because of the rejection of some or all of the traditional main parties in the context of the current economic crisis and resulting austerity. Here we refer to both Greece and Ireland, where volatility is now at or above the EU-wide average. Indeed, in Greece from the election of 2009 to that of May 2012, it was 48.0 per cent, an enormously high level matching the most volatile elections of post-communist Europe.

Table 3: Average Inter-Election Volatility for all Elections since 1990 and 2000

	SINCE 1990		SINCE 2000	
	Number of Election Pairs	**Average Volatility**	**Number of Election Pairs**	**Average Volatility**
Current European Union Members				
Malta	4	2.8	1	2.5
Cyprus	4	6.5	2	7.1
Luxembourg	3	6.8	1	4.8
United Kingdom	4	7.7	2	6.8
Germany	5	8.6	2	10.3
Spain	5	9.0	3	10.1
Finland	5	9.4	2	10.8
Portugal	5	10.6	2	10.8
Denmark	6	10.8	3	9.8
Austria	6	11.9	2	12.1
Belgium	5	12.0	2	13.8
Ireland	4	13.0	2	18.0
Sweden	5	13.0	2	12.0

Greece	8	14.3	5	17.6
France	4	17.1	2	17.2
Italy	5	17.7	2	6.5
Czech Republic	6	19.9	2	25.3
Netherlands	5	20.5	3	19.3
Romania	4	20.9	2	19.8
Hungary	5	21.8	2	18.4
Estonia	5	28.3	2	16.3
Slovakia	7	29.5	3	24.1
Slovenia	5	31.0	3	31.7
Bulgaria	6	32.7	2	40.1
Poland	6	33.9	3	22.8
Latvia	5	36.7	2	28.2
Lithuania	4	43.6	2	40.9
Mean percentage		**18.1**		**16.9**
European Union Acceding Country and Candidate Countries				
Iceland	5	13.8	2	16.2
Croatia	4	15.1	2	14.5
Turkey	4	25.7	1	18.6
Macedonia	6	27.2	3	19.4
Montenegro		n.a.	3	16.3
Serbia		n.a.	3	15.7
Potential European Union Candidate Countries				
Albania	3	18.5	2	20.2
Bosnia and Herzegovina	5	23.2	3	21.8
Kosovo		n.a.	3	18.3
Other European Free Trade Association (EFTA) States				
Liechtenstein	5	6.5	2	6.8
Norway	4	18.5	2	12.7
Switzerland	5	8.1	2	8.3

A Combined Classification

Figure 1 combines the two broad measures in this analysis. It looks at the core four party groups (thus giving national parties an additional "option" of the Greens where they might "fit in") and suggests a break point of whether or not the mean share of national seats in these four groups has been at least 80 per cent (averaged for the last two EP elections). It also divides national electoral volatility into two categories, with the break point at 20 per cent. What do we find with this combination? The most institutionalised countries in this sense are those in the upper right – where the national parties fit into the main EP groups and the low or medium-low level of national volatility allows us to assume that said national parties are "here to stay". In this quadrant, one finds some of the founding states (Belgium, France, Germany, Luxembourg), but also members from the new(er) "Catholic South" (Malta, Portugal, Spain) and perhaps more interestingly, Finland and Sweden. However, one does not find any post-communist countries. The opposite quadrant is that of the lower left, the least institutionalised and thus the most "problematic" for the development of the EP party system. Here one finds three post-communist countries (Latvia, Lithuania and Poland) but also the Netherlands – which can be seen as the key West European outlier here. Mair (2008) explains the Dutch electoral volatility in terms of the openness of the Dutch party system in the Western European context, especially in terms of governments (that is, innovative coalitions and openness to new parties joining government). Though post-communist countries are not in Mair's analysis, they, too, tend to have these party system features. The three post-communist countries noted here are obviously not the majority of post-communist countries. Where one does find the majority of post-communist countries is in the lower right quadrant combining a good fit into the four core EP groups but with high national volatility (and thus no guarantee of the previous point lasting); indeed, this quadrant is uniquely comprised of post-communist countries. This confirms that the post-communist EU Member States are problematic in terms of national volatility but not in terms of (trans)national party families.

Figure 1: Combined Measures of Institutionalisation

	Mean (Share of) Seats in the Core Four Party Groups (Core Three Plus Greens) (Average of Last Two EP Elections)	
	Below 80 per cent	**80 per cent or more**
Average National Volatility since 1990		
Less than 20 per cent	Austria	Belgium
	Cyprus	Finland
	Czech Republic	France
	Denmark	Germany
	Greece	Luxembourg
	Ireland	Malta
	Italy	Portugal
	United Kingdom	Spain
		Sweden
20 per cent or more	Latvia	Bulgaria
	Lithuania	Estonia
	Netherlands	Hungary
	Poland	Romania
		Slovakia
		Slovenia

Implications of Further Widening

The European Union is now set to widen further, at least to take in Croatia. There are also now (as of 2012) five candidate countries: Iceland, Macedonia, Montenegro, Serbia and Turkey. We can call these six the 'short list' expansion countries. The issue here is not how many of these will actually join, but rather how well their national party systems would fit into EP institutionalisation assuming they did join. In terms of fitting into the core EP groups, this can be assessed at least for the EPP, the PES and the ELDR in terms of member parties or associate member parties found in these non-EU European states (this latter status does not seem to exist for the Greens/EFA group).[5] For Croatia, there is an excellent fit: An overwhelming majority (more than 80 per cent) of the seats currently held in its *Sabor* belong to parties that are members

[5] Information on group membership et cetera is taken from the group websites as well as the Parties and Elections in Europe website.

or associate members of the core three groups. This includes Croatia's two main parties, the Social Democratic Party of Croatia (SDP), which is an associate member of the PES, and the Croatian Democratic Union (HDZ), which is an associate member of the EPP. Macedonia is similar in this regard to Croatia. It has two main parties, a conservative one which has observer status with the EPP and a social democratic one which is an affiliate of the PES. (This is also true for Albania.) Macedonia's other parties are all of its Albanian minority. Montenegro is less clear, but it is also likely to be unproblematic. The key political divide is ethnicity; that is, almost all parties in Montenegro are focussed on Montenegrin voters, Serbian voters, Bosnian voters, Albanian voters or Croatian voters (in rough descending order of collective size). The Montenegrin-oriented parties are social democratic and affiliated with the PES. However, though not affiliated with any EP party group, the other key (medium-sized) parties in Montenegro are generally clearly pro-European.

Iceland would be much more of a problem in terms of its parties. Although the governing Alliance is an associate member of the PES, it is the only Icelandic party affiliated with one of the core EP groups. The main opposition party – and traditionally the largest party in Iceland – the conservative Independence Party affiliated with the anti-federalist European Conservatives and Reformists Group (ECR) in November 2011, is against Iceland joining the EU and, obviously, would be Eurosceptic if Iceland were a member. The Alliance's coalition partner, the Left-Green Movement, is also Eurosceptic and thus is affiliated with the European United Left/Nordic Green Left group in the EP, not the Greens/EFA. The last of the main Icelandic parties is the rural-based Progressive Party, which one presumes would find a home somewhere in the EP centre-right. Still, one must conclude that if Iceland were in the EU, its membership in the core EP groups would be towards the very bottom of Table 2. (Of course, this makes it more doubtful that it would join.)

Serbia is also problematic. Parties affiliated with or members of the PES, the EPP or the ALDE won (only) about 40 per cent of the seats in the 2012 election, similar to earlier results. Indeed, the single largest party up through the 2008 Serbian election was the far right Serbian Radical Party. However, soon after the 2008 election, more moderate elements in the party broke away and formed the Serbian Progressive Party that led the coalition that came first in the 2012 parliamentary election. Moreover, the Serbian Progressive Party leader was elected president in May 2012 – defeating, however, the pro-EU incumbent.

Last in this regard is the case of Turkey. With the exception of the far-right National Movement Party (MHP), all the parties in the Turkish

Grand National Assembly are associate or observer members of either the EPP or the PES. If Turkey were in the EU, it likely would be somewhere in the middle of Table 2. Yet the question for Turkey is really the situation of the ruling Justice and Development Party (AKP), which has observer status with the EPP. As a moderate right party with religious supporters (but not only these), the AKP is a "logical" member to be in the EPP, except, of course, that there is a difference in religion here between the Islam of the AKP and the Christianity of the EPP. Moreover, some of the key EPP parties – the CDU/CSU in Germany, the UMP in France, the ÖVP in Austria – are the very parties that want to keep Turkey out of the EU.

Thus, there would be clear variations on the first measure of institutionalisation from admitting all these "short-listed" countries into the European Union. The country with the best fit on this first measure, Croatia, is also the one to join next. Regarding the second measure, that of volatility Table 3 also provides volatility scores for these various countries, as well as the remaining Balkan countries (not that these are likely European Union members for some time) and the remaining three EFTA countries. None of the "short list" countries have high volatility, and, indeed, all – even the post-communist countries – have had medium-low volatility since 1990. Consequently, overall one would expect Croatia to be in the "desirable" upper right quadrant of Figure 1. So at least the next (single country) expansion of the European Union will not hurt party system institutionalisation in the European Parliament.

Conclusions

This chapter has examined two specific institutionalisation problems regarding the party politics of new and forthcoming European Union members: (i) "fitting" certain national parties into the various transnational party groups, and (ii) the level of volatility from national election to election (and thus the stability of the actual parties). These two variables were then combined into a two-dimensional model. It was shown that Latvia, Lithuania and Poland are problematic on both dimensions of institutionalisation. However, most post-communist countries are problematic only on the second dimension of institutionalisation, that of national volatility. Moreover, the Catholic legacy of European integration seems to reassert itself in that new member Malta is institutionalised on both dimensions and acceding state Croatia is likely to be as well. Given that some longstanding, indeed original, members are also problematic (for example, the Netherlands), one must conclude that the differences between East and Southeast Europe versus Western Europe should not be overemphasized in this regard.

References

Bardi, Luciano. 1996, "Transnational Trends in European Parties and the 1994 Elections of the European Parliament". *Party Politics*, 2: 1 (January): 99-114.

Bardi, Luciano. 2002. "Parties and Party Systems in the European Union". In *Political Parties in the New Europe: Political and Analytical Challenges*, eds. Kurt Richard Luther and Ferdinand Müller-Rommel. Oxford: Oxford University Press.

Bielasiak, Jack. 2002. "The Institutionalisation of Electoral and Party Systems in Postcommunist States", *Comparative Politics*, 34: 2 (January): 189-210.

Hix, Simon, and Christopher Lord. 1997. *Political Parties in the European Union*. New York: St. Martin's Press.

Judge, David, and David Earnshaw. 2008. *The European Parliament*. 2nd ed. Basingstoke: Palgrave Macmillan.

Kuenzi, Michelle, and Gina Lambright. 2001. "Party System Institutionalisation in 30 African Countries", *Party Politics*, 7: 4 (July): 437-468.

Lane, Jan-Erik, with Svante Ersson. 2007. "Party System Instability in Europe: Persistent Differences in Volatility between West and East?" *Democratisation*, 14: 1 (February): 92-110.

Lightfoot, Simon. 2010. "The 2009 European Parliamentary Elections and the Party Groups". In *The 2009 Elections to the European Parliament*, ed. Juliet Lodge. Basingstoke: Palgrave Macmillan, 30-42.

Mainwaring, Scott, and Timothy R. Scully. 1995. "Introduction: Party Systems in Latin America". In *Building Democratic Institutions: Party Systems in Latin America*, eds., Scott Mainwaring, and Timothy R. Scully. Stanford: Stanford University Press, 1-34.

Mainwaring, Scott, and Edurne Zoco. 2007. "Political Sequences and the Stabilization of Interparty Competition: Electoral Volatility in Old and New Democracies". *Party Politics*, 13: 2 (March): 155-178.

Mair, Peter. 2008. "Electoral Volatility and the Dutch Party System: A Comparative Perspective". *Acta Politica*, 43: 235-253.

Marks, Gary, *et al.* 2006. "Party Competition and European Integration in the East and West: Different Structure, Same Causality". *Comparative Political Studies*, 39: 2 (March): 155-175.

Millard, Frances. 2010. *Democratic Elections in Poland, 1991-2007*. London and New York: Routledge.

Payne, J. Mark, *et al.* 2002. *Democracies in Development: Politics and Reform in Latin America*. Washington, DC: Inter-American Development Bank.

Raunio, Tapio. 2001. "The Party System of the European Parliament after the 1999 Elections". In *The 1999 Elections to the European Parliament*, ed. Juliet Lodge. Basingstoke: Palgrave, 231-51.

Reif, Karlheinz, ed. 1985. *Ten European Elections: Campaigns and Results of the 1979/81 First Direct Elections to the European Parliament.* Aldershot: Gower.

Reif, Karlheinz, and Hermann Schmidt. 1980. "Nine Second Order National Elections: A Conceptual Framework for the Analysis of European Election Results". *European Journal of Political Research,* 8: 3-44.

Rose, Richard. 2008. *Understanding Post-Communist Transformation: A Bottom Up Approach.* London and New York: Routledge, Chapter 15: "A floating system of parties".

Rose, Richard, and Neil Munro. 2009. *Parties and Elections in New European Democracies.* Colchester: ECPR Press.

Schmitt, Hermann, and Jacques Thomassen. 2010. "The EU Party System after Eastern Enlargement". In *European Parliament Elections after Eastern Enlargement,* ed. Hermann Schmitt. London and New York: Routledge, 43-61.

Tavits, Margit. 2005. "The Development of Stable Party Support: Electoral Dynamics in Post-Communist Europe". *American Journal of Political Science,* 49: 2 (April): 283-298.

von Beyme, Klaus. 1985. *Political Parties in Western Democracies.* Trans. Eileen Martin. New York: St. Martin's Press.

EU-Scepticism vs. Euroscepticism

Re-assessing the Party Positions in the Accession Countries towards EU Membership

Seçkin Bariş GÜLMEZ

Introduction

This paper attempts to develop a coherent analytical framework in order to explain party positions towards European Union (EU) membership in candidate countries. With this objective, this chapter starts by challenging the explanatory power of the term 'Euroscepticism' in terms of analysing party positions towards EU membership during the accession process. Outlining the limitations of the concept and scholarship on Euroscepticism, the study will introduce a new term 'EU-scepticism' that could be defined as criticism of, or reluctance towards, EU membership, as a reaction to the EU's accession conditionality. Introducing three different forms of EU-scepticism (standard, conditional and substantive), the study will empirically discuss how these three forms are applied to former and current candidate countries. Finally, the study will discuss the three main findings concerning EU-scepticism in political parties: it is not entirely an opposition party phenomenon, ideological party positioning has no explanatory power over EU-scepticism, and the mitigation or elimination of EU-scepticism is contingent upon the restoration of EU's legitimacy in the eyes of the candidate country.

Euroscepticism and its Critics

The prevailing literature mainly defines Euroscepticism as "the idea of contingent or qualified opposition, as well as incorporating outright and unqualified opposition to the process of European integration" (Taggart, 1998 p. 366). Szczerbiak and Taggart (2004) argue that Euroscepticism involves two different forms of opposition to European integration: "hard" and "soft" Euroscepticisms. Hard Eurosceptics reject the idea of EU membership, since they have no desire to be a part of such a Union. On the other hand, soft Eurosceptic parties are generally in favour of European integration, but oppose a particular policy within the integration process, or exert opposition with the motivation to preserve national interest in a specific domain (Szczerbiak and Taggart, 2004 p. 4).

Kopecky and Mudde (2002) suggest an alternative classification for Eurosceptic tendencies in Europe. In this respect, they differentiate between Eurosceptics and Euro-rejects by advancing four new categories: 'Europhiles' vs. 'Europhobes' (depending on the level of one's support of European integration), and 'EU-optimists' vs. 'EU-pessimists' (depending on one's attitude towards the current and future directions of the EU as a polity). In this context, Euroscepticism refers to a combination of Europhiles and EU-pessimists while 'Euro-rejects' are simultaneously both Europhobes and EU-pessimists. In other words, Eurosceptics are not against what they see as realistic advantageous cooperation among various groups of European states for greater peace and prosperity (Kopecky and Mudde, 2002 p. 304), but they are pessimistic about the current and/or future direction in which European integration is heading.

However, extant typologies suffer from crucial limitations. First of all, as the analytical distinction between "principled opposition" and "qualified objection" is fuzzy (Mudde, 2011 p. 6), it is difficult to determine a party's political stance along the soft-hard Euroscepticism scale. In particular, when political parties involve simultaneously both soft and hard Eurosceptic elements, for instance, in the Communist Party of Bohemia and Moravia (KSCM) in the Czech Republic (Hanley, 2008 p. 254), the soft/hard distinction is insufficient to grasp such overlapping Eurosceptic tendencies. Furthermore, there is still no consensus on how to study Euroscepticism in political parties. Thus, the same parties are often studied under different categories (Mudde, 2011 p. 6). For example, the ultranationalist Nationalist Action Party (MHP) in Turkey has been deemed both hard Eurosceptic (Günes-Ayata, 2003 p. 212) and soft Eurosceptic (Gülmez and Buhari-Gülmez 2008).

Additionally, Euroscepticism categories have been mainly formulated as applicable to member states. Scholars interested in Euroscepticism in candidate countries have failed to develop new models and frameworks, and have often attempted to replicate the same categories in candidate countries (Szczerbiak and Taggart, 2004 p. 2). However, this suggests serious limitations. For instance while defining "hard Eurosceptics", Szczerbiak and Taggart (2008a p. 2) specifically refer to "parties who think that their countries should withdraw from membership". Since candidate countries are not yet EU members, it is not possible to think that political parties would to ask to withdrawal from membership. Rather, they would ask to withdraw their candidacy. Application of the Kopecky and Mudde (2002) typology to candidate countries is even more problematic. For instance, defining Eurosceptics as being both Europhile and EU-pessimist does not make sense if you are a candidate country (Batory, 2008 p. 267). If you are pessimistic about the EU's current or future projection, why would you wish to join the EU in the first place?

In response to critics, particularly Kopecky and Mudde (2002), Szczerbiak and Taggart (2008b) refined their typology, which in the end better emphasized its focus on member states at the expense of candidate states. Accordingly, the priority in determining the party stances has been ultimately given to "underlying support for or opposition to the European integration project as embodied in the EU" and "attitudes towards further actual or planned extensions of EU competencies" rather than "a party's support for or opposition to their country's membership at any given time" (Szczerbiak and Taggart, 2008b p. 242). In other words, Euroscepticism would only be used to categorise parties which oppose European integration project, not for the parties which oppose their own membership. Hence, numerous academic pieces, which used the same typology for analysing party reactions during the accession negotiation process, have become problematic. An important reason for that is that, rather than the idea of integration or certain policy fields, it is the membership prospects which gather much attention in candidate states. The views of political actors towards the EU before and after membership might turn out to be quite different as "the political and economic dimensions of the EU project for member states differ considerably from the political and economic Copenhagen criteria, which related solely to the internal reforms necessary in candidates" to become an EU member (Henderson, 2008b p. 109). Even Szczerbiak (2008), who initially suggested the hard and soft Euroscepticism typology, admitted that with the reformulation of the concept it became nearly impossible to identify who was Eurosceptic in Poland, as political parties focused on membership prospects rather than European integration and its trajectory.

Apart from the need to develop a new approach for EU candidate countries, there is another problem associated with the general tendency to treat Eurosceptic categories as a-temporal and static. It is hard, if not impossible, to (1) grasp whether Eurosceptic attitudes derive from past preconceptions against, and experiences with, Europe and the EU, or emerge as a reaction to current discourse and policies of the EU, and (2) analyse 'change' in Eurosceptic attitudes. On the last point, Szczerbiak and Taggart (2002 p. 30) acknowledged the need for analysing 'change' in Eurosceptic patterns, but they have not yet specified ways of looking at shifting positions between soft and hard Euroscepticisms. Overall, this study aims to go beyond mainstream theorizing by studying attitudes towards EU membership in candidate countries, and focusing on the accession process rather than the post-accession phase. In so doing, the paper offers a new term, 'EU-scepticism', in order to specifically scrutinize party attitudes towards EU membership. Finally, this study's ontological approach allows for studying shifting attitudes towards the EU in pre- and post-accession phases.

EU-scepticism vs. Euroscepticism

The extant frameworks limit the application of Euroscepticism to member states since they aim to measure the views towards overall European integration and its trajectory, while political parties in candidate countries mainly stress concerns over membership. In this respect, there is a need to differentiate between opposition to Europe and opposition to EU membership as they imply two distinct meanings and yet the latter is ruled out from the mainstream's equation of Euroscepticism. Therefore, in order to better evaluate party positions in the accession countries, I propose the term 'EU-scepticism', which involves criticisms of, and reluctance for, EU membership in candidate countries, as a reaction to the EU's membership conditionality.

EU-scepticism differs from Euroscepticism because its focus is limited to the temporal phase that follows the officialization of a country's EU candidacy and ends with the officialization of its EU membership. Hence, it scrutinises a candidate country's active efforts to comply with EU membership conditionality For its part, Euroscepticism involves opposition to the idea of European integration, seeing it perhaps as moving towards a federal Europe (Euroscepticism in a broader sense) and particular EU policies such as the European Monetary Union (EMU) (Euroscepticism in a narrow sense).

Euroscepticism is therefore the reflection of a negative preconception about what 'Europe' and/or the idea of a 'Union' stand for due to historical memories or ideological standpoints. This preconception fuels nationalist sentiments and thus triggers strong reservations towards joining the EU in the first place. Therefore, the opposition does not stem from the EU's membership conditionality, but from the previous experiences of the country with Europe, Europeans, and/or the other Unions before the EU accession process. For instance, due to past experiences with the Soviet Union, Baltic States in general, and Estonia in particular, were hesitant towards the idea of joining another union, for example, the European 'Union' (Mikkel and Kasekamp, 2008). Vetik *et al.* (2006, p. 1086) claim that the fear of Germanization led the Estonian public to forge a 'reactive identity' against assimilation under the EU umbrella.

EU-scepticism, on the other hand, is a reaction. It stands for the reluctance of candidates to becoming a member because of unfavourable accession criteria, and/or as a reaction against the EU's own reluctance towards the candidate country's membership. This opposition is strategic and reversible because the main motivation underpinning EU-scepticism is to gain/guarantee membership with full benefits. It therefore materialises after the EU starts to apply official membership conditionality and it reaches its peak during the negotiations which precede accession to the EU. In this respect, EU-scepticism emerges out of candidate country's concerns related to the complicated negotiation process with the EU. This study argues that in most cases (except the League of Polish Families [LPR] and the Czech Civic Democrats [ODS]), political parties in the accession countries reflect EU-scepticism rather than Euroscepticism. Thus they react to the complications that derive from their state's negotiations with the EU. Their mention of preconceptions is mostly instrumentalised and reversible. The EU could respond in at least two ways to dissipate EU-scepticism: either it could convince EU-sceptics to embrace the reforms by guaranteeing membership or it could withdraw the additional and problematic criteria from its membership negotiations. Otherwise, it often triggers domestic preconceptions that usually work against the EU process and further complicate negotiations.

Overall, EU-scepticism is a helpful category because it reveals the fact that (1) domestic political actors are more likely to concentrate their energy on membership conditionality rather than on general European integration discussions, and (2) as compliance becomes costly for the candidate, or the EU fails to give enough incentives for membership, political actors may react against the EU and show reluctance towards membership.

Varieties of EU-scepticism

Although contested, EU enlargement is essentially depicted in the literature as a top-down process, in which a candidate country carries out reforms and adopts norms that the EU dictates in order to become a member. During this process, according to Schimmelfennig (2008 p. 921), the success of political conditionality is contingent on three factors: (a) credible membership conditionality in which the EU promises eventual membership provided that candidate complies with the accession criteria; (b) normative consistency which dictates that the EU should be "guided only by the democratic and human rights performance of the target countries", without any discrimination based on nationality or culture; and finally (c) low political costs of domestic compliance. He argues that most of the times, (a) and (b) are met, but serious problems arise in EU-candidate state relations when (c) is not met, in other words, when candidate states perceive compliance with the EU as too costly.

Schimmelfennig's analysis might be better scrutinised in conjunction with the issue of the EU's pragmatic legitimacy in the eyes of candidate countries. According to Suchman (1995 p. 578), the pragmatic legitimacy of an organization (the EU) rests on "the self-interested calculations of [its] most immediate audiences/constituents (candidate countries)". Pragmatic legitimacy is divided into three types: exchange, influence and dispositional. Exchange legitimacy stands for the support for an organisation's policy based on the expected benefits for the audience, while influence legitimacy refers to the support for an organisation which rests on the willingness of the organisation to incorporate the constituent into its policy-making structure (*Ibid.*). Finally, dispositional legitimacy attaches personal traits to organisations to determine their legitimacy. For instance, constituents are more likely to consider an organisation as legitimate if it is 'honest', 'trustworthy', 'decent' and 'wise' (*Ibid.*). Accordingly, the EU's credible membership incentive (a) contributes to its influence legitimacy in the eyes of candidates, since by promising membership the EU declares its willingness to incorporate the candidate country into its policy-making structure. The EU's normative consistency (b) empowers its dispositional legitimacy since candidate countries perceive it as 'trustworthy' and 'fair'. Finally, low political costs of domestic compliance (c) increases the EU's exchange legitimacy, as low costs imply comparably higher benefits for the candidate. In his analysis, Schimmelfennig (2008) points to the fact that the EU's exchange legitimacy decreases only when candidates fail to comply with the membership conditionality, because non-compliance mainly stems from higher costs calculated by candidates (c). However, non-compliance might also constitute a stronger challenge to the EU's pragmatic legitimacy when the EU fails to meet the conditions (a) and (b) outlined by Schimmelfennig (2008).

EU-scepticism, therefore, stems from two factors: first, it is a reaction against the EU's standard conditional pressures and derives from endogenous considerations namely, cost-benefit calculations (c) and/or cultural reservations of candidate country. Second, it materialises against non-standard exogenous pressures from the EU and its member states (a) and (b). In either case, EU-scepticism is the projection of the EU's declining pragmatic legitimacy in the eyes of candidate country. Depending on whether it derives from endogenous or exogenous factors, EU-scepticism has three different forms: 'standard', 'conditional' and 'substantive'. When endogenous considerations determine domestic reactions, we observe standard EU-scepticism. This type of EU-scepticism is a reaction against EU-led reforms associated with the Copenhagen criteria. It develops during the negotiation process whereby domestic political actors oppose certain EU reforms, either due to high costs of compliance or to the threats that these reforms pose to national sovereignty and identity (Schimmelfennig 2008, Hooghe and Marks, 2008). Therefore, albeit non-discriminatory, the conditionality may spark scepticism in the candidate country. The reaction observed in such situations would be considered as standard for it might be witnessed in most candidates having to fulfil the Copenhagen criteria. Certain EU-sponsored reforms may be perceived as a threat to the country's sovereignty and/or costly to national interests since the reforms may challenge established domestic social and political norms and practices, and thus have the potential to make significant changes in people's daily lives. In many accession countries, as the negotiations continued political parties reacted against the EU's 'imposition' of certain reforms. A favourite motto of the political parties, which reflects standard EU-scepticism, may be 'No to second-class membership', 'No to unfair membership negotiations' and 'Yes to full membership with equal rights' (Riishøj 2007). In the case of standard EU-scepticism, in line with Schimmelfennig (2008), high compliance costs draw domestic reaction and render the fulfilment of the EU conditionality problematic. Since the calculated cost of compliance with EU reforms outweigh the expected benefits, the EU's exchange legitimacy declines in the eyes of the candidate, as does its capacity to encourage the candidate to fulfil the membership criteria.

EU-scepticism may also derive from exogenous factors, further diminishing EU legitimacy. EU-scepticism becomes conditional when the EU applies additional conditions due to a bilateral issue with a member state. It is a particular reaction to the instrumentalization of the EU accession negotiations by an individual member state which seeks to get concessions from the candidate country on a bilateral issue that is not directly related to the EU's official membership criteria. The EU thus inherits the extant bilateral problem and fails to act as an impartial problem solver. It either remains indifferent to the constraints inflicted upon the candidate by the member state or puts extra conditions on the candidate country to solve the bilateral problem before joining the Union. In order to get concessions on the bilateral issue, the member state may use its veto power to block the initiation of accession negotiations, or even freeze an ongoing negotiation process by blocking the negotiation chapters. Political parties in the accession country resist these new reforms or the constraining acts of the member state, showing strong reluctance to join the EU. The mitigation of this EU-scepticism is directly contingent upon the solution of the bilateral issue, either through reciprocal compromise or unilateral concession by the candidate in return for a membership guarantee by the EU.

Finally, EU-scepticism becomes substantive when reluctance for membership emerges due to the fact that domestic political actors perceive strong reluctance or indecisiveness in the EU towards their membership. Evidence of the EU's non-standard attitudes towards the candidate may be observed in either of two instances. First, the EU puts additional preconditions which may either specifically target the candidate country in question, or seek to generally slow down EU's widening process in the near future. The introduction of additional provisions, such as 'absorption capacity', 'open-ended negotiations' and 'permanent derogations' to the official documents regarding the candidate's accession may spark strong domestic reactions in the country and be interpreted as indications of EU reluctance towards its membership. Second, the statements of leading European politicians and Eurocrats against the accession of the country and the discussion of propositions alternative to membership such as 'privileged partnership' might be perceived as evidence of the existence of such reluctance.

Conditional and substantive EU-scepticisms challenge the credibility of the argument that the EU is normatively consistent and non-discriminatory in its enlargement strategy (Schimmelfennig, 2008). Political actors in candidate countries resist EU reforms and show reluctance for membership because of the increasing perception that the EU's strategy towards them is 'unfair' thus discriminatory. Therefore, not only the EU's exchange legitimacy, but also its dispositional legitimacy comes under the threat of eroding in the eyes of the candidate. Moreover, the EU's influence legitimacy declines as well, since inconsistencies in the EU's discourse and policies reinforces uncertainty towards the candidate country's full membership in both cases Hence, the EU risks losing its pragmatic legitimacy and its influence over the candidate country.

Empirical Discussion, EU-scepticism in Accession Countries

In this part, the study aims to apply the three categories of EU-scepticism (standard, conditional, and substantive) to selected EU candidate countries. The selection is based on the application of the Copenhagen criteria, which significantly changed how EU enlargement was approached. Compliance with such norms as minority rights has become part of the official preconditions for membership (Wiener and Wobbe, 2002). Non-compliance with the Copenhagen criteria is strictly punished by the rejection of membership (Schimmelfennig 2008). In this context, this study looks at EU-scepticism in countries whose EU candidacy has been assessed under the Copenhagen criteria.

Standard EU-scepticism

Standard EU-scepticism is a reaction against EU-led reforms associated with the Copenhagen criteria in all candidate countries. Hence, the EU's discourse and policies towards candidates are assumed standardised. Thus, those who resist compliance with the EU membership conditionality tend to resort to endogenous factors, such as national sovereignty and pride, national and sectoral interests as well as identity, in order to justify their opposition (rather than blaming the EU for its inconsistency or unfairness). In comparison to conditional and substantive EU-scepticisms, standard EU-scepticism is the most common tendency in candidate countries. During their accession negotiations with the EU, many candidate countries have witnessed the rise of political party protests against particular reforms associated with Copenhagen criteria.

1. Foreign Land Ownership

One of the reforms that draw EU-scepticism is ensuring free movement of capital through lifting restrictions against foreigners/non-nationals. There are numerous reasons for opposing foreign land ownership, ranging from purely economic fears that foreign ownership will increase land prices enormously at the expense of local buyers, to patriotic concerns over the loss of national sovereignty and the fears of "re-Germanisation" (Tesser, 2004 p. 214).

In the Polish case, most of the opposition parties, all with different ideological backgrounds, stood against this reform. The Polish Peasant Party (PSL), an agrarian party with 8.98 per cent popularity in the 2001 elections, supported Polish membership. However, with the particular motivation to protect the rights of local farmers, the PSL strongly opposed the foreign acquisition of land, forests, or areas containing water sources (Tesser, 2004 p. 220). Party officials even demanded an 18 year prohibition on foreigners purchasing agricultural land in Poland (Zuba, 2009 p. 332).

The centre-right Solidarity coalition (AWS) also opposed land liberalization, fearing the return of Germans to Poland (Tesser, 2004 p. 220). Similarly, the centre right parties, Law and Justice (PiS), and Civic Platform (PO), with respectively 9.5 per cent and 12.68 per cent popularity in 2001 during the accession negotiations, have shown standard EU-scepticism in their opposition of foreign land ownership. The PiS proposed a "land turnover law" in order to protect Polish farmers from foreign land speculators (Szczerbiak, 2008 p. 232) and party officials threatened to vote NO in the referendum unless the membership package offered to Poland was substantively improved (*Ibid.*).

Hungary is another example of a state with EU-sceptic political parties opposing land liberalisation during accession negotiations. The Fidesz-Hungarian Civic Party, a mainstream right wing party with 41.1 per cent popularity in the 2002 elections, was one of the most Euro-enthusiast political actors in Hungary, endorsing the 'return to Europe' motto. However, their eagerness shifted to EU-scepticism as the country started EU membership negotiations. Defending "hard bargaining with Brussels", the party declared itself the protector of Hungarian land, and proposed a referendum to prevent EU reforms that would enable foreign land ownership in Hungary (Batory, 2008 p. 270-271). The Hungarian Justice and Life Party, a rather fringe right-wing party with 4.4 per cent popularity in 2002, also reflected an EU-sceptic stance, conditioning its support for EU membership on the full guarantee of national survival, culture and independence (Batory, 2008 p. 272). In particular, the party demanded a full guarantee regarding the issue of foreign land ownership, and wage parity with existing members; in the absence of this they proposed the postponement Hungary's membership (*Ibid.*).

EU-scepticism in the form of opposition to land liberalisation is also applicable to Slovenia, a strong pro-EU country, which had already determined its "return to Europe" as a strategic goal, even before the dissolution of Yugoslavia (Krasovec and Lipicer, 2008 p. 316). The Slovenian National Party and the New Party, far-right fringe parties with 4.38 per cent and 0.59 per cent popularities in the 2000 election, opposed the foreign land ownership stipulation, claiming that this EU reform made them realise the true nature of the EU (Krasovec and Lipicer, 2008 p. 318).

2. Agricultural Subsidies

Another issue that raises tension in candidate countries is the question of agricultural subsidies. The EU offered the candidates only 25 per cent of what farmers in older member countries received. In particular, the countries that heavily rely upon the agricultural sector, such as Poland, Estonia and Czech Republic protested against the EU's reform of subsidies. In Poland, the PSL, the main party defending the rights of local farmers, strongly opposed the EU's offer to Polish farmers and demanded full subsidies for them (Szczerbiak, 2008 p. 237, Riishoj, 2007 p. 517, Zuba 2009 p. 332).

The Self-Defence (Samoobrona), a nationalist right-wing party with 10.20 per cent popularity in 2001, also prioritized agricultural subsidies in its EU policy. Denoting the negotiations as a threat to Polish farmers, party leaders claimed that with the deal offered by the EU, Poland would be permanently relegated to second-class EU member (Zuba 2009 p. 333, Szczerbiak, 2008 p. 228-229). Instead, the party explicitly demanded that Polish membership be based on equal rights (Szczerbiak, 2008 p. 230).

Although Euroscepticism is rather more visible in Czech politics compared to other candidate countries, it is also plausible to talk about EU-scepticism especially concerning the issue of agricultural subsidies. The Communist Party of Bohemia and Moravia (KSCM), which is generally accepted as hard Eurosceptic for its opposition to EU membership (Szczerbiak and Taggart, 2004), actually stressed the importance of Czech membership under equitable conditions and denounced the EU's unbalanced agricultural subsidies for new-comers (Hanley, 2008 p. 252).

In Estonia, although the public was known as being highly Eurosceptic, all political parties regarded EU membership as a necessity for Estonia's development hence they supported its accession (Mikkel and Kasekamp, 2008 p. 300). The parties, however, also stressed the importance of conducting fair negotiations with the EU, upholding national interests (*Ibid.*). Therefore, many political parties in the country, including the mainstream Centre Party with 25.4 per cent popularity in the 2003 elections, reacted to certain EU reforms, especially the level of agricultural subsidies for Estonian farmers, and blamed the government for being too submissive to such EU demands (Mikkel and Kasekamp, 2008 p. 309).

3. Other Issues

Standard EU-scepticism has also been observed during the adoption of reforms associated with identity, human rights and minority rights, which triggered opposition in candidate countries. In Slovakia, even pro-EU parties, the Christian Democratic Movement (KHD) (8.25 per cent) and the Social Democrat Smer (13.46 per cent), criticised the negotiation process intensively. While the KDH attacked particular EU reforms, such as same sex partnership and abortion (Henderson, 2008a p. 287), in its election campaign the Smer party defended the preservation of Bohunice's nuclear reactor, standing firm against EU pressures to close it down, and depicted it as "a pillar of Slovak economy" and national pride (Ivanov, 2008 p. 161). The Smer even demanded the reopening of various negotiation chapters that had already been closed, in order not to accept EU membership at all costs (Henderson, 2008a p. 288).

In Estonia, the Centre Party opposed the EU-led reforms on the citizenship rights of minorities and the removal of the Estonian language requirement for minority candidates in national elections. Claiming that such reforms would constitute a threat to Estonian identity, party officials condemned the government for "giving in" to western institutions on such sensitive issues (Feldman, 2001 p. 16). Minority rights became a source of intense opposition in Romania as well. The far-right nationalist Greater Romania Party, although giving strategic support to Romania's EU membership, stood against the reforms on the rights of Hungarian and Roma minorities. Vadim Tudor, the party leader, even demanded that all Gypsies be put in jail, for there was no other solution (Goldston, 2002 p. 155). Opposition to minority rights also engulfed Latvian politics. The For Fatherland and Freedom/Latvian National Independence Party, a far right nationalist party, opposed the EU-led reforms which enabled the naturalisation of non-Latvians living in the country. The reason for this opposition originated from the fear that "if all the non-citizens were suddenly given voting rights they would vote to destabilise Latvia's shaky political scene and even re-annex Latvia to Russia" (Morris, 2004 p. 554). The party even demanded a referendum in order to prevent the reforms. However, after becoming member of the coalition government in 1998, the party revised its hard-line stance on the citizenship issue, since party officials announced that it was in Latvia's strategic interest to become an EU member to offset future threats from Russia (Morris, 2004 p. 558).

During the accession process, political party views towards EU integration in candidate countries were mainly formed through the prism of membership negotiations and there was no tangible reference to the European project as a whole and its trajectory (Szczerbiak, 2008 p. 237). Because of this the criticisms discussed above qualify for EU-scepticism rather than Euroscepticism. Their actions can be categorized as standard EU-scepticism, because while parties reacted to the reforms, the EU remained impartial and consistent in its approach to candidate countries. For instance, the governments had to agree to a maximum seven-year transition period before granting land ownership rights to foreigners, although the Polish government demanded 18 years, and Hungarian, Czech and Slovak governments asked for ten years of postponement of this reform (Tesser, 2004 p. 228). Moreover, the EU offered all newcomers the same rate (25 per cent) of agricultural subsidies.

Conditional EU-scepticism

Contrary to standard EU-scepticism, the existence of conditional EU-scepticism indicates a more problematic accession process for the candidate country, due to a bilateral conflict with an EU member state. The member state which is party to the ongoing bilateral issue with the candidate country could block the initiation of the accession negotiations and thus use its veto power as a blackmailing device. Although there have been some milder versions of conditional EU-scepticism in the former candidates, this type of EU-scepticism has become particularly visible in the current accession countries. For instance, the Republic of Macedonia, a candidate since 2005, has been put under pressure by Greece, an EU member since 1981 which has a historical claim on the name 'Macedonia'. Greece has been blocking Macedonia's EU accession talks since 2009, despite the European Commission's recommendation to initiate the negotiations with the country. Political actors in Macedonia, including the government, have reacted strongly to Greece and condemned "Brussels' one-sidedness" which has been precluding Macedonia's EU bid (Marusic, 2011). Accusing the EU of inflicting double standards, officials of the ruling party, the VMRO-DPMNE, even likened the EU's Macedonian policy to "the Holocaust" (Balkan Insight, 2011).

A member state in conflict with a candidate may even curtail an ongoing negotiation process by blocking the negotiation chapters. For instance, the Exclusive Economic Zone issue between Croatia and Slovenia caused the curtailment of Croatia's EU membership negotiations for up to ten months due to the Slovenian veto. Correspondingly, reluctance towards membership rose among all Croatian political actors, who felt threatened by the Slovenian-led EU pressure to choose either the fisheries zone or membership (Zorić, 2008). The Croatian Prime Minister, Ivo Sanader, even accused Slovenia of blackmailing them, and asserted that they did not intend to "buy the EU membership with the territory" (EUobserver, 2008). The negotiations resumed only after Croatia and Slovenia agreed to the EU plan of bringing the issue to an *ad hoc* international arbitration court. Croatia consented to the plan since the fisheries zone stood as the final obstacle to Croatia's realization of full EU membership.

Similarly, not only the member state party to the conflict but also the EU and other member states might freeze the negotiations by blocking certain chapters. For instance, the EU pressured Turkey to open its harbours and air space to Cyprus (an EU member since 2004) having ongoing bilateral issues with Turkey. Upon Turkey's refusal to comply with this precondition, the EU partially froze the Turkish accession negotiations by blocking eight chapters. Later France and Cyprus decided to block several other chapters and today 18 negotiation chapters remain frozen, which has practically halted the entire accession process. This has sparked a significant amount of reaction in both the government and the opposition in Turkey (Gülmez and Buhari-Gulmez, 2008). The main opposition party in Turkey (the CHP) criticised that the Cyprus problem took Turkey-EU relations 'hostage', prohibiting Turkey's eventual EU membership. Deniz Baykal, the party leader, claimed: "If Turkey fails or is prevented from becoming a member, this is not the end of the world" (Hürriyet, 2005). The governing party (the AKP) threatened to freeze its relations with the EU for six months should Cyprus be granted the EU Presidency (Vatan, 2011).

Problems for the accession countries, caused by bilateral issues, have often resulted in intense EU-scepticism.

As stated above, its mitigation is directly contingent upon the solution of the bilateral issue either through reciprocal compromise or unilateral concession by the candidate. Moreover, conditional EU-scepticism is adopted by both opposition and government, attracting parties from different ideological backgrounds. This is because the EU's non-standard membership pressures, resulting from a bilateral problem with a member state, decreases its pragmatic legitimacy in the eyes of many of the candidate country's political parties. Therefore, unless the EU restores its legitimacy either by guaranteeing membership or by withdrawing additional conditions to solve the bilateral issue prior to accession, EU-scepticism remains among the political elite of the candidate country under discussion.

Substantive EU-scepticism

Substantive EU-scepticism is an exceptional phenomenon in the accession countries, which signals almost no membership incentive for the candidate and jeopardises the future relations with the EU. Turkey stands out as the only candidate country whose political actors reflect substantive EU-scepticism. As previously discussed, the EU introduced additional provisions such as 'absorption capacity', 'open-ended negotiations' and 'permanent derogations' to the official documents regarding Turkey's accession. These expressions constituted a novelty for the EU's enlargement policy since they were first introduced to Turkey. Another novelty is that a number of top EU politicians[1] overtly stood against Turkey's accession and instead offered cooperation short of full membership such as 'privileged partnership'. In the meantime, due to Turkey's persistent refusal to open its harbours and airspace to Cyprus, an EU member, its membership process remains frozen. The EU cannot even credibly promise eventual membership to Turkey even if it agrees to open its market to Cyprus. This stalemate has had a very negative impact on the Turkish political elite since new provisions and the lack of clear membership impetus decreases the EU's legitimacy in the eyes of the Turkish. Therefore, especially after the postponement of the

[1] Such as French President Nicholas Sarkozy, German Prime Minister Angela Merkel, Austrian Chancellor Wolfang Schussel and the EU President Herman Van Rompuy.

accession negotiations, the Turkish government became even less motivated to continue with the EU's reforms. Top government officials accused the EU of being indecisive for accepting Turkey's membership. The Prime Minister and the leader of the governing AKP party, Tayyip Erdoğan, argued that the EU has been dragging its feet over Turkey for more than fifty years and he urged EU officials to clearly announce whether they really want Turkey or not (Hürriyet, 2011). Erdoğan claimed that no other candidate country had faced unfair treatment such as Turkey had been suffering from (Vatan, 2011) and accused the EU of becoming a unified block against Turkey's accession (Erdoğan, 2011). Baykal, leader of the CHP, the main opposition party, criticised the open-ended nature of the negotiations, the absorption capacity of the EU and permanent safeguard clauses against Turkey. The CHP leader claimed that these expressions were proof that the EU had only considered 'privileged partnership' for Turkey not membership (Hürriyet, 2004).

Substantive EU-scepticism in Turkey transcended the notion of strategic reaction to certain reform areas and changed the overall rhetoric of the major political actors towards the EU. Condemning the EU's reluctance for Turkey's accession has become a daily practice of domestic political actors, voicing their stance on Turkey's EU accession.

The Turkish case confirms that substantive EU-scepticism is embraced by both opposition and government. It also indicates that party ideology does not directly affect their behaviour towards the EU, since both a centre right party (the AKP) and a social democrat party (the CHP) adopted similar stances against the EU. It also holds true for the GAL/TAN dyad, since both the AKP as a right GAL party and the CHP as a left TAN party during Baykal's leadership, and left GAL under Kilicdaroglu, all reacted against the EU. This is due to the fact that the EU had lost its pragmatic in the eyes of Turkish political actors, since it both failed to provide credible membership perspective and to remain non-discriminatory towards Turkey.

Conclusion

This chapter aimed to offer a new framework from which to analyse the oppositional stances of political parties against EU membership in recent (post-Copenhagen criteria) candidate countries in general, and in Turkey in particular. With this goal, the study highlighted the limitations of the prevailing approaches based on 'Euroscepticism', in explaining political party positions towards EU membership during the accession negotiations. Accordingly, the study offered 'EU-scepticism' as a more useful term in terms of emphasizing that the critical attitudes of political parties during the negotiation process do not reflect a wholesale opposition to the idea of Europe. Accordingly, the study offers three main findings. First of all, it sought to grasp whether EU-scepticism was generally limited to opposition parties. Empirical findings (discussed above) reflect the fact that while standard EU-scepticism is mainly observed in opposition parties, conditional and substantive forms of EU-scepticism have been a broader political phenomenon and have involved both government and opposition. Not only fringe parties such as the Hungarian Justice and Life Party, the Slovak National Party and the New Party in Slovenia, but also mainstream parties such as the ODS and the KSCM in Czech Republic, the PO and the PiS in Poland, the Fidesz-Hungarian Civic Party in Hungary, the MLP in Malta and the Progressive Party of the Working Peoples (AKEL) in Cyprus resorted to standard EU-scepticism during the accession process, especially when they were in opposition. On the other hand, as the cases of Turkey, Macedonia and Croatia indicate, three factors triggered conditional and substantive EU-scepticism, which has spread to the government and even to some previously Europhile segments of the political elite. These are: (1) additional conditionality by the EU, (2) interruption or changes in accession negotiations due to bilateral issues between an EU member state and the candidate state, and (3) the EU's perceived reluctance to proceed with the negotiations (as well as widespread political speeches/criticisms against the candidate country's membership by particular EU member countries).

The second finding suggests that ideological positioning has no explanatory power to determine party preferences for EU-scepticism. Since EU-scepticism implies reaction to the membership conditionality rather than deep-seated resentment against Europe, political parties from different ideological perspectives might stand against particular reforms that are perceived as violating national and sectoral interests as well as culture and national identity. In such cases, not only left wing or right wing parties, but also GAL as well as TAN parties demonstrate EU-sceptic reflexes.[2] The empirical evidence confirms this claim with various examples derived from candidate countries. For instance, Fidesz-Hungarian Civic Party, a mainstream Right/GAL party, as well as the Justice and Life Party, a fringe Right/TAN party, showed similar reactions to the EU reform concerning foreigners' right to own land in Hungary. Major right wing GAL parties in Poland, the PO and PiS, as well as the left/TAN Self-Defence Samoobrona criticised similar EU reforms during the Polish candidacy. Moreover, the SMER, a major left/GAL party and the radical right/TAN Slovak National Party too

2 For *GAL* (green/alternative/libertarian) – *TAN* (traditionalism/authority/nationalism) categorization of European political parties, see Marks *et al.*, 2006.

adopted EU-sceptic rhetoric during the negotiation process. This is also true for the current EU candidate, Turkey. For example, not only the conservative governing AKP (right/GAL), but also the main opposition, the social democrat CHP (left/TAN before 2010 and left/GAL afterwards) and ultra-nationalist MHP (right/TAN) reflected EU-scepticism as regards the EU's Cyprus conditionality.

Finally, empirical evidence demonstrates that EU-scepticism in most candidate countries is mitigated or disappears when the EU has restored its pragmatic legitimacy over the country by guaranteeing EU accession via the signature of the accession treaty and the national referendum. EU-scepticism, therefore, mostly changed into Euro-supportiveness after membership. Even in the case of the KSCM in the Czech Republic, whose officials had shown a hard-line stance towards the EU, the party said YES to the referendum and revised its critical stance towards the EU because the party officials admitted that membership was imminent and that the majority of the Czech public was in favour of membership (Riishoj, 2007 p. 527).

In some other cases, it has been witnessed that EU-scepticism was replaced with Euroscepticism. For instance, it is plausible to argue that the PO and the PiS in Poland become Eurosceptic after the Polish referendum, since they started to raise substantive criticisms against the European Constitution. 'Nice or Die' became a popular motto spearheaded by PO after the referendum (Zuba, 2009 p. 332). After Polish EU membership, the PiS particularly reflected a 'soft [E]urosceptic' image as the party officials focused their criticisms on the EU's energy policy (Riishøj, 2007 p. 522).

As the nature of standard EU-scepticism indicates, domestic reaction to certain reform areas only challenged the EU's exchange legitimacy due to concerns over national interests and sovereignty. Nevertheless, the credible membership perspective enabled the EU to maintain its legitimacy over the candidate countries, which fulfilled the EU reforms despite domestic resistance from the opposition. Even in the case of Croatia, which showed a conditional EU-scepticism due to the Slovenian veto, the EU restored its practical legitimacy over the domestic elite by guaranteeing Croatian accession and proposing a joint solution to the bilateral conflict. However, in other cases concerning conditional and substantive EU-scepticism, the lack of membership perspective, along with the sense of being discriminated against by the EU plummeted both the EU's influence and its dispositional legitimacy in the eyes of the candidates such as Turkey and Macedonia, whose membership prospects are still slim. The EU's dwindling legitimacy resulted in the crystallisation of EU-scepticism in their domestic political elite.

Amongst the others, Turkey stands out as the only case in which all three forms of EU-scepticism have been observed. At the beginning of accession negotiations, the opposition parties showed standard EU-scepticism by criticizing certain EU-led reforms, while the government was mostly pro-EU. However, after the curtailment of the accession negotiations due to the bilateral issue with Cyprus, the Turkish government joined the opposition in questioning the fairness of the EU in terms of its additional conditionality towards Turkey's Cyprus policy. The Cyprus problem has not only precluded Turkey's advancement in the negotiations, but also contributed to the eroding Turkish trust in the EU's willingness for Turkish accession. Moreover, the introduction of new provisions for Turkey's membership along, with overt oppositional stances of certain European statesmen against Turkey, increased perception among the Turkish political elite that Turkey is not wanted by the EU. Therefore, while Turkey-EU relations both reached its zenith and hit the bottom during the last decade, Turkish political actors reflected all three forms of EU-scepticism in their EU policies. Such an intensive reaction was highlighted because Turkish political actors believe that the EU lost its pragmatic legitimacy in all three aspects. Unless the EU takes resolute steps to restore its overall pragmatic legitimacy over Turkey as it did for Croatia, Turkey's exceptional EU-scepticism will remain unabated, as will the stalemate over the bilateral relations.

References

Balkan Insight (2011) 'Macedonia Harshens Tone Towards EU and US Critics' 14 March. Available online: http://www.balkaninsight.com/en/article/macedonia-boosts-negative-remarks-towards-eu-and-usa (accessed 18 May 2012).

Batory, A. (2008) 'Euroscepticism in the Hungarian party system: Voices from the wilderness?'. In Taggart, P. and A. Szczerbiak (eds.), *Opposing Europe? The Comparative Party Politics of Euroscepticism*, Vol. 1, Oxford University Press, Oxford.

Erdoğan, R.T. (2011) Interview with Erdoğan. Vatan, 8 June: http://haber.gazetevatan.com/Erdogandan-ahmet-altana-yanit/382348/9/Siyaset (accessed 15 May 2012).

EUobserver (2008) 'Slovenia to block Croatia EU accession talks', 18 December. Available online: http://euobserver.com/15/27314 (accessed 17 May 2012).

Feldman, M. (2001) 'European Integration and the Discourse of National Identity in Estonia', *National Identities*, Vol. 3, No. 1, pp. 5-21.

Goldston, J.A. (2002) 'Roma Rights, Roma Wrongs', Foreign Affairs, Vol. 81, No. 2, pp. 146-162.

Gulmez, S. B. and Buhari-Gulmez, D. (2008) 'The EU conditionality in the Cyprus problem: Catalyzing Euro-scepticism in Turkey?' *Journal of Cyprus Studies*, Vol. 14, No. 1, pp. 1-38.

Gunes-Ayata, A. (2003) 'From Euro-scepticism to Turkey-scepticism: changing political attitudes on the European Union in Turkey'. *Journal of Southern Europe and the Balkans*, Vol. 5, No. 2, pp. 205-22.

Hanley, S. (2008) 'Embracing Europe, Opposing EU-rope? Party-based Euro-scepticism in the Czech Republic'. In Taggart, P. and A. Szczerbiak (eds.), *Opposing Europe? The Comparative Party Politics of Euroscepticism*, Vol. 1, Oxford University Press, Oxford.

Henderson, K. (2008a) 'The Slovak Republic: eurosceptics and phoney euro-philes'. In Taggart, P. and A. Szczerbiak (eds.), *Opposing Europe? The Comparative Party Politics of Euroscepticism*, Vol. 1, Oxford University Press, Oxford.

Henderson, K. (2008b) 'Exceptionalism or Convergence? Euroscepticism and Party Systems in Central and Eastern Europe', In Szczerbiak, A. and P. Taggart (eds.), *Opposing Europe? The Comparative Party Politics of Euroscepticism*, Vol. 2, Oxford University Press, Oxford.

Hooghe, L. and Marks, G. (2008) 'A Postfunctionalist Theory of European Integration: From Permissive Consensus to Constraining Dissensus'. *British Journal of Political Science*, Vol. 39, pp. 1-23.

Hürriyet (2004) 'Bu müzakerelerden tam üyelik çıkmaz' [These negotiations won't bring EU membership], 8 October. Available online: http://webarsiv.hurriyet.com.tr/2004/10/08/533744.asp (accessed 15 May 2012).

Hürriyet (2005) Baykal: Türkiye'nin AB üyeliği ikinci sınıf olacak [Baykal: Turkey's EU membership will be a second-class membership]. 18 October: http://hurarsiv.Hürriyet.com.tr/goster/ShowNew.aspx?id=3401627 (accessed 15 May 2012).

Hürriyet (2011) Erzurum'da AB atışması [Quarrel over the EU in Erzurum]. 7 January: http://www.Hürriyet.com.tr/gundem/16709762.asp?gid=373 (accessed 15 May 2012).

Ivanov, K. (2008) 'Legitimate Conditionality? The European Union and Nuclear Power Safety in Central and Eastern Europe', *International Politics*, Vol. 45, pp. 146-167.

Kopecky, P. and C. Mudde (2002) 'The Two Sides of Euroscepticism: Party Positions on European Integration in East Central Europe'. *European Union Politics*, Vol. 3, No. 3, 297-326.

Krasovec, A. and S.K. Lipicer (2008) 'Euroscepticism and Slovenian political parties: A case of weak party-based Euroscepticism'. In Taggart, P. and A. Szczerbiak (eds.), *Opposing Europe? The Comparative Party Politics of Euroscepticism*, Vol. 1, Oxford University Press, Oxford.

Marks, G., L. Hooghe, M. Nelson and E. Edwards (2006) 'Party Competition and European Integration in the East and West: Different Structure, Same Causality', *Comparative Political Studies*, Vol. 39, No. 2.

Marusic, S.J. (2011) 'Macedonia Leader Renews Attacks on EU Critics', *Balkan Insight*, 18 October. Available online: http://www.balkaninsight.com/en/article/macedonian-pm-renews-criticism-of-brussels.

Mikkel, E. and A. Kasekamp (2008) 'Emerging party-based euroscepticism in Estonia'. In Taggart, P. and A. Szczerbiak (eds.), *Opposing Europe? The Comparative Party Politics of Euroscepticism*, Vol. 1, Oxford University Press, Oxford.

Morris, H.M. (2004) 'President, Party and Nationality Policy in Latvia, 1991-1999', *Europe-Asia Studies*, Vol. 56, No. 4, pp. 543-569.

Mudde, C. (2011) 'Sussex v. North Carolina: The Comparative Study of Party-Based Euroskepticism', Sussex European Institute Working Paper, No. 121.

Riishøj, S. (2007) 'Europeanization and Euroscepticism: Experiences from Poland and the Czech Republic', *Nationalities Papers*, Vol. 35, No. 3, pp. 502-535.

Schimmelfennig, F. (2008) 'EU political accession conditionality after the 2004 enlargement: consistency and effectiveness', *Journal of European Public Policy*, Vol. 15, No. 6.

Suchman, M.C. (1995) 'Managing Legitimacy: Strategic and Institutional Approaches', *Academy of Management Review*, Vol. 20, No. 3.

Szczerbiak A. and P. Taggart (2002) 'The Party Politics of Euroscepticism in EU Member and Candidate States'. SEI Working Paper No. 51.

Szczerbiak A. and P. Taggart (2004) 'Contemporary Euroscepticism in the party systems of the European Union candidate states of Central and Eastern Europe'. *European Journal of Political Research.* Vol. 43, No. 1, pp. 1-27.

Szczerbiak, A. (2008) 'Opposing Europe or Problematizing Europe? Euroscepticism and 'Eurorealism' in the Polish Party System'. In Taggart, P. and A. Szczerbiak (eds.), *Opposing Europe? The Comparative Party Politics of Euroscepticism*, Vol. 1, Oxford University Press, Oxford.

Szczerbiak, A. and P. Taggart (2008a) 'Introduction: Researching Euroscepticism in European Party Systems: A Comparative and Theoretical Research Agenda'. In Szczerbiak, A. and P. Taggart (eds.), *Opposing Europe? The Comparative Party Politics of Euroscepticism*, Vol. 2, Oxford University Press, Oxford.

Szczerbiak, A. and P. Taggart (2008b) 'Theorizing Party-Based Euroscepticism: Problems of Definition, Measurement, and Causality'. In Szczerbiak, A. and P. Taggart (eds.), *Opposing Europe? The Comparative Party Politics of Euroscepticism*, Vol. 2, Oxford University Press, Oxford.

Taggart, P. (1998) 'A touchstone of dissent: Euroscepticism in contemporary Western European party systems'. *European Journal of Political Research*, Vol. 33, pp. 363-88.

Tesser, L.M. (2004) 'East-Central Europe's new security concern: foreign land ownership', *Communist and Post-Communist Studies*, Vol. 37, pp. 213-239.

Vatan (2011) Erdoğan'dan çok sert mesajlar'[Harsh criticisms by Erdoğan]. 7 January: http://haber.gazetevatan.com/Erdoğandan-cok-sert-mesajlar/351458/9/Siyaset (accessed 15 May 2012).

Vetik, R., G. Nimmerfelft and M. Taru (2006) 'Reactive identity versus EU integration'. *Journal of Common Market Studies*, Vol. 44, No. 5, pp. 1079-102.

Wiener, A. and T. Wobbe (2002) 'Norm Resonance in Global Governance – Contested Norms in the Process of EU Enlargement', Paper prepared for presentation at the Annual Meeting of the International Studies Association, New Orleans, 24-27 March.

Zorić, K. (2008) 'ZERP ili EU – recept za širenje "euroskepticizma' [ZERP or the EU – a recipe for the spread of "euro-skepticism"]. Nacional, 2 March: http://www.nacional.hr/clanak/43248/zerp-ili-eu-recept-za-sirenje-euroskepticizma.

Zuba, K. (2009) 'Through the Looking Glass: The Attitudes of Polish Political Parties towards the EU before and after Accession', *Perspectives on European Politics and Society*, Vol. 10, No. 3, pp. 326-349.

Ideological Families and Party Attitudes toward the EU in Serbia and Croatia

Marko STOJIĆ

Introduction

The Council of the EU reaffirmed in December 2011 its unequivocal commitment to the European prospect of the Western Balkans. It particularly welcomed the successful completion of the accession negotiations with Croatia, which brought a new momentum to the European integration of this region. However, some of the key parliamentary political parties in Serbia have consistently expressed strong opposition to further integration into the EU, while Croatian party-based Euroscepticism, although less politically relevant, was rather vocal at the January 2012 referendum on Croatian accession into the European Union. On the other side, a large majority of parties in both countries have demonstrated a broad, although often qualified, pro-EU orientation.

The purpose of this chapter is to examine party ideologies, conceptualised through the form of ideological families, as one of the key factors identified in the comparative literature that may impact party stances on the EU. The study aims to answer whether it is possible to predict a party's attitude toward the EU on the basis of its ideological family. It also intends to offer more general arguments and contribute to the debate about the importance of ideology as a factor that may explain how parties respond to European integration by examining the two former Yugoslav countries.

The chapter argues that ideology is an important explanatory variable that may determine party stances on the EU, although not *per se*. Its effect is not straightforward and depends on a number of other factors related to a party's strategic and pragmatic considerations as well as its intrinsic characteristics, namely whether it is more goal-oriented or office-seeking. The study also finds that adherence to an ideological family may create a certain predisposition for parties to have particular attitudes towards the EU, with social democrats being more consistently pro-European than conservative, demo-Christian and agrarian families. However, belonging to a particular ideological family does not seem to be an indicator or a predictor of a party's stance, given that parties from the same family expressed rather opposing positions on this issue, most evident in the case of the conservatives. The analysis also shows that two party families are the outliers, namely the liberal and radical right, since they uniformly and consistently supported and opposed the EU, respectively, throughout the analysed period.

The main data sources for this qualitative analysis are the parties' key programmatic documents published since 2000 as well as interviews conducted with senior party officials. The chapter first reviews the literature on ideology as an explanatory factor. The second section briefly discusses the methodological issues as well as the main features of parties' ideologies in Serbia and Croatia. The study then examines in greater detail the individual ideological families and their attitudes towards the EU. The final conceptual and empirical findings are summarised in the conclusion.

Ideology and Party Attitudes toward the EU in the Comparative Literature

Ideology as an explaining variable has received considerable attention in the literature, but with varying opinions among scholars on how and to what extent it shapes party positions on Europe. As Batory (2002) argued, it is perhaps most controversial among the driving forces addressed by the comparative literature, since the long-term impact of ideological colouring, party histories and identities does not easily transfer across political systems.

This analysis focuses on the literature that looked at the nature of a relation between ideological families and party stances on Europe, and it identifies two broad camps. One group of authors specifically argued that stances on Europe are not directly related to parties' general ideologies, given that "the EU can in principle engender allegiance or hostility from any ideological perspective" (Gaffney, 1996, p. 19). Taggart (1998) asserted that placing parties in party families does not allow us to predict with any certainty their position on the EU, since different party families adopt different positions in different countries. However, Taggart also pointed out that some types of parties seem to be predisposed towards opposition (new politics and extreme left parties), while others towards support (social democrats, Christian democrats and liberals), but that ideology, although an important component, alone does not predict Euroscepticism.

Szczerbiak and Taggart (2001, p. 21) also argued that Euroscepticism in Central and Eastern European states draws from a range of party families and that "attempting to lever the European issue into a left-right framework is at least difficult and possibly even fruitless". In a later study, they further found that there is no straightforward relationship between general party ideology and stances on Europe, since “it is not possible to ‘read off’ a party’s position from whatever ideological family it belongs to” (Szczerbiak and Taggart, 2008, p. 257). Sitter (2001) similarly claimed that Euroscepticism emerges as a phenomenon potentially linked to a range of ideologies and noted that party-based Euroscepticism is mainly driven by party strategy. Batory (2002) also emphasised that ideology does not determine party positions as far as a clear-cut choice between support and outright rejection of EU membership is concerned.

On the other side, Marks, Wilson and Ray (2002) argued that the party family is a stronger causal factor than strategic competition, national location, participation in government or the position of a party’s supporters. They also demonstrated that the party families most favourably oriented towards the EU are the liberal and Christian democratic parties, followed by the social democrats and regionalists. The agrarian, conservative and green party families are less supportive, while the protestant, extreme right and extreme left/communist families are the most Eurosceptic. These authors hence claimed that parties assimilate and exploit European issues within existing ideologies, which are the result of key social cleavages that give rise to party families. Similarly, Hooghe, Marks and Wilson (2002) found that extreme left and right parties, and to a lesser extent the green parties, share Euroscepticism, while parties in the middle – including most social democratic, Christian democratic, liberal and conservative parties – are generally much more supportive of European integration. Kopecký and Mudde (2002) made the case that ideology determines a party’s support for the general ideas that underlie the EU, and argued that all parties belonging to one party family have the same general position on Europe. They found evidence for such a claim for all but the agrarian party family in the Central and Eastern European states, and also argued that all social democrats and liberals were Europhiles, while all extreme right and unreformed or hard-line communist parties were Europhobes.

This analysis finds that, although ideology is an important factor that shaped stances of some political parties across both countries, belonging to a certain party family does not seem to be an indicator of their positions on Europe. The study does, however, find that extreme right parties were all Eurosceptic, while the liberals were strongly pro-European, as well as that there is a tendency of some families to be more pro-European (social democrats), while others have more complex and changing positions on Europe (conservatives, Christian democrats).

Ideology of Serbian and Croatian Political Parties

The following section briefly addresses the methodological issues, specifically how to examine ideology of Serbian and Croatian parties as well as their multifaceted attitudes towards the EU. It also discusses the main features of parties' ideologies across both countries.

The notion of party ideology is generally not easy to define. Gaffney (1996) wondered whether it is possible to identify the true underlying organising principle of political parties, while Mair and Mudde (1998) argued that it is difficult to specify party ideology with any precision. Identifying party ideology is particularly difficult in the context of Serbian and Croatian party politics, given that these parties were founded relatively recently and did not have a long history of firmly established fundamental ideological principles. The key methodological issue is what indicators to use in order to identify party ideologies, given their rather vague and unsettled nature. Nevertheless, this study, drawing on the comparative literature, conceptualises party ideology as a system of fundamental ideas and values that underpin all segments of party policies, and uses three indicators to identify it: party origins and genesis, key party policies and stances, and transnational links (Mair and Mudde, 1998).

Furthermore, there are two widely used concepts in the comparative literature that conceptualise party ideologies: party family classification (von Beyme, 1985) and a model of dominant patterns of party competition, whereby authors classify parties by locating them on the dominant axes of party competition (Batory, 2002; Siaroff, 2000). In order to conduct a cross-country analysis of party ideologies and stances on Europe in Serbia and Croatia, this chapter employs a classification into party families. This approach seems to be more suitable for a comparative analysis of party ideologies, particularly given a tendency of some core parties in both countries to converge with the Western concept of party families, which has served as the model for their ideological reinventions since 2000. Nevertheless, in applying this concept, one needs to be aware that traditional social and political groupings based on classical political cleavages – which are the key to this conceptualisation – were distorted by growing nationalism and a war at the time these parties emerged, and, therefore, significantly influenced their ideological profiles. As a result, classification into party families is largely conditional in these countries and rather represents an attempt to synthesise prevailing parties' fundamental values and identities given their slow political profiling.

This model specifically makes a distinction between nine party families: liberal or radical, conservative, socialist or social democratic, communist, Christian democratic, agrarian or centre, regional or ethnic, ecological or new left, and right-wing extremist (von Beyme, 1985). The chapter, however, identifies five party families in Croatia – socialist/social democrat, Christian democrat, agrarian, liberal and radical right-wing – while there was a conservative, but no Christian democrat or agrarian family in Serbia (Table 1). This was primarily a consequence of the fact that the dominant Orthodox Christian church in Serbia had no tradition of political organisation in the same manner as Catholic and Protestant churches. Additionally, farmers were not a politically articulate social group in Serbia, which, as a result, did not give rise to the traditional rural-urban conflict and development of agrarian parties. Ecological or new left parties based on post-materialist values are neither identified, since these were not Western-style, post-industrial societies. Finally, the non-existence of communist parties may be explained by a deeply compromised left in Serbia, given that the left-wing parties were implementing far right, nationalist policies throughout the 1990s (Pavlović, 2011).

With regard to parties' ideologies, this study primarily finds that a large number of core Serbian and Croatian parties were not fully ideologically rooted and some of them have fundamentally shifted ideology since the early 1990s. That was particularly the case with a highly fragmented and unsettled party scene in Serbia, where parties tended to change key policies, including their fundamental principles, in a search for the most suitable and politically cost-effective ideological position. The Democratic Party in Serbia, for example, was founded as a centre-right and liberal party, whose socio-economic programme was a consistent concept of a liberal market economy, and it was the only relevant party that explicitly stood in favour of capitalism (Vukomanović, 2007). However, after coming to power in 2000, this party started shifting its ideology, formally adopted social democratic principles and became a member of the Party of European Socialists. This move was pushed personally by the then-party president, Zoran Djindjić, who ceased contact with the centre-right parties from the European People's Party and aimed at getting closer to social democratic parties that at that time had a majority in the European parliament (Pack, interview, 2011).[1] On the other side, the Socialist Party of Serbia, a successor of the Serbian Communist Party, was the left-centre national populist party (Siaroff, 2000) throughout the 1990s. This party also expressed an ideological suspicion towards private property and perceived privatisation of public properties as general extortion (Vukomanović, 2007). However,

---

1 Doris Pack, MEP, EPP, member of the EP Delegation for relations with Albania, Bosnia and Herzegovina, Serbia, Montenegro and Kosovo. Interview, July 2011.

it has undergone a substantial ideological transformation and adopted a formula of 'the plural left' modelled on the French Socialist Party (Vukomanović, interview, 2011)[2] in an effort to reinvent itself as a modern European social democratic party since the mid-2000s, as a result of a strategically motivated decision from the new party leadership.

Similarly, the Serbian Progressive Party was founded by a group of moderate members that broke away from the radical right Serbian Radical Party in 2008. This party clearly abandoned the nationalist ideology of a 'Great Serbia' in order to present itself as a modern, conservative, pro-European party that aimed to become a member of the European People's Party. Senior party official Marko Djurić (interview, 2011)[3] thus argued that the Serbian Progressive Party was a centre-right party, although "ideology was not its priority". This party, therefore, may be conditionally characterised as a conservative party whose ideological position has not been fully developed. Finally, the Croatian Democratic Union was considered rather nationalist and populist right-wing in the 1990s (Šedo, 2010), before it underwent an ideological re-orientation in the early 2000s due to strategic electoral concerns. The party may be therefore categorised as a Christian democratic, traditionalist and conservative party (PEE, 2012) that expressed a pronounced concern for national issues.

On the other side, in order to categorise parties' stances on Europe, the study employs the concepts of "hard" and "soft" Euroscepticism developed by Szczerbiak and Taggart (2008). The first term implies "a principled opposition to the EU and European integration and therefore can be seen in parties who think that their countries should withdraw from membership, or whose policies towards the EU are tantamount to being opposed to the whole project of European integration as it is currently conceived". The second terms refers to a party position "where there is not a principled objection to the European integration or EU membership, but where concerns on one (or a number) of policy areas leads to the expression of qualified oppositions to the EU, or where there is a sense that 'national interest' is currently at odds with the EU trajectory" (Szczerbiak and Taggart, 2008, p. 2). These authors later argued that attitudes towards a country's membership of the EU should not be seen as a key variable determining a party's underlying stances on the EU (Szczerbiak and Taggart, 2008). However, given that parties

2 Dijana Vukomanović, vice president of the Socialist Party of Serbia. Interview, March 2011.

3 Marko Djurić, member of the Executive Committee of the Serbian Progressive Party. Interview, March 2011.

in Serbia and Croatia almost exclusively perceived the EU through the prisms of these countries' EU membership, the study employs these authors' initial concepts. Moreover, it classifies pro-European parties as hard and soft pro-European based on the level and the nature of support for EU membership and (indirectly) the EU – that is, to what extent these parties' affirmative stances are principled and whether they are limited by positions on other related issues (such as the status of Kosovo, national identity issues or the cooperation with the International Criminal Tribunal for the former Yugoslavia [ICTY]).

Party Ideology and Attitudes toward the EU in Serbia and Croatia

The following section examines the attitudes toward the EU of individual political parties in both countries grouped into party families (Table 1). It seeks to establish whether there is a link between their ideology and position on Europe, and whether parties belonging to the same party family express the same or similar attitudes towards the EU.

Table 1: Party families and attitudes of Serbian and Croatian political parties toward the EU

Serbian parties	Croatian parties	Attitudes toward the EU/ EU membership	Number of MPs	
			Dec. 2011	Nov. 2012
1. Socialist/social democratic				
Democratic Party (strong liberal legacy)		Hard pro-European	64	51
Socialist Party of Serbia (left-centre national populist until the mid-2000s)		Hard/soft Eurosceptic until 2008 Soft pro-European since 2008	11	24
	Social Democratic Party	Hard pro-European	53	60
2. Conservative				
Democratic Party of Serbia (national conservatism)		Soft pro-European until 2008 Soft Eurosceptic since 2008	21	21

New Serbia (national conservatism)		Soft pro-European until 2008 Soft Eurosceptic 2008-2010 Soft pro-European since 2010	9	8
Serbian Progressive Party (weakly ideologically profiled)		Soft pro-European	21	64
3. Christian democratic				
	Croatian Democratic Union (nationalist populist until the early 2000s)	Hard/soft Eurosceptic until the early 2000s Soft pro-European since the early 2000s	65	45
4. Agrarian				
	Croatian Peasants' Party	Soft pro-European	6	1
5. Liberal				
G17 Plus		Hard pro-European	24	15[4]
Liberal Democratic Party		Hard pro-European	12	14
	Croatian Peoples' Party – Liberal Democrats (social liberalism)	Hard pro-European	5	14
6. Radical right				
Serbian Radical Party		Hard Eurosceptic	57	0
	Croatian Party of Rights	Hard Eurosceptic	1	0

Source: party programmes, interviews with party officials, Serbian Parliament (2012) and Croatian Parliament (2012).

Socialists/Social Democrats and the EU

There were three socialist/social democratic parties in Serbia and Croatia, and all of them expressed pro-European orientations and sup-

4 In the coalition United Regions of Serbia with seven regional parties.

ported the EU accession of their countries. That has always been a characteristic of the Democratic Party in Serbia and the Social Democratic Party in Croatia, while the Socialist Party of Serbia fundamentally changed its position and started advocating Serbian EU integration in 2008.

The European credentials of the Democratic Party, unlike its social democratic orientation, have never been contested, since the party has consistently been pro-European. The party programme (DS, 2009) stated that its goal was Serbian accession into the EU. The Democrats argued that they wanted "European structures and standards to become a part of Serbian society, and Serbia to become an equal member state of the EU" (DS, 2009, p. 23). Its public policies may also be interpreted as strongly pro-European. Even in the period after 2008, when a majority of EU member states recognised Kosovo as an independent state and consequently the Serbian public expressed a high level of disillusionment with the country's EU integration, this party promoted the idea of Europe and pleaded for Serbian EU accession. Given this party's origins and genesis as well as its key policies and stances, the party orientation toward the EU was an essential element of its identity. An initial pro-European position unambiguously adopted by the party founders in the early 1990s has remained a constant, fundamental feature of this party, regardless of its strategic ideological reinventions.

Similarly, the Social Democratic Party of Croatia has constantly been pro-European. In its 2003 election manifesto, the party declared that it would meet all demands during the Croatian EU accession and that there should be no hesitation and reservations about this process (SDP, 2003). The 2011 election programme (SDP, 2011) similarly argued that the party's policies have been based on the traditions of a social Europe as the fundamental value of the EU. It also stated that the Social Democratic Party and its coalition partners are "originally pro-European parties" and that their "coalition is Euro-optimistic today[,] as it was yesterday and as it will be tomorrow" (SDP, 2011). This was the party that most consistently expressed social democratic and pro-European principles, given that 'social democracy was its historical choice' (SDP, 2004). This party's positive attitude towards the EU was therefore primarily grounded in its social democratic identity, which provided a framework through which this party perceived itself and determined its key policies.

On the other side, the Socialist Party of Serbia underwent a fundamental transformation since 2000. Throughout the 1990s, it was a ruling party characterised by nationalism, anti-globalism and anti-Westernism. The party also expressed a strongly critical stance on the EU, although it did not articulate outright rejection of Serbian EU membership. It did not endorse a 2004 parliamentary resolution on Serbian accession into the EU, even though it formulated the accession of Serbia into the EU as a political goal at the 2003 congress. The key change came after the death of its authoritarian leader, Slobodan Milošević, in 2006, when Ivica Dačić was elected as the new party president. As a result, the party embarked on a transformation in an effort to legitimise itself as a modern social democratic party. The transformation reached a climax in 2008, when the Socialists helped to form a pro-European government with former political enemies of the Serbian Democratic Opposition. Its 2010 programme also demonstrated a radical break with the party's troublesome past and showed the new pro-European orientation of the Socialists. The party specifically argued that "Serbia should give a contribution to building a common European home, from the Atlantic to the Urals", and therefore it "gives full support and contribution to the negotiations on Serbian EU membership" (SPS, 2010).

Social democratic parties appeared to have been more consistently pro-European than the right-wing parties, given that both the Democratic Party and the Social Democratic Party were essentially and ideologically pro-European parties. The Social Democratic Party was a fully ideologically profiled party that perceived the EU in the context of its social democratic identity. The Democratic Party, however, formed its position to a much lesser extent as a result of its adherence to social democratic principles, given that the party itself was not fully profiled as social democratic. On the other side, the ideological transformation of the Socialist Party of Serbia was primarily the result of pragmatic decisions of a new party leadership that realised the party needed to adopt a new policy orientation if it were to politically survive, particularly in relation to Serbian EU accession. The case of this party thus shows the strong power that the EU exerts on the political landscape of the Western Balkan countries and how the process of EU accession creates strong incentives for parties to change and adapt to 'the new reality'.

In conclusion, although all social democratic parties were pro-European after 2008, the position of the Socialist Party of Serbia was primarily strategically driven, while the attitude of the Democratic Party was based on a rather general, not specifically social democratic, positive ideological perception of the EU. It seems, therefore, that there was no direct link between this ideological family and party attitudes toward the EU, except in the case of the Social Democratic Party. However, the newly formed position of the Socialist Party of Serbia also demonstrates that adherence to the principles of this family party ruled out the possibility that parties have a distinct (hard) Eurosceptic outlook.

Conservatives and the EU

Conservatives, unlike social democrats, expressed a variety of stances on the EU, spanning the strong Euroscepticism of the Democratic Party of Serbia, the conflicting and changeable stances of New Serbia, and the pro-European position of the Serbian Progressive Party.

The most Eurosceptic conservative party was the Democratic Party of Serbia. This party has always expressed a complex attitude towards the EU. On one side, it demonstrated mistrust of the West and particularly contested the legitimacy and cooperation with the ICTY, which was a key precondition for Serbian EU accession (Goati, 2009). On the other side, it in principle supported Serbian EU accession and significantly contributed to the negotiations on the Stabilisation and Association Agreement with the EU. However, recognition of Kosovo's independence by a large majority of EU member states fundamentally affected the party position. After 2008, this party argued for stopping further EU integration until the EU explicitly recognises the international borders of Serbia. In the run-up to the 2012 elections, it further hardened its position and declared support for political and military neutrality as its key programmatic principle.

This party's position on Serbian EU integration may be thus interpreted as a consequence of its traditional, conservative and national ideological conviction that territorial integrity and sovereignty are prime European values. At the same time, the Democratic Party of Serbia was not a party with an anti-European ideology. It advocated "a new national policy that will have as its main objectives Serbia itself, but based on the best European values and standards that are in the interest of the country" (DSS, 2010). The key factor that shaped the party's position was substantially idiosyncratic – that is, the policy of the EU toward Kosovo. The party positioned itself as an authoritative interpreter of the fundamental national principles, and its negative attitudes towards Serbian EU membership were therefore grounded in its conservative and traditionalist, not anti-European, identity and ideology.

On the other side, the Serbian Progressive Party has also undergone a fundamental transformation regarding attitudes towards Serbian EU membership. Specifically, the leaders of this party had expressed opposition to Serbian EU integration for almost 20 years before they broke away from the Serbian Radical Party in 2008. The decision to take a radically new position and support Serbian EU membership as long as this does not entail the recognition of Kosovo as an independent state was highly strategic. It rests upon the fact that the vast majority of voters were in favour of Serbian EU membership and that, without reorienting itself, the party could not win the election. The party leader,

Tomislav Nikolić, openly argued that "the Radicals have never had a desire to come to power and that the Serbian Progressive Party is something else. We are a pro-European party. If we stand against the EU, we will never be able to win the elections in Serbia" (SNS, 2011). This was confirmed in the 2012 elections, when this party got the highest number of votes. The party aimed to present itself as a modern, conservative and centre-right party, although it is difficult to reliably establish its ideological profile. As a consequence, the party position on the EU, characterised as soft pro-European, seems to be not directly linked to its still-emerging ideology. It was, rather, a result of repeated attempts to come to power advocating nationalism and anti-Europeanism as well as the relatively advanced level of Serbian integration to the EU, which created strong incentives for the party leadership to become pro-European.

Finally, the New Serbia programme argued that "Serbia belongs to the United Europe", and that it supported "the transformation of the EU from commercial to political society" (NS, 2010, p. 3). The party, however, had rather different politics after 2008. It firmly opposed the signing of the Stabilisation and Association Agreement and accused the government of betraying national interests (NS, 2010). Nevertheless, it again shifted attitudes in 2010, abandoned its coalition with the Democratic Party of Serbia and returned to its soft pro-European, pre-2008 policy due to a fear of political marginalisation. The party vice president, Dubravka Filipovski (interview, 2011),[5] confirmed that voters' support had been in steady decline, and given that Kosovo was not a priority issue for voters, the party decided to "follow what the citizens think" and return to its original pro-European principles.

The case of the Serbian conservative parties thus demonstrates that this ideological family may adopt (and change) a wide range of attitudes towards the EU. The politics of the Serbian Progressive Party and New Serbia represent clear examples of pragmatic and strategic party positioning regarding the EU, devoid of any deep conservative ideological belief in the principles that underpin the process of European integration. On the other side, as a pronounced conservative and value-based party, the Democratic Party of Serbia expressed ideologically driven Euroscepticism. Therefore, the study does not identify the positive correlation between this ideological family and these parties' responses to the EU. What it did find was the tendency of conservative parties to be more sceptical towards the EU and to have difficulties expressing a definite stance on this issue. However, it was the intrinsic characteristics of individual conservative parties – that is, if they are more value-based

5 Dubravka Filipovski, vice president and spokeswoman of New Serbia. Interview, March 2011.

or office-seeking – as well as the specific context of domestic party politics and the nature of the country's relation with the EU that may have decisively shaped their attitudes towards the EU.

Christian Democrats and Agrarians and the EU

Christian democratic and agrarian families were each represented by one relevant party in Croatia: the Croatian Democratic Union and the Croatian Peasants' Party, respectively.

Throughout the 1990s, the Croatian Democratic Union had a negative stance on EU policy towards the Western Balkans, as well as on the conditions for Croatia's accession to the EU, primarily cooperation with the ICTY (Jović, 2006). Following an electoral defeat and the death of its founder and autocratic president, Franjo Tudjman, Ivo Sanader became a moderate leader that declared accession to the EU as party's main goal. The party, therefore, has expressed a pro-European orientation since the early 2000s, although not as strongly and unambiguously as Croatian social democratic and liberal parties, which was expected given what drove the party's reinvention. Specifically, senior party official Marija Pejčinović Burić (interview, 2011)[6] pointed out that the party's transformation was a deeply pragmatic and strategic decision made by a party leadership that realised "the policy of isolation and nationalism had no future". This party was therefore another example of strategic, rather than ideological, positioning regarding the EU as a result of electoral incentives in the run-up to the 2003 parliamentary election. At the same time, the party underwent an ideological transformation from a nationalist and populist (Šedo, 2010) to a pro-European, Christian democratic party, which demonstrates how parties may strategically choose ideology in order to fit into the European political mainstream and legitimise in the eyes of the West.

However, the party successfully negotiated the terms for Croatian EU membership in 2011, and its pro-European orientation has not been widely questioned, despite occasionally hardened nationalist rhetoric during the 2007 and 2011 election campaigns. It also appears that over the years the party has become somewhat an ideological supporter of the demo-Christian concept of Europe and Croatian membership of the EU, largely under the influence of members of the European People's Party. The Croatian Democratic Union was thus committed to the "spiritual and cultural heritage of the Croatian people, as part of a common European civilisation and cultural heritage" (HDZ, 2002). Nevertheless, it

6 Marija Pejcinović Burić, MP, Croatian Democratic Union, chair of the Joint Parliamentary Committee EU-Croatia. Interview, May 2011.

was difficult to assess to what extent European demo-Christian values permeated all segments of this conservative and traditional party, given its autocratic and illiberal legacy.

The agrarian Croatian Peasants' Party similarly stood for "a principle of Christian solidarity and traditional, Croatian values", including preservation of the national identity and culture (HSS, 2009). It also expressed sceptic attitudes towards the common agricultural policy of the EU, as well as concerns for the position of the Croatian agricultural and fishing industry after the country enters the EU. Nevertheless, the party's vice president, Marijana Petir (interview, 2011),[7] argued that this party supported joining the EU, but also noticed that Croatia "uncritically accepted everything that the EU demanded". Thus, as a traditionalist and conservative party focused on the protection of national identity, traditional family and peasants' rights (Petir, interview, 2011), it expressed concerns about the EU as a consequence of its ideological profile, although it in principle never objected to Croatian EU accession.

In summary, the Croatian Democratic Union shared the characteristics of similar conservative parties in Serbia (the Serbian Progressive Party, New Serbia) that have also adopted strategic attitudes towards the EU. As a result, these parties in both countries tended to perceive EU membership largely positively, but also instrumentally and pragmatically. On the other side, though, the position of the Democratic Party of Serbia, the Croatian Peasants' Party and, to a lesser extent, the Croatian Democratic Union after 2002 may point to the importance of ideological motivation for these parties' responses to the EU. However, this led to fully opposing views on this issue, with the Democratic Party of Serbia being strongly Eurosceptic, and Croatian parties being softly pro-European. As a result, the ideological affiliations to these families, which share a number of similar characteristics, appear not to predispose party attitudes towards the EU, even though there was a tendency for demo-Christians and agrarians to express pronounced concerns for national issues and therefore take an affirmative but cautious approach to the EU.

Liberals and the EU

There were three relevant liberal parties in these countries: the G17 Plus, the Liberal Democratic Party and the Croatian Peoples' Party. All have consistently been the strongest advocates of European integration.

7 Marijana Petir, MP, vice president of the Croatian Peasants' Party. Interview, May 2011.

The G17 Plus was a firm supporter of Serbian EU integration. In its programme, the party specified that historically, culturally and economically, Serbia is already a part of Europe, so the party's main goal is to achieve EU membership as soon as possible (G17 Plus, 2004). The mission of the G17 Plus was the "creation of [an] economically strong and democratically stable Serbia that will become a leader in the Balkans, ready to accept European standards and able to preserve and protect the best from its own traditions and culture" (G17 Plus, 2004, p. 2). The Liberal Democratic Party was also a vocal proponent of European integration among Serbian political parties. Although in opposition throughout the analysed period, this party supported legislative proposals of the government in the parliament aimed at speeding up European integration of the country. The Croatian Peoples' Party (HNS, 2011) similarly proclaimed in its programme that accession to the EU as soon as possible was the most important national interest, which should be an absolute priority of Croatian foreign policy, and argued that it was strongly and unreservedly committed to fulfilling all the criteria. In conclusion, unlike other families, these parties' liberal ideology can be seen as a factor that predisposes them to adopting a hard pro-EU orientation and makes them consistently the most pro-European ideological family in these two countries.

Radical Right Parties and the EU

Until the Croatian 2011 and Serbian 2012 parliamentary elections, there were two relevant radical right parties in these countries, namely the Serbian Radical Party and the Croatian Party of Rights, which were also the most relevant hard Eurosceptic parties.

The Serbian Radical Party was the strongest opponent of Serbian EU integration and cooperation with Western countries, as well as a proponent of close relations with the Russian Federation. The party fully crystallised its position – an absolute and unconditional opposition to Serbian EU integration – in 2008 after a declaration of Kosovo independence was sponsored by key EU member states. The party position was deeply grounded in the pronounced ideology of nationalism and anti-Westernism. It expressed hostility, a deep-seated animosity, and sometimes even hatred towards the EU and the West in general. As a radical right and nationalist party, whose ideology of a 'Great Serbia' was by no means compatible with the liberal values of modern Europe, the Serbian Radical Party was a natural ideological opponent of Serbian EU membership. The party position may have been seen as a reflection of traditionally anti-European sentiments, which have been a feature of a considerable part of Serbian society and politics since the early 2000s.

On the other side, the Croatian Party of Rights demonstrated anti-EU attitudes based on the ideology of 'anti-Yugoslavism' rather than anti-Westernism. It proclaimed as one of its key principles that, given the experience of the Yugoslav federation, any form of state union with other countries without the consent of the Croatian people was unacceptable (HSP, 2012). This party argued that Croatian people had a fundamental right to a fully sovereign and independent state (HSP, 2012). Therefore, the Croatian Party of Rights, "in accordance with the Croats' nine century striving for independence", believed that accession to any form of state union that would endanger its sovereignty is unsupportable (HSP, 2010). Although in the mid-2000s this party moderated its rhetoric on the EU, in early 2011, "when the negative results of the accession negotiations had become public", it adopted the policy of an outright opposition to Croatian EU membership and called on citizens to vote against it at a referendum on EU accession (Srb, interview, 2011).[8] The case of these two parties thus demonstrates that hard Euroscepticism was exclusively expressed by radical right, nationalist parties, as well as that it was largely ideologically driven, particularly in the case of the Serbian Radical Party. Therefore, similar to the liberal family, it appears that there was a correlation between the radical right family and its party positions on Europe.

Conclusion

The purpose of this chapter was to examine whether ideologies of Serbian and Croatian parties impacted their attitudes toward the EU, and whether it is possible to predict party responses to Europe on the basis of its affiliation to an ideological family. Table 2 summarises party stances on the EU and their ideological positions. It indicates that the liberal parties stood out as unreserved supporters of EU membership of these countries, while the radical right parties expressed outright opposition. Between the two opposing poles are the socialist/social democratic parties, which expressed more consistent pro-European orientations than the conservative, Christian democratic and agrarian parties. The table, however, also shows that some parties from the same family expressed different positions on Europe – such as the conservative family, which adopted a wide range of attitudes, spanning from strong rejection (the Democratic Party of Serbia) to support for Serbian EU membership and indirectly the EU (the Serbian Progressive Party, New Serbia).

What general conclusions can be drawn about ideological families and party stances on Europe based on the analysis of Serbian and Croa-

[8] Daniel Srb, MP, president of the Croatian Party of Rights. Interview, May 2011.

tian cases? First, ideology seems to be an important explanatory variable that may determine and change party stances on the EU, although not per se, given that its effect is not straightforward and depends on a number of other factors. These are primarily each party's strategic and pragmatic considerations related to the logic of domestic political contestation, maximising chances of coming to power or getting legitimisation in the eyes of the West. Also, whether a party develops ideologically driven stances on the EU seems to depend on its intrinsic characteristics, namely whether it is more goal-oriented or office-seeking, with the former adopting firmer, value-based policies, and the latter acting pragmatically and combining different ideological principles and practical policies (including those on Europe) in order to come to power.

Party ideology may therefore provide a framework through which parties determine key attitudes and policies, as it was the case with the most consistent supporters of EU integration, the Social Democratic Party and Croatian Peoples' Party in Croatia, and the Liberal Democratic Party and G17 Plus in Serbia, as well as a traditional opponent, the Serbian Radical Party. It may be reasonably assumed that their ideological profiles have become rooted since the 1990s, given that the social democratic, liberal or radical right-wing identity of these parties, as well as stances on the EU, have not changed since they were founded. In addition, it seems that party ideology and the peculiar context of Serbian EU integration can also induce changes in party stances, as shown in the transformation of the Democratic Party of Serbia from a soft pro-European to substantially Eurosceptic party.

Conversely, other parties tended to strategically change ideological profiles (the Democratic Party, the Socialist Party of Serbia), pragmatically modified ideology for the sake of tangible electoral benefits (the Croatian Democratic Union) or were reluctant to adopt a definite ideological position in order to avoid expressing opinion on politically sensitive issues (the Serbian Progressive Party). Likewise, these parties' positions on the EU were mainly a consequence of strategic political calculations, post-electoral negotiations impacted by Western countries and repeated, failed attempts to come to power advocating anti-Europeanism. As a result, the majority of these parties did not have firmly established attitudes towards the EU that may have been grounded in their fundamental values and identity.

Second, the Serbian and Croatian cases demonstrate that adherence to a certain family may create a predisposition for parties to have particular attitudes towards the EU. Social democrats appeared to find it easier to accept the supranational principles of the EU, whereas this was a rather difficult issue for conservative, demo-Christian and agrarian parties. Strong traditionalism and pronounced concerns for national issues – such as the preservation of sovereignty, national culture and traditional values that primarily characterise these three ideological families in Serbia and Croatia – significantly impacted their attitudes toward the EU.

Table 2: Support and opposition to EU/EU membership by party families in Serbia and Croatia

Party families: (1) socialist/social democrat; (2) conservative; (3) Christian democrat; (4) agrarian; (5) liberal; and (6) radical right

	Serbian parties	Croatian parties
Support for EU/ EU membership	(5) Liberal Democratic Party	(5) Croatian Peoples' Party
↑	(5) G17 Plus	(1) Social Democratic Party
	(1) Democratic Party	
	(1) Socialist Party of Serbia	(3) Croatian Democratic Union
	(2) Serbian Progressive Party	(4) Croatian Peasants' Party
	(2) New Serbia	
↓	(2) Democratic Party of Serbia	
		(6) Croatian Party of Rights
Opposition to EU/ EU membership	(6) Serbian Radical Party	

Source: party programmes and interviews with party officials

However, belonging to a particular ideological family does not seem to be an indicator or a predictor of a party's stances on this issue. As shown in Table 2, the conservative parties tended to express a wide range of mutually opposing positions on the EU. On the other hand, social democrats were all pro-European, but their position was rather strategically driven (the Socialist Party of Serbia) or was not based on elaborated social democratic principles (the Democratic Party), which indicates that their orientation was not necessary grounded in social democratic ideology. Similarly, it is difficult to establish a direct, causal relation between the Christian democratic ideology of the Croatian Democratic Union and its post-2002 pro-European orientation. Two party families, however, are an exception, namely the liberal and radical right, since these parties uniformly and consistently supported and opposed the EU, respectively.

References

Batory, A. 2002. "Attitudes to Europe: Ideology, strategy and the issue of European Union membership in Hungarian party politics." *Party Politics* 8(5): 525-39.

Croatian Parliament. 2012. Parliament composition. www.sabor.hr/Default.aspx?sec=4577 (20 May 2012).

DS. 2009. *Party programme*. www.ds.org.rs/dokumenti/ds-program.pdf (15 August 2010).

DSS. 2010. *Party statement*. www.dss.org.rs/newsitem.php?id=9471 (25 September 2010).

G17 Plus. 2004. *Party programme*. www.g17plus.rs/v2/images/stories/dokumenti/program-g17-plus.pdf (25 July 2010).

Gaffney, J. 1996. *Political parties and the European Union*. London: Routledge.

Goati, V. 2009. "State Interest through the Prism of the Commitments of Ruling Parties." In *Between authoritarianism and Democracy: Serbia at the Political Crossroads*, eds. D. Vujadinović and V. Goati. Belgrade: CEDET, FES, 283-302.

Hooghe, L., G. Marks and C. Wilson. 2002. "Does Left/Right Structure Party Positions on European Integration?" *Comparative Political Studies* 35: 965-89.

HDZ. 2002. *Party programme*. www.hdztresnjevka.com/hdz/index.php?option=com_content&view=article&id=51&Itemid=58 (10 October 2011).

HNS. 2011. *Party programme*. www.hns.hr/index.php?option=com_content&view=article&id=185:programi-hns-a&catid=56:programiiprojekti&Itemid=62 (1 November 2011).

HSP. 2010. *Vukovar Declaration*. http://hsp.hr/content/view/997/138/ (5 January 2012).

HSP. 2012. *Party principles*. http://hsp.hr/content/view/12/30/ (5 January 2012).

HSS. 2009. *Political principles*. www.hss-smz.org/joomla-overview/ciljevi-stranke (15 October 2011).

Jović, D. 2006. "Croatia and the European Union: a Long Delayed Journey." *Journal of Southern Europe and the Balkans* 8(1): 85-103.

Kopecký, P. and C. Mudde. 2002. "The two sides of Euroscepticism: Party positions on European integration in Central Eastern Europe." *European Union Politics* 3: 297-326.

Mair, P. and C. Mudde. 1998. "The party family and its study." *Annual Reviews of Political Science* 1: 211-29.

Marks, G., C. Wilson and L. Ray. 2002. "National political parties and European integration." *American Journal of Political Science* 46(3): 585-94.

NS. 2010. *Party programme.* www.nova-srbija.org/index1.htm (20 October 2010).

Pavlović, V. 2011. "Programski identitet politickih partija." In *Partije i izbori u Srbiji, 20 godina*, ed. S. Orlović. Beograd: Friedrich Ebert Stiftung, Fakultet političkih nauka, 137-52.

PEE. 2012. *Parties and Elections in Europe.* www.parties-and-elections.de/content.html (5 February 2012).

SDP. 2003. *Election manifesto.* http://hidra.srce.hr/arhiva/407/10502/www.sdp.hr/content/download/253/1131/file/program2003.pdf (19 October 2011).

SDP. 2004. *Političko-programska deklaracija 9. konvencije SDP-a, Naš put socijaldemokracije.* http://hidra.srce.hr/arhiva/407/407/www.sdp.hr/download/deklaracija-9kon.pdf (1 November 2012).

SDP. 2011. *Party programme.* http://www.kukuriku.org/plan21/clanstvo-u-europskoj-uniji-i-vanjska-politika/ (19 October 2011).

Serbian Parliament. 2012. *Parliament composition.* www.parlament.gov.rs/narodna-skupstina-/sastav/poslanicke-grupe.901.html (20 May 2012).

Siaroff, A. 2000. *Comparative European Party Systems (An Analysis of Parliamentary Elections Since 1945).* New York: Garland Publishing, Inc.

Sitter, N. 2001. "The politics of opposition and European integration in Scandinavia: Is Euro-scepticism a government-opposition dynamic?" *West European Politics* 24(4): 22-39.

SNS. 2011. *Party news.* www.sns.org.rs/%D1%81%D1%80/srpska-napredna-straka-vesti/85-glavne-vesti/3367--srpska-napredna-stranka-tanjug.html (20 June 2011).

SPS. 2010. *Party programme.* http://spspetrovac.rs/nacrt-novog-programa-sps.html (15 January 2011).

Szczerbiak, A. and P. Taggart. 2001. "Parties, Positions and Europe: Euroscepticism in the EU Candidate States of Central and Eastern Europe." *SEI Working Paper* 46.

Šedo, J. 2010. "The party system of Croatia." in *Party Politics in the Western Balkans*, eds. V. Stojarova and P. Emerson. Oxon: Routledge, 73-85.

Šedo, J. 2008. *Opposing Europe? The comparative party politics of Euroscepticism* (2). Oxford: Oxford University Press.

Taggart, P. 1998. "A touchstone of dissent: Euroscepticism in contemporary Western European party systems." *European Journal of Political Research* 33: 363-88.

von Beyme, K. 1985. *Political Parties in Western Democracies.* Aldershot: Gower Press.

Vukomanović, D. 2007. "Ideološke Matrice Političkih Partija u Srbiji (1990-2007)." In *Ideologija i Političke Stranke u Srbiji*, ed. Z. Lutovac. Belgrade: Friedrich Ebert Stiftung, 67-113.

Part IV

The Western Balkans and EU Enlargement

Weak Conditionality and Uncertain Membership Perspective

Discussing EU Integration of the Western Balkans

Gentian ELEZI

Introduction

The European Union has been and still is very active in promoting democracy and economic development internationally, especially in the post-communist countries. In the case of the Balkan area, its presence became very important after 2000 when the EU offered a clear path towards membership. Although the Copenhagen European Council in December 2002 had already confirmed the European perspective of the countries of the Western Balkans as potential candidates, the Thessaloniki Summit of 2003 made it clear that the future of the Western Balkans is within the European Union and claimed the Union's full support to the efforts of the countries of the region to consolidate democracy and stability and to promote economic development (Thessaloniki Agenda 2003). It was declared that "the Balkans will be an integral part of a unified Europe. The ongoing enlargement and the signature of the Treaty of Athens in April 2003 should inspire and encourage the countries of the Western Balkans to follow the same successful road of reforms and to increase their efforts in that direction" (EU Commission 2004).

Considering that these countries faced multiple challenges ahead and suffered from important institutional legacies from the past regimes, the European Union set up a well-defined framework under the Stabilization and Association Process. Each country of the region aspiring EU membership would undergo this process. To make it even more feasible and attractive, the EU started designing European Partnerships, which were inspired by the Accession Partnerships for candidate countries, but adapted to the Western Balkan countries. These instruments would be used as checklists to monitor and evaluate progress for each country (Grabbe 2006).

During the first years of this process, the European Union's policy of Stabilization and Association has been a major contributor to the progress achieved throughout the region in promoting stability and in bringing the countries closer to membership (Henderson 1999). Except for the case of Kosovo, due to its status dispute during those years, the countries of the region advanced in the integration process, both formally and substantially. Since each country represented different specific patterns and stages of development, achievements and pace of integration were also diverse. It is well known that the EU principle fundamental to this process is that the pace of further integration steps of the Western Balkan countries towards the EU depends on each country's performance in implementing reforms, thus respecting the criteria set by the Copenhagen European Council of 1993 and the Stabilization and Association Agreement (SAA). Since proper implementation of the SAA was considered by the EU as a necessary condition for later accession, countries were firmly committed in complying with it. Despite the success of the process in the early years, this chapter argues that the EU's attractiveness has decreased in the region and that the process has experienced a slowdown due to poor conditionality of EU policy and its effects. Consequently, public support for integration has decreased in the last year. Main democratic consolidation indicators have deteriorated, according to EU reports and the studies of other international institutions. In addition, despite good pace of acquis adoption, implementation deficit has increased, creating a problematic gap in all the countries. This chapter will try to show and explain these negative elements and argue on the impact of poor conditionality.

The Integration Process of Western Balkans

As mentioned above, all Western Balkan (WB) countries, except Kosovo, were offered a clear perspective for EU membership at the beginning of the last decade. Since the start of the Stabilization and Association Agreement, the EU was committed in supporting these countries in several ways. First of all, the institutional building process was in the centre of the program. The instrument of twinning, which was adopted in the case of the Central and Eastern European (CEE) countries, was extended to all WB countries (Haughton 2007). In order to achieve results in the integration process, major reforms were needed. For these reforms to be implemented, institutional capacities have proved to be crucial (Hille and Knill 2006). Especially when taking into account these countries' specific situations, the EU started to support financially capacity building through the Community Assistance for Reconstruction, Development and Stabilization program CARDS. This has been one of the major challenges because reforms needed to cope with resistance that comes from institutional and cultural legacies from the communist regime (Fowkes 1999). There are many authors who have developed different theses on the importance of institutional legacies and their influence (Holmes, 1997; Ekiert and Hanson, 2003), structural and institutional characteristics, number of actors involved, the decision-making process, administrative capacities and patterns, the coordination level of the management of this process, etc. For the purpose of supporting the implementation of necessary reforms in the field of public administration, the EU tried to advance different financing schemes and trainings, not only through improving infrastructure, but also by providing expertise from the new Member States in the light of their own successful transition process and preparations for EU membership.

Since organized crime and corruption were real obstacles to democratic consolidation, stability, sound and accountable institutions and economic development in the Western Balkans and a source of serious concern to the EU, the fight against these phenomena was another important criterion (Jensen 2007). The EU urged countries of the region to commit themselves in Thessaloniki to adopt, within a specified time frame, all necessary legislation in order to tackle problems in this area. Achieving results in this field was a condition for an important element for the WB countries: the perspective of liberalization of the visa regime. After the fall of the Berlin wall, a new isolation had started, and visa regimens had turned into a blockade for the citizens of these countries. Especially in the case of Albania, whose communist regime did not permit citizens to travel abroad, removing the visa barrier was a very attractive issue and a big "carrot" in the EU's hands (Hoffmann 2005).

All the criteria, together with regional co-operation, were part of the Stabilization and Association Agreement. The Western Balkan countries needed to develop regional co-operation, which constituted an essential element of the Stabilization and Association Process. More specifically, this included the need for the development of regional free trade among the Western Balkan countries (Sanjay 2008). They committed themselves to complete the network of bilateral Free Trade Agreements through necessary ratifications, on the basis of the 2001 Memorandum of Understanding. This meant the harmonization of the dispositions of their FTAs, with a view of establishing a free-trade zone in full respect of World Trade Organization rules, within a specified time frame.

With this framework set up, the countries of the WB experienced different trajectories in complying with EU requirements. As shown in Table 1.1, the main stages of moving forward with the integration agenda were not the same for all five countries. Macedonia and Albania were first to start the process, and both are now stuck, for different reasons. While Serbia and Montenegro have experienced a quick pace in achieving the consequent steps, if compared to the other countries. For Bosnia, however, due also to the internal specific situation, little progress has been achieved so far.

Table 1.1 Main steps in the integration agenda of WB countries

	Albania	Bosnia and Herze-govina	Macedonia	Montenegro	Serbia
SAA (sign)	2006	2008	2001	2007	2008
Application for membership	2009	-	2004	2008	2009
SAA (in force)	2009	-	2004	2010	-
Candidate status	-	-	2005	2010	2012
Visa liberalization	2010	2010	2009	2009	2009

Source: DG Enlargement, EC Commission

Considering the overall picture of the integration process of the region, is conditionality succeeding in influencing these countries' performances, or has the EU lost its leverage in the Western Balkans?

Conditionality and its Limitations in the Case of the Western Balkans

When it comes to the EU and its influence in the neighbourhood countries, conditionality is the key word for explaining these relationships. A vast literature, which tries to explain and build theories on this concept, has developed in the past decades.

Conditionality has been used as an explanatory instrument for the effects that international actors, such as the EU, have on third countries' democratic consolidation (Vachudova 2002; Schimmelfennig and Sedelmeier 2005; Grabbe 2006; Lavenex and Schimmelfennig 2010). These theories claim that incentives given by international actors, especially the EU, have been a main mechanism for a positive performance and change in post-communist countries of Eastern Europe. The European Union has identified institution building and legislation adoption efforts as a priority for achieving these goals and bringing these countries closer to the EU (Pridham 2001; Vachudova 2005; Grabbe 2006; Schimmelfennig 2006). Yet, while literature on the EU influence on democratization, compliance, economic development and institution building has proliferated during the last two decades, taken as a whole, empirical studies have been characterized by a rather selective geography that has focused largely on Central Eastern Europe and not on the Balkan countries. Most of the existing research work on EU conditionality is based in Central European countries (Kaiser and Elvert 2004), leaving in the shadow the role of this instrument in the Balkan region. In the case of the Western Balkans, although the literature is under development, it was still early for confirming the same findings as in the CEE case (Kubicek 2003). With reference to the last years, we can tell that, while the CEE integration processes are considered to be successful (especially after accession in 2004), the outcomes of conditionality that the EU has adopted on the WB case remains uncertain.

"By conditionality, one refers to the linking of perceived benefits – e.g., political support, economic aid, membership in an organization – to the fulfilment of a certain program, in this case the advancement of democratic principles and institutions in a 'target state'" (Kubicek 2003, p. 7). With the use of incentives as "carrots", the EU strives to influence the reform process in third countries. As Hoffman has pointed out, "in this context, the EU relies on a wide range of instruments to affect institutional and policy transformation. These can be categorized as 1) the access to negotiations, 2) the provision of legislative and institutional templates, 3) aid and technical assistance, 4) policy advice, and 5) monitoring" (Hoffman 2006). Furthermore, "access to negotiations and other stages of the accession process is the EU's strongest conditionality lever, and hence its most powerful political tool for institutional change" (Grabbe 2002, p. 257).

However, the use of conditionality does not guarantee success. Not always do changes go in the direction intended by the EU, in terms of reforms and democratic consolidation. In some cases, EU assistance has actually produced weak economic reforms and institutions, with legitimacy problems and without having substantial impact in the overall environment (Hughes, Sasse and Gordon 2005). For example, one interesting hypothesis that Kubicek advances is that in case the leaders of a country are relatively certain that they would lose under fair democratic contestation, they will be less likely to push ahead with democratization and integration, even in the face of EU pressure (2003).

But most important, the "sticks" that the EU threats use have to be credible in order to be effective. That means that it has to be willing and able to fulfil its commitments. Related to this last point, in the case of Albania, conditionality has shown major deficiencies. Although the country has been rejected two times in the candidate status (2010 and 2011), because of the domestic political crisis, little has changed. Rejecting the candidate status has been seen by the EU as using the stick, but it was not perceived in the same way by domestic actors and public opinion. Blocking the next step is not seen necessarily as a form of punishment, rather than a stand-by. Despite harsh declarations and calls from Brussels for solving the political crisis, the EU couldn't influence the country's internal situation. This gave a weak image of its power and loss of credibility, in the best case, and created a perception of its lack of interest in Albania. Of course this case might seem not representative of the region due to its specific domestic stalemate, but if we refer to surveys on public support for EU integration, a clear trend of decrease can be noticed. According to Balkan Monitor Survey (2010), important changes were recorded in terms of public support for EU integration in the region for 2010. Albania and Serbia were the two countries with the major fall of support, by 7 and 6 per cent, respectively. Except for Montenegro, which has also proved to be the most "successful" in the integration agenda of the last years, all other countries have experienced a decrease of support (Balkan Monitor 2010).

Democratic Consolidation or Stagnation?

The EU has invested in the support of democratic consolidation of the region through capacity-building programs. Free and fair elections, rule of law, independence of judiciary and press freedom are some of the elements that are part of the political criteria that EU institutions monitor in the Western Balkan countries. While economic reforms have experienced an improvement in the last years, fulfilling some of the criteria of political requirements show a different picture. According to the Progress Reports of the European Commission, political criteria are the most problematic field in the region, especially in terms of democratic standards and independence of institutions. The performance differs among the countries, but all of them represent major problems in at least some of the political requirements.

An important set of indicators on political criteria is related to the Nations in Transit report, published by the Freedom House. Although its findings and scores given to the countries can be questionable, especially in terms of methodology, they still provide a remarkable overview of countries in the democratic transition process. As shown in Table 1.2, it is interesting to notice that specific results in the integration process of each country seem to match with the change of score that the Freedom House has assigned. Without going into details on each country's performance in the chosen indicators, for the purpose of this chapter we are looking at the performance in the last five years – from 2006 to 2011. This time period is chosen because most of the countries started the integration process late, especially when we refer to the Stabilization and Association Process. The entry into force of the Stabilization and Association Agreements in these years marked a qualitative new stage in bilateral relations of these countries with the EU, entailing significant new obligations and engagement in many areas. In most cases, cooperation has focused mainly on priorities related to the EU *acquis* in the relevant fields, with countries committing to gradually introduce EU *acquis* in their legislation, to implement related policies and to co-operate with the EU on joint policy objectives. This agreement has also offered a clear path and roadmap for the region, by describing specific objectives and time frame for adoption.

Using Freedom House indicators, Table 1.2 shows the differences (between 2006 and 2011) of six different elements studied. As indicated in Table 1.1 regarding integration process performance, we can confirm that, except for the rapid improvement of Montenegro and, partially, of Serbia, other countries are stuck. Bosnia and Herzegovina represent the worst case, recording only negative changes during these five years. Very similar patterns are presented in the case of Albania and Macedonia. Although these two countries started the integration process much earlier than the others, they are now experiencing a major break in terms of advancing with the integration agenda. Albania has not been able to comply with the requirements needed for the candidate status (for two consecutive years now), and Macedonia has not been able to progress in the accessions' negotiations stage. In both cases, although different interventions have taken place by EU institutions, results have been poor and conditionality instruments have not provided the necessary incentives.

Table 1.2 Democratic consolidation indicators of WB countries (change, 2006-2011)

	Albania	Bosnia and Herzegovina	Macedonia	Montenegro	Serbia
Electoral Process	- 0.5	- 0.25	0	+ 0.25	0
Independ-ent Media	- 0.25	- 0.75	- 0.25	- 1.00	- 0.75
National governance	- 0.75	- 0.50	- 0.25	+ 0.25	+ 0.25
Judicial independ-ence	0	- 0.25	- 0.25	+ 0.25	- 0.25
Corruption	+ 0.25	- 0.25	+ 0.75	+ 0.25	+ 0.50
Democracy Score	- 0.25	- 0.25	0	+ 0.07	+ 0.05

Source: Nations in Transit, Freedom House

Despite few positive performances of Montenegro and Serbia, if we refer to the average figures for the entire region and compare between 2006 and 2011, all main indicators show negative performance. Especially, electoral processes, freedom of the media and democratic governance are the variables that represent the highest decrease.

Five years later, these countries are almost in the same situation or worse, despite some formal recognition of progress in terms of moving forward. It looks as if EU conditionality has not worked properly in substantively improving standards and supporting reforms in the region. Formal adoption of required measures and legislation has not brought real change and compliance. The implementation deficit, which will be discussed in the next part, has grown and is becoming a real issue in terms of membership perspective. There are other reports and indices such as European Bank for Reconstruction and Development (EBRD), World Bank, National Democratic Institute (NDI), etc. assessing these countries in a similar way, showing that the pace of development is really slow (especially if compared to CEE countries at the end of their first decade in the integration process). Ten years after the beginning of the process and five years after the Instrument for Pre-Accession and SAA entered into force, all countries represent serious problems in the political field. Albania has not been able to hold free and fair elections and presents concern in terms of judiciary independence. Bosnia represents the worst case, experiencing many difficulties on state building, democracy, human rights, etc. In Serbia, where political criteria seem to be doing slightly better, the most pro-European candidate did not win the last elections in May 2012. Although the country is formally following the integration agenda, there are several opened issues (such as Kosovo) that will keep holding it back. Montenegro and Macedonia have also had troubles with the negotiations process. In the case of Macedonia, the increase of ethnic conflicts between Macedonians and Albanians has once again affirmed the powerless role of the EU in influencing and stopping the deterioration of the situation. The region appears to be stuck, and the EU has not showed strong commitment in using its leverage but rather has only observed and reported the situation.

Implementation Deficit: The Biggest Challenge

The Western Balkan countries are showing an increasing deficit in implementation performance of EU legislation. Legislation and directives are adopted rapidly, but actual implementation and enforcement is low or even missing. Literature suggests that administrative capacity is one key element that explains this. The fact that the countries were granted visa liberalization and that public support for integration is decreasing makes the process less attractive for domestic political actors, and, therefore, that influences political willingness necessary for implementation. The EU Commission, through the annual progress report for each country, has marked the implementation deficit in different policy areas.

When looking more in detail at the process of complying with the EU, Falkner is among those authors who have contributed in policy compliance. More specifically, she has been focused on lack or distortion of compliance, which is an important aspect that explains the deficit. As she calls it, noncompliance is a concept that has been explored especially in the CEE countries (Falkner *et al.* 2005). She elaborated other related factors such as non-transposition, non-enforcement and non-application. Especially the motives for non-compliance are a salient issue and have a major role in explaining conditionality failures.

Schimmelfennig is also a main contributor in this field. What Schimmelfennig calls "rule adoption" is a complex process of transposition of EU law into domestic law, which requires the restructuring of domestic institutions according to EU rules or the change of domestic political practices according to EU standards (Schimmelfennig 2005). In his work, he analyses the main factors that link conditionality and policy implementation. This helps in analysing and explaining patterns of institutional and policy adoption practices and can give a more helpful framework in order to identify the main factors that influence the process of policy implementation. As Bardach (1984) explains in his work *The Implementation Game*, "the implementation process is a process of assembling the elements required to produce a particular programmatic outcome". He studies and explains the elements that influence the process of policy implementation under the political pressure (or commitment).

The first of these elements is domestic political stability and internal political factors. More specifically, political stability seems to be a key issue in the process of European integration in these countries. As the region has some gaps in terms of consolidating institutional culture, all institutions are sensitive to political events and their performance is in correlation with the stability of the political debate. There are several precedents that indicate the role of political conflicts in the speed of integration and compliance with the EU (Albi 2005; De Bardeleben 2008). There is already some evidence (EU progress reports), such as in the case of Albania, that confirm this as a major issue. For three years, there has been an on-going political crisis in Albania where the opposition has continually been boycotting the Parliament. This has had direct and immediate impact on the policy implementation process because several directives, reforms and main laws have to be passed in order to advance with the integration agenda. It happens often that this process gets stuck because of this political instability. In the case of Albania, political instability has had direct impact in the process. The opposition's long term boycott had considerable repercussions in the process of achieving the candidate status. The political stalemate in Albania, the tensions in Macedonia or internal dilemmas in Serbia influence directly the pace of reforms and, therefore, the implementation performance. In the case of the Western Balkans, the EU has showed its weakness and incapacity for influencing political processes (as in the case of Meciar in the CEE). The relationships between state institutions are also a very important issue. Trying to observe and understand the dynamics of relations among the government, the parliament and the judiciary is very important in order to understand how this environment can influence the process of complying with the EU. Especially, continual clashes with the judiciary have proved to undermine the process and be harshly criticized by the EU. However, other than as critics, the EU has not been able to influence and incentivise change in this direction, despite its attempts.

State capacity is also a complex factor and very incisive in the integration process. First of all, it is related to the administrative capacity that the country requires in order to comply with EU policies (Hille and Knill 2006). This is related mainly to the administrative capacities that are engaged directly with adopting and implementing EU policies. In order to face the challenges coming from EU integration, the largest share of the burden falls over the public administration and its capacities (Schimmelfennig 2005). In the case of the Western Balkans, administrative capacity represents one of the weakest points of institutional performance. This is due to several structural reasons, but also mainly due to lack of a proper civil service law, low level of expertise and instability because of political appointments (Schimmelfennig 2005). The administration performance is important in all stages of policy adoption, from the transposition to implementation (Toshkov 2008; Thomson 2009). This is why it is crucial to try to understand its influence in the whole process. Despite the fact that the EU has spent hundreds of millions of euros in capacity building for the region, it has not been able to help create a stable and efficient public administration, and it has not prevented frequent changes due to political appointments (this has further undermined EU efforts).

Coordination is also an important aspect, part of state capacity. The type of institutional coordination applied for the management of the EU policy adoption process has proved to be relevant (Kassim, Peters and Wright 2000). There is an on-going debate on the efficiency of institutions in charge for coordinating this process. Due to lack of institutional tradition and, therefore, legitimacy of coordinative bodies, coordination has been shown to be weak and has not responded preventively to the requirements coming from the integration agenda (EU Commission

2009). These problems have emerged even clearer during the challenges that these countries have faced in crucial moments of the integration process. For example, coordination shortcomings were demonstrated in each of the countries, especially when responding to the EU questionnaire for the status candidate (in the case of those countries that have already applied for EU membership). Different types of coordination produce different results in different countries, but the construction of hierarchies and competences are important for the legitimacy of these coordination institutions and, thus, for their credibility in relation to other partner institutions. For example, the case of the Ministry of Integration in Albania, which is still weak and does not have a political power to exercise pressure among other institutions for complying with EU policies, shows that EU conditionality has not been translated as important in terms of empowering domestic institutions in charge of the integration process. The process of coordination can influence and determine the outcome of overall compliance with EU. But what is the role and responsibility of the EU in these latter shortcomings? How can conditionality influence and change countries' performances?

The EU often fails to capture properly the various ways in which recipients respond to the efforts of the EU. Many of such efforts carried out by the EU fail just because they are designed at their headquarters in Brussels and applied to a variety of local settings. The background and the specific conditions can determine the performance of complying with Europe (Giuliani 2003). The EU has adopted a very similar strategy in all Balkan countries, although they differ from each other, and they are at different stages of development and democratic consolidation. Failing to recognize their differences and neglecting to reflect those diversities in terms of strategies employed can influence the process of adoption and compliance in these countries (Cini 2003). The fact that EU integration is offered as a full package with little space for negotiation interferes with the adaptability and suitability of the whole process in the Balkans. Some scholars argue that if the policies applied are first discussed thoroughly with the national officials that will implement them, we can expect a better result. The requirements of the agenda need also to be more specific in order to leave little space for misinterpretations and misunderstandings. A more scheduled strategy could help in this case, as the visa liberalization roadmap showed successfully. In that case, the EU offered a comprehensive and detailed path for the countries. Conditionality was strong, clear and with attractive incentives. All countries, though with different timing, fulfilled the requirement and met the criteria in short time.

Establishing whether or not the EU has adopted adequate strategies in the WB countries would require an in-depth research and a more inclusive study. However, what seems to be certain from the evidence and reports offered is that conditionality as the CEE and WB have known it so far is not delivering as it used to. The EU has continued to use the same framework in all the countries of these two regions, and different results were seen (Martin and Winkler 2009). Especially in terms of political conditionality, the EU's influence seems to be less powerful. This has caused the creation of a new landscape in the region, and there is a risk of membership becoming merely political rhetoric. If we refer to the Regional Approach launched more than a decade ago, the EU declared its commitment to support the whole region in moving towards membership; therefore, there is direct responsibility for this. If classic conditionality instruments did not work, probably the EU should have paid more attention in analysing and finding new ways how to influence these countries' trajectories rather than wasting money and losing credibility. The fact that the countries are advancing differently in this process might signify that the regional approach of integration needs also to be revised. It is exactly in this kind of situation that the EU needs to give credibility and legitimacy to the European project and not to reflect uncertainties (Vachudova 2005). The way conditionality has been used and the way internal problems of these countries have impeded implementation have been major obstacles for achieving better results.

Conclusions

This chapter tried to give an overview of the EU integration process of Western Balkans countries, with particular attention to conditionality shortcomings. After looking into the different stages that each country has gone through, the study focused on the conditionality concept and its limitations in the case of the WB. It was argued that classic conditionality instruments have not always been successful in the region and, in most cases, the integration process has experienced important slowdowns. The EU has appeared to be powerless in influencing domestic political agendas of these countries and has slowly lost public support. This has blocked the process, especially in terms of implementation of the acquis. Political will, administrative capacities and EU pressure are known to be necessary elements for implementing successfully the EU legislation in candidate or potential candidate countries. In the case of Albania, Macedonia and Bosnia and Herzegovina, these variables have suffered deficiencies, and their progress towards EU membership has experienced negative evaluations. There might also be a potential risk of splitting the region in "two speeds" areas, where Serbia and Montenegro would advance and the others would be left behind (although they started implementing the integration agenda many years before). Each country's merits and achievements are the basis of this evaluation, but there is also an EU responsibility for poor conditionality instruments and mismanagement of the process. Especially political conditionality has experienced the worst period, showing that the EU is losing its leverage in some of the countries. If political conditionality does not work, all integration processes will suffer, from approximation with the EU acquis to full implementation of the requirements. In order to avoid the increase of distance between the EU and the region, a new medium term strategy should be studied. Instead of using few "carrots" and even less "sticks", the EU needs to increase its efforts and maintain its credibility in the region and strengthen the membership perspective. Almost 10 years after the Thessaloniki Agenda, there is a need for new political motivation and engagement. Domestic stability of WB countries is still fragile, and the EU can play a major role in keeping the pace of reforms towards democratic consolidation through more direct "interventions". The results achieved so far in the integration agenda have been impressive, but the last years have shown that a new and more incisive strategy is needed. The success of the Regional Approach launched many years ago depends on the reforming capacities of the whole region, rather than risking to create considerable differences among the countries.

References

Albi, A. 2005. *EU Enlargement and the Constitution of Central and Eastern Europe*. Cambridge: Cambridge University Press.

Bardach, E. 1984. *The Implementation Game: What Happens When a Bill Becomes a Law*. Cambridge, MA: MIT Press.

Balkan Monitor. 2010. "Insights and Perceptions: Voices of the Balkans". *European Fund for the Balkans*.

Cini, M. 2003. *European Union Politics*. Oxford: Oxford University Press.

De Bardeleben, J. 2008. The Boundaries of EU Enlargement Finding a Place for Neighbours, New York: Palgrave Macmillan.

Ekiert, G., and S. E. Hanson. 2003. *Capitalism and Democracy in Central and Eastern Europe*. Cambridge: Cambridge University Press.

European Commission. 2009. Commission Staff Working Paper. Albania. Stabilisation and Association Report 2009. Brussels.

Falkner, G., O. Treib, M. Hartlapp, and S. Leiber. 2005. *Complying with Europe? The Impact of EU Minimum Harmonisation and Soft Law in the Member States.* Cambridge: Cambridge University Press.

Fowkes, B. 1999. *The Post-Communist Era. Change and Continuity in Eastern Europe*. London: MacMillian Press Ltd.

Giuliani, M. 2003. "Europeanization in Comparative Perspective: Institutional Fit and National Adaptation." In *The Politics of Europeanization*, eds. K. Featherstone and C. M. Radaelli. Oxford: Oxford University Press.

Grabbe, H. 2002. "European Union Conditionality and the Acquis Communautaire". *International Political Science Review* 23 (3): 249-268.

Grabbe, H. 2006. *The EU's Transformative Power. Europeanization through Conditionality in Central and Eastern Europe*. New York: Palgrave MacMillan.

Haughton, T. J. 2007. "When Does the EU Make a Difference? Conditionality and the Accession Process in Central and Eastern Europe". *Political Studies Review* 5 (2), 233-246

Henderson, K. 1999. *Back to Europe: Central and Eastern Europe and the European Union*. London: UCL Press.

Hille, P. and C. Knill. 2006. "It's the Bureaucracy, Stupid: The Implementation of the Acquis Communautaire in EU Candidate Countries, 1999-2003". *European Union Politics* 7, 531-552.

Hoffmann, J. 2005. "Integrating Albania: the Role of the European Union in the Democratization Process". *Albanian* Journal of Politics I (1): 55-74.

Holmes, L. 1997. *Post-Communism, an Introduction*. Oxford: Polity Press.

Hughes, J., G. Sasse, and C. Gordon. 2005. *Europeanization and Regionalization in the EU's Enlargement to Central and Eastern Europe: The Myth of Conditionality*. New York: Palgrave Macmillan.

Jensen, C. B. 2007. "Implementing Europe: A Question of Oversight". *European Union Politics* 8, 451-477.

Kaiser, W. and J. Elvert. 2004. *European Union Enlargement: A Comparative History*. London: Routledge.

Kassim, H., G. Peters, and V. Wright. 2000. *The National Co-Ordination of EU Policy*. New York: Oxford University Press.

Kubicek, P. J. 2003. *The European Union and Democratization*. New York: Routledge.

Lavenex, S. and F. Schimmelfennig. 2010. *EU External Governance. Projecting EU Rules Beyond Membership*. New York: Routledge.

Linden, R. H. 2002. *Norms and Nannies. The Impact of International Organizations on the Central and East European States*. Lanham, MD: Rowman & Littlefield Publishers, Inc.

Martin, R. and A. Winkler. 2009. *Real Convergence in Central, Eastern and South-Eastern Europe*. New York: Palgrave Macmillan.

Pridham Geoffrey, and A. Agh. 2001. *Prospects for Democratic Consolidation in East-Central Europe*. Manchester: Manchester University Press.

Sanjay, K. 2008. *Western Balkan Integration and the EU: An Agenda for Trade and Growth*. Washington, DC: World Bank.

Schimmelfennig, F., S. Engert, and H. Knobel. 2006. *International Socialization in European Organizations: Political Conditionality and Democratic Change*. New York: Palgrave.

Schimmelfenning, F. and U. Sedelmeier. 2005. The Europeanization of Central and Eastern Europe. New York: Cornell University Press.

Thomson, R. 2009. "Same Effects in Different Worlds: The Transposition of EU Directives". *Journal of European Public Policy*, 16, 1-18.

Toshkov, D. 2008. "Embracing European Law: Transposition of EU Directives in Central and Eastern Europe". *European Union Politics*, 9, 379-402.

Vachudova, M. A. 2005. *Europe Undivided. Democracy, Leverage, and Integration after Communism*. Oxford: Oxford University Press.

Is There a Future for the Western Balkans in the European Union?

Shirley CLOYES DIOGUARDI

Introduction

The EU High Representative for Foreign Policy and Security, Catherine Ashton, said in advance of the European Union-Western Balkans high-level meeting in Sarajevo on 2 June 2010 that "integrating the Western Balkans into the European family of nations remains one of the last challenges to building a democratic and unified Europe" (Europa, 2010). Echoing this outlook a year later, US Assistant Secretary of State Philip H. Gordon testified at a 15 November 2011 hearing before the Subcommittee on Europe and Eurasian Affairs in the US House of Representatives: "[t]he Obama Administration remains as committed as ever to helping the Western Balkans on their path to Euro-Atlantic integration… [because] this is the best means of ensuring long-term peace, stability, and prosperity" (Gordon, 2011, pp. 9-10).

I agree with EU High Representative Ashton and Assistant Secretary of State Gordon that ultimately all of the nations in the Western Balkans – which emerged from almost fifty years of communist dictatorship in the early 1990s, followed by a decade of ethnic cleansing and genocide at the hands of the late Serbian dictator and war criminal, Slobodan Milosevic – should be included in the EU zone of peace and prosperity. Nevertheless, I believe that this should not happen before the countries in question meet the Copenhagen criteria, including the "stability of institutions guaranteeing democracy, the rule of law, human rights, regional cooperation and respect for and protection of minorities" (EUABC.com, n.d.), not just a functioning market economy.

While there have been noteworthy achievements (for which the West can claim some credit) in the political, economic and social progress of the Western Balkans after the Balkan wars of the 1990s, Albania and most of the countries of the former Yugoslavia remain unstable and, in the case of Bosnia and Kosovo, at risk of future conflict. This chapter will argue that Albania, Bosnia and Kosovo need to make significant reforms before they are granted candidate status, and that Serbia, Macedonia and Montenegro must do the same before they are given dates for accession negotiations.

In March 2000, a year after the Balkan wars ended, the Lisbon European Council made it a priority to sign Stabilisation and Association agreements with countries in the Western Balkans as a first step toward EU integration. Every year since, Albania and the countries of the former Yugoslavia have been given the prospect of EU membership as a stimulus to prevent future conflicts and to establish genuine democracies. But twelve years later, in 2012, the changes have not been wide-ranging enough to warrant integration into a union that is already severely threatened by the collapse of the financial markets in the West and by what is now understood as the premature inclusion of Greece in the euro zone in 2001 (Polychroniou, 2011). Apart from Croatia, which will join the EU as its twenty-eighth member state in 2013, the countries of the Western Balkans face severe, external challenges to their admission to the EU because of the economic recession in the West, which began with the collapse of the financial markets in the United States in September 2008 and the debt crisis that ensued in western Europe.

In addition, while both the European Union and the US government have used the prospect of EU membership as a catalyst for reform in the post-war nations of the Western Balkans, reforms are unlikely to materialise as long as both the European Union and the US government cling to foreign policy approaches that have undermined the very possibility of essential political, economic and social change in the region. In short, change needs to occur not only in the Western Balkans, but also in the foreign policy institutions of Europe and the United States if there is to be an outcome that would warrant future EU enlargement. Pivotal to that change is the resolution of the conflict between Serbia and Kosovo – a resolution that is stymied not only by Belgrade's refusal to recognise Kosovo's sovereignty and territorial integrity, but by internal divisions within the European Union about Kosovo's status and often intermittent diplomatic interventions by a US government that is more focused on the Middle East and northern Africa than it is on southeast Europe.

Serbia

Serbia, which received EU candidate status on 1 March 2012, has made substantial gains in establishing the rule of law since the end of the Balkan wars of the 1990s, with 11 rounds of free and fair elections, two fully democratic referenda on changes to its constitution, a major effort to combat corruption in its state enterprises and its military, and the end of suppressing internal dissent. But there is another side to Serbia's postwar story that has profound implications for regional development and for the integration of the Western Balkans into the

European Union. Serbia was told by the EU that it would not be able to obtain candidate status until it captured and extradited to the International Criminal Tribunal for the Former Yugoslavia (ICTY) in The Hague the remaining indicted war criminals Ratko Mladic and Goran Hadžić (which it did in 2011), and until it ended its adversarial relationship with Kosovo (see European Council decision 2008/213/EC, 2008). Although it has yet to do the latter, Belgrade entered into EU-sponsored talks with Prishtina in March 2011 as a signal to the EU that it was willing to comply with the Copenhagen criteria, which require a country's commitment to the peaceful resolution of conflicts and regional cooperation, in order to gain EU membership. Nevertheless, new developments in 2012, which demonstrate that Serbia expects to maintain its sovereignty over Kosovo and still be admitted to the European Union, indicate that if the depth of the problem between Serbia and Kosovo is left unaddressed, it will jeopardise regional progress and undermine the EU's credibility.

The Serbia-Kosovo Impasse

Thirteen years after NATO air strikes against Serbia ended Slobodan Milosevic's genocidal campaign against Kosovar Albanians in 1999 and four years after 'supervised independence' began in 2008, Serbia is a candidate for admission to the European Union even though it simultaneously acts as a destructive force in the region. This is true in relation to Kosovo, but also to a lesser extent in Bosnia, where it has supported Republika Srpska in its discrimination against non-Serbs and rejection of the authority of the central government. When all is said and done, Belgrade has yet to fully dismantle the Milosevic system and to come to grips with its racist and ultranationalist past, which led to the deaths of more than 250,000 Bosnian Muslims and Kosovar Albanians and the displacement of 4 million people in the region between 1989 and 1999.

Instead, Serbia has spent tremendous amounts of time and money trying to destabilise Kosovo. According to the International Crisis Group (2011), Belgrade spends some 200 million euros annually on the creation and financing of illegal parallel structures in northern Kosovo. Serbia has actively manipulated Kosovo Serbs since war's end to boycott Kosovo's elections and institutions, and to reject integration into Kosovo's new reality. The day after Kosovo declared its independence in February 2008, for example, UN officials stood idly by as Belgrade-supported extremists burned Kosovo's border crossing, customs checkpoints and courthouses in the north. Since NATO air strikes ended the Kosovo war in June 1999, Belgrade has also implemented an unrelenting propaganda campaign in the media and in the courts to block the resolution of Kosovo's final status. Belgrade has used the media to warn the West that Kosovo's independence would lead to the creation of a 'Greater Albania' and that Kosovo's large Muslim population would lead to the incursion of radical Islam into the heart of Europe, neither of which has transpired in a pro-Western population where Albanians are Muslims, Roman Catholics, Orthodox Christians and Jews, and have lived side by side in harmony for centuries (International Crisis Group, 2001).

Belgrade has also made use of international legal venues to undermine support for Kosovo's independence. It has colluded with pro-Serb elements in the European Union to steer the International Criminal Tribunal for the Former Yugoslavia (ICTY) in The Hague toward creating a false parity between the perpetrators and the victims of the Balkan wars, when there is no moral equivalence between Serbia's orchestrated state-sponsored terrorism against Kosovar Albanians and the Kosovo Liberation Army (KLA), the grassroots defense force that defended the civilian population against Serbian aggression. As recently as 2010, this resulted in the re-incarceration of KLA commander Ramush Haradinaj, who was acquitted on all charges by the ICTY in 2008 and, based on misinformation by Serbian intelligence officials (Emmerson, 2011), is the first defendant since the tribunal was established in 1993 to have his acquittal overturned.

After Kosovo declared its independence in February 2008, Serbia mounted a challenge to the declaration in the International Court of Justice (ICJ), which made it more difficult for Kosovo to secure recognitions from EU and UN member states (thus far, 98 countries have recognised Kosovo's independence) and nearly impossible to attract foreign investors of significance. When, two years later, on 22 July 2010, the ICJ affirmed the legality of Kosovo's sovereignty, Serbia attempted to override the court by introducing a draft resolution at the UN General Assembly that would invalidate the ICJ's opinion. Following pressure from leading EU member states, Serbia was forced to create a new draft. But by the time the negotiations were over, Serbia had received more pledges for a 'fast-track' EU integration process and assurances that Kosovo would be summoned to negotiate with Belgrade again (Cloyes DioGuardi and Gjoni, 2010). These EU-sponsored talks, purportedly limited to technical issues, began in March 2011.

Although only a few agreements were reached on paper (such as freedom of movement, return of Kosovo's cadastral registries, and joint border patrol), a year later Serbia received candidate status for admission to the European Union. It was conferred, even though Belgrade-backed Serb extremists in the north had spent months erecting barricades to block the central government in Prishtina (which was helped by KFOR, NATO's force in Kosovo) from extending its jurisdiction over all of Kosovo's territory. The confrontations that ensued ultimately left an Albanian policeman dead, and four NATO soldiers and sixteen Serb civilians seriously injured.

Leading up to the consideration of Serbia's candidate status in December 2011, only German Chancellor Angela Merkel insisted that Belgrade first had to normalise its relationship with Kosovo and dismantle the barricades and its parallel structures in the north. According to Balkan expert Elisabeth Pond, the resulting postponement of Serbia's status until March 2012 was an indication that "the era of EU passivity on Kosovo was over, not least thanks to Merkel's new-found bluntness" (Pond, 2012, p. 3).

Nevertheless, once the March date approached, Merkel, apparently at the Obama administration's insistence, withdrew her requirement that Serbia stop funding the parallel structures in the north.

This paved the way for Belgrade to achieve another victory: Kosovo, under pressure from the European Union and the US government, agreed, in exchange for access to regional meetings (previously blocked by Belgrade), to allow the word "Republic" to be removed from its name plate and replaced with an asterisk and a footnote. The footnote refers to UN Resolution 1244 and the opinion of the International Court of Justice that Kosovo's 2008 declaration of independence did not violate international law.[1] With the addition of the footnote, it will be that much more difficult for Kosovo to gain additional recognitions and much-needed foreign investment. It also gives Serbia a seemingly legal sovereignty over Kosovo. As David Kanin, professor of international relations at Johns Hopkins University, has observed, the reinstitution of UN Resolution 1244 "underscores Serbia's insistence that 1244 remains the practical, as well as the legal, basis for the international status of what was a province of Serbia, Yugoslavia, and Serbia again from 1913 through 1999" (Kanin, 2012).

Kanin's assessment was borne out on the ground a week after the agreement requiring the footnote was signed on 23 February 2012, when both Kosovar and Serb representatives started walking out of regional meetings because Serbia insisted that the footnote referring to UN Resolution 1244 must not only appear on Kosovo's nameplate, but must also be read aloud to reinforce Kosovo as a province of Serbia (Barlovac, 2012). Then Serbia's speaker of the parliament, Slavica Djukic Dejanovic, announced that Belgrade expected Serbia's local and parliamentary elections on 6 May 2012 to be held in northern Kosovo as

---

1 Resolution 1244 remains nominally in force, since Kosovo's declaration of independence greatly reduced the scope of the UN Mission in Kosovo. See Sperabauer, 2008.

well. The United Nations warned Serbia that this was a violation of international law, but the international community generally retreated to the sidelines.

At the end of March, Kosovo police arrested four Serbs working for Serbia's Interior Ministry when they entered the north carrying voting lists and election materials. In retaliation, Serbian police officers arrested two Kosovo police officers assigned to patrol the joint border (in violation of a previous EU-brokered agreement on the integrated management of borders). Preliminary reports from NATO and EU investigators on the ground indicated that the men were ambushed 130 metres inside Kosovo's territory (Bytyci, 2012). Outrage in Kosovo subsided when the officers were finally released from a Serbian prison on 2 April, but the controversy is far from over.

Whether EU members will continue to call for fast tracking Serbia into EU accession talks in the face of Belgrade's continual adversarial relations with Prishtina remains to be seen. To do so would be a blow to EU credibility, since Belgrade's actions amount to a flagrant disregard of the Copenhagen criteria. At the same time, the reinstitution of UN 1244 is a potentially perilous setback not only for Kosovo, but for the region. The European Union and the US government – now in a final push to resolve the long-standing conflict between Belgrade and Prishtina and to exit the region – are turning their attention to northern Kosovo. Ever since the Prishtina-Belgrade talks commenced in March 2011, Western officials repeatedly assured Kosovo that the negotiations would be confined to a discussion of 'technical issues'. However, once the agreement about 'the footnote' was signed – an agreement that was rigorously pushed by US Secretary of State Hillary Clinton and Deputy Secretary William Burns – the EU and the United States called for the renewal of talks after Serbia's local and parliamentary elections and with a focus on resolving the issue of the north. The stage was now set for Belgrade's oft-repeated intention to make the *de facto* partition of the Serb majority area in the north a *de jure* reality.

Belgrade has been successful in convincing the international community that Kosovo Serbs in the north are at risk. No one seems to be paying attention to the fact that the majority of Kosovo Serbs (80,000 out of 120,000) live in the centre and southern parts of the country and enjoy local self-government unimpeded. Integration of Serbs has worked everywhere in Kosovo except in the north, where radical Serb leaders have been operating without even the semblance of responding to the central government in Prishtina (Cloyes DioGuardi, 2008). Since war's end, the Kosovo government, KFOR and EULEX (the EU entity responsible for overseeing the police and the judiciary in Kosovo) have been reluctant to establish the rule of law there. In reality, the conflict in the north has always been about Belgrade's expansionist aims. Ever since Milosevic's troops invaded Kosovo in 1998, Serbia's endgame has been the partition of the mineral-rich north, just as it was in Bosnia, where it was able to create an ethnic Serb enclave called Republika Srpska.

The European Union is itself part of the problem because of its uninterrupted policy of appeasement of Serbia and its lack of unity in relation to Kosovo. Five member states – Spain, Greece, Cyprus, Romania and Slovakia – refuse to recognise Kosovo's independence, and EULEX is 'status neutral'.[2] I believe that its lack of unity causes the EU to put pressure on the weakest link in the Western Balkans, the country that is the least likely to create problems, namely Kosovo.

The EU has assured Prishtina that it will not allow Serbia to embark on membership negotiations until it resolves its conflict with Kosovo. And yet, in preparation for the resumption of the Prishtina-Belgrade talks in May (which the political opposition in Kosovo is rejecting), the European Union and the United States have put the onus on Kosovo to assemble a coalition of all political factors in the country to develop a resolution for the north, while still not making Serbia's full recognition of Kosovo's sovereignty a requirement for EU admission. The European Parliament has claimed that negotiations are "the only way to permanently remove tensions in the region" (Adnkronos International, 2012). But with the aim of intensifying the pressure on Kosovo to find a solution for the north, one that might include changing the status of the north from 'non-territorial autonomy' to 'territorial autonomy', the resumption of negotiations will not produce lasting peace in the region. Instead, they will help Serbia challenge the finality of Kosovo's status and its functionality as a state in its pursuit of more territory, while increasing the potential for open conflict.

Unfortunately, Kosovo's political elite has contributed to the decline in the country's fortunes on the international stage. With the exception of Ramush Haradinaj's government in 2004 and some members of the political opposition today, Prishtina has been too willing to satisfy the West's interest in appeasing Serbia since the war ended in 1999. In order to gain "supervised independence"[3] for a country that is 92 per cent

---

2 This makes it difficult for the EU to pressure Serbia to recognize Kosovo, and it is also one of the reasons why Kosovo does not yet have the 128 out of 193 members of the United Nations it needs to be admitted to this body. See Stinner (2012), who was a member of the German Bundestag, and Bugajski and Conley (2010).

3 "Supervised independence" was the core recommendation made by Ambassador Martti Ahtisaari, as the Special Envoy of the UN Secretary General on Kosovo's future status. It is the first recommendation in his "Comprehensive Proposal for the Kosovo Status Settlement", submitted on 26 March 2007. It became known interna-

Albanian and 5 per cent Serb, the Kosovo government under Hashim Thaci accepted compromises through the "Ahtisaari plan", including changing the Albanian name of the Republic of 'Kosova' to the Serbian 'Kosovo'; replacing the Albanian flag with a flag and national anthem devoid of any historical and cultural meaning; and giving Kosovo Serbs more rights than any other ethnic minority in Europe, including some that undermine the strength of the central government, such as establishing direct links between Kosovo Serb municipalities and Belgrade, and requiring the vote of two-thirds of the minority members of parliament to make any changes in the constitution (see Cloyes DioGuardi, 2007).

Perhaps even more important, Kosovo's political elite has failed to properly govern and meet the needs of their citizens. There is a lack of a robust, democratic government, a high level of corruption, insufficient rule of law and freedom of the press, a pattern of rigged elections, substandard educational institutions and little economic development. While some of this is the result of Kosovo having spent nine years as an international protectorate and four years without genuine independence, blame must be placed on the Kosovar Albanian leadership. While Serbia has been working since war's end to destabilise northern Kosovo, Belgrade has also been working to meet standards for admission to the European Union. If Kosovo expects to sign a EU Stabilisation and Association Agreement in the near future, it needs to concentrate on fulfilling criteria for EU membership.

Macedonia

The European Union's awarding of candidate status to Macedonia in 2005, and the beginning of preliminary high-level talks in 2012 in advance of formal negotiations, may eventually be seen as premature in light of increasing interethnic strife. Candidacy status was conferred following Macedonia's purportedly successful negotiations to implement the Ohrid Agreement. The agreement was designed to end the conflict between the country's ruling ethnic Macedonians and the ethnic Albanian minority (which makes up at least one-third of the population) in the wake of the armed conflict of 2001. Both groups were willing to enter into the negotiations leading to the Ohrid Agreement because both Washington and Brussels promised that it would lead to a more equitable distribution of power and, with it, admission to the European Union and to NATO.

---

tionally as "the Ahtisaari plan". See www.unosek.org and also Hill and Linden-Retek (2010).

While European Commission President José Barroso and the EU's enlargement commissioner, Stefan Füle, agreed to enter into preliminary talks with Macedonia's leadership in 2011 in the interest of keeping institutional reforms on track (Taleski, 2012), the country remains deeply divided along ethnic lines and, to this day, only a few parts of the Ohrid Agreement have been implemented. In 2011, Macedonian nationalists and Albanian protesters clashed, leaving eight seriously injured, over the construction of a museum in the form of an Orthodox church at the site of an ancient Albanian fortress in Skopje. For a long time, Macedonian sports fan clubs have been using slogans such as 'Gas Chambers for Shiptars' (a pejorative term for Albanians) and burning Albanian flags at stadiums domestically and abroad. However, in 2012, interethnic violence intensified to a level not seen since the incidents that led to the armed conflict of 2001, and this now threatens to turn Macedonia into nothing more than a dysfunctional enclave within democratic Europe – a deteriorating situation that should give the European Union pause about proceeding with accession talks.

In January 2012, Albanian Muslims torched an Orthodox church in the ethnically mixed city of Struga, after ethnic Macedonians arrived at a nearby annual village carnival wearing masks that were deemed offensive to Muslims. The tipping point came with two terrible acts of violence in February and March. Clashes ensued across the country, with police moving in to quell the unrest. The first involved the murder of two young Albanian men in Gostivar by an off-duty ethnic Macedonian police officer in a feud about a parking space. While Western officials in Skopje called for calm, a cycle of violence ensued: groups of ethnic Albanian youths retaliated by attacking Macedonians at public transportation sites, and then thirty masked ethnic Macedonians boarded a bus with baseball bats and metal bars and severely beat 10 ethnic Albanian minors, some of whom were female (Marusic, 2012).

Prime Minister Nikola Gruevski, who is also the leader of the ruling ethnic Macedonian party, VMRO-DPMNE, and his coalition partner, Ali Ahmeti, the leader of the ethnic Albanian Democratic Union for Integration (DUI), have denied any responsibility for the surge in street violence. Nevertheless, both parties have contributed to whipping up nationalist rhetoric in their communities, the deterioration of human rights, suppression of independent media, an absence of the rule of law, a corrupt justice system, rampant governmental corruption, and widespread unemployment and poverty.[4] According to Xhabir Deralla, head of the Civil Center for Freedom in Skopje, "In order to divert society's reaction from these alarming problems, the ruling party imposed a rapid

4 The unemployment rate is 33.8 per cent. See Marusic, 2010.

growth of populism and national-chauvinist rhetoric and action and has raised nationalism and discrimination to institutional levels" (Deralla, 2012).

In addition, Macedonia has been unable to obtain a membership negotiation date with the European Union because of its protracted struggle with Greece over the country's name. Hence, Macedonia is referred to as the Former Yugoslav Republic of Macedonia (FYROM) in the United Nations, where it is a member state. The dispute between Macedonia and Greece has intensified ever since Prime Minister Gruevski decided to spend millions of dollars on renovating the capital of Skopje in the image of Alexander the Great, beginning with a 20-metre-high statue of Alexander on horseback in the heart of the city. Albanians in Macedonia are also upset because of the expense, because Alexander was an Illyrian (an ethnic Albanian) and because the refusal to resolve the name is blocking admission to the European Union. According to the Fitch Ratings Agency:

> Further delays in the EU accession process could undermine interethnic relations, as the Albanian minority does not share the intransigent stance taken by the ethnic Macedonians on the dispute with Greece about Macedonia's constitutional name. This dispute, centered on Greek fears that Macedonia's proposed formal name implies a claim on its northern territory of the same name, has caused Greece to block the start of formal accession talks since 2009 (Reuters, 2012).

Greece's blockade over Macedonia's name will remain the biggest obstacle to Macedonia's admission to the European Union and to NATO. While waiting for a resolution with Greece, Brussels and Macedonia began the first round of 'high-level' talks on 15 March 2012, with teams led by Prime Minister Gruevski and the EU's enlargement commissioner, Stefan Füle, for the purpose of instituting reforms that will ensure rule of law, freedom of speech, a free press, a sound market economy and a viable public administration.

The bigger, long-range problem and hurdle to overcome may turn out to be the failure to grant equal human and civil rights to the Albanian population and the concentration of power in the hands of a small group of political leaders in both Macedonian and Albanian ethnic groups. This has resulted in little public trust in state institutions and a hobbled civil society.

Montenegro

In a 12 October 2011 report, the European Commission recommended the opening of accession talks with Montenegro. This was surprising on several counts, beginning with the fact that the division between ethnic groups and the struggle for power among political parties in Montenegro is even greater than in Macedonia. The Albanian minority, only 6 per cent of Montenegro's population, also experiences severe discrimination and repression.[5]

Instead of curtailing the marginalisation of the Albanian minority, the ruling Macedonian party has intensified its historical policies of forced assimilation, land confiscation, the economic underdevelopment of Albanian majority areas, a lack of adequate health care, substandard education and a criminal justice system infected by racism. This strategy, which has its roots in the first annexation of Albanian land to Montenegro in 1878, has led to more than half of the population of Albanians from Montenegro living outside the country today, primarily in the United States and western Europe. Interethnic divisions were brought to a head in September 2006, when the Montenegrin government arrested, tortured and imprisoned fourteen Albanians, three of whom were American citizens, on suspicion of terrorist activity. The Americans were finally released at the end of 2009. Another assault on ethnic Albanian rights occurred in 2012 with the passage of a law prohibiting the display of national flags in both private and public places, and the ruling party's refusal to give the Albanian majority Malesia/Tuzi region the communal status it once enjoyed along with the 21 other municipalities that make up Montenegro.

Lack of protection for minorities (a protection that is a core principle of the Copenhagen criteria) is coupled with weak enforcement of the rule of law, institutional corruption, a high level of unemployment and lack of a free press. The latest example of the latter was shockingly illustrated on 7 March 2012 when journalist Olivera Lakic, after receiving repeated threats for her series of articles in the daily newspaper *Vijesti* about the production of counterfeit cigarettes in Montenegro, was attacked with repeated blows to the head. Almost 1,000 Montenegrins signed a petition asking the European Union to pressure the Montenegrin government to take steps to protect journalists and fight organised crime (Radio Free Europe/Radio Liberty, 2012).

The European Commission stressed the problem of corruption in Montenegro in its annual report of November 2011. There is also well-documented activity of organised criminal groups in Montenegro engaged in narcotics and arms trafficking, the money from which is being laundered through the purchase of real estate, especially hotels and

---

5 I documented the latter in a 2003 report to the late Congressman Tom Lantos, then ranking Democratic Member of the House International Relations Committee, who led a fact-finding mission sponsored by the Albanian American Civic League to the Albanian lands in Montenegro. See Cloyes DioGuardi, 2003.

resorts along the Montenegrin coastline (Večernje novosti, 2012). Prime Minister Milo Djukanovic, who stepped down from his position in December 2010 after more than two decades in power but who remains head of Montenegro's main political party (and who was named as prime minister designate by Montenegro's President Filip Vujanovic on 9 November 2012), has been widely known to have a hand in tobacco smuggling and money laundering, and has been sought in the past by Italian prosecutors without success. The current prime minister, Igor Luksic, said in his first interview with foreign media after assuming power that he did not see a case "where any member of the government would deserve to go before the prosecutor's office" (Tanner and Komnenic, 2011).

Bosnia-Herzegovina

More than 250,000 Bosnian Muslims died at the hands of the Serbian military and paramilitary troops under Slobodan Milosevic while the EU and the United States collaborated on a policy of appeasement, containment and non-intervention. With the murder of some 8,000 men and boys in Srebrenica, the largest genocide in Europe since the Nazi era, that policy was temporarily suspended. The Dayton Accords ensued in 1995 and brought an end to Serbian ethnic cleansing and war in Bosnia. But at the same time, the accords, which brought Milosevic to the table as a peacemaker, carved up the territory and left the country in a *de facto* partition along ethnic lines. The result was a political structure that weakened the central government. In particular, the creation of a Bosnian Serb entity called Republika Srpska allowed the hardliners to maintain their power at the expense of political and economic progress in Bosnia. Seventeen years after war's end, the leader of Srpska, Milorad Dodik, has rejected reform and continues to brandish the threat of holding a referendum on secession.[6]

As Sonja Biserko, head of the Helsinki Committee for Human Rights in Serbia, has observed, Serbia's "continual ambition for a predominant influence" over its neighbours, includes not only Kosova but Bosnia and Herzegovina, where Belgrade "officially encourages and supports not only the status quo there, but also the secessionist policies of the Serb entity leadership" (Biserko, 2011, pp. 4-5). Without a strong central government in Sarajevo, Bosnia continues to suffer from interethnic rivalries. But it also is unable to undertake the kind of reforms that would enable it to measure up to the Copenhagen criteria and gain

---

6 EU High Representative Ashton convinced Dodik to drop his plans to hold a referendum in May 2011; see Hadzovic, 2011.

admission to the European Union. As Morton Abramowitz and James Hooper observed in "Re-Repairing Bosnia" (2010):

> The Bosnians lack the capability to modify the iron corset bequeathed to them at Dayton. ...Leaving Bosnians to explore the options that befall a failed state (with a Muslim plurality) – located within Europe, but on the margins of its prosperity, unity, and relative social cohesion – is to acknowledge policy bankruptcy and let others roll the dice on ways to end the current stalemate.

The United States long ago took a backseat to the European Union when it comes to Bosnia, even though it continues to champion the Dayton Accords. Less than a year ago, US Assistant Secretary of State Philip Gordon said, "The United States continues to strongly support this framework: one state, two vibrant entities, three constituent people" (Gordon, 2011, p. 9). However, it is impossible to achieve robust entities in the kind of decentralised structure that Dayton established. Thus, it is left to the European Union to revise the Dayton agreement so that the central government is strengthened and democracy can take root. Apart from this, the EU accession process will never work in Bosnia. And since the EU has granted Serbia candidate status, it can and should also use its leverage to pressure Belgrade into reforming the obstructionist behaviour of the leadership in Srpska as a condition of entering into accession negotiations.

Albania

The Stabilisation and Association Agreement between the European Union and Albania was signed in June 2006, and it entered into force on 28 April 2009 when Albania made its formal application for membership. In December 2010, the European Parliament granted Albanian citizens 'visa liberalisation' to travel freely in the Schengen zone covering 25 European countries. The following year, as Albania was preparing to take the next step towards EU accession, Albanians across the globe were shocked when a protest in the capital of Tirana on 21 January 2011 turned violent, leaving three dead and 39 wounded. The Socialist Party, chaired by Edi Rama, had conducted a door-to-door campaign to drive Albanians into the streets after Deputy Prime Minister Ilir Meta, chairman of the Socialist Movement for Integration, was caught on tape trying to fix a public tender for a hydropower plant granted to one of his friends. But the public reaction went far beyond two decades of stark division between the country's reigning democratic and socialist political camps.

By the time the violence was quelled, it was clear that the crowd of more than 20,000 represented a citizenry filled with pent-up anger about uninvestigated and unpunished corruption among the political elite and an ever worsening economic downward spiral for the majority of Albanians. The Socialist Party had contested the results of the parliamentary elections in June 2009, left the government, and would not return until September 2011. In 2010, the European Union rejected Albania's application to become a member state, insisting that the country had to bring an end to corruption and establish rule of law and a viable democracy. With the 21 January uprising, admission to the European Union became more elusive than ever before. According to the European Commission's Albania 2011 Progress Report, "the longstanding political stalemate has also hampered the establishment of a consensus enabling the implementation of relevant EU reforms" (European Commission, 2011, sec. 2.1, pp. 7-8).

The Berisha government's lack of progress in ensuring the independence of the judiciary and the eradication of corruption has been troubling to both EU officials and Albanian citizens.[7] The unresolved matter of the March 2008 ammunitions factory explosion in Gerdec, in particular, has been a festering wound for Albanians of all political persuasions, because it demonstrated that oligarchs in politics and business are exempt from the rule of law. Twenty-six workers died and 309 were injured at the Gerdec plant, where they were prying open thousands of artillery shells with metal rods and bare hands on a daily basis as part of a national program to dismantle ammunition and sell the components. It was later revealed that the explosions began when workers were moving old cartridges from China and Russia, amassed by the communist-era dictatorship of Enver Hoxha, and that these stocks were being repackaged and sold to the Afghan army and police forces.

To make matters worse, the money from this enterprise was being diverted to Albanian officials, including the son of Prime Minister and Democratic Party leader Sali Berisha, according to an investigative report conducted by *The New York Times*. Although former Defense Minister Fatmir Mediu resigned, neither he nor any other government or company officials were charged with wrongdoing. Instead, after the national elections on 29 June 2009, Mediu was reinstated in the government as the minister of the environment, a position that gives him immunity from criminal prosecution (Cloyes DioGuardi, 2011).

And so, even though the Socialist Party initiated the demonstration on 21 January 2011, they tapped into the sense of helplessness and hopelessness engulfing the Albanian public in the face of endemic governmental and judicial corruption on the part of the elite, weak

[7] Currently, high-level officials enjoy full immunity from prosecution. See European Commission, 2011, p. 11.

institutions, lack of rule of law, elections that are not fully free and fair, media constrained by the political persuasions of their owners, and the failure of both Socialist and Democratic Party leaders to bring the nation out of poverty. As former US Ambassador to Albania John Withers stated in a March 2012 interview in Tirana's JAVA magazine, "What needs to change most among Albania's political elite is its mentality. Today, Albania's governing class clings to the bygone, indeed regressive notion that it is privileged above the common people, that it is immune from the rule of law, and that it does not have to submit to the will of the people" (Withers, 2012).

The European Union and the United States also need to change by ceasing to give the government in Tirana a pass. While Albania was busy violating democratic norms, it was prematurely accepted into NATO (in 2008) because it had been willing for many years to do the bidding of the West, especially the United States – by not joining Kosova in its fight for independence, not supporting the struggle of Albanians in the Presheva Valley and in Macedonia to gain equal rights, and not mounting any serious challenges to Greece's violation of the civil rights of its Albanian minority population, at least one million in number.

Parliamentary elections in Albania on 11 June 2012, maintained the political status quo. The ruling Democratic Party retained its grip on power, and the protracted struggle between democratic and socialist leaders led to four rounds of voting before the parliament reached a consensus to elect Bujar Nishani as the country's president. Nothing in the way of fundamental change can be expected in Albania until conditions are created that allow new political leaders and new political parties to emerge, and specifically ones not tainted by the last 20 years of embezzlement and hidden political party collaboration. EU and US government representatives in Tirana should do more than try to broker stability; they should hold politicians accountable, help new political movements emerge, and in this way support the Albanian population's yearning for genuine democracy and economic viability. Before Albania can be accepted into the European Union, it is essential that today's corrupt politicians are replaced by a new political bloc rallied around democratic values and prepared to lead Albania into a productive future with the rest of Europe.

Conclusion

Is the EU enlargement plan really on track in the Western Balkans? And, if so, is it undergirded by a political strategy that will successfully integrate Serbia, Kosova, Macedonia, Montenegro, Bosnia and Albania? Will the outcome be one that brings lasting peace and prosperity to the region, on par with the reality enjoyed by western Europe since the end of World War II?

For those who believe that leaving the countries of the Western Balkans out of the EU enlargement process may increase the possibility of interethnic conflict and extreme nationalism, I believe that accelerating the accession process before the requirements of Copenhagen are met will lead to what Fareed Zakaria has called the entrenchment of "illiberal democracies" in southeast Europe, to the detriment of both the Western Balkans and the European Union. He rightly includes the region in his list of "democratically elected regimes [that] are routinely ignoring constitutional limits on their power and depriving their citizens of basic rights and freedoms (Zakaria, 1997, p. 22).

While the European Union has been bearing the burden of expending the resources to reform the Western Balkans and integrate the region into its membership, the United States has been pouring most of its resources into a post-9/11 fight against Islamic terrorism in Afghanistan and Iraq. As long as the Obama administration remains engaged in military intervention in Afghanistan and does not develop a policy based on demilitarising the 'war on terror' – thereby eliminating the possibility of military intervention in Iran and elsewhere – it will not be able to focus on the Western Balkans or develop a foreign policy approach based on prevention and diplomacy. The US government's approach to the Western Balkans since Kosova's declaration of independence in 2008 has been one of taking a backseat to Europe. Ever since 1999, after America led NATO air strikes against Serbia to end the Balkan wars, US policy has pursued the status quo and 'stability' at all costs, using robust international executive powers to accomplish this end. I would argue that this policy is increasingly misguided and unproductive for the region and for the West.

This presents an opportunity for the European Union to do more than "strengthen their political engagement in the region beyond a mere institutional restructuring" (Sebastian, 2011, p. 5) by putting social justice and human rights at the forefront of its foreign policy objectives and increasing domestic ownership. It would be a mistake for the European Union to leapfrog over interethnic strife and lack of human rights perpetrated by Slav-dominated countries over Albanians in order to bring the Western Balkans into the European Union. This is the time to adopt a comprehensive, regional approach to come to terms with violations of human rights and the rule of law.

The Western Balkans will only benefit from the process of accession to EU membership when the process values human rights and interethnic tolerance on par with economic advancement. The staggering unemployment rates (45 per cent in Kosova, for example) and pervasive poverty side by side the excessive wealth of the political elites who have concentrated power in a few hands in most of the countries in the Western Balkans is increasingly untenable. But "even if the region's economies were put forth on a better footing," according to political analyst Ekrem Krasniqi, "the European Union and the United States must... come up with a new concept for minority rights on a region wide basis" (2010). This is where I believe that the European Union should be concentrating its efforts: supporting civil society to promote mutual coexistence and universal human rights throughout the region in anticipation of the day when all borders and visas in the Balkans will be removed.

This will require publicly opposing Serbia's expansionist appetite, the severe interethnic tension in Bosnia, Macedonia and Montenegro, and political elites in Albania and throughout the region intent on enriching themselves at the expense of their citizens. This will also require the European Union to convince its five hold-out member states to recognise Kosova's sovereignty, without which there will never be regional cooperation.

The concept of regional cooperation must be taken seriously, not just because it is a component of the Copenhagen criteria but because it is essential to avoiding future conflict. As Nevena Jovanović has asserted:

Regional cooperation should not be considered only as a part of the EU conditionality policy. On the contrary, it should be perceived as a real and honest necessity. The Western Balkans can, through sincere partnership and open regional cooperation, be a relevant actor in European policy and successful not only in the process of European integration, but also in further internal reforms. If Western Balkan countries succeed in that, getting precise dates for becoming EU member states...is of less importance (2012).

References

Abramowitz, M. and J. Hooper. 2010. "Re-Repairing Bosnia." *Project Syndicate*, March 11. http://www.project-syndicate.org/commentary/re-repairing-bosnia (29 October 2012).

Adnkronos International. 2012. "Balkans: European parliament adopts resolutions on Kosovo, Serbia." 29 March. www.adnkronos.com/IGN/Aki/English/Politics/Balkans-European-parliament-adopts-resolutions-on-Kosovo (22 November 2012).

Barlovac, B. 2012. "EU urged to save crumbling Kosova-Serbia deal." *Balkan Insight*, March 22. http://www.balkaninsight.com/en/article/kosovo-Serbia-interpret-brussels-deal-differently (29 October 2012).

Biserko, S. 2011. "Western Balkans – towards a more integrated Europe." Speech to the Joint Parliamentary Meeting, European Parliament. Brussels, 13-14 April.

Bugajski, J. and H.A. Conley. 2010. "Kosovo at the Crossroads: Impact of the International Court Ruling." Washington, DC: Center for Strategic & International Studies, 22 July. www.csis.org/publication/Kosovo-crossroads-impact-international-court-justice-ruling (22 November 2012).

Bytyci, F. 2012. "Serbia releases Kosovo police officers to EU." Reuters World Service, 2 April.

Cloyes DioGuardi, S. 2003. "Montenegro: An Apartheid State in the Heart of Europe." Report to Congressman Tom Lantos, Ranking Member of the House International Relations Committee. Published in *Illyria* 1268, 22 August.

Cloyes DioGuardi, S. 2007. "The Ahtisaari Plan: Caveat Emptor." *Illyria* 1624, 23-26 February.

Cloyes DioGuardi, S. 2008. "Saving Kosova." *Illyria* 1803, 28 November-4 December.

Cloyes DioGuardi, S. 2011. "Albanians Stand at a Perilous Crossroads." *Balkan Insight*, 3 February.

Cloyes DioGuardi, S. and R. Gjoni. 2010. "It's Time to End the Appeasement of Serbia." *Balkan Insight*, 29 October.

Deralla, X. 2012. "Who wants War in Macedonia?" *Balkan Insight*, 14 March. http://www.balkaninsight.com/en/article/who-wants-war-in-macedonia (29 October 2012).

Emmerson, B., QC. 2011. Opening statement, pre-trial conference. ICTY, Prosecution *versus* Ramush Haradinaj, Idriz Balaj, and Lahi Brahimaj. 17 August. http://www.icty.org/x/cases/haradinaj/trans/en/110817ED.htm (22 November 2012).

EUABC.com. n.d. "Copenhagen Criteria." http://uk.euabc.com/word/230 (22 November 2012).

Europa. 2010. "EU to reaffirm its commitment to Western Balkans at Sarajevo meeting." Press releases RAPID, IP/10/647, 6 January. http://europa.eu/rapid/press-release_IP-10-647_en.htm (22 November 2012).

European Commission. 2011. "Albanian 2011 Progress Report." Commission Staff Working Paper, *Communication from the Commission to the European Parliament and the Council, Enlargement Strategy and Main Challenges.* Section 2.1: Democracy and the Rule of Law, Judicial System.

European Council. 2008. "European Partnership with Serbia, including Kosovo." 2008/213/EC. 18 February. http://europa.eu/legislation_summaries/ enlargement/western_balkans/r18015_en.htm (29 October 2012).

Gordon, P.H., 2011. "The State of Affairs in the Balkans." Hearing before the Subcommittee on Europe and Eurasia of the Committee on Foreign Affairs, House of Representatives, 112th Congress, First Session, No. 112-112, 15 November.

Hadzovic, E. 2011. "Bosnian Serb MPs Set to Withdraw Referendum Decision." *Balkan Insight*, 31 May. www.balkaninsight.com/en/article/rs-national-assembly-to-withdraw-its-decision-on-referendum (22 November 2012).

Hill, S. and P. Linden-Retek. 2010. "Supervised Independence and Post-Conflict Sovereignty: The Dynamics of Hybridity in Kosovo's New Constitutional Court." *Yale Journal of International Law Online* 36 (Fall). http://www.yjil.org/docs/pub/o-36-hill-linden-retek-hybridity-in-kosovo.pdf (22 November 2012).

International Crisis Group. 2001. "Bin Laden and the Balkans: The Politics of Anti-Terrorism." *ICG Balkans Report* No. 119. www.crisisgroup.org/~/media/Files/europe/Balkans%202.pdf (30 October 2012).

International Crisis Group. 2011. "North Kosovo: Dual Sovereignty in Practice." *Europe Report* No. 211, 14 March. http://www.crisisgroup.org/en/ regions/europe/balkans/kosovo/211-north-kosovo-dual-sovereignty-in-practice.aspx (22 November 2012).

Jovanović, N. 2012. "A European Future for the Western Balkans – challenges and perspectives." FutureLab Europe, 18 January. http://www.futurelabeurope.eu/blog/a-european-future-for-the-western-balkans-challenges-and-perspectives/ (22 November 2012).

Kanin, D.B. 2012. "Kosovo – Serbia: Two Concessions, One Winner." *Eurasia Review*, 29 February. http://www.eurasiareview.com/29022012-kosovo-serbia-two-concessions-one-winner-analysis/ (30 October 2012).

Krasniqi, E. 2010. "A wake-up call for the EU on Kosovo." euobserver.com, 20 December. http://euobserver.com/opinion/31548 (30 October 2012).

Marusic, S.J. 2010. "Macedonia Leads World Unemployment Study." *Balkan Insight*, 25 June. www.balkaninsight.com/en/article/macedonia-leads-world-unemployment-study (22 November 2012).

Marusic, S.J. 2012. "Church Almost Burned in Struga, Macedonia." *Balkan Insight*, 31 January. http://www.balkaninsight.com/en/article/ethnic-tensions-surge-in-macedonian-town (30 October 2012).

Polychroniou, C.J. 2011. "An Unblinking Glance at a National Catastrophe and the Potential Dissolution of the Eurozone: Greece's Debt Crisis in Context." Working Paper No. 688, September. Annandale-on-Hudson, NY: Levy Economics Institute. http://www.levyinstitute.org/pubs/wp_688.pdf (30 October 2012).

Pond, E. 2012. "Kosova's Endgame." *Illyria* 2132, 16-19 March.

Radio Free Europe/Radio Liberty. 2012. "Suspect Arrested in Beating of Montenegrin Journalist." 13 March. http://www.rferl.org/content/montenegro_journalist_beating_suspect_arrested/24514718.html (30 October 2012).

Reuters. 2012. "Text-Fitch: EU dialogue could boost Macedonia reforms, stability." 21 March. http://www.reuters.com/article/2012/03/21/idUSWNA305020120321 (30 October 2012).

Sebastian, S. 2011. "A new start in the Balkans?" Policy Brief, FRIDE: A European Think Tank for Global Action, No. 89, August.

Sperabauer, M. 2008. "EULEX Kosovo: The Difficult Deployment and Challenge." *German Law Journal* 11(8): 769-802. www.germanlawjournal.com/pdfs/FullIssues/PDF_vol11_no_8_08Complete%20 (22 November 2012).

Stinner, R. 2012. "Debating Europe: Should Kosovo Join the European Union?" 5 July. http://www.debatingeurope.eu/2012/07/05/should-kosovo-join-the-eu/ (22 November 2012).

Taleski, M. 2012. "Macedonia Begins EU Accession Talks." *Eurasia Review*, 13 March. http://www.eurasiareview.com/13032012-macedonia-begins-eu-accession-talks/ (30 October 2012).

Tanner, A and P. Komnenic. 2011. "Montenegro PM to address EU Corruption Concerns." Reuters, 21 January. http://www.forexyard.com/en/news/Montenegro-PM-to-address-corruption-concerns-2011-01-21T145021Z-INTERVIEW-EU (22 November 2012).

Večernje novosti. 2012. "35 criminal groups active in Montenegro." Reprinted in *B-92*, 1 April.

Withers, J.L. 2012. Interview with Skender Minxhozi in *JAVA* magazine, Tirana, Albania. 17 March. http://news.albania.de/2012/03/17/ex-us-botschafter-john-withers-uber-die-gerdec-ermittliungs-sabotage-salih-berisha-und-lulzim-basha-sind-keine-demokraten/print/ (22 November 2012).

Zakaria, F. 1997. "The rise of illiberal democracy." *Foreign Affairs* 76(6): 22-43.

EU Enlargement and Kosovo's Europeanization

European Union and Shaping Kosovo's Representative or 'Represented' Democracy

Faton Tony BISLIMI

Introduction: A New State with a Complex Political System

After decades of civil unrest, demonstrations, protests, and finally the war of 1998-99, Kosovo became a UN-administered territory in June 1999. After nine years of UN administration, on 17 February 2008, Kosovo declared its independence, which so far has been recognized by 92 nations worldwide, including most of the European Union (EU) Member States (except for Cyprus, Greece, Romania, Slovakia and Spain), most of NATO and OECD members. About a year after independence, Kosovo became a member of the World Bank Group and the International Monetary Fund. It aspires to join the EU, UN and NATO in the future.

Independence, however, did not resolve Kosovo's mounting problems such as the lack of economic development, poor infrastructure and health care, a weak education system and above all, a political system that is hard to define. While Kosovo is a democracy and allows for the existence and operation of a multitude of political parties and interest groups with a stake in policymaking, its political and governing systems are quite complex to fit within one single definition of a conventional political system. What makes Kosovo's political system unique in this sense is the fact that Kosovo is still, at least formally, under the auspices of the UN, albeit being an independent state. Apart from the UN, there is one European Union mission and one international civilian mission in Kosovo as well, both of whom have executive powers and are under the leadership of the EU. And, on top of everything, there is still a NATO-led peacekeeping mission, KFOR, which holds executive power in the area of security and border control.

Clearly, Kosovo's political system is complex, and the EU plays a crucial role in it. There exists a myriad of actors that not only affect, but also have executive powers over the policymaking process in Kosovo.

Some of these actors are domestic; some are international, namely EU-based. Their goals and objectives do not always match, and their views can sometimes be contradictory.

As a result, what Kosovo has today is a multifaceted political system that is shaped and influenced by domestic as well as international layers of governance. In a country in which the democratic world (especially the West) has heavily invested with the objective of making it a liberal democracy with a European future, in which the will of the people reigns over the political process, the institutions are functional and in service of the citizens and politicians respond to citizen demands, and a pluralist society, in which people of all ethnicities and other backgrounds (social, cultural, religious, etc.) would be free and equal, both of these concepts, democracy and pluralism, seem to be highly talked about but little acted on.

Thus, from the theoretical perspectives of pluralism and democratization, this chapter looks at the political system of Kosovo and its Europeanization process, based on the *democratic conditionality* framework set forth by Schimmelfennig and Sedelmeier (2005a), in an effort to better understand the roles of the actors that shape both the political and policymaking processes of a newborn country in the middle of Europe that aspires to join the EU. The complexity of Kosovo's political system, however, seems to go beyond the conventional boundaries of theories of both pluralism (and neo-pluralism) and democratization, and Europeanization has played a key role in it.

Therefore, Kosovo provides a unique case study for the understanding of contemporary representation of interests and the process of democratization along with that of Europeanization where actors – domestic and foreign/international – interact, argue and sometimes even agree with one another. Indeed, the creation of such multifaceted political systems, where a combination of domestic and international governing structures exists, has been studied through the lens of neo-trusteeship (see Fearon and Laitin 2004). But, neo-trusteeship focuses on the immediate post-conflict reconstruction and state-building efforts as opposed to the processes of internal politics and policymaking, including Europeanization. Therefore, the study of Kosovo's political system in terms of theories of pluralism (and neo-pluralism) and democratization can provide more meaningful insights about the internal processes of politics and policymaking in light of the Europeanization of the country, which is the purpose of this chapter.

The chapter has been divided into six sections, the first one being this introduction. The second section provides some background to the process of Europeanization in Kosovo, while the third section gives an overview of the kind of democracy that has been established in Kosovo after the 1998-99 war. Considering the political system in which Kosovo operates, the fourth section provides an analysis of interest representation from a pluralist perspective. The fifth section provides a brief overview of Kosovo's current state of politico-economic affairs in the view of its people. Finally, the sixth section offers some concluding remarks.

The Europeanization Process in Kosovo

Europeanization has become a rather significant concept in political studies with the ever growing – both geographically and in terms of influence – European Union. Most generally, it is defined as the impact that the EU has on domestic politics and policies (Cowles *et al.* 2001). For a country like Kosovo, this impact is quite significant, given two key facts: the EU's mission in Kosovo (EULEX) and Kosovo's aspirations to join the EU. Indeed, Schimmelfennig and Sedelmeier (2005a) argue that the desire of countries to join the EU and the high volume of EU-based rules and regulations (*acquis communitaire*) that aspiring countries have to adopt give the EU an "unprecedented influence in restructuring domestic institutions and the entire range of public policies" in these countries.

The Ahtisaari Plan, upon which Kosovo got its independence, among others, called for major and substantial EU involvement in the fields of justice, rule of law and customs and for an International Civilian Office (ICO) to ensure the full implementation of the plan. The chief of ICO, the International Civilian Representative (ICR), would still have executive powers and could intervene to override legislation or other decisions of the Kosovo authorities if they were deemed in violation of the letter or spirit of the plan. The EU rule of law, justice and customs mission would also have a rather limited executive mandate. KFOR's presence was deemed necessary to continue while the Kosovo Protection Corps would be dissolved, and a new, modern but small military force called the Kosovo Security Force would be created under KFOR's guidance and direction. The plan also suggested that continuation of international administration in Kosovo was not sustainable (UNOSEK 2007).

Once the Ahtisaari Plan was introduced in the UN Security Council, a sharp divide ensued among Western powers on one side and Russia and China on the other. The United States and the European Union were fully in support of the plan, but Russia firmly opposed it, claiming that without Serbia's consent, Kosovo cannot become independent as it would set a dangerous precedent for other separatist movements around the world and especially in Eurasia (Antonenko 2007). As no progress was in near sight at the UN Security Council given Russia's threat to veto any new UN Security Council resolution giving way to Kosovo's independence, the Kosovo authorities, in close coordination with Washington and Brussels, unilaterally declared Kosovo an independent and sovereign state on 17 February 2008. Kosovo's Declaration of Independence, however, made specific mention of the Ahtisaari Plan and pledged that Kosovo would fully implement it (Assembly of Kosovo 2008).

Thus, without a new UN Security Council resolution, the existence of the UN Mission in Kosovo (UNMIK) continued, despite the fact that its role as an all-powerful entity expired with Kosovo's declaration of independence. A new international presence, however, was established in post-independence Kosovo: the EU Rule of Law Mission (EULEX) and ICO, headed by the ICR/EU Special Representative (EUSR). At first glance, it may seem that indeed the UN Mission in Kosovo (UNMIK) was replaced by an EU Mission. But, there are substantial differences between the two.

Let us recall that the EU was given a role within UNMIK as well – tasked with reconstruction (William 2005), but that was not because of the EU's political importance but rather because of the UN's need for the EU's economic and development resources necessary for the post-war Kosovo (King and Mason 2006). EULEX, however, represents the most ambitious EU mission ever and the largest of all twenty-two European Security and Defence Policy (ESDP) missions to date (Pond 2008). As opposed to UNMIK, EULEX does not have a civil administration mandate, and it cannot adopt legislation or regulations on behalf of Kosovo. The EULEX mission statement stipulates that "EULEX is not in Kosovo to govern or rule". Its legal basis stems from the European Council Joint Action 2008/124/CFSP of 4 February 2008 (EULEX: URL). While EULEX does not enjoy a UN mandate, it deployed at the invitation of the Kosovo government (Pond 2008). Despite the fact that EULEX is an EU mission, non-EU Member States such as the United States, Canada, Turkey and Norway have also contributed police officers to it (EUSR 2009).

The International Civilian Office, on the other hand, is headed by a double-mandated International Civilian Representative (ICR)/EU Special Representative (EUSR). The ICR/EUSR reports to the European Council and the International Steering Group (ISG) on Kosovo. The purpose of the ICO, however, is "international support for a European future" for Kosovo, and its aims include "ensuring full implementation of the Kosovo's status settlement and supporting Kosovo's European integration". ICO strives to achieve its purpose and aims by "advising Kosovo's government and community leaders" (ICO: URL).

Even though both EULEX and ICO are relatively new in their presence in Kosovo, opinion polls indicate a favourable assessment of their roles by the Kosovo public. Approval ratings for EULEX, for instance, in the beginning of its mission in May 2008 were relatively low, only about 12 per cent, while by April 2009, the approval ratings more than tripled to about 40 per cent, which was slightly higher than approval ratings for either the government or Assembly of Kosovo (UNDP 2009).

Considering the context and missions of both EULEX and ICO, it seems that Kosovo's way forward as an independent state, recognized by 92 countries as of November 2012, is inseparably connected to its prospects of a European future. Given Kosovo's aspirations for a European future and the fact that democracy is at the core of EU values, a full-fledged and functioning democracy in Kosovo is required, among others, before Kosovo can join the EU. Whether Kosovo has come to meet this criterion yet remains to be seen as Kosovo conducts itself and its policies as an independent state from now on. But democracy must be promoted and nourished even though Kosovo may not be a "well-functioning state" yet (Carothers 2007).

Furthermore, in their elaboration of the impact of Europeanization on accession seeking countries, Schimmelfennig and Sedelmeier (2005a) define "two main contexts of Europeanization in Central and Eastern Europe – democratic conditionality and acquis conditionality". Democratic conditionality is concerned with an accession-seeking country's general ability to uphold EU rules of liberal democracy, while acquis conditionality deals more specifically with the EU body of rules and regulations that an accession-seeking country must adopt before becoming a full EU member.

While both democratic conditionality and the acquis conditionality are important, for the purposes of this chapter, the focus of the analysis will be placed on the former. Democracy and democratization usually require societal and ideological changes, whereas adopting a body of new rules and regulations is more of a technocratic process than an ideological one. Hence, in the following section, a comparative theoretical analysis of democratization in Kosovo is provided to see whether the international involvement in Kosovo has helped or hindered Kosovo's ability to attain a European-type liberal democracy and, therefore, to meet the democratic conditionality of Europeanization.

Representative Democracy versus 'Represented' Democracy

As any other post-communist and post-occupied state, Kosovo also is striving to build a good state with a good government and a good political system. But to get a good government, Kosovo needs a good and democratic political system. In light of Kosovo's unique political circumstances, its strategic position in the heart of the Balkans, the increasing ambitions and efforts of the region's states to acquire EU membership and the general trend of globalization, it becomes even more important to study the evolution of politics in Kosovo, its political system and the role that the international community has played in shaping the process of Kosovo's democratization.

When the international community first intervened in Kosovo in 1999, it did so with the objective of establishing peace and prosperity as well as democracy (IICK 2000). But what kind of democracy did it have in mind? A democracy in which all the people of Kosovo regardless of their ethnicity or other background differences (cultural, social, religious, etc.) would live freely and equally.

Representative democracy sounds like the one that would match the goal of the international community's involvement in Kosovo. Kosovo, under the UN administration from 1999, has moved towards democratization in an effort to create a political system that is accountable to the people, guarantees a set of basic individual rights and liberties (through a constitution, for example) and creates a government based on regular fair and free elections. A representative democracy with guaranteed (usually constitutionally) individual liberties is known as a liberal democracy (Dryzek and Dunleavy 2009).

While Kosovo has regularly held free and fair elections (both at the local and national levels) since 2000, and has approved a constitution that guarantees human rights and individual liberties with special focus on the rights of ethnic minorities, it remains questionable whether the country is truly a representative democracy. In a representative democracy, or any functioning democracy for that matter, the basic principle is that the will of the people (as expressed through fair and free elections) matters. In Kosovo, that may not be the case. According to the Ahtisaari Plan,[1] to which the Constitution of Kosovo has given legal prevalence

1 Martti Ahtisaari, former Finnish president and winner of the Nobel Peace Prize 2009, was appointed by the UN Secretary General Ban Ki-Moon to lead the negotiations process between Pristina and Belgrade in an effort to find a mutually acceptable settlement for the political status of Kosovo. After two years of negotiations between 2005 and 2007 and no agreement achieved by the parties, Ahtisaari proposed a Comprehensive Settlement for the Political Status of Kosovo, which would give Kosovo "supervised independence" under the European Union. The document, known as the Ahtisaari Plan, included specific provisions that were to be guaranteed by Prishtina – such as extensive minority rights, the establishment of an EU rule of law mission and the establishment of an international mechanism to supervise independence and the full implementation of the Ahtisaari Plan.

over itself (see the Constitution of the Republic of Kosovo, 2008), two new missions have taken place in post-independence Kosovo: the EU Rule of Law Mission (EULEX) and the International Civilian Office (ICO) headed by the EU Special Representative (EUSR)/International Civilian Representative (ICR) in Kosovo. While EULEX is a an EU-mandated mission and reports directly to Brussels, the ICO is an international mission, albeit primarily funded and directed by the EU, and reports to the Kosovo International Steering Group that includes the European Union, the United States, Switzerland, Norway, Canada, and others.

Similar to the UN Mission in Kosovo (UNMIK) that had executive powers over Kosovo in all fields of life from 1999 to 2008, both of these missions also have executive powers, despite the fact that their executive powers in comparison to those of UNMIK are significantly limited. As noted above, EULEX has executive powers in the police, judiciary and customs domains, while the ICO can overrule any decision of the Kosovo institutions (government, parliament) that is found to be in violation of the letter or the spirit of the Ahtisaari Plan (EULEX, ICO: URL). The ICR can also remove elected people from office if he or she finds that the elected person is not suitable for the given office in light of the Ahtisaari Plan. How is that for a democracy? What happened to the *will of the people*? Why bother to have elections if an EU-appointed diplomat who heads the ICO can overrule your vote?

Huntington (1991) argues that free, fair and competitive elections form the core of a democratic system. Such elections are essential to distinguishing democracies from other authoritarian regimes. Moreover, Simensen (1999) also stresses the fact that a real democracy is based on a plural society, the rule of law, individual liberties and a neutral military. So, in a political system where an externally appointed actor can overrule decisions of a domestically elected body, the importance of political parties seems to decrease. Given that political parties are considered decisive players in a democracy (Cappocia and Ziblatt 2010) however, one can see how the current political system in Kosovo may lower the level of its democratization.

In a more recent article, Huntington (1997) also notes that there is correlation, if not necessarily a causal relationship, between economic development and democracy. Kosovo's continued lack of significant economic development (which will be explored in section four) since the end of the war can be considered as another indicator of its low level of democracy.

Furthermore, Kosovo's democratization process, at present, seems to be unable to meet several of the fifteen key and critical findings about democracy that Schmitter (2010) has identified based on twenty-five years of democratization research. For instance, Schmitter (2010) highlights that while decentralization and other forms of horizontal accountability (checks and balances) have been thought to be "magic ingredients of successful [democratic] consolidation" (p. 24), countries that have implemented other forms of institutions have done just as well. This finding brings into question the decentralization process that Kosovo has taken upon itself to implement in accordance with the Ahtisaari Plan so as to give the Serb minority a local government dominated by them in certain areas of Kosovo where they mostly live. This decentralization plan has been conceived based on ethnic lines and as such will not do much to increase Kosovo's level of democratization but can perhaps further invigorate ethnic divisions. Another finding that Schmitter (2010) highlights states that "democratization continues to rely on a political unit with a capacity for exercising legitimate public coercion and implementing collective decisions within a distinct territory – that is, a state" (pp. 25-26). Given the inability of Kosovo authorities to exercise full power in the northern part of Kosovo, north of the Iber river in the ethnically divided city of Mitrovica, and the lack of willingness of the international presence in Kosovo to do so on behalf of the Kosovo authorities so as to avoid ethnic tensions between the local Serbs who predominantly inhabit that part of the territory and ethnic Albanians south of the Iber river, one can see how this multi-layered governance structure in Kosovo has failed to exercise public authority over the whole of Kosovo and, as such, has hindered the level of democratization of the country.

In a country where democracy is so much preached by the very actors (in this case the international representation in the form of UNMIK, ICO and EULEX) with mandates that are completely antidemocratic, it seems that the form of political system in place is what I call "represented democracy". While a *represented democracy* may include some symptoms mainly associated with the notion of democratic deficit (for a detailed list of what constitutes the democratic deficit, please see Dryzek and Dunleavy 2009), these two notions are different. Represented democracy is also different from all other forms of democracy (such as pseudo democracy, low intensity democracy, partial democracy) that are associated with Zakaria's (1997) notion of illiberal democracy. A represented democracy is a form of democracy that is managed by external actors that primarily come from representative democracies. It looks like a representative democracy – since it allows for regular free and fair elections, a competitive multiparty system and existence of various interest groups (pluralism), and is based on a constitution that guarantees civil liberties and human rights – but its very essence is only a proclaimed form of democracy as opposed to a real one. In a represented democracy, external actors have executive powers that can override the powers of domestically elected bodies. This fact diminishes the importance of elections and, consequently, that of political parties as well. Furthermore, the existence of such powerful external actors also diminishes the capacity of the domestic institutions (the political unit) to exercise full authority over the whole of its territory. As such, represented democracy seems to be the kind of the political system that the international community has established in Kosovo.

The represented democracy that we are seeing in Kosovo has numerous effects on the pluralism of its society as well. Indeed, in a represented democracy, just like in any other form of democracy, interest representation remains a critical way of influencing policymaking. However, the role of actors and their respective weight of influence are different under a represented democracy as opposed to a representative or liberal democracy.

A Pluralist Society as a Basis for Fair Interest Representation?

Pluralism, as a philosophical and political term, was first used to acknowledge diversity in the work of William James (1909). Since then, it has been developed into a theory of politics. In a diverse society, interest groups emerge as one way to influence policymaking. The influence of interest groups in political life has been approached and studied in a variety of ways. Pluralism and its modified version of neopluralism, however, have served as dominant frameworks of such analysis.

As a theory, pluralism had its heyday in the decade following World War II. While critics of pluralism claim that there is no clear definition of what pluralism really is (Jordan 1990), generally speaking, pluralism as a theory of politics sees interest groups as being of equal influence, with access to the state always being open and the state as neutral in relation to interest groups (Smith 1990). As a normative theory, pluralism "stresses the beneficial consequences of social and cultural diversity, of having many different institutions, values, groups and ways of life", while as an explanatory theory, it "shows how policy gets made in interactions across diverse actors and institutions" (Dryzek and Dunleavy 2009).

What these definitions miss, however, is to account for another, quite special, interest group in a political system such as that of Kosovo. This group is the group of external actors with executive powers over the domestic policymaking process of a country. I consider them an interest group because they cannot be considered part of the government since they are neither elected by the people nor appointed by elected representatives of Kosovo, despite the fact that they do govern in some areas (such as police and judiciary under EULEX, for example).

Moreover, critics of pluralism made the point that business groups or groups of economic interests would always be better positioned to influence the state (government) than other groups (Jordan 1990; Smith 1990; Dryzek and Dunleavy 2009). In an effort to answer the challenges levelled at the core assumptions of pluralism, proponents of this theory made room for the inevitable inequality of groups, respectively, the privileged position of business and the fact that not all groups have equal access to the state. This new form of pluralism became known as neo-pluralism (Dryzek and Dunleavy 2009). Once a government comes to power, it wants to stay in power by winning the next round of elections. If the state is to serve as a platform that helps broker policy setting deals with a variety of interest groups, the government will certainly have to be more attuned to the interests and preferences of the business than any other group (Dryzek and Dunleavy 2009). This is because, as Lindblom (1982) explains, the business (market) controls the economy: It decides where and when to invest and how production and distribution are organized. So if the government decides to pursue a policy that is not market-friendly, the economy will suffer, and when the economy suffers, the people suffer because of increased unemployment and loss of income. Therefore, chances are that a government that caused suffering by way of making the economy sluggish if not recessive will not be re-elected. Governments want to be re-elected, and, therefore, business has a privileged position in terms of its influence in policymaking.

This all seems realistic for a representative democracy. In a represented democracy, however, as is the case with Kosovo, the group best positioned to influence the state is the group of external actors with executive powers over the domestic policymaking process. The influence of EULEX or ICO over the state of Kosovo, for instance, is far greater than the influence of any domestic economic interest group.

For example, while many business associations and other business groups as well as the government of Kosovo have continually called for reopening and fully operationalizing the Trepca Mining Complex located in the outskirts of Mitrovica, because of political issues and the unwillingness of the international presence to deal with this issue (given Serbia's claims of ownership over this conglomerate), this mining complex remains mostly closed. Nevertheless, a 1999 International Crisis Group report notes that the Trepca Mining Complex, "famous since Roman times", makes the basis for the economy of Kosovo given its vast mineral wealth.

Moreover, in terms of interest groups' access to the state, Dryzek and Dunleavy (2009) distinguish between a passive and active inclusion form that states may adopt in relation to interest groups. The United States is an example of a passively inclusive state: Access is available, but groups have to find the appropriate way and opportunity to make use of it. On the other hand, Norway is an example of an actively inclusive state: The government formally includes interest groups and gives them the means necessary to design certain policies on its behalf.

In a represented democracy, external actors place special restrictions on the domestic government and other state structures in regards to the inclusiveness of certain interest groups. While for some groups, access to the state is privileged and constitutionally guaranteed, others have to fight to get it. The represented democracy in Kosovo, for example, does not fit either the definition of a passively or an actively inclusive state. It falls in between the two and includes elements from each of these forms of inclusiveness. In Kosovo, on one hand, access to the state is available, but groups have to find the right way to get it and make use of it: A civil society organization or a network of NGOs, for instance, can advocate for a particular issue through members of the Kosovo Assembly to put the issue on the government agenda and influence the policy in response to it as was the case with the Youth Participation and Empowerment Law (Bislimi 2010). On the other hand, access for some groups is constitutionally guaranteed, making Kosovo an actively inclusive state. According to the Kosovo Constitution, Kosovo ethnic minorities are reserved twenty out of one hundred twenty Kosovo Assembly seats, whether they vote in an election or not. Kosovo Serbs are guaranteed ten of these twenty reserved parliamentary seats. If they decide to vote in a national election, Kosovo Serbs may win an additional ten seats or more. But, if Kosovo Albanians do not vote in a national election, they will be left out of the legislature, since they have no guaranteed parliamentary seats. Thus, access to the state in the represented democracy in Kosovo is dependent on one's ethnic background more so than anything else. How is that for a pluralist society?

Therefore, unless we are talking about a dictatorship or a totalitarian state, for example, group influence is normally felt in policymaking and politics, especially in liberal democratic states. The ability of people to organize in groups or associations and to express, promote and defend their preferences and interests is a basic feature of liberal democracy. These features make it possible for interest groups to have influence in both political and policymaking processes (Dryzek and Dunleavy 2009).

Nevertheless, we have seen that under a represented democracy, as in the case of Kosovo, the representation of interests and the degree to which such interests can influence policymaking are dependent on whether one belongs to a domestic or external (international/foreign) interest group. Furthermore, whether one has to fight to get access to the state or one enjoys free access is dependent on one's ethnicity more than any other characteristic.

Kosovo's Political System in the View of the People

When the first internationally organized, supervised and recognized free and fair local elections took place in post-war Kosovo in October 2000, representatives of the international community working in Kosovo – either for the UN or the EU or NATO – were positively surprised with the high voter turnout of 79 per cent (KAM 2000). However, what we see after the 2000 elections is a significant drop in voter turnout in only one year's time. The voter turnout in Kosovo's national elections of 2001 was not higher than 64 per cent (CEC: URL) – down by 15 percentage points from a year before. This negative trend of voter turnout continued all the way to the latest national Kosovo elections of 12 December 2010, in which the level of voter turnout did not pass 48 per cent (CEC: URL) despite the fact that these were the first national elections being held in an independent Kosovo, and two new parties entered the political scene for the first time.

One major reason that may help us understand why the Kosovo electorate has been seemingly losing its trust in the power of the vote and thus turning away from one of the fundamental rights of democracy is related to the executive roles of UNMIK in particular and the international presence in Kosovo in general, including ICO and EULEX.

Whether the political institutions of post-war Kosovo had any real power or not, people's satisfaction with their work seems to have decreased along with voter turnout. According to the UNDP's Kosovo Early Warning Report, one can see that from a record-high satisfaction level of some 70-80 per cent in 2002, people's satisfaction with the work of either the government of Kosovo or the Assembly of Kosovo continually dropped on average all the way to 2007 (UNDP 2009).

While between October 2007 and September 2009, there was an increase on average in people's satisfaction with Kosovo's institutions (namely, the Assembly of Kosovo and the government), the trend seems to have reversed. The latest UNDP Public Pulse Report notes that people's satisfaction with these institutions decreased on average between November 2009 and November 2010 to only 32 per cent for the Assembly of Kosovo and an all-time low of only 25 per cent for the Government of Kosovo (UNDP 2010). This decrease in people's satisfaction with governing institutions in Kosovo can be linked to the inability of these institutions to meet high expectations for much more progress post-independence and the continued executive role of the international presence, namely the ICO and EULEX.

Therefore, while the international community tried to develop a representative democracy and a pluralist society in Kosovo by keeping executive mandates within external actors, such as UNMIK initially and now ICO and EULEX, it shot itself in the foot. By doing so, the international community gave Kosovars no good reason to believe in their own institutions, and it gave these very institutions a free pass on crucial issues of responsibility and accountability.

Not only are the Kosovo institutions legally obligated to respect ICO and EULEX decisions, but they also sometimes prefer to have important political decisions be made by ICO and EULEX even though they could make such decisions on their own. It seems as if the international presence knows better and thus should be allowed to make those decisions on behalf of Kosovo. However, there are no guarantees that the international presence knows better or always has right and good motivations to make the correct decisions (Bain 2007).

For example, Kosovo has its own Anti-Corruption Agency, but it has never acted against much-talked-about corruption affairs within government ministries and other public institutions. On the other hand, EULEX used its executive mandate and carried out several search operations in an effort to shed some light on claims of corruption involving high-ranking government officials (Telegrafi 2010). Another example would be the government of Kosovo's decision to announce a political strategy for integration of Kosovo's North only when such strategy was approved by the ICO, and a European ambassador in Kosovo took the lead in supporting and monitoring its implementation (Koha Ditore 2010). Both of these examples are indicators of the unwillingness of Kosovo's political institutions thus far to act as independent actors.

Things do not seem any better in terms of Kosovo's economic performance either. The latest UNDP Public Pulse Report shows that 72 per cent of Kosovars are either dissatisfied or very dissatisfied with the current economic situation of the country, and exactly the same number of them is ready to join public protests organized due to economic reasons (UNDP 2010). Moreover, since the resolution of Kosovo's final political status (i.e., declaration of independence in February 2008), unemployment and poverty have been continually identified as the two top paramount problems that Kosovo faces (UNDP 2010).

The unemployment rate has reached levels as high as 48 per cent, while Kosovo's economic growth albeit positive (between 3 per cent and 6 per cent) has been so mainly because of foreign aid and remittances, which cannot be the foundation of sustainable economic development. The newest country in Europe is also the poorest one, and foreign direct investment (FDI) is considered one key input that Kosovo's economy needs for further growth (World Bank 2010).

For FDI inflows to Kosovo to increase, however, there need to be political stability and a clear definition and implementation of ownership rights and contractual obligations. In a country with a multifaceted political system where both domestic and external actors have executive mandates over the policymaking process, it is hard to figure out who is truly in charge of what. This very fact, on top of all the other problems that Kosovo faces, including a weak rule of law, corruption, unreliably energy supply, etc., make any significant FDI quite unlikely.

Concluding Remarks

It seems like a noble goal to help someone to achieve democracy and a plural society in which everyone can live freely and equally. As noble as it may be, this was the goal of the international community when it intervened in Kosovo in 1999. More than ten years have passed since then, and this goal seems, at best, far from being achieved anytime soon.

In its efforts to establish a representative democracy and a pluralist society, the international community (first under the auspices of the UN and now under those of the EU) has established a "represented" democracy and neither an actively nor a passively inclusive state in Kosovo. The represented democracy established in Kosovo is a form of democracy that is managed by external actors that primarily come from representative democracies. While it looks like a representative democracy, in its very essence a represented democracy is only a proclaimed form of democracy as opposed to a real one because external actors have executive powers that can override the powers of domestically freely and fairly elected bodies.

Furthermore, while a truly pluralistic society could provide a good foundation for representations of a variety of groups, in a represented democracy such as that of Kosovo, the external actors have put in place conditions that privilege one particular group against another and consequently hinder the pluralistic society by invigorating differences among certain groups and by increasing ethnic tensions.

Under this kind of a political system, neither true democracy nor sustainable economic development can be achieved even though both are required before Kosovo can actually move beyond its dark past and into a brighter European future. But as long as Kosovo remains a "represented democracy", it will not meet the democratic conditionality as defined by Schimmelfennig and Sedelmeier (2005b) and, therefore, it will not be able to move ahead with its Europeanization process so as to get closer to fulfilling its aspirations for EU membership.

References

Antonenko, Oksana. 2007. *Russia and the Deadlock over Kosovo*. Brussels: IFRI.

Assembly of Kosovo. 2008. Declaration of Independence [17 February 2008]. Available from http://www.assembly-kosova.org/?cid=2,128,1635.

Bain, William. 2007. "In Praise of Folly: International Administration and the Corruption of Humanity". In *State-Building: Theory and Practice*, eds. A. Hehir and N. Robinson. Oxford: Routledge.

Bislimi, Faton. 2010. *Youth Volunteerism in Kosovo: An Opportunity to Learn*. Pristina, Kosovo: UNDP/UN Volunteers.

Capoccia, Giovanni, and Daniel Ziblat. 2010. "The Historical Turn in Democratization Studies: A New Research Agenda for Europe and Beyond". *Comparative Political Studies* 43 (8/9): 931-68.

Carothers, Thomas. 2007. "How Democracies Emerge: The 'Sequencing' Fallacy". *Journal of Democracy* 18 (1): 12-27.

CEC – Central Elections Commission. Available from http://www.kqz-ks.org/SKQZ-WEB/al/zgjedhjetekosoves/zgjedhjetepergjitshme.html.

Cowles, Maria, James Caporaso, Thomas Risse, eds. 2001. *Transforming Europe: Europeanization and Domestic Change*. New York: Cornell University Press.

Dryzek, John, and Patrick Dunleavy. 2009. *Theories of the Democratic State*. London: Palgrave.

EU Rule of Law Mission. 2012. EULEX Kosovo. "*What is EULEX?*" Available from http://www.eulex-kosovo.eu/?id=2.

EUSR in Kosovo. 2009. "*EULEX Kosovo Fact Sheet*". Available from http://www.eusrinkosovo.eu/pdf/090406%20EULEX%20FOC.pdf.

Fearon, James D., and David D. Laitin. 2004. "Neo-trusteeship and the Problem of Weak States". *International Security* 28 (4): 5-43.

Heritier, Ardienne. 2005. "Europeanization Research East and West: A Comparative Assessment". In *The Europeanization of Central and Eastern Europe*, eds. F. Schimmelfennig and U. Sedelmeier. New York: Cornell University Press.

Huntington, Samuel P. 1991. "How Countries Democratize". *Political Science Quarterly* 106 (4): 579-61.

Huntington, Samuel P. 1997. "After Twenty Years: The Future of the Third Wave". *Journal of Democracy* 8 (4): 3-12.

International Civilian Office/EU Special Representative. 2011. Mission Statement. Available from http://www.ico-kos.org//

International Independent Commission on Kosovo (IICK). 2000. *The Kosovo Report: Conflict, International Response, Lessons Learned*. Oxford: Oxford University Press.

International Crisis Group. 1999. *Trepca: Making Sense of the Labyrinth*. Europe Report No. 86. Brussels: ICG.

James, William. 2008. *A Pluralistic Universe*. Rockville, MD: Arc Mannor Press.

Jordan, Grant. 1990. "The Pluralism of Pluralism: An Anti-Theory?" *Political Studies* 38 (2): 286-301. KAM – Kosovo Association of Municipalities. 2000. "Municipal Elections 2000". Available from http://komunat-ks.net/wp-content/uploads/2011/11/zgjedhjetkomunale_2000.pdf.

King, Iain, and Whit Mason. 2006. *Peace at Any Price How the World Failed Kosovo*. Ithaca, NY: Cornell University Press.

Koha Ditore. 2010, 24 March. "*Brukseli me Strategji te vet per Veriun e Kosoves*" [Brussels Has Its Own Strategy for the North of Kosovo]. Available from http://www.kohaditore.com/index.php?cid=1,22,15649.

Lindblom, Charles. 1982. "The Market as Prison". *The Journal of Politics* 44 (2): 324-36.

Pond, Elizabeth. 2008. "The EU Test in Kosovo". *The Washington Quarterly* 31 (4): 97-112.

Schimmelfennig, Frank and Ulrich Sedelmeier, eds. 2005a. "Introduction". In *The Europeanization of Central and Eastern Europe*, ed. F. Schimmelfennig and U. Sedelmeier. New York: Cornell University Press.

Schimmelfennig, Frank and Ulrich Sedelmeier. 2005b. "Conclusions: The Impact of the EU on the Accession Countries". In *The Europeanization of Central and Eastern Europe*, eds. F. Schimmelfennig and U. Sedelmeier. New York: Cornell University Press.

Schmitter, Philippe C. 2010. "Twenty-Five Years, Fifteen Findings". *Journal of Democracy* 21 (1): 17-28.

Simensen, Jarle. 1999. "Democracy and Globalization: Nineteen Eighty-Nine and the 'Third Wave'". *Journal of World History* 10 (2): 391-411.

Smith, Martin J. 1990. "Pluralism, Reformed Pluralism and Neopluralism: The Role of Pressure Groups in Policy-Making". *Political Studies* 38 (2): 302-22.

Telegrafi News Agency. 2010, 28 April. "*Policia e EULEX-it bastis zyrat e MTPT-se*" [EULEX Police Raids Offices of the Ministry of Transport and Telecommunications]. Available from http://www.telegrafi.com/?id=2&a=8349.

UNDP. 2009, November. *Early Warning Report No. 26, Fast Facts*. Available from http://www.ks.undp.org/repository/docs/Fast_Facts_26_English.pdf.

UNDP. 2010, December. *Kosovo Public Pulse Report: Fast Facts*. Pristina, Kosovo: UNDP.

UNOSEK. 2007. *UN Office of Special Envoy for Kosovo: Status Settlement Proposal*. Available from http://www.unosek.org/unosek/en/statusproposal.html.

William, Garland H. 2005. *Engineering Peace: The Military Role in Post Conflict Reconstruction.* Washington DC: United States Institute of Peace Press.

World Bank. 2010. *Kosovo – Unlocking Growth Potential: Strategies, Policies, Actions.* Report No. 53185-XK. Washington, DC: World Bank.

Zakaria, Fareed. 1997. "The Rise of Illiberal Democracy". *Foreign Affairs* 76 (6): 22-43.

Part V

Turkey and the End of Enlargement?

The Institutional Impact of Turkish EU Accession

Nanette NEUWAHL

Introduction

Croatia is scheduled to be the next country acceding to the EU. Although it applied only in 2009, it is anticipated to become a full member on 1 July 2013.[1] Turkey, on the other hand, which applied for membership back in 1987, is still negotiating and has no date of entry. As George Orwell (1996, p. 133) ironised in his novel *Animal Farm*, all animals are equal but some animals are more equal than others. Transposed to the European Union, this would read: all candidates are equal but some are more equal than others.

Among the reasons it is suggested that Turkey would be special, it is sometimes advanced that Turkey would be too big, too poor and too different a country to be integrated or 'absorbed' into the EU from an institutional and political viewpoint. Turkish accession would be unrealistic, unworkable or unacceptable because it would give the current member states a feeling of loss of control, or because it would immobilise the EU or slow down its decision-making processes. I am going to dismiss this point of view as far as the institutional set-up of the EU is concerned.

The reason for addressing the question is twofold. On one hand, it will be seen that institutional aspects of Turkish accession are to be taken seriously. It would be silly to dismiss any problems in the institutional context as mere excuses on the part of the EU, as pretexts for rejecting or delaying any prospect of membership. The question of how

1 At the time of writing, the EU has 27 member states: Germany, France, Italy, Belgium, the Netherlands, Luxembourg, the United Kingdom, Ireland, Denmark, Greece, Spain, Portugal, Finland, Sweden, Austria, Poland, Hungary, the Czech Republic, Slovenia, Slovakia, Estonia, Latvia, Lithuania, Cyprus, Malta, Romania and Bulgaria. Accession negotiations are underway with Turkey (which applied in 1987); those with Croatia (applied 2003) have been concluded and an accession treaty is being ratified. There are four more recognised candidates for membership: Macedonia (applied 2004), Montenegro (applied 2008), Serbia (applied 2009) and Iceland (applied 2009).

to fit this country into the European Union's institutional structure is certainly legitimate. On the other hand, it will be argued that any arising difficulties can be overcome and that, with the right attitude, the institutional argument should therefore not be a major stumbling block in EU-Turkey accession talks. Because institutional amendments required by EU accession are to be addressed in a distinct chapter of EU-Turkey accession negotiations, the issue will invariably come up in the not too distant future, even if the moment – or, indeed, the materialisation – of Turkish accession is at the present time highly uncertain.

The Main Political Institutions of the EU and their Working under the Treaty of Lisbon

The main political institutions of the EU are the European Council, the Council of Ministers, the European Commission and the European Parliament. They will be briefly described in turn before the impact of Turkish accession will be addressed in more detail. Apart from these, it should also be mentioned that the national parliaments play a role in the EU decision-making process (Art. 12 TEU). The European Union institutions that will be considered in this chapter are the legislative ones, and they can be briefly characterised as follows:

The European Council, which is at the top of the EU hierarchy, is essentially composed of heads of state or government along with the president of the European Commission. Its task is to give impetus to the integration process, but it can also decide issues that remain without a solution on a lower level.

The Council of Ministers is composed of representatives of the member states at the ministerial level. Under the 'normal' legislative procedure that applies in most areas, it co-decides with the European Parliament on the basis of qualified majority voting, but certain issues considered more sensitive are subject to unanimity.[2] The rules for determining the majority are currently those of the Nice Treaty, which will remain in force until 31 October 2014. After that date, simpler voting rules will apply in accordance with the Treaty of Lisbon. These are specifically designed to increase the decision-making efficiency of the Union.

The European Commission is the European executive, composed of 27 commissioners that are nominated by the member states. This body

2 Citizenship, taxation, EU membership, EU finance, social protection, some issues of justice and home affairs (the European prosecutor and family law, among others.), the flexibility clause of Article 352 TFEU, most of the common foreign and security policy and the common security and defence policy, as well as certain institutional issues such as the EP electoral system or revision of primary law.

has the right of legislative initiative in the European Union, except in matters of foreign affairs, where they share it with the High Representative. The number of commissioners equals the number of member states (Art. 17(4) TEU), but they do not receive a mandate from them (Art. 17(3) TEU): being independent implies that they are the most supranational institution.

The European Parliament is currently composed of 736 directly elected members of Parliament. It co-decides with the Council on most EU legislation and represents the peoples of the member states. Seats are distributed among member states on the basis of population size, it being understood that the small states are advantaged over the big member states. Elections are held every five years, and the latest one was in June 2009.

There is considerable agreement on the fact that the size of Turkey is a puzzle in institutional terms. The impact of Turkish accession on EU institutions has been analysed by several authors before the entry into force of the Lisbon Treaty (Baldwin and Widgren, 2005; Emerson, 2006; Gidisoglu, 2007; Müftüler Baç, 2004; Toksabay Esen, 2007). The present overview is therefore an update as well as the adoption of a point of view.

The Impact of Turkish Accession on the European Parliament

Michael Emerson and his co-authors of a 2006 CEPS report opine that the "deliberative quality of the Parliament would be undercut by an ever growing and increasingly impersonal chamber of elected representatives" (Emerson, 2006, p. 15). At the same time, they suggest that the Parliament is the institution best prepared for continuing enlargement because the Lisbon Treaty contains provisions allowing for a growth in the number of seats, up to a maximum of 750 plus the president of the European Parliament. The relevant provisions (contained in Art. 14(2) TEU) have been adopted with a view to, on one hand, cap the number of MEPs and, on the other hand, enable an expansion of the Parliament in line with the enlargement and the increase of the population of the EU. The process by which MEP seats are apportioned at any given time among member states has also been facilitated. Previously it was the case that the allocation of numbers between the member states was fixed in the treaties and, therefore, could be changed only through negotiations, at the time of the accession of new member states or otherwise. Today, the allocation of seats can be done through (unanimous) Council decision at the initiative and with the consent of the Parliament itself. In theory, therefore, a renewed allocation can be adopted after every new accession or before every EP election. The treaty merely provides the framework within which this allocation should be situated: in particular, it is provided that the number of MEPs of any member state should 1) be digressively proportional to its number of citizens; and 2) be a minimum of six and a maximum of 96.[3]

Table 1 provides the distribution of seats after the 2007 enlargement, the 2009 elections (held under the Nice provisions because the Treaty of Lisbon had not yet entered into force at the time of the elections) and the Lisbon corrections that would apply at the next elections if nothing else is decided. In particular, the projections for the future presented in this table presuppose that the number of member states will remain the same in the 2014 EP elections – which is most likely not the case, given that accession by Croatia is scheduled for 1 July 2013.[4] The effect of Turkish accession will have to be considered against this background.

It does not take a mathematical genius to see that under the current rules, the accession of Turkey would affect the number of seats of the medium sized and large countries, because the population of Turkey is currently second only to Germany, and somewhere between 2015 and 2020 the relative population sizes of those countries will invert (see Table 3). Turkish membership before that time will require the Council to carve out for Turkey a number of seats roughly equal to those of Germany. Since these cannot come from the 15 seats available before the ceiling of 751 is reached, it is clear that the bigger and medium sized member states will have to sacrifice an average of eight seats each to accommodate Turkey.

A side effect of this is that the constituencies in these countries will become even bigger than they were previously, with a member of parliament in a large member state representing nearly a million voters each. This situation is of course acceptable only because the European Parliament cannot be compared to a national parliament, and because national parliaments equally fulfil a role in the EU decision-making process. Apart from the fact that national parliaments scrutinise their representatives in the Council, they play an important role in the evaluation of the principle of subsidiarity.[5]

---

3 The Treaty of Lisbon has thus brought about changes for Germany, which saw its number of MEPs decrease to 96, and for Estonia, Cyprus, Luxembourg and Malta, which have obtained an increase to six MEP seats each.

4 Croatia is expected to have 12 MEPs, bringing the total up to 748.

5 *Subsidiarity* is the principle whereby the EU, in matters outside its exclusive powers, should act, only to the extent that action by the Union has added value by comparison to action by the member states individually or collectively. The national parliaments have a say in the determination of whether this criterion is met.

Table 1: MEPS under the Lisbon Treaty

Member State	Outgoing parliament 2009 (Nice Treaty including 2004 and 2007 enlargements)	2009 election (before entry into force of Lisbon)	Lisbon Treaty (from 2014 election)
Germany	99	99	96
France	78	72	74
Italy	78	72	73
United Kingdom	78	72	73
Spain	54	50	54
Poland	54	50	51
Romania	35	33	33
Netherlands	27	25	26
Belgium	24	22	22
Czech Republic	24	22	22
Greece	24	22	22
Hungary	24	22	22
Portugal	24	22	22
Sweden	19	18	20
Austria	18	17	19
Bulgaria	18	17	18
Finland	14	13	13
Denmark	14	13	13
Slovakia	14	13	13
Ireland	13	12	12
Lithuania	13	12	12
Latvia	9	8	9
Slovenia	7	7	8
Cyprus	6	6	6
Estonia	6	6	6
Luxembourg	6	6	6
Malta	5	5	6
Total	**785**	**736**	**751**

Source: http://www.europarl.europa.eu/aboutparliament/en/004a50d310/Composition-of-Parliament.html#legislature_6_incoming

The Impact of Turkish Accession on the European Commission

Currently the Commission is composed of one commissioner per member state. The intention was to reduce the number of commissioners to a *rata* of 0.66 per cent per member state by 2014 – which can still be seen in Article 15(5) TEU – but this was prevented, in accordance with Article 17(5) TEU, by a European Council decision. If the same arrangement applies at the moment of accession, Turkey will therefore nominate one commissioner. If, in the meantime, states accede and the dossiers of the commissioners become too ‘light’, it may be necessary to revert to the original provision of the Lisbon Treaty. This issue, however, is not specific to Turkish accession.

The Impact of Turkish Accession on the European Council

After Lisbon, the European Council gained importance, and the fact that there are new areas of majority voting in the European Council should add to the dynamics of this institution. However, the question of voting in the European Council does not pose itself any differently than in the context of the Council (see the fourth section of this chapter). The European Council does not normally take any legally binding solutions unless matters are specifically referred to it and it decides as a special formation of the Council. In that case, the decision-making rules and practices of that body apply. For reasons we will set out below, there is no ground for believing that Turkey would have an undue share of influence in the European Council.

The Impact of Turkish Accession on the Council of Ministers

Under the Lisbon Treaty, most matters are decided on the basis of qualified majority rules for voting in the Council of Ministers (QMV). Since in this system population size of a country matters, the effect of Turkish accession is expected to have a significant impact on the distribution of power within this institution, and it is therefore expedient to look into this matter in somewhat greater detail. The influence of Turkish accession will be looked at after a concise description of the different arrangements for QMV provided under the Treaty of Lisbon.

QMV Arrangements Provided for Under the Treaty of Lisbon

Triple majority with weighted voting (potentially applicable until 31 March 2017)

The current voting arrangements – which, in accordance with Article 16 TEU, remain in force at least until 31 October 2014 – provide for the following pass rules:

- a majority of countries (more precisely, a simple majority of member states when acting on the initiative of the Commission, otherwise 67 per cent of member states),
- representing 67 per cent of the population and
- 74 per cent of the voting weights.

In the case of weighted voting, the relative weights of the votes of each member state are determined grossly according to population size, but with a strong bias towards the small member states, as can be seen from Table 2.[6] The intricate voting rules are designed so as to ensure that no single country can dictate its will on the others and every country has some leverage in the decision-making process.

Double majority with population size – applicable in principle from 31 October 2014, with a transition period until 31 March 2017

The arrangements described in the previous section remain of interest well after 31 October 2014 because until 31 March 2017, any member state can request that the current (Nice) rules be used for a particular vote. Otherwise, a different arrangement will apply, notably in which the third condition (voting weight) will no longer be applicable.

A vote in the Council on a matter subject to QMV is then passed on the following Conditions:

- 55 per cent of member states when acting on the initiative of the Commission, otherwise 72 per cent;
- representing 65 per cent of the population or
- no blocking minority (understood as four countries against, or, in a procedure of enhanced cooperation procedure, one member and 35 per cent of the population voting against).

Table 2: Comparison of voting weights

Country	Population		Votes	
	Population in millions	% pop.	votes	% votes
Germany	82	16.5%	29	8.4%
France	64	12.9%	29	8.4%
United Kingdom	62	12.4%	29	8.4%
Italy	60	12.0%	29	8.4%
Spain	46	9.0%	27	7.8%
Poland	38	7.6%	27	7.8%
Romania	21	4.3%	14	4.1%
Netherlands	17	3.3%	13	3.8%
Greece	11	2.2%	12	3.5%
Portugal	11	2.1%	12	3.5%

6 Source: http://en.wikipedia.org/wiki/Voting_in_the_Council_of_the_European_Union (4 May 2012). Population is listed in millions on 1 January 2009. Croatia will, upon accession, get seven votes, bringing the total up to 352.

Belgium	11	2.1%	12	3.5%
Czech Republic	10	2.1%	12	3.5%
Hungary	10	2.0%	12	3.5%
Sweden	9.2	1.9%	10	2.9%
Austria	8.3	1.7%	10	2.9%
Bulgaria	7.6	1.5%	10	2.9%
Denmark	5.5	1.1%	7	2.0%
Slovakia	5.4	1.1%	7	2.0%
Finland	5.3	1.1%	7	2.0%
Ireland	4.5	0.9%	7	2.0%
Lithuania	3.3	0.7%	7	2.0%
Latvia	2.2	0.5%	4	1.2%
Slovenia	2.0	0.4%	4	1.2%
Estonia	1.3	0.3%	4	1.2%
Cyprus	0.87	0.2%	4	1.2%
Luxembourg	0.49	0.1%	4	1.2%
Malta	0.41	0.1%	3	0.9%
Total	**498**	**100%**	**345**	**100%**

Voting in the Council after Turkish Accession: Efficiency and Distribution of Power

If Turkish accession is to take effect before 31 March 2017, the impact of Turkish accession on the Council is rather more difficult to predict than that on the European Parliament, exactly because the weight of Turkey's vote for the purpose of the triple majority procedure would have to be negotiated: weighted votes are negotiated votes, and the practice with large member states is that they would accept a cap on their voting power. If Turkish accession takes effect after 31 March 2017, negotiation is, strictly speaking, not necessary because there will be no more talk of weighted votes. There will be no more capping of voting power, either, because influence is directly related to population size. In the double majority process applicable under the Lisbon system, what counts most for QMV is the population size. On this account, the impact of Turkish accession on Council proceedings is potentially more direct than its influence on the distribution of seats in the European Parliament. If arrangements remain as they are under the Lisbon Treaty (that is, no other arrangements are made between Turkey and the other member states during the accession negotiations), it is clear that the sheer size of the Turkish population will give it an important share in the decision-making power of the Council. Moreover, as voting power in the Council is directly related to population size, it can be deduced from Table 3 that this influence is projected to grow over time. But just how important is this?

Baldwin and Widgren, in their CEPS paper, have been doing some number crunching. They distinguish between the impact of Turkish accession on the EU's capacity to act and its impact on the distribution of power (Baldwin and Windgren, 2005, p. 4). They argue that under the arrangements of the Treaty establishing a Constitution for Europe – similar to the Lisbon double majority context explained in above – the Union's ability to act would hardly be affected by Turkish accession, because the decision-making power of the EU would have been greatly improved by the removal of the weighted voting system. However, their calculations are based on a crude measure – namely, the mathematical probability that a proposed measure passes the voting requirements. It is hardly surprising that, when one of three conditions for passing a measure has been eliminated, the chances that a proposal passes are greatly increased.

A more significant finding of these authors is that the distribution of power would be significantly affected by Turkish accession because, whatever the majority requirements, Turkey would be the second-most powerful member state on the basis of population size alone (Baldwin and Windgren, 2005, p. 9) and that, as power loss occurs progressively in accordance with member size, under the double majority system accession would mostly affect the relative power of Germany. It would have a lesser effect on Poland, Spain, Italy, France or the UK because they are smaller. However, the latter countries still would have to accept a more powerful actor next to them.

The real question is therefore why a member state would accept a powerful player next to it in the Council (in addition to a relative loss of power in the European Parliament). The answer to that is complex and may vary from state to state. We will turn to that next.

Evaluation

Criteria that may persuade member states include the following (in descending order of importance):

- a positive cost/benefit analysis of Turkish accession overall;
- the perceived capacity of building alliances with this country and others in the decision-making process;
- the obsolescence, in practice, of voting in the Council.

The Perceived Benefits of Turkish Accession Overall

Turkish accession is impossible without an evaluation of costs and benefits by all member states, because EU enlargement presupposes the positive agreement of all of them. This means in practice that all the governments and the parliaments need to be in favour of accession after weighing all sorts of issues, including economic impact, demographic impact, free movement implications, security impact and even socio-cultural issues (Neuwahl, 2005).

If opinion polls are anything to go by (they are not necessarily determining), then the outlook for Turkish accession is rather bleak (cf. van der Veen, 2009). *Eurobarometer* indicated in Autumn 2010 that while support for Turkish accession in the European Union is low (30 per cent in favour and 59 per cent against), the population in some countries is more supportive than in others. In five member states, opinions are relatively in favour:

Romania is 61 per cent in favour of Turkish accession, in Hungary it is 52 per cent, in Sweden 52 per cent, in Slovenia 48 per cent and in Lithuania 41 per cent. The people interviewed in the other countries were relatively against Turkish accession.[7] The reason for the lack of support may in part have to do with the economic crisis, because the countries that were hit hardest or that feel most under threat displayed the greatest reduction in support for EU enlargement in general as compared to the last census in spring 2008.[8] However, the populations from other countries such as Finland and Denmark have also shown a growing enlargement fatigue.[9]

The electorates of the member states are rarely asked to express themselves in a referendum on the question of the accession of particular applicants, and if they are, then the outcome of a referendum is not necessarily binding on the government.

Some of the reasons for ratifying an accession treaty may have to do with issues that are not immediately in the minds of the people when they are called to vote, such as the strategic importance of the accession, the timing of the enlargement or the perceived common destiny of the countries concerned. For such reasons, the opinion of the people is no true indicator of what a country will do.

---

7 *Eurobarometer* standard 74: "l'opinion publique dans l'Union europeenne." Automne 2010, pp. 59-60. The attitude of people interviewed in Turkey itself was still favourable (59 per cent).

8 Which was scored as follows: -14 points in Greece, -13 points in Ireland, -11 points in Spain and -9 points in Portugal. *Eurobarometer*, p. 60.

9 Finland at -11 points and Denmark at -9 points in comparison to spring 2008. *Eurobarometer*, p. 60.

One of the reasons for Turkish accession may be its potential contribution to a European security and defence policy.[10] Interestingly, more EU presence in this sector is favoured by a large part of the EU population. The support for a European security and defence policy is overwhelming in all of the member states, including the big ones.[11]

Ultimately, on a deeper, philosophical level, political leaders are being asked to overcome nationalistic thinking ('what is in there for our country?') – a vision according to which the EU is a rare commodity that is to be partitioned – and to instead adopt a meta-perspective according to which the EU is a capital that is worth more when bestowed on a larger number of beneficiaries, be they states or populations. This has helped to rationalise past enlargements even though they were, economically speaking, more difficult to stomach (Davignon, 2003).

The Perceived Capacity of Building Alliances with this Country and Others in the Decision-making Process

A second incentive for some member states to be in favour of Turkey's admission to the EU is that they perceive Turkey as an ally on matters of concern to them. Some early research on this matter by Professor Müftüler Baç is of interest here (Müftüler Baç, 2004). This researcher points out that there are three dominant axes of interests in the EU: big states' versus small states' interests, federalists' versus intergovernmentalists', and 'poor' versus 'rich' member states' interests (here, contradistinguishing net contributors to the EU budget from net receivers of the budget – see Müftüler Baç, 2004, p. 33). The fact that Turkey would be relatively poor (and capable of blocking decisions) may induce the more integrationist member states (such as France) to have reservations about Turkish accession, while states with intergovernmental preferences (such as the United Kingdom) would view Turkish accession more favourably (Müftüler Baç, 2004, p. 34). The governments of small, poor states will quickly see the benefit of Turkish accession as this country might take their side against the interests of the biggest member states: France, Germany, the UK and Italy (Müftüler Baç, 2004, p. 35).

However, a word of caution is required here. It would be a mistake to think that member states always vote in the same way, as the system of decision-making in the EU is designed to encourage compromise. For instance, the fact that, under the Nice rules (valid until 31 March 2017),

---

10 Thus, the German foreign minister stated in 2004: "In order for the EU to be more powerful and for our children and grandchildren to live in peace, Turkey needs to be a member in the EU." *Hiirriyet*, Turkish daily newspaper, September 2004.

11 *Eurobarometer*, p. 56.

the weighted votes of states are subject to caps and thresholds forces all states, great or small, not only to seek alliances but also to reach compromise. Furthermore, in practice, the ambassadors of the member states in Brussels, who prepare the Council meetings and who are capable of bridging the different constellations of the Council, have a real opportunity to broker deals between the different representatives of the member states. A member state can therefore acquiesce on a specific subject matter of interest in return for a favour obtained in another domain.[12] As a result, Union policy is therefore not merely the sum of national positions and one can truly speak of a general community or Union interest, even though it may be difficult to discern. Further ways in which the EU encourages compromise will be mentioned below (point 4).

While this does not diminish the force of the argument that some member states may be in favour of Turkish accession because it suits their particular direction of the EU best, it does indicate that votes in Council are not always exercised in a linear way. Because positions of member states are 'tradable' in the interest of the general, supranational good, the distinctive character of any particular member state, including Turkey, is at best relative.

The Obsolescence, in Practice, of Voting in the Council

A further reason why voting power is not immediately threatening for individual member states is that voting in the Council is relatively rare. Ordinary decision-making in the Council is by consensus, a vote being used practically only as an incentive for member states to take positions. In the particular decision-making culture of the Council, it is not so much votes but the threat of voting that has to be considered. However, as pointed out above, there are many ways for politicians and diplomats to 'play this game', if they wish.

If a member state representative believes that a proposal concerns a matter on which a blocking minority can be reached, they may, for instance, try to obtain a watering down of the proposal. However, the spectre of enhanced cooperation (now possible on most issues in accordance with Art. 20 TEU) is another tool for persuading reluctant

12 The six-month rotating presidency was also designed to induce compromise. As the presidency has to provide results, it is customary for it to be more flexible in its positions so as to induce other member states to accept a compromise position. Obviously, with the creation of the president of the European Council, the rotating presidency has lost its importance as a motor of integration.

member states into line.[13] It may be more fruitful to engage in trade-offs of the type described in the previous section.

A fortiori, if member states see that in the event of a vote, they may not be able to block a proposal, they will be likely to give up their position in exchange for an advantage on another matter rather than prevent the adoption of the measure. Accordingly, it seems difficult to build a strategy, even for small states, on the possibility of building voting alliances with Turkey. It simply would not work in many cases.

All this goes to say that the population size of Turkey does not immobilise the Council of Ministers, nor does it give this country the power to dictate its will on the institution or to force the EU in a direction that would be easily determined in advance. On this basis it would seem that the building of alliances between governments on individual legislative acts would not constitute a factor of overriding concern for countries.

Conclusion

The thesis according to which the EU's institutions would become unmanageable with the accession of Turkey can be dismissed; the argument that this particular state would be too big, too poor and too different to be integrated into the Union has not at all been corroborated.

There is nothing in the system of institutions to suggest that Turkey cannot be a EU member. The institutions would not collapse. Turkey could be given a significant number of MEPs and a significant share in the qualified majority voting system designed under the Lisbon Treaty.

Table 3: Population growth projections, Turkey and current EU member states

Population/ Year	2010	2015	2020	2025	2030
Turkey	75.705.000	79.966.000	83.873.000	87.364.000	90.375.000
EU-27	**499.389.380**	**50.7726.736**	**513.837.632**	**517.810.844**	**519.942.079**
Belgium	10.783.738	11.069.711	11.321.733	11.547.489	11.744.723
Bulgaria	7.564.300	7.382.440	7.187.743	6.974.375	6.752.644
Czech	10.394.112	10.496.514	10.543.351	10.515.540	10.420.166
Denmark	5.512.296	5.591.046	5.661.099	5.736.195	5.807.527

13 Many matters are today shared competences of the Union and the member states, leaving the latter the possibility to act individually or jointly as long as the Union has not acted.

Germany	82.144.902	81.857.964	81.471.598	80.907.345	80.151.642
Estonia	1.333.210	1.323.261	1.310.993	1.291.670	1.267.356
Ireland	4.614.218	5.051.992	5.404.231	5.673.287	5881.335
Greece	11.306.765	11.475.669	11.555.829	11.575.097	11.573.142
Spain	46.673.372	49.381.307	51.108.563	52.100.856	52.660.674
France	65.606.558	66.845.909	67.982.012	69.021.061	69.898.298
Italy	60.017.346	60.928.533	61.420.962	61.683.410	61.868.177
Cyprus	820.709	888.003	954.522	1.016.523	1.071.966
Latvia	2.247.275	2.200.033	2.151.445	2.095.092	2.032.593
Lithuania	3.337.008	3.275.272	3.219.837	3.157.667	3.082.993
Luxembourg	494.153	523.024	551.045	578.966	606.654
Hungary	10.023.453	9.964.433	9.892.967	9.790.312	9.651.197
Malta	413.542	4.20.933	427.045	430.963	431.601
Netherlands	16.503.473	16.717.366	16.895.747	17.069.057	17.207.677
Austria	8.404.899	8.569.899	8.723.363	8.866.425	8.988.139
Poland	37.959.838	37.612.061	36.974.977	36.140.706	35.218.897
Portugal	10.723.195	10.947.334	11.108.159	11.223.610	11.317.257
Romania	21.333.838	21.102.552	20.833.786	20.483.994	20.049.059
Slovenia	2.034.220	2.052.980	2.058.003	20.46.651	2.022.872
Slovakia	5.407.491	5.426.588	5.432.265	5.402.185	5.332.069
Finland	5.337.461	5.428.612	5.500.929	5.549.470	5.569.395
Sweden	93.056.31	9.588.259	9.852.965	10.093.742	10.270.173
United	61.983.950	63.791.983	65.683.056	67.542.953	69.224.059
Norway	4.816.156	5.000.252	5.177.999	5.351.189	5.506.470
Switzerland	7.694.796	7.946.823	8.192.198	8.424.039	8.631.216

Sources: ec.europa.eu/Eurostat and esa.un.org/UNPP

Overstretching the institutions is not in the cards. This need not come as a big surprise: if in 2004 the EU was able to absorb the entry of 10 new member states and nearly double in number of countries, it is hard to maintain that one state, even with a population the size of Germany, is too big a piece to swallow.

It is true that Turkey would have a sizeable say in the Council decision-making process. Table 3 allows us to extrapolate the share Turkey would have in any given timeframe in the formation of a blocking minority. This makes it a potential ally, especially for smaller member states. Yet we are reminded that the decision-making process is much more sophisticated than can be expressed by mere reference to majority voting in the Council. In particular, it is the distinct character of the EU decision-making process to balance the interests of peoples and countries, and in doing so, the impact of large countries is purposely diluted. Just as Germany cannot dictate its will on the rest of Europe, so too would Turkey be part of a system that is greater than the sum of its component parts. If the institutional argument is then out of the way, it is clear that Turkish entry is really a cost/benefit analysis, implying that if Turkish accession is delayed, this is most likely the case because the cost/benefit analysis was so far considered unsatisfactory in some of the member states.

It seems right that the accession of Turkey is seen in light of the perceived advantages, or otherwise, for the member states. However, membership should not be presented just as the question of how to divide a cake of well-defined dimensions, but rather more broadly as a question of what is to be gained when admitting a member of this calibre into the EU circle. The security impact of Turkish accession, whether it would be a boost to the European market and innovation capacity, and the potential rejuvenation of the population are all factors that count as much as initial financial implications (Domaniç, 2006; Hug, 2008; Nas, 2006; Rumelili 2011). Furthermore, regarding the fact that most of the population in Turkey is Muslim, one may acknowledge that the accession of Turkey stretches the EU slogan 'unity in diversity', and that it puts the European Union in front of a dilemma. As one commentator put it:

> Those who hold a principled objection to Turkey's accession express the concern that its inclusion would dilute the particularistic norms of European society rooted in its Judeo-Christian heritage. In response, those who support Turkey's accession argue that rejection would challenge the multilateral and universalistic foundations of European norms and identity (Rumelili, 2011, p. 237).

These are the real issues, and a decision should be taken from there.

References

Baldwin, R. and M. Widgren. 2005. "The Impact of Turkish Membership on EU Voting." CEPS Policy Brief 62, February.

Davignon, E. 2003. "L'Europe dans le monde d'aujourd'hui." Conference held at Université de Montréal, 8 May.

Emerson, M. 2006. "Just what is this Absorption Capacity of the European Union?" CEPS Policy Brief 113, September.

Domaniç, S. 2006. "The Turkish Accession to the European Union: Mutually Beneficial? Mutually Possible?" Institute of Public Affairs, Centre for Economic and Foreign Policy Studies, Turkey. http://pasos.org/wp-content/archive/Turkish+accession.pdf (9 March 2011).

European Union. 2010. "Consolidated versions of the Treaty on European Union and the Treaty on the functioning of the European Union." *Official Journal of the European Union C 83.*

Gidisoglu, S. 2007. "Understanding the 'Absorption Capacity' of the European Union." *Insight Turkey* (October).

Hug, A. 2008. *Turkey in Europe: The Economic Case for Turkish Membership of the EU.* London: The Foreign Policy Centre.

Müftüler Baç, M. 2004. "Turkish Accession to the European Union: Institutional and Security Challenges." *Perceptions*: 29-43.

Nas, C. 2006. "Intercultural Dialogue Between Civilizations: Turkey as a Bridge." In *European Union and Turkey: Reflections on the Prospects for Membership*, eds. N. Neuwahl and H. Kabaalioglu. Istanbul: Marmara University Publication 730, 157-81.

Neuwahl, N. 2005. "What Borders for Which Europe?" In *Soft or Hard Borders? Managing the Divide in an Enlarged Europe*, ed. J. Debardeleben. London: Ashgate, 23-41.

Orwell, G. 1996. *Animal Farm*. New York: Penguin Books.

Toksabay Esen, A. 2007. "Absorption Capacity of the EU and Turkish Accession: Definitions and Comments." Tepav-Epri, Policy Brief, 9 May.

Rumelili, B. 2011. "Turkey: Identity, Foreign Policy and Socialization in a Post-Enlargement Europe." *Journal of European Integration* 33: 235-49.

van der Veen, M. 2009. "Who can Join? Public Opinion and EU Enlargement." 15 March. http://www.maurits.net/Research/EB_enlargement_full.pdf (9 March 2011).

The Non-accession of Turkey to the European Union

Implications for Cyprus Reunification, Eastern Mediterranean Natural Gas Exploration and Regional Stability

Demetrios NICOLAIDES

Introduction

On July 1, 2012, the divided island nation of Cyprus will assume the six-month rotating presidency of the single greatest example of state integration and cooperation in the world. It is indeed ironic that a state that has been plagued with internal divisions since its independence will lead the European Union (EU) toward greater integration. This significance has not gone unnoticed. Candidate country Turkey is threatening to freeze all relations with the EU should Cyprus assume the presidency in July (Demiris, 2012). While much of Europe's population generally disapproves of Turkey's accession to the EU due primarily to populist fears of an increase in immigration and economic destabilization (Gerhards and Hans, 2011; De Vreese *et al.*, 2008; McLaren 2007), it is likely that most of Europe would in fact be largely apathetic to the non-accession of Turkey to the EU. However, should Turkey indeed freeze its diplomatic negotiations with the union on July 1, such an action could have irreversible repercussions for the reunification of Cyprus and eastern Mediterranean security and stability.

Drawing on recent events and an analysis of the positive effects of Turkey's EU accession negotiations, this paper will suggest that while the non-accession of Turkey to the EU may indeed have little or no repercussions for the vast majority of Europeans, inversely, it would have significant implications for Cyprus and the eastern Mediterranean. With the recent discoveries of large oil and natural gas deposits in the eastern Mediterranean Basin, tensions in the region have increased significantly. Turkey is keen to take its fair share of the natural resources that the region has to offer and its failure to accede to the EU could act as a catalyst for heightened regional tensions and instability. This is not to suggest that Turkey is the sole destabilizing force in the region; on the contrary, neither Cyprus nor Israel is contributing to a climate of cooperation, friendship and peace. However, before an investigation into the possible implications of Turkish non-accession to the EU can begin, a summary of the historical tensions between Cyprus and Turkey in particular is necessary.

Background – The Cyprus Problem

The Cyprus conflict is one of the most intricate and protracted ethno-nationalist conflicts of the last fifty years (Anastasiou, 2007; Morag, 2004; Reiterer, 2003) and although no violence has erupted on the island in more than 30 years, the issue remains unresolved. In the early 1950s, nationalist elements swept the island as both the native Greek and Turkish Cypriot communities began lobbying for greater social, cultural and political association with their respective motherlands (Anastasiou, 2006; Peristianis, 2006). Amongst the Greek Cypriots, nationalist aspirations developed into the idea of *enosis* (union) with the Greek mainland (Coughland and Mallinson, 2005) and a Hellenization of Cyprus. Amongst the Turkish Cypriots, the idea of *taksim* (partition or double-*enosis*) was born, which aimed to divide the island along historical ethno-nationalist lines (Pollis, 1973; Markides 1974). The colonial British scuttled the diplomatic manoeuvring of the Greek Cypriots, who attempted to raise the matter before the United Nations General Assembly (Xydis, 1968), and instead relied on their policy of divide-and-rule. Frustrated with their failed diplomatic attempts, on April 1, 1955, the Greek Cypriots launched a violent liberation struggle to achieve *enosis.* Greek and Turkish Cypriot paramilitary forces soon engaged one another. While the liberation struggle did not succeed in achieving *enosis*, it did succeed in forcing the colonial authorities to the negotiating table. In 1959, the British authorities granted Cyprus independence under the auspices of a delicate power-sharing government, which would prove overly complicated and largely non-functional (Adams, 1966). The government was described as being, "Unique in its tortuous complexity and in the multiplicity of the safeguards that it provides for the principal minority; the Constitution of Cyprus stands alone among the Constitutions of the World" (Smith, 1964). Turkey, Greece and Great Britain were permitted to station forces on the island and were charged with maintaining the island's neutrality, independence and sovereignty.[1] Independence was not enough for the ardent Greek Cypriot *enosis* supporters and on July 15, 1974, Greek junta and Cypriot

1 For a complete account of the events including establishment, internal-strife and invasion of the RoC, see Markides, C. Kyriacos (1977) *The Rise and Fall of the Cyprus Republic*. Yale University Press, London: UK.

National Guard forces staged a *coup d'état*. A few days later, on July 20, Turkey, quoting its duties and obligations under the Treaty of Guarantee to safeguard the independence of the Republic, launched a military intervention in Cyprus. When the violence subsided, Turkey controlled more than 37 per cent of the northern areas of the Republic. A massive population exchange followed as Turkish Cypriots fled north and Greek Cypriots fled south. The Turkish north eventually declared its independence on November 13, 1983 and to this day, only Turkey recognizes the country.[2] The legal Republic of Cyprus (the Greek south) has enjoyed economic prosperity following the violence of 1974. In 2004, it acceded to the EU, creating new legal and practical challenges for the EU as countless reunification negotiations have failed (Anastasiou, 2009).

Today, the Republic of Cyprus (RoC) is preparing to take over the EU's six-month rotating presidency and has recently made a significant discovery of natural gas off its southern coast (Wethe & Orphanides, 2011). The RoC has also, over many years, managed to garner favourable international opinion and keep the Turkish Republic of Northern Cyprus (TRNC) from securing international recognition. However, with the failure of the current reunification negotiations between Greek and Turkish Cypriot leaders a continuance of the *status quo* appears inevitable for the foreseeable future (Dabilis, 2012).

Current Dynamics and the Need for Momentum

While many commentators and analysts suggest that the discovery of natural gas by the RoC may in fact act as a motivating force to bring about a successful resolution of the Cyprus issue (International Crisis Group, 2012), the degree of increased security and defence cooperation between Israel and Cyprus offers tangible factual evidence to the contrary.

Furthermore, some scholars link the successful resolution of the Cyprus issue to the application and enforcement of international law (Melakopides, 2006 & 2009) while others have more faith in slow evolutionary approaches (Hadjipavlou and Trigeorgis, 1993; Prodromou, 1998; Nicolaidis, 1998; Olgun, 1998; Bahcheli, 2000) or suggest a model of neo-functional integration between the two communities, similar to that of the EU itself (Nicolaides, 2011). Regardless of the various theories and approaches surrounding a successful resolution of the Cyprus problem, the willingness of Turkey will certainly play a

2 The Turkish Federated State of Cyprus was announced in 1975 as a measure to secure the political equality of the Turkish Cypriot community. The TFSC later announced its independence as the Turkish Republic of Northern Cyprus (TRNC).

determining role, and it is on this premise that a solution should be sought. It is ultimately Turkey that will need to remove over 40,000 troops from the island and thus any reunification efforts that are not supported by Turkey are destined to fail. Following the accession of the RoC to the EU in 2004, the dynamics of the reunification negotiations have changed drastically. The impeding entry of Cyprus to the EU in 2004 led to the reversal of the decades-old hard-line policies of the Turkish Cypriot community and the adoption of more moderate and conciliatory approaches. This was a milestone in the Turkish Cypriot reunification process. The result for the Greek Cypriot community, however, was the opposite; the community hardened its nationalist views (Anastasiou, 2007). The next foreseeable significant regional event, which could be used as impetus to resolve the Cyprus dispute, is in fact the accession of Turkey itself to the EU. On this premise, it can reasonably be suggested that the accession of Turkey to the EU will have significant negative or positive implications for Cypriot reunification. Many believed that the entry of the RoC to the EU in 2004 would be the ultimate impetus to resolving the Cyprus issue; in hindsight, they were correct (Vassiliou, 2003). The impending accession of Cyprus to the EU brought the two communities the closest they have ever come to achieving reunification. A comprehensive proposal (commonly referred to as the Annan Plan) was finalized and put forward to both the Greek and Turkish Cypriot people in two separate and simultaneous referenda. Although the Annan Plan failed due to a Greek Cypriot "No" vote, it still represents the closest the communities have come to reunification. It can thus be argued that the entry of Turkey to the EU may have similar effects. While this idea can only be hypothesized, the one aspect that can indeed be argued scientifically is the probable implications of Turkey's non-accession to the EU.

Implications of Turkish Non-accession to the EU

This section will highlight evidence of social, economic, political and military reforms in Turkey that have occurred largely due to the impetus of EU accession. This reforming trend is commonly referred to as Europeanisation, and the central argument explored here is the suggestion that failure to accede to the EU may leave the door open to a de-Europeanisation of Turkish policies. A de-Europeanised Turkey may mean less civilian control over foreign and military matters, as has traditionally characterised the state, and may thus lead to the transformation of Turkey into a destabilizing force in the region. This is due in part to four critical factors: a de-Europeanisation of foreign and security policy, an increase in unilateralism and less cooperation with the Common Foreign and Security Policy (CFSP), deteriorating relations with Israel, and growing Israeli-Cypriot cooperation.

De-Europeanisation and Shifting Turkish Foreign Policy

A key component of this analysis is the possible de-Europeanisation of Turkish foreign policy as recently evidenced by shifting foreign policy objectives. Developments in the region suggest that Turkey is exploring new foreign policy objectives. This changed foreign policy has included closer cooperation and friendlier relations with its Arab neighbours at the expense of Israel and an increasing military presence in the region, contradicting previous policies (Farley, 1995). Turkey boasts a large population and a strong military and with the support of neighbouring Arab nations, Turkey would quickly find itself in a position of prominence and power in the Middle East. With the last of the U.S. forces having departed from Iraq, a new balance of power may indeed be taking shape in the region (Akram, 2010). Despite the aforementioned changes, Turkey's recent track record as a regional mediator and influential player has been notable (Bechev, 2011; Altunisik and Cuhadar, 2010). More specifically, positive developments have included the country's participation in the UN-led peacekeeping mission in southern Lebanon (Oguzlu and Gungor, 2006). However, the question that remains is who will step in to take advantage of the new *status quo*. With its relations with Turkey deteriorating, Israel appears to have lost a significant friend and ally in the region. Thus, will Israel prepare to increase its presence and keep the Middle East in check? Or will Iran eye a bigger role in the region? What about Turkey? Still engaged in a continued offensive against Kurdish rebels in Northern Iraq, will Turkey step up to take on the task? These questions remain unanswered, but one thing is certain: should Turkey turn its back on the EU (or the EU on Turkey), then its attention will most certainly turn to the eastern Mediterranean and the Middle East. Many scholars, commentators and analysts have taken note of the shift in Turkish foreign policy, which has been described as Neo-Ottomanism (Inbar, 2011; Koprulu, 2009; Oguzlu, 2008; Kassimeris, 2010; Alessandri, 2010; Pope, 2010; Ozel & Ozcan, 2011; Ari & Pirincci, 2010). Aspects of this new foreign policy direction include support for Arab popular uprisings, support for the rights of Palestinians, increased military presence in the eastern Mediterranean, and a deterioration of relations with Israel.

As stated earlier, one area where the EU has made considerable progress is in the development of democratisation and social reform amongst prospective member states (Anastasiou, 2007). It is for this reason that non-accession to the EU may hamper regional peace and stability. Evidence of positive socio-political changes and the general

Europeanisation of Turkey's foreign policy can be found in a number of selected works (Oguzlu & Ozpek, 2008; Diez *et al.*, 2005; Ergun, 2010; Ertugal, 2010; Bac, 2005; Gursoy, 2010). More critical however is the extent to which military and security decision-making has been Europeanised in Turkey (Bilgic, 2009). A constant source of tension between EU leaders and Turkey is the country's less-than-complete control over its armed forces. Without delving too deeply into the relationship between the government and the military, it is commonly noted that the military generally views itself as the protector of Turkish secularism and identity and its government and constitution. It is in these contexts that Turkish armed forces intervened in 1960, 1971, 1980 and 1997. Inclusion in the European family requires that the democratic Turkish government exert greater control over its armed forces. Doing so would undoubtedly increase the amount of democratic decision-making with respect to military matters (Onis, 2010; Ulusoy, 2008). Turkey is now at a crossroads and must implement additional reforms with respect to its management of foreign and defence affairs. Improved Turkish political and civilian control over the armed forces is evidenced by a 2010 nation-wide referendum that resulted in the people of Turkey voting to replace the ailing 1980 constitution that had been put in place by military leaders who had seized power in a *coup d'état*. In addition to changes to the judiciary and individual freedoms, the referendum also led to reform of the armed forces (*Economist*, 2010). More specifically, *coup* leaders would no longer be protected under the 1980 constitution and could be prosecuted by the government. Military officers who participate in the planning and/or execution of a military *coup* would also no longer be tried in military courts (Bali, 2010).

Turkey is also reluctant to integrate into the EU's Common Foreign & Security Policy (CSFP) due primarily to its overall desire to maintain sovereignty and exclusive decision-making in all foreign policy matters. This may in fact be due in part to the less than complete civilian control over the military.

As of yet, Turkey has failed to align its policies with common EU positions with respect to the International Criminal Court, and it still prosecutes conscientious objectors in violation of the European Convention of Human Rights. Turkey also disputes large sections of its border with its EU neighbours. It also has unresolved disputes with Greece over territories in the Aegean and fails to recognise the sovereignty and independence of the RoC. Turkey's record of violating UN Security Council resolutions was second (after Israel) for the period between 1968 and 2002, with 24 violations, all of which related to Cyprus (Zunes, 2002). Such issues are highlighted in the works of Ipek Ruacan (2007), who suggests that complete socialisation with the CFSP is certain to prove a major stumbling block to Turkish accession to the EU. While considered inappropriate, given the conditions of cooperation – and although still commonplace in the union – it is certain that Turkey will find it difficult to restrict its unilateralism. This is not to suggest that Turkey is by any means naturally unilateral or aggressive; on the contrary, it has been argued that geopolitical foundations require such a policy (Jung & Piccoli, 2000).

Increase in Unilateralism

Should Turkey's EU aspirations fail and some degree of de-Europeanisation occur with respect to its foreign policy, it can be expected that elements of unilateralism may creep back into Turkish politics. As discussed earlier, the Europeanisation process, and specifically increased civilian control over the armed forces, has been effective in curbing Turkish military unilateralism. As discussed earlier, the EU accession process has indeed had a positive effect in bringing about a greater degree of, if not complete, civilian control over the military. While Turkey may not necessarily revert back to complete military dominance over foreign policy decision-making, it can be expected that with EU hopes lost it may lapse into old habits. For example, many commentators and analysts have referred to Turkey's recent actions in the eastern Mediterranean as 'gunboat' tactics. Following the commencement of exploratory drilling in late September, Turkey dispatched naval forces to the shores of Cyprus and loudly proclaimed that its military forces were preparing to increase their presence in the region. Due in part to the 2009 Gaza Flotilla fiasco, Turkey has also been flexing its military muscle toward Israel (Villelabeitia, 2011).

Deteriorating Relations with Israel

Another significant factor that will undoubtedly add to regional instability should Turkey not accede to the EU is its rapidly deteriorating relationship with Israel. Although previously allies and friendly neighbours, relations have recently reached an all-time low. While the specific events that have contributed to this deterioration have been well documented what remains somewhat unclear are the motivations behind these actions. Examining the underlying motivations, one may quickly deduce that Turkish foreign policy is shifting. We have seen evidence earlier in this paper to support such a claim and thus a shifting foreign policy is re-emphasised. Should EU accession fail, coupled with de-Europeanisation and an increase in unilateralism, it is plausible that Israeli-Turkish relations will continue to deteriorate. This can also be attributed to growing Cypriot-Israeli cooperation, which will be discussed further below. In his analysis of the dynamics of Israeli-Turkish relations, Tarik Oguzlu argues that Turkey-Israeli relations are largely based on short-term objectives rather than long-term ideological similarities and therefore, friendly relations come with a time limit (2010). Oguzlu further concludes that shifting foreign policy objectives will continue to strain Israeli-Turkish relations.

Israeli-Cypriot Cooperation

Although not directly linked to Turkey's EU ambitions, the recent positive developments between Israel and Cyprus are also significant contributing factors to regional instability. While traditional Cypriot foreign policy has generally followed a policy of non-alignment and solidarity with its Arab neighbours (Ker-Lindsay, 2008 and 2010; Mallinson, 2011), the discovery of over 7 trillion cubic feet of natural gas of the south coast of the island has significantly changed Cypriot foreign policy objectives. After the commencement of exploratory drilling on September 20, 2011, Turkish fighter jets reportedly violated the Nicosia Flight Information Region (FIR). In a separate incident, various regional news sources reported that Israeli fighter jets were dispatched toward the Turkish research vessel, the Piri Reis. The research vessel had been sent to the area by Turkey to signal their displeasure with Cypriot oil & gas exploration and to conduct explorations of their own (Doss, 2011). Following the dispatch of Israeli fighters, it was also reported that Turkey scrambled its own aircraft in response. The situation concluded without incident, but is a strong indication of the increasing tensions in the region. There are also un-confirmed reports that Israel has discussed with the Cypriot government, the possibility of accessing its Andreas Papandreou air base, near Paphos. Earlier in September, opposition *Dimokratikós Sinayermós* (DISY) second-in-command called on Cypriot Defence Minister Demetris Eliades, to visit Israel and propose military cooperation between the two countries, stating, "He [the President of Cyprus] should immediately put the Andreas Papandreou air base and Evangelos Florakis naval base at Israel's disposal" (Evripidou, 2011). In his analysis of Cypriot foreign policy, Daniel Pipes, President of the Middle East Forum and Taube distinguished visiting fellow at the Hoover Institution, stated that, "In conjunction, these two developments – growing Turkish ambitions and possible gas deposits in the trillions – link Cyprus and Israel in self-defence. Leading Greek Cypriot figures in the government, the media, and business told me during a just-concluded trip to the island about their urgent wish to build economic and security relations with Israel" (Pipes, 2011). He further states that, "Cyprus would gain from Israel's much greater military, economic, and diplomatic prowess….Such an alliance would terminate the Cypriot legacy of non-alignment and low-key diplomacy designed to convince governments not to recognize the TRNC, though that strategy, arguably, has not brought it much benefit." In early February, 2012 media in Cyprus, Israel, Greece and Turkey reported that Israel was preparing to officially request permission from the Cypriot government to station military jets at the Andreas Papandreou airbase. If such a requested was granted, it would be the first-ever stationing of Israeli military forces abroad. Immediately after the announcement of the discovery of over 7 Tcf of natural gas in Block 12 of Cyprus' exclusive economic zone (EEZ), Cypriot Defence Minister Eliades visited his counterpart, Ehud Barack, in Israel, where agreements on common defence and exchange of intelligence were signed. This was the first-ever visit of a Cypriot defence minister to Israel. In February 2012, Israeli Prime Minister Benjamin Netanyahu visited Nicosia to sign a joint oil and natural gas venture between the two nations. Netanyahu's visit marked another significant milestone in Israeli-Cypriot relations as it was the first-ever visit of an Israeli head of state to Cyprus. The deal also allowed Israel to use Cypriot airspace and territorial waters for aerial and naval search and rescue drills. A more notable outcome of his visit was the beginning of discussions to create a common pipeline to deliver natural gas from the region into Europe, via Greece.

The Cyprus Question

Although it is not yet clear whether the EU or Cyprus will ultimately reject Turkish EU membership due to a failure to resolve the Cyprus issue, it is certain that little progress will be made unless Turkey shows a considerable amount of positive progress toward resolving the problem. Previous actions of the EU seem to support this argument. In 2004, both Turkey and the Turkish Cypriot community received international praise for their positive stance and for the Turkish Cypriot community's ultimate vote in favour of the Annan Plan for the reunification of the island. Immediately following the referendum, the European Commission issued a press statement in which it outlined its disappointment with the Greek Cypriot community for its "No" vote and "warmly congratulated" the Turkish Cypriot community for its "Yes" vote. The European Commission further stated that, "This signals a clear desire of the community to resolve the island's problem. The Commission is ready to consider ways of further promoting economic development of the northern part of Cyprus" (European Commission, 2004). The United Kingdom responded in a similar manner, with then Prime Minister Tony Blair stating, "The UK government believes steps should be taken as quickly as possible to end the isolation of the Turkish Cypriots" (Helm,

2004). Other foreign dignitaries and leaders from nations such as Germany, France, Czech Republic, Bangladesh, Sweden, Austria and the United States all made similar statements in support of 'rewarding' the Turkish Cypriot community for the its positive stance. The EU in particular was swift in dispensing its 'reward' to the Turkish Cypriot community. On February 27, 2006, the EU approved over €259 million in development assistance for the Turkish Cypriot community, which was scheduled to be implemented over the course of five years. In March 2012, the aid program celebrated its sixth anniversary, and has so far seen over €292 million injected into the Turkish Cypriot economy (European Commission, 2012). EU rewards were also issued to Turkey. However, Turkey had its own internal restructuring challenges to overcome before it could receive a favourable opinion on accession from the European Commission. These challenges included the implementation of the Ankara Protocol, which was signed at the European Council summit on December 16, 2004, and in which EU leaders agreed to begin accession negotiations with Turkey on October 3, 2005. However, this positive atmosphere was short-lived and on December 11, 2006, EU leaders agreed to suspend accession negotiations on eight chapters of the acquis, due primarily to the failure of Turkey to completely implement the Ankara Protocol. Although the EU in general was in favour of 'rewarding' Turkey, the Cypriot government was able to successfully persuade its EU counterparts that Turkey's failure to completely implement the Ankara Protocol with respect to Cyprus could not legally be ignored.

While the current peace negotiations show little promise of a breakthrough, Turkey is set to suspend negotiations with the EU should Cyprus take over the bloc's six-month rotating Presidency on July 1, 2012. For the purposes of this analysis, I assume that the current deadlock with respect to the Cyprus negations will persist and may even break down completely in the coming months. The status quo will almost certainly continue unless another significant international event or local development occurs. In all of Cyprus' history, only its pending accession to the EU in 2004 brought the two communities to a referendum and to the closest they have ever come to achieving reunification. It can thus be expected that Turkey's imminent accession to the EU could be a major catalyst in bringing both communities and regional players close to reunification (Tocci, 2010). Prior to Cyprus' accession to the EU in 2004, the Turkish Cypriot community recognized the inevitability of Cypriot accession and this resulted in a substantial deviation from traditional Turkish Cypriot reunification policies. Since the Turkish invasion of 1974 the Turkish Cypriot community, under the leadership of Rauf Denktash, maintained a hard-line position in the negotiations and was consistently labelled as the primary stumbling block to reunification negotiations (Denktash, 1982). In December 2003, with Cypriot entry to the EU mere months away, Denktash's party suffered heavy losses in legislative elections. Thousands of demonstrators had taken to the streets since 2002 to demand an end to Denktash's rule and call for reunification, peace and EU entry. Denktash was eventually ousted in the February 2004 presidential election by moderate Mehmet Ali Talat, who subsequently replaced Denktash as the main negotiator for the Turkish Cypriot community. This was a positive and historic development and it is possible that the pending accession of Turkey to the EU could have similar effects. The nature of these hypothesised future developments is of course impossible to know for certain; however, it is probable that Turkey would not jeopardize EU entry for the sake of the Turkish Cypriot community. Such a move might lead the Turkish Cypriots, perceiving a betrayal by Turkey, to fear that they are entering an era of complete diplomatic isolation, with Turkey's back effectively turned on Cyprus. Faced with the prospect of being left out in the cold, the Turkish Cypriots may turn once again to their Greek Cypriot compatriots and seek reunification. Whether the reunification would succeed or not is a matter for further research and outside the scope of this paper; however, the conclusion still holds true that Turkey's pending EU entry may indeed spur reunification sentiments within the Turkish Cypriot community.

There are significant implications for Cyprus should Turkey fail to join the EU and the island remains divided. Should the Greek and Turkish Cypriots achieve a breakthrough in the current negotiations, pave the way for a future settlement to the Cyprus problem and actually achieve reunification, the failure of Turkey to join the EU would have little consequence to a united Cyprus. While it is difficult to predict with certainty, it can be hypothesized that under a reunified Cyprus, the Turkish Cypriot component state would have a high degree of sociopolitical and cultural relations with Turkey, using the Annan Plan as a point of reference. A Turkey excluded from the EU may become more involved in local affairs in Cyprus and concern itself with the preservation of Cyprus' Turkish identity. Doing so would undoubtedly strain relations with the Greek Cypriot community and could become a destabilizing force. As specified by the Annan Plan, a constituent state of the United Cyprus Republic, "could conclude and enter into agreements on commercial and cultural matters with states that have relations with the United Cyprus Republic" (Annan, 2004). Furthermore, it is conceivable that in a reunified Cyprus, the 1960 treaties of Guarantee and Alliance would still be in force and thus Turkey would retain both the ability to station military forces on the island and the right and responsibility to maintain and guarantee the status quo of the independent republic. Whether Turkey would decide to flex its legal and political muscle with respect to Cyprus is a matter that should be given great thought within Cyprus.

If, however, Cyprus remains divided and Turkey is subsequently rebuffed from EU membership, it can be expected that the Cyprus problem could reach a different stage. With Turkey already threatening to pursue the international recognition of the TRNC more vigorously and suspend relations with the EU should Cyprus take over its six-month rotating presidency in July it is highly probable that Turkey would be less conciliatory about removing its forces from the island. While the annexation of Northern Cyprus by Turkey is not a completely implausible scenario, it becomes more likely if little or no incentive exists for Turkey to cooperate toward reaching a compromise over the Cyprus impasse. In the earlier hypothetical scenario whereby Turkey enters the EU, there appears to be ample international and regional momentum for a viable solution to the Cyprus problem. Thus, if Turkey is not permitted to join, it can be assumed that little to no momentum will be generated toward the reunification of the island. On the contrary, it may spark a move away from current moderate Turkish Cypriot policies to more traditional hard-line positions (Webster, 2005). Evidence of such a shift can already be seen in the Turkish Cypriot community. In April 2009 for example, the National Unity Party (UBP) of past hard-line leader Rauf Denktash, which was ousted in 2003 during the public outcry for peace, unification and EU entry, was elected back into power. The party gained seven parliamentary seats and managed to secure a majority in the TRNC House of Representatives. A year later, nationalist politician and UBP leader Dervis Eroglu claimed victory over the moderate Mehmet Ali Talat, in the presidential elections. While the era of Turkish Cypriot political modernism appears to be coming to an end, should Turkey be rejected by the EU, this event could give greater support to nationalist and hard-line politicians in the TRNC in a divided Cyprus. For the Turkish Cypriot community in particular, the failure of Turkey to join the EU would be significantly damaging. Having already missed the opportunity to join the EU alongside their Greek Cypriot compatriots in 2004, they would have missed a second opportunity to become EU citizens through a formal annexation of Northern Cyprus by Turkey. While Turkey is quite capable of sustaining economic growth and protecting its foreign interests unilaterally, the Turkish Cypriots are not quite so lucky. Should reunification fail and Turkey be denied EU entry, the Turkish Cypriot community would be forced to lean heavily on the Turkish motherland for economic and diplomatic support. Turkey could conceivably pursue international recognition for TRNC or annex the TRNC as a province of Turkey.

Conclusion

Due primarily to Turkey's aspirations to join the EU, the nation has undergone a great deal of social, political, economic and even military reform. The Europeanisation of many facets of Turkish society has been well documented. However, many scholars, analysts and commentators are beginning to interpret recent actions and policies by Turkey as a shift away from the EU. Some have gone further to suggest a degree of Neo-Ottomanism and believe that recent developments are only the beginning.

With respect to Cyprus, the current reunification negotiations appear destined for failure. Greek and Turkish Cypriot leaders, as well as the UN and the EU, have all but given up hope that the current round of negotiations will end with success. The closest the two communities have come to reunification was prior to the accession of the RoC in 2004. Mere weeks before the RoC acceded to the bloc, a referendum was held to accept or reject the Annan Plan. With the dream of becoming European citizens overnight, the Turkish Cypriots threw out previous hard-line leaders and adopted more conciliatory positions. While the Turkish Cypriots ultimately voted in favour of the UN peace proposal, the Greek Cypriots, comfortable in the fact that EU accession was imminent, opted to reject the proposal (Tocci and Diez, 2010; Michael, 2007).

It can also be expected that, at a time where the accession of Turkey to the EU is imminent, momentum may once again bring the Greek and Turkish Cypriots close to reunification. Faced with either diplomatic exile (as Turkey would be forced to abandon the Turkish Cypriots if it were to accede to the EU) or annexation and amalgamation into Turkey, The Turkish Cypriots may indeed favour reunification.

Apart from the aforementioned positive implications for the Cypriot communities, negative implications abound should Turkey either turn its back on the EU or be rejected by European leaders. A European rejection may reverse recent advancements in social, political and, most importantly, foreign and security matters and leave the gate open for renewed unilateralism and heightened regional tensions. With the recent discoveries of oil and natural gas deposits in the eastern Mediterranean, additional 'fuel' has certainly been added to the fire. In order to ensure its place on the world stage and reaffirm its role as a proponent of peace and stability, EU leaders must take such developments into consideration when discussing the accession of Turkey to the EU. In his analysis of Cyprus-EU-Turkey relations, Ahmet Sozen, a Turkish Cypriot academic, comes to a similar conclusions, stating, "A Turkey slipping away from the EU will have less motivation to undertake further reforms in the area of democracy; it will have less incentive to solve the Cyprus problem; and it will fail to become a model of 'consensus civilizations' in the post-September 11 era, as well as a democratic model for the 'post-Arab Spring' Middle Eastern and North African states" (Sozen, 2012).

References

Adams, W. T. 1966. "The First Republic of Cyprus: A Review of an Unworkable Constitution." *The Western Political Quarterly* 19(3): 475-490.

Akram, Sarah. 2010. "Turkey and the Middle East." *Strategic Studies* 30(1, 2). Accessed April 5, 2012. http://go.galegroup.com.ezproxy.lib.ucalgary.ca/ps/i.do?action=interpret&id=GALE%7CA239794386&v=2.1&u=ucalgary&it=r&p=AONE&sw=w&authCount=1.

Alessandri, Emiliano. 2010. "Turkey's New Foreign Policy and the Future of Turkey-EU Relations." *The International Spectator: Italian Journal of International Affairs* 45(3): 85-100.

Altunisik, Meliha and Ersa Cuhadar. 2010. "Turkey's Search for a Third Party Role in Arab-Israeli Conflicts: A Neutral Facilitator or a Principal Power Mediator?" *Mediterranean Politics* 15(3): 371-392.

Anastasiou, Harry. 2009. "Cyprus as the EU Anomaly." *Global Society* 23(2): 129-151.

Anastasiou, Harry. 2008. *The Broken Olive Branch: Nationalist, Ethnic Conflict and the Quest for Peace in Cyprus. Volume 1: The Impasse of Ethnonationalism*. Syracuse: Syracuse University Press.

Anastasiou, Harry. 2007. "The EU as a peace building system: Deconstructing Nationalism in an era of globalization." *International Journal of Peace Studies* 12(2): 31-50.

Anastasiou, Harry. 2007. "Nationalism as a Deterrent to Peace and Interethnic Democracy: The Failure of Nationalist Leadership from The Hague talks to the Cyprus Referendum." *International Studies Perspectives* 8: 190-205.

Annan, K. 2004. *Comprehensive Settlement of the Cyprus Problem.* UN Official Paper, March 31. New York: UN Headquarters. Accessed April 4, 2012. http://www.zypern.cc/extras/annan-plan-for-cyprus-2004.pdf.

Ari, Tayyar and Ferhat Pirincci. 2010. "Turkey's new foreign policy towards the Middle East and the perceptions in Syria and Lebanon." *Journal of Gazi Academic View* 4(7): 1-16.

Bac, Muftuler Meltem. 2005. "Turkey's Political Reforms and the Impact of the European Union." *South European Society & Politics* 10 (1): 17-31.

Bahcheli, T. 2000. "Searching for a Cyprus Settlement: Considering Options for Creating a Federation, a Confederation, or Two Independent States." *Publius: The Journal of Federalism* 30(1-2): 203-216.

Bechev, Dimitar. 2011. "Turkey's ruse as a regional power." *European View* 10 (173): 173-179.

Bilgic, Tuba. 2009. "The Military and Europeanization Reforms in Turkey." *Middle Eastern Studies* 45(5): 803-824.

Chrysostomos, Pericleous. 2012. "Cyprus: A Last Window of Opportunity? Natural Gas Revives Solution Dynamic." *Insight Turkey* 14(1): 93-108.

Coughland, Reed and Mallinson. 2005. "Enosis, Socio-Cultural Imperialism and Strategy: Difficult Bedfellows." *Middle Eastern Studies* 41(4): 575-614.

Dabilis, Andy. 2012. "Cyprus stalemate continues as EU presidency looms." *Southeast European Times*, March 27, 2012 Accessed March 28, 2012. http://www.setimes.com/cocoon/setimes/xhtml/en_GB/features/setimes/features/2012/03/27/feature04.

Demiris, V. "EP regrets Turkey's remarks to freeze relations with Cyprus' EU Presidency." *East Media Group*, March 20, 2012. http://www.emg.rs/en/news/region/177560.html. Accessed April 4, 2012.

De Vreese, C. H., H. F. Boomgaarden and H. A. Semetko. 2008. "Hard and Soft: Public Support for Turkish Membership in the EU." *European Union Politics* 9: 511-530.

Diez Thomas, Apostolos Agnantopoulos and Alper Kaliber. 2005. "Turkey, Europeanization and Civil Society." *South European Society & Politics* 10(1): 1-15.

Diez, Thomas and Nathalie Tocci. 2010. "The Cyprus Conflict and the Ambiguous Effects of Europeanization." *The Cyprus Review* 22(2): 175-186.

Economist, The. 2010. "Is Turkey Turning? Turkey's foreign policy." June 12, 2010. Accessed March 12, 2012. http://go.galegroup.com.ezproxy.lib.ucalgary.ca/ps/i.do?id=GALE%7CA228521184&v=2.1&u=ucalgary&it=r&p=AONE&sw=w.

Ergun, Ayca. 2010. *Civil Society in Turkey and Local Dimensions of Europeanization. European Integration* 32(5): 507-522.

Ertugal, Ebru. 2010. "Europeanization and multi-level governance in Turkey." *Southeast European and Black Sea Studies* 10(1): 97-110.

Evripidou, Stefanos. 2011. "UN urges resolution of gas dispute." *Cyprus Mail*, 2011. Accessed April 5, 2012. http://www.cyprus-mail.com/cyprus/un-urges-resolution-gas-dispute/20110917.

Famagusta Gazette, 2011. "Cyprus president calls for end to Turkish gunboat diplomacy." Accessed March 27, 2012. http://famagusta-gazette.com/cyprus-president-calls-for-end-to-turkish-gunboat-diplomacy-p13927-69.htm.

Farley, Jonathan. 1995. "Turkey's Foreign Policy." *The Round Table: The Commonwealth Journal of International Affairs* 84(333): 81-88.

Gerhards, Jurgen and Silke Hans. 2011. "Why not Turkey? Attitudes towards Turkish Membership in the EU among Citizens in 27 European Countries." *Journal of Common Market Studies* 49(4): 741-766.

Gursoy, Yaprak. 2010. "Democratization and Foreign Policy Reforms in Turkey: Europeanization of Turkish Politics?" *International Journal of Legal Information* 38(2): 227-234.

Hadjipavlou, M. and L. Trigeorgis. 1993. "Cyprus: An Evolutionary Approach to Conflict Resolution." *The Journal of Conflict Resolution* 37(2): 340-360.

Inbar, Efraim. 2011. "Turkey's changing foreign policy and its international ramifications." *Foreign Policy Research Institute.* Accessed March 25, 2012 http://www.fpri.org/enotes/201102.inbar.turkey.html.

International Crisis Group. 2012. "Aphrodite's Gift: Can Cypriot Gas Power a New Dialogue?" Accessed April 2, 2012. http://www.crisisgroup.org/en/regions/europe/turkey-cyprus/cyprus/216-aphrodites-gift-can-cypriot-gas-power-a-new-dialogue.aspx.

Jung, D. and W Piccoli. 2000. "The Turkish-Israeli alignment: Paranoia or pragmatism?" *Security Dialogue* 31(1): 91-104.

Koprulu, Kemal. 2009. "Paradigm shift in Turkey's Foreign Policy." *The Brown Journal of World Affairs* 16(1): 185-201.

Lindsay-Ker, James. 2010. "Shifting Alignments: The External Orientations of Cyprus since Independence." *Cyprus Review* 22(2): 67-74.

Lindsay-Ker, James. 2008. "Europe's Eastern Outpost: The Republic of Cyprus and the Middle East." *The Round Table: The Commonwealth Journal of International Affairs* 97(397): 535-545.

Mallinson, William. 2011. "Foreign Policy Issues of a Part-Occupied EU states." *Cyprus Review* 23(1): 155-160.

Markides, Kyriacos C. 1977. *The Rise and Fall of the Cyprus Republic*. London: Yale University Press.

Markides, C. K., 1974. "Social Change and the Rise and Decline of Social Movements, The Case of Cyprus." *American Ethnologist* 1(2): 309-330.

Michael, S. Michalis. 2007. "The Cyprus Peace Talks: A Critical Appraisal." *Journal of Peace Research* 44(5): 587-604.

McLaren, L. M. 2007. "Explaining Opposition to Turkish Membership of the EU." *European Union Politics* 8: 251-278.

Morag, Nadav. 2004. "Cyprus and the Clash of Greek and Turkish Nationalisms." *Ethnic Politics* 10(4): 595-624.

Nicolaides, Demetrios. 2011. "Applying Conflict Transformation in Cyprus: A Neo-Functional Approach." *Cyprus Review*, 23(1): 49-63.

Nicolaidis, K. 1998. "Exploring Second-best Solutions for Cyprus." Response to Prodromou, H. E. 1998. "Reintegrating Cyprus: The Need for a New Approach." *Survival* 40(3): 5-24.

Oguzlu, Tarik. 2010. "The Changing Dynamics of Turkey-Israel Relations: A Structural Realist Account." *Mediterranean Politics* 15(2): 273-288.

Oguzlu, Tarik and Ozpek, Burak. 2008. "Turkey's Europeanization." *International Journal* 63(4):991-1009.

Oguzlu, Tarik and U. Gungor. 2006. "Peace operations and transformation of Turkey's security policy." *Contemporary Security Policy* 27(3): 472-788.

Olgun, E. 1998. "Recognising Two States in Cyprus Would Facilitate Co-existence and Stability." Response to Prodromou, H. E. (1998) "Reintegrating Cyprus: The Need for a New Approach." *Survival* 40(3): 35-24.

Onis, Ziya. 2010. "Domestic Politics, International Norms and Challenges to the State: Turkey-EU Relations in the post-Helsinki Era." *Turkish Studies* 4(1): 9-34.

Onis, Ziya and Suhnaz Yilmaz. 2009. "Between Europeanization and Euro-Asianism: Foreign Policy Activism in Turkey during the AKP era." *Turkish Studies* 10(1): 7-24.

Ozel, Soli and Gencer Ozcan. 2011. "Do New Democracies Support Democracy? Turkey's Dilemmas" *Journal of Democracy* 22(4): 124-138.

Peristianis, Nicos. 2006. "Cypriot Nationalism, Dual Identity, and Politics." In *Divided Cyprus: Modernity, History and an Island in Conflict*, edited by Yiannis Padadakis, Nicos Peristianis, and Gisela Welz, 100-120. Bloomington: Indiana University Press.

Pipes, Daniel. 2011. "Cyprus on the world stage." *National Review*. Accessed April 4, 2012. http://www.cceia.unic.ac.cy/index.php?option=com_content&task=view&id=212&Itemid=212.

Pollis, Adamantia. 1973. "Intergroup Conflict and British Colonial Policy: The Case of Cyprus." *Comparative Politics* 5(4): 575-599.

Pope, Hugh. 2010. "Pax Ottomana? The mixed success of Turkey's foreign policy." *Foreign Affairs* 89(6): 161.

Prodromou, H. E. 1988. "Reintegrating Cyprus: The Need for a New Approach." *Survival* 40(3): 25-29.

Reiterer, F. Albert. 2003. *Cyprus: Case Study about a Failure of Ethno-National Understanding*. Peter Lang Publishing.

Ruacan, Ipek. 2007. "A Study in State Socialization: Turkey's EU Accession and CFSP." *Southeast European and Black Sea Studies* 7(4): 573-590.

De Smith, S.A. 1964. *The New Commonwealth and its Constitutions*. London: Stevens & Sons.

Sozen, Ahmet. 2012. "Heading Towards the Defining Moment in Cyprus: Public Opinion vs. Realities on the Ground." *Insight Turkey* 41(1): 109-129.

Tocci, Nathalie. 2010. "Unblocking Turkey's EU Accession." *Insight Turkey* 12(3): 27-31.

Tocci, Nathalie. 2003. "Towards Peace in Cyprus: Incentives and Disincentives." *The Brown Journal of World Affairs* 10(1): 199-212.

Ulusoy, Kivanc. 2008. "Turkey and the EU: Democratization, Civil-Military Relations, and the Cyprus Issue." *Insight Turkey* 10(4): 51-76.

Vassiliou, George. 2003. "EU Entry: Catalyst for a Cyprus Solution." *Global Dialogue* 5(3, 4). Accessed March 12, 2012. http://www.worlddialogue.org/content.php?id=262.

Villelabeitia, Ibon. 2011. "Turkey's gunboat diplomacy makes waves in the region." *Reuters*, September 8. Accessed April 1, 2012. http://www.reuters.com/article/2011/09/08/us-turkey-israel-gamble-idUSTRE7871WZ20110908.

Wethe, David and Stelios Orphanides. 2011. "Noble Announces Natural-Gas Discovery off Coast of Cyprus." *BloombergBusinessweek*, December 29. Accessed April 2, 2012. http://www.businessweek.com/news/2011-12-29/noble-announces-natural-gas-discovery-off-coast-of-cyprus.html.

Xydis, Stephen. 1968. "*The UN General Assembly as an Instrument of Greek Foreign Policy: Cyprus, 1954-58.*" *The Journal of Conflict Resolution* 12(2): 141-158.

Zunes, Stephen. 2002. "United Nations Security Council Resolutions currently being violated by countries other than Iraq." *Foreign Policy in Focus*, October 1, 2002. Accessed February 20, 2012. http://www.fpif.org/articles/united_nations_security_council_resolutions_currently_being_violated_by_countries_other_than_iraq.

The End of Enlargement?

The Case of Turkey, or Thinking Beyond the Widening versus Deepening Dichotomy

Boyka STEFANOVA

Introduction

In the wake of its 2004-07 eastward enlargement, the EU descended into "enlargement fatigue" (Bindi and Angelescu, 2011a). This situation is puzzling, despite the variety of explanations drawn from the everyday politics of European integration and integration theory. Geographic expansion has been a continuity in the history of the European Union. The functionalist argument subsumes enlargement under the premise of regional integration as a working peace system. Building upon the formative case of Franco-German reconciliation through European integration, all rounds of EU enlargement have reaffirmed European values of democracy, unification and regional peace (Bindi and Angelescu, 2011b). Enlargement has completely reconfigured the original European Economic Community (EEC) from a West-centric to a pan-European union (Nugent, 2006)[1] and is viewed as a catalyst for European integration. At the same time, enlargement has emerged as one of the most contested EU policies. Against the background of economic and financial crises, and the rising costs of adding new members, the claim that a further expansion of the EU membership base will destroy the attained level of integration has emerged into a widely held assumption. It is thus uncertain whether the lack of impetus for further EU enlargement is due to the absence of a sense of historical legacy and obligation that has characterised most enlargement rounds (Bindi and Angelescu,

1 By the late 1990s, enlargement had consolidated into three parallel frameworks. First, with respect to the Central and East European countries, candidates since the mid-1990s, the EU pursued a gradual, tiered approach. The Czech Republic, Estonia, Hungary, Latvia, Lithuania, Poland, Slovakia and Slovenia became EU members in 2004. Bulgaria and Romania joined the EU in 2007. Second, in 2003, the EU embarked on an integration strategy towards the Western Balkans. Croatia signed an accession treaty in 2011 with a view of accession in July 2013. Third, accession negotiations with Turkey commenced in 2005 and with Iceland in 2010.

2011b), or whether it marks a significant pause and withdrawal from the systemic rationale of integration and the EU's normative agenda.

What explains the apparent mismatch between historical continuity and political uncertainty with regard to enlargement? This question is important due to the profound international implications of European integration for broader regional dynamics. If "enlargement fatigue" prevails, the EU borders to the east may become the ultimate geopolitical and cultural definition of Europe. Conversely, if enlargement is pursued in a path-dependent process, its *finalités politiques* will need to be defined. Is the EU's enlargement sustainable, and how far can the EU expand?

The problem with the EU enlargement is that there is no theoretically necessary link between the deepening and widening of integration beyond a politically contested relationship. The conventional view posits actors' preferences for territorial growth and further deepening of integration as non-separable. Enlargement and the movement towards 'a closer union' are regarded either as a single systemic process or as a trade-off between enlargement and the hollowing-out of integration, or yet as a dialectical push-pull rebalancing between territorial expansion and institutional deepening. Because it brings more diversity and disparity within a broader membership base, enlargement tends to lower the efficiency of EU decision-making, thus creating incentives to deepen integration in order to reverse such trends. Such propositions suggest that the EU is conceptualised as a one-dimensional space characterised by a dynamic equilibrium between territorial expansion and vertical integration. While such propositions are consistent with both the neo-functionalist and intergovernmentalist varieties of integration theory, they offer little insight into enlargement as a historical and political process. There are few theoretically informed arguments suggesting that enlargement is a systemic process, inherent to integration, that it is context specific, or that it has yet reached a state of overextension. Neither the continued enlargement nor the enlargement fatigue argument can be rigorously tested. The sources of both integration and enlargement are endogenous (Jupille *et al.*, 2003) and no clear prediction about the strength and direction of their association can be made. The deepening versus widening dichotomy may be useful in determining the EU's optimal size as an international organisation or a multi-product club (Sandler and Hartley, 1999) but is less amenable to explain its evolution as a political system, or the quality and legitimacy of the outcomes it generates.

This chapter presents a more contextualised view of the relationship between enlargement and integration. It argues that the link between deepening and widening is historically contingent: the product of endogenous political preferences along multiple dimensions – economic, political and systemic – that shape state interests not necessarily in an additive or order-ranked manner. Both enlargement and deepening are equilibrium-producing mechanisms along the principal objectives of European integration, such as economic prosperity, democratic legitimacy and political unification. Depending on their relative salience, the relationship between enlargement and the deepening of integration is contextually determined at each stage. There is no standing or uniform preference for enlargement and therefore no permanent trade-off, push-pull dynamic or path dependency between enlargement and institutional deepening.

The EU's enlargement history provides consistent evidence of the claim about the multi-dimensionality of member state preferences. That these preferences are separable is revealed in the piecemeal approach to enlargement on behalf of the member states. Each round of enlargement has induced demands for adjustment, reform and joint decision-making, redefining integration from a process of progressive deepening into a multi-modal process of regional governance. Building on the historical record, the chapter demonstrates the validity of the separable preferences model by examining the aftermath of the 2004/07 East European enlargement, in the case of Turkey's EU accession negotiations. It explains the lack of a common preference for continued enlargement beyond the deepening/widening dichotomy by reflecting on the role of domestic, geopolitical and institutional factors. Based on the evidence, the chapter draws conclusions regarding the need to theorise about enlargement beyond the dichotomy of rational choice versus reflexive premises, or material versus ideational arguments.

Enlargement and Integration in Theory

The relationship between widening and deepening is not a simple contrast between horizontal versus vertical institutionalisation, as the theoretical literature contends (Schimmelfennig and Sedelmeier, 2002). Besides a process of territorial expansion, enlargement is also an extension of the EU's governance system. By contrast, deepening is an expansion of the domain of joint policymaking, a shift from economics to political choices and, in terms of decision rule, a process of "automatic politization", whereby initially technical-economic decisions become progressively more controversial and lead to the transfer of competences to the central organs of the union (Schmitter, 1969, p. 166).

The conventional argument on enlargement is drawn from the principal theoretical perspectives on European integration: neo-functionalism, intergovernmentalism, federalist theorising, as well as economic theories of clubs and international unions, and international negotiation

(Alesina *et al.*, 2005; Sandler and Hartley, 1999). These perspectives regard enlargement either as an autonomous process – an instance of regionalism or an element of the EU's external policy – or as a systemic process inseparable from the institutional development of integration. The former view explains enlargement as progressive territorial expansion in the context of asymmetric interdependence; the latter considers it either as a trade-off to institutional deepening or as an impetus for more integration.

From a macro-political perspective, enlargement is subsumed under regionalist premises – the idea that global politics should be organised in regional blocs, as it is territorial in nature. State preferences are explained by propositions about the cohesiveness of regions and economies of scale (Hurrell, 1995). Enlargement is thus territorially confined within the boundaries of the region. The problem with the regionalist perspective is that Europe does not have a clear-cut geopolitical definition and, due to the openness of EU enlargement, the boundaries of structural interdependence are not coterminous with its regional geography. As a policy action, enlargement involves strategic calculations under conditions of structural interdependence, underlying values and institutional choices, which then require the study of preferences (Moravcsik, 1993). A theory of actors' preferences is thus better positioned to explain enlargement as a form of integration policy rather than regionalist theorising, which ultimately regards the EU as the shorthand for Europe.

Moravcsik and Vachudova (2002) have argued that enlargement is a consistently pursued policy because the EU member states have a long-term economic and geopolitical interest in territorial expansion. As every enlargement round represents a significant event in the evolution of European integration, the mechanism of the process should be amenable to the premises of liberal intergovernmentalism (Moravcsik, 1998). The dynamics of enlargement fit well into the three-stage model of outcome creation valid for the significant events in European integration: domestic state preference formation, inter-state bargaining and institutional choice. In reality, however, the domestic preferences model advanced by liberal intergovernmentalism is only partially applicable to enlargement due to both the secondary place it grants to the possibility of converging or shared preferences among all EU member states and the significance it places on institutional input. Enlargement takes place in a more cooperative framework and is more profoundly affected by the policy initiatives of the EU institutions than rationalist theorising suggests, although in practice it may be reduced to individual domestic preferences due to the growing 'nationalisation' of the process (Hillion, 2010).

Rationalist theories do not exclude the possibility that enlargement may reflect the common preference of the EU member states, but rationalism limits such outcomes to conditions of homogeneity or high levels of inner cohesion. In the case of heterogeneity, enlargement is the outcome of international bargaining in which their diverging preferences are reconciled through side payments. Rationalist theorising is based on several assumptions: first, that state preferences for enlargement are transferable – that is, derived from the same sources as preferences for integration; second, that current political preferences are anchored in the status quo; and third, and that enlargement is possible when the marginal benefits from adding a new member exceed the costs. As all policies with an overall positive effect may create distributive outcomes, some members may incur short-term losses. According to Alesina *et al.* (2005), the marginal cost proposition determines the optimal size of international unions, unless the negative externalities associated with a growing membership base are internalised either through side payments for the 'old' members or reduced benefits for new members.

Enlargement does not compromise the attained level of integration as long as the median member states (including new members) prefer joint policymaking and a majority-based decision rule (Alesina *et al.*, 2001). According to this view, enlargement is always possible, and therefore its rationale is independent from the deepening of integration. Schneider (2009) contends that the accession of new members is preceded by the resolution of distributional conflicts among the 'old' member states by means of internal transfers or side payments. This system of internal redistribution is complemented by external adjustment: a temporary suspension or reduction of membership benefits for the new members, most frequently in the area of market freedoms, the Common Agricultural Policy, and the EU's structural funds. Schneider (2009) has argued that such adjustments make enlargement possible by lowering the opportunities for member state veto when the costs of adding new members exceed the benefits for individual states. The compensatory mechanism results in a form of discriminatory membership that ensures the reconciliation of diverging member states' preferences on enlargement.

The main issue with the cost-benefit conceptualisation of this form of 'differentiated' membership is that it is concerned exclusively with the economic costs of enlargement and has no adequate estimate of the scope of political costs and benefits. Rational choice theory assumes a repetitive redistribution of benefits as a method of compensating old members for losses they may incur in the process, without taking into account policy innovation that may balance out the increasing heterogeneity of an expanded EU membership base. Even if the accommodation of diversity takes place by means of limited membership benefits, it is amenable to policy innovation and learning. New policy instruments – such as regional and cohesion policies, external and political conditionality, and post-accession monitoring – create linkages between asymmetric negotiation and policy innovation in the area of market liberalisation, policy compliance and geopolitical consolidation. Furthermore, enlargement is affected by developments pertaining to several other EU projects: the Schengen Agreement, conflict resolution and neighbourhood relations, institutional reform, elections and voting, citizenship, and fundamental rights.

Similarly, rationalist theories underestimate the causal influence of non-material factors – the classical functionalist and normative argument about European integration as a working peace project – although they include conditions of incomplete negotiation. By contrast, social constructivism examines the role of ideational factors in European integration. Constructivism posits enlargement as a project of European unification (Parsons, 2003). Cultural factors, ideas, common visions, and political and normative entrepreneurship are as important determinants of the enlargement preferences of the EU member states as economic benefits and geopolitical interests. Following constructivist premises, Jacoby (1999) and Schimmelfennig and Sedelmeier (2002), among others, regard enlargement as a process of incomplete negotiation dominated by political and ideational factors. The incomplete negotiations model is hierarchical rather than horizontal and linkage-based. It is defined by enhanced conditionality, political conditions and multi-dimensional benefits, as shown in the 2004/07 East European enlargement.

Theories focused on the relationship between the deepening and widening of integration explain enlargement as an intermediate outcome of the dialectical push-pull dynamic of European integration. The deepening of integration creates incentives for widening as the attractiveness of the integrated core increases. In turn, enlargement creates incentives for deeper integration because of the political commitment to preserve the attained level of cooperation. As Preston (1997, p. 9) contends, enlargement reflects a new member's commitment to apply "an ever-expanding rule book". The limitations on state sovereignty after enlargement represent an automatic deepening of integration as an open-ended process. Conversely, by dealing predominantly with the conditions of membership, enlargement isolates the accession negotiations from the big debates in integration, which in turn slows down enlargement "even further" (Preston, 1997, p. 9). It is obvious that the theoretical claim of a deepening/widening trade-off stands in contrast to the rationalist proposition on enlargement as an autonomous process, a proposition that holds enlargement as not necessarily diluting integration or causing a gridlock of decision-making. Based on the evidence of the East European enlargement, the EU's most recent and complex territorial expansion, Moravcsik and Vachudova (2002) have argued that enlargement has not slowed down integration, as the EU's fundamental problem is the persisting diversity of member state preferences, not the size of the union.

Modelling Enlargement and Integration Beyond Dichotomous Preferences

In contrast to propositions about enlargement as an autonomous process or a trade-off to integration, the argument for the multi-dimensional relationship between the deepening and territorial expansion of European integration is based on several premises: about the significance of political, rather than primarily economic distributional effects for the old member states; about the separability of actor preferences for enlargement along economic, domestic and geopolitical objectives; and about the evolving, rather than fixed, nature of political preferences. Its central claim is that enlargement is a political process. It reflects power asymmetries, values, preferences and issue positions. Enlargement is also a process of incomplete negotiation. It takes place by means of open commitments, transitional periods, mid-term adjustment and enhanced monitoring, which suggests that integration, while aspiring to correct for heterogeneity and problematic diversity, may lead to disequilibria and the unequal distribution of costs and benefits. As a classical integration process, enlargement both corrects for internal disequilibria and creates new imbalances: by increasing the heterogeneity of club membership, by opening integration to uncharted waters, or by revealing its limitations to resolve distributional conflicts. The dual contingency of the process defies deterministic claims. A political approach permits the examination of the relationships between actor preferences and environmental constraints, otherwise in line with the tenets of rational institutionalist theorising, and further contextualises outcomes relative to values and power asymmetries.

From a political perspective, there is no standing preference for enlargement, or a 'price' of obtaining member state support for it through side payments and reduced benefits for new members. Actors' preferences along the individual dimensions are separable. Enlargement may create incentives for more vertical integration if the median of member state preferences represents a majority preference for common policies. The relationship between enlargement and the deepening of integration is context specific and equilibrium-based, rather than path dependent. It corresponds to a view on European integration as a historical process, which takes place in terms of cycles of actor preferences, interests and priorities. Accordingly, an understanding of its dynamics must be informed by its historical evolution (Katzenstein, 1997).

The proposition that state preferences for integration are neither fixed nor transferable suggests that they may be differentiated based on the fundamental values and objectives of European integration, which reflect functional expediencies (economic benefits, coherence), domestic legitimacy (an 'ever closer union', democracy and diversity) and geopolitical stability (peace rationale, regional order). The preferences of the member states change historically along these core dimensions. All individual rounds of territorial expansion have resolved – to varying degrees – functional, geopolitical and legitimacy priorities. The claim that these priorities are flexible and driven by ecological influences is based on the fact that enlargement originates as a result of the preferences and interests of non-members. While the preferences of the 'old' member states may be assumed as stable, anchored in the status quo, and reflected in the requirement for full adoption of the *acquis communautaire* as a condition for membership, such preferences are not fixed. Depending on the historical and geopolitical context, they are likely to be formed along multiple dimensions, altering the overall cost-benefit calculation by adding preferences for more versus fewer common policies, and a variable degree of approval for delegating more (or less) power to the community institutions.

Enlargement is both a systemic process anchored in treaty provisions and a policy area within the EU's external domain. As a systemic process, enlargement is affected by the attained level of cohesion, decision-making and institutional capacity. The mix of preferences at each stage determines the model of outcome creation, ranging from asymmetric negotiation implemented through trade-offs and accommodation to consensus for community-building with secondary redistribution of benefits, to a strictly veto players' framework.

The EU's enlargement history is consistent with the claim about the multi-dimensionality of member state preferences. Every enlargement round has required a consensus on the feasibility and normative value of the process beyond a simple redistribution of costs and benefits among the 'old' members, as well as between 'old' and 'new' member states. Every round has opened European integration to a strengthened regional policy and presented new demands for problem solving (such as the UK budget rebate, the quality of democracy in southern Europe, the post-communist transition, human rights and the protection of minorities, conflict resolution, neighbourhood relations, and so on). None of these issues has been resolved exclusively through redistribution but has required a renewed value consensus, including on issues such as solidarity, the desired level of supranationalism and the direction of integration. In the wake of the East European accession, the case study of Turkey's negotiations for EU membership provides evidence of the consolidation of the political approach to enlargement, which is reflected in the growing significance of political rather than economic cost-benefit calculations, multi-dimensional preferences, and linkage politics beyond accommodation and side payments. The following section demonstrates the proposition of separability of preferences, enhanced conditionality, an open-ended enlargement model, and veto player politics as factors explaining the stalemate in Turkey's EU accession negotiations beyond rational choice and cultural arguments.

Historical Referents for Enlargement and the Deepening/ Widening Dichotomy: Not a Simple Trade-off

Territorial expansion is compatible with and was anticipated by the founding treaties of European integration. The EU is governed by open-ended treaties that reflect the idea that it is not only an ever-deepening system ('an ever closer union') but also a system permanently open to membership expansion. According to Article 237 of the Rome Treaty, Article 98 of the ECSC Treaty and Article 205 of the Euratom Treaty, "every European state may demand to join" (that is, to become a member of the Community). The preamble to the Rome Treaty links enlargement to the political objective of European integration by restating the commitment of the signatory states: "by thus pooling their resources to preserve and strengthen peace and liberty, and calling upon the other peoples of Europe who share their ideal to join in their efforts" (Olmi, 1978, p. 77). Article 49 of the Treaty on European Union (1993) stipulates that any European state may become a EU member. The Laeken Declaration of 2001 determined that the only boundary of the Union is democracy and the respect for human rights (European Council, 2001). The Treaty on the functioning of the European Union (TFEU, 2008, Art. 212) also confirms the EU's openness to future members (European Union, 2007).

Viewed through a political lens, the EU's enlargement policy is embedded in the political priorities of the member states prevalent at each consecutive stage of European integration. The topic of enlargement was originally discussed in connection with European unity, and the EEC's movement towards unification. Although enlargement may be explained by a common preference to enhance economic prosperity, one of the foundational goals of European integration, it is also relevant to the European construction as a political project. Accession has always amounted to more than international negotiation for joining a club.

While the salience of political (relative to economic) objectives has varied, the rationale for enlargement has been embedded in the EU's systemic objectives, which are political in nature.

The first European enlargement (1973) – in which Denmark, Ireland and the UK joined the EEC – was shaped by the idea about European unity. Even though redistributive issues ranked high in the negotiations, the debate among the six 'old' member states was primarily about the political differentiation between continental Europe and the UK, the Europeanist and Atlanticist powers in European politics, and the interface between them. The economic dimension was negotiated separately and acquired salience only at a later stage. The UK entry introduced a renewed consensus on the necessity of joint action to reduce regional disparities through the creation of the European Regional Development Fund. The key objective in the Mediterranean enlargement (1981-86) was the consolidation of democracy in Greece, Portugal and Spain. Economic preferences were accommodated beyond a simple trade-off, by means of prescriptions for structural reform implemented under the Integrated Mediterranean Programmes. European integration was seen as a way to overcome southern Europe's exceptionalism and instability through participation in European governance.

Political costs, ideational arguments and geopolitical gains ranked high in the collective EU preference for a robust East European enlargement (2004-2007). The accession of ten new Eastern European states took place within a multi-dimensional enlargement model combining economic, political, institutional and identity issues (Nugent, 2006). The application of conditionality became increasingly political and institutional in nature.[2] In the context of the East European accession, the framework of negotiations was not only incomplete due to the extensive reference to political conditionality; it also redefined the meaning of membership from a concept indicating status (with or without reduced access to benefits) to one reflecting an open-ended process of adjustment through instruments for post-accession monitoring, commitment to participation in integration projects subject to change and reform (for example, the euro zone and the Schengen Agreement), and compliance with norms not fully internalised by the 'old' member states (minority rights).

In the aftermath of the East European accession, the negative outcomes of the 2005 referendum on the EU Constitutional Treaty in France and the Netherlands demonstrated that as a result of domestic

---

2 The political criteria for accession stipulate that the countries must have achieved "stability of institutions guaranteeing democracy, the rule of law, human rights and respect for and protection of minorities" (European Council, 1993).

politics, the preferences of the member states for continued enlargement had weakened. Although the enlargement issue was not essential to the ratification process, the rejection of the Constitutional Treaty in the national referenda in France and the Netherlands (29 May-1 June 2005) produced significant retrenchment among the EU member states.[3] Only 7 per cent of voters in the Netherlands believed that the EU constitution would have negative effects on the country due to enlargement-related relocation of Dutch businesses and the loss of jobs. Three per cent rejected the constitution because it would make possible a future Turkish membership in the EU. Disagreement with an EU membership for Turkey accounted for 6 per cent of the 'no' vote in France; another 3 per cent of the negative vote was associated with fear of future EU enlargements (European Commission, 2005b; 2005c).

Although references to Eastern Europe were not explicit in either case, as a result of the constitutional referenda, enlargement emerged as a diminished priority for the EU member states (Stefanova, 2006). The common view was that the Union needed a reflection pause in order to respond to the citizens' appeal for better functioning European institutions. The debates of the European Parliament re-examined the rationale of enlargement in order to "reflect the political realities of the European nations" (European Parliament, 2005). Prominent French politicians reintroduced the rhetoric of a multi-speed Europe of the early 1990s.[4] The diverse and often conflicting views on the appropriate policy response led to political uncertainty over enlargement rather than to an engaging process of treaty revision. "Europe should have borders" became a key political message beyond the argument that the EU needs to function as a defined territorial entity (Stefanova, 2006, p. 254).

The enlargement policy of the Union formally remained unchanged. Croatia and Turkey officially opened accession negotiations. Macedonia acquired the status of a candidate country. Substantively, however, the diverging positions of the member states, repeated rounds of compromise and last-minute concessions have diminished the principled character of the policy. The debate among national governments, the Euro-

3 By the time of the referenda, European public opinion on enlargement had become increasingly divided. Support for future enlargements fell to around 50 per cent in 2005. In Germany, 40 per cent opposed any future enlargement; 74 per cent were against Turkey commencing accession negotiations. Support for enlargement was below the EU average both in France (32 per cent) and in the Netherlands (45 per cent) (European Commission, 2005a, p. 27).

4 Nicolas Sarkozy, then president of the governing Union for a Popular Movement, suggested that a leading "G6" group of the largest EU members should become the new EU core to advance integration where common policies are impossible among all countries. See Stefanova (2006, p. 254).

pean Commission and the European Parliament in regard to Turkey's accession negotiations demonstrates the prevalence of bureaucratic politics and veto power, replacing previously implemented frameworks for the resolution of distributional conflicts under the EU's enlargement policy.

The Case of Turkey: An Open-Ended Enlargement Model

The EU made a decision to open accession negotiations with Turkey in 2004. Although the negotiation process, which began in 2005, replicated the mechanism of the East European enlargement, its geopolitical, economic and temporal scale remains unprecedented. It may not be subsumed under a framework based on side payments and discriminatory membership as one-dimensional rationalist models posit, or under the premises of a trade-off between the deepening and widening of European integration.

Turkey has a long history of relations with the EU. It applied for associated status with the EEC in 1959 and signed an Association Agreement in 1963. In 1964, Turkey established a customs union, which entered into force in 1995. Turkey submitted an application for membership in 1987. It was acknowledged as a candidate country in 1999 (failed in 1997) and became subject to monitoring under the Copenhagen political and economic criteria for membership. Since then, the EU has applied a mechanism of enhanced conditionality, which reflects flexible political preferences on behalf of the EU member states, virtually transforming the accession process into an open-ended negotiation framework.

The premises of political conditionality *vis-à-vis* Turkey were formulated progressively, in the course of its *rapprochement* with the EU. Recognition of the Republic of Cyprus and effective contribution to the resolution of the Cyprus conflict emerged as the two most significant membership conditions. Due to the persistence of unresolved issues pertaining to the conflict, Turkey's EU accession has been subject to strict political conditionality, increasingly subsumed under a negotiating framework based on veto players' politics. As the linkages between conflict resolution in Cyprus and general political conditionality under the Copenhagen criteria demonstrate, the EU enlargement model no longer involves direct redistribution of benefits and, accordingly, may not be completed by means of side payments and differentiated membership alone.

The Cyprus Issue Through the Lens of Turkey's Negotiations for EU Membership

The Republic of Cyprus, represented by the Greek Cypriot government, applied for EC membership in 1990. The European Commission issued a positive opinion on the eligibility of the candidacy in 1993. The Commission viewed the separation between the Greek and Turkish Cypriot communities as a violation of the sovereignty of Cyprus forced by the presence of Turkish troops; however, issues critical to the resolution of the conflict, such as the federal form of government and intercommunal relations, were not relevant to the community *acquis* at the time.[5] The main preoccupation of the EU institutional actors was the ability of Cyprus' government to assume responsibilities under the treaties, its membership in the non-aligned movement, and its capacity to affect the relationship between the EU and Turkey (European Commission, 1993, p. 12, Art. 22). Despite the seemingly technical nature of the review, the opinion of the European Commission was political (Stefanova, 2011). The Commission recommended negotiations with the objective of "sending a positive signal" by endorsing Cyprus' European vocation (European Commission, 1993, p. 23).[6]

The first linkage between the Cyprus candidacy for membership and the EU-Turkey relationship emerged at the Corfu European Council (1994) when Greece threatened to stop the eastward enlargement and the customs union with Turkey unless Cyprus was included in the first wave of candidates. France brokered an agreement in the General Affairs Council (6 March 1995) and Greece lifted its veto on the EU-Turkey customs union. The Council concluded that Cyprus was eligible to begin membership negotiations six months after the 1996 intergovernmental conference. In a parallel development, it approved the customs union with Turkey.

---

5 The Cyprus conflict was the result of a long-standing constitutional impasse that had produced a breakdown of the constitutional order in 1963. In 1974, the Greek junta organised a coup against Cyprus' President Makarios with the objective of a union with Greece. The coup was followed by a Turkish invasion justified under the constitutive Treaty of Guarantee to protect the Turkish Cypriots. The coup and the subsequent invasion resulted in a mass refugee wave and established areas of Greek Cypriot and Turkish Cypriot control, leading to the partition of control over the territory of Cyprus. This outcome was reinforced through the creation of a quasi-independent Turkish Federated State after the 1974 Turkish invasion. The Turkish Republic of Northern Cyprus (TRNC) was declared in northern Cyprus in 1983, but it did not receive international recognition except from Turkey. The legal framework for conflict resolution was established under the United Nations with an emphasis on issues of sovereignty, territorial integrity and occupation.

6 The chronology below is based on Stefanova 2011 (p. 127 40).

The decisions of the 1995 Council limited the opportunities for political conditionality *vis-à-vis* Turkey prior to the Cyprus accession. Individual member states (the UK, France and Germany) and the European Parliament (EP) had proposed to link the customs union to the state of human rights in Turkey but the issue was downplayed by the Commission and the Council in 1995. The EU institutions did not take into account Turkey's military presence and, as in the Cyprus case, used the argument of engaging Turkey and encouraging its European vocation (Council of the European Union, 1995). The EU's policy preference was to treat Turkey's EU membership separate from the conflict resolution issue. However, the lack of conditionality allowed for multiple linkages to develop, leading to sub-optimal outcomes rather than intermediate internal trade-offs, side payments or transitional discriminatory membership. The work of the European Council evolved in the direction of a veto players' model.

Greece emerged as a major player in the negotiation framework when it rejected a connection between conflict resolution and EU membership. At the Helsinki European Council (1999), Greece agreed to candidate status for Turkey only if the conditionality of conflict resolution was removed from the accession negotiations with Cyprus. In a parallel development, the EU did not consistently apply conditionality *vis-à-vis* Turkey (Nugent, 2006). The Council granted Turkey the status of a candidate country and established the improvement of relations with Greece as a condition for the opening of accession negotiations (European Council, 1999). The recognition of Turkey's status as a EU candidate country made no reference to its military presence in Cyprus or to the requirement to recognise the Republic of Cyprus as a EU member state. The accession model only subsequently incorporated these issues due to their practical meaning for the *acquis*-based content of the negotiations.

The EU's willingness to address conflict resolution in Cyprus by engaging Turkey transformed the accession process into a pluralist framework comprised of the diverse and often contradictory preferences of the EU member states and EU institutional actors. The Accession Partnership (December 2000) included a condition for Turkey to encourage the Turkish Cypriot community to take a more conciliatory stance toward the Greek Cypriot community and support UN mediation. As Turkey acquired an interest in its own accession, it was selectively adjusting to EU pressures to assume a constructive role in the Cyprus conflict. In November 2002, Turkey's Prime Minster Erdogan acknowledged that the resolution of the Cyprus question would increase Turkey's chances for membership: "No matter how much we say they're not related, solving the Cyprus issue will not just accelerate our EU process, it will also be a concrete and useful step to overcoming the problems between Greece and Turkey."[7] The resolution of the conflict was not a single issue for Turkey. The country had no motivation to end the conflict, as its primary concern was the protection of the Turkish Cypriot community, which was ensured through the presence of Turkish troops. For this reason, Turkey continued to oppose Cyprus' EU accession, as well as any connection between conflict resolution in Cyprus and the prospects of its own EU candidacy.[8]

Public discourse on Turkey's place in the EU was negatively affected by the failed referenda on the ratification of the EU Constitutional Treaty in France and the Netherlands. Although the discussion on the desirability of enlargement as a permanent integration policy was not restricted to the Constitutional Treaty, Turkey's roadmap to EU accession experienced major policy reconsideration as a result of the national referenda (Stefanova, 2006).

France questioned the sustainability of the EU open-door enlargement policy: "Is the EU able to expand if we do not have the institutions providing for the smooth functioning of this enlarged Union?" asked President Chirac (Gouillaud, 2005). Such rhetoric implicitly questioned the wisdom of the planned accession negotiations with Turkey. France demanded that Turkey recognise Cyprus as a condition for the opening of accession negotiations.[9] Political circles in Austria and Germany, among others, supported a reformulation of the EU enlargement policy towards Turkey. Austria demanded that Turkey be instead granted a privileged partnership. A last-minute Franco-British compromise extended the timeframe for Turkey's recognition of Cyprus as a condition for accession negotiations (Browne, 2005). The European Parliament postponed its vote on the commencement of official negotiations with Turkey and proposed additional conditions to Turkey's roadmap to membership, such as the recognition of the killings of Armenians in 1915 as genocide. In a declaration on the opening of the accession negotiations, the president of the European Commission, José Manuel Barroso, stated: "Europe must learn more about Turkey. And Turkey must win the hearts and minds of European citizens. They are the ones who at the end of the day will decide about Turkey's membership" (European Commission, 2005d).

---

7 "Change of Turkish mood on Cyprus." *Irish Times*, 18 November 2002, p. 9.

8 "Turkish Premier: Cyprus issue, EU should not be linked." *Anatolia News Agency* (in Greek), 19 November 2003; BBC Worldwide Monitoring (English translation).

9 The conditions set by the European Council in December 2004 required that Turkey extend its customs union with the EU (effective since 1995) to the new member states, including Cyprus, prior to opening accession negotiations.

The issue of the recognition of Cyprus became critical to the accession *acquis* in the area of the customs union and the political conditions on relations with neighbours. While political discourse in the EU later downplayed these requirements, in addition to the question about the presence of Turkish troops in northern Cyprus, Turkey's accession negotiations were strongly linked to the resolution of the Cyprus issue.

An important reference to the Cyprus conflict re-emerged in connection with the process of extending the EU-Turkey customs union, operational since 1995, to include the new member states of the East European enlargement (the Ankara Protocol). The view of the European Commission was that the customs union was part of the membership conditionality and therefore non-negotiable. The negotiating framework included a requirement for Turkey to support the UN efforts, contribute to a comprehensive settlement and normalise relations with all countries. Turkey signed the Ankara Protocol, extending the customs union with the EU to the 10 new members, but included a unilateral declaration (dated 29 July 2005) to the effect that the signature did not constitute a formal recognition of Cyprus. As a result of Cyprus' pressure, the EU issued a declaration condemning the statement and stating that Turkey's declaration would not change its obligations under the Additional Protocol. The declaration referred to the principle of recognition of all member states as a necessary component of the accession process (Council of the European Union, 2005). Regional issues were to remain a standing reference point for evaluating Turkey's progress under the Copenhagen political criteria. Cyprus further blocked Turkey's accession negotiations by directly opposing discussions on eight policy areas related to the customs union. The initial process had neutralised a Cyprus veto by obtaining consensus of the opening of accession negotiations with Turkey; however, issues related to the implementation of the customs union allowed for continued conditionality in line with the community *acquis*.

Cyprus was not the only country blocking the process in exchange for Turkish cooperation in the Cyprus issue. In December 2004, the EP expressed concern about Turkey's non-recognition of Cyprus and did not support the position of the European Commission and the Council on Turkey's Progress Report. The EP Foreign Affairs Committee criticised Turkey for its lack of progress on human rights and "persistent shortcomings" with regard to Cyprus.[10] In 2005, the EP endorsed the beginning of membership negotiations with Turkey but stated that it would not ratify the EU-Turkey customs union because Cyprus was denied access to Turkish ports. Although Turkey had signed the Ankara

---

10 European Parliament, news report, 30 November 2004.

Protocol, it did not implement it. France blocked five policy areas of negotiation under the membership *acquis*. In 2006, a parliamentary report urged Turkey to recognise Cyprus or face possible suspension of the accession negotiations.

Yet another stream of linkage politics developed in the Council outside Cyprus, where several member states (Austria, France and Germany) saw another opportunity to link Turkey's intransigence on Cyprus to reaffirm their uncertainty about a fully-fledged EU membership for Turkey. The European Commission recommended suspending negotiations on chapters of the *acquis* related to the customs union in November 2006 (European Council, 2006).[11] By 2012, the accession negotiations had stalled at a level of 13 open out of 33 negotiation chapters. All but three chapters – on social policy and employment, competition policy and public procurement – have been blocked due to issues that link the EU-Turkey customs union to the recognition of Cyprus and the resolution of the conflict.[12]

The fluidity of member state preferences in the case of Turkey's accession negotiations, informed primarily by political considerations, has limited the ability of the EU institutional actors to pursue enlargement by conventional means. The diversity of preferences, no longer limited to economic costs or reduced benefits for the 'old' member states, makes the enlargement process less predictable and politically sustainable. While serving as an illustration of the need to study the preferences of the EU member states more seriously (Moravscik, 1997), it also suggests that, despite its reliance on rigorous conditionality, the EU's enlargement policy is closer to the politics of international negotiation than to the mechanism of a policy process.

Conclusion

The EU's enlargement history and, more recently, the case of Turkey's accession negotiations both demonstrate that there is no unequivocally defined relationship between the deepening and widening of European integration. Enlargement is a mechanism to extend the system of EU governance, values and benefits to a growing number of countries outside the original West European design. This process is more complex than horizontal institutionalisation or a negotiated mechanism of benefit sharing.

---

11 The chapters were: free movement of goods, right of establishment and freedom to provide services, financial services, agriculture and rural development, fisheries, transport policy, customs union and external relations.

12 Vogel, T. 2012. "EU membership losing its appeal" *European Voice*, 9 June.

Enlargement has territorial, efficiency (functional) and sustainability aspects. Certain rounds of enlargement, such as the eastward enlargement, have been significant events in the history of European integration (Rosamond, 2000); others have demonstrated the repetitive logic of enlargement, compatible with the view that enlargement is inevitable and necessary to integration. On the one hand, enlargement grants new momentum to integration. On the other, it has led to substantial resource transfers and institutional restructuring.

All individual rounds of territorial expansion have resolved, to varying degrees, functional, geopolitical and legitimacy priorities. That these priorities may be flexible and driven by external influences is due to the fact that enlargement originates as a result of the preferences of non-members. While member state preferences may be assumed as stable, anchored in the status quo and reflected in the requirement for full adoption of the *acquis communautaire* as a condition for membership, they are also flexible. Depending on the historical and geopolitical context, they are likely to be formed along multiple dimensions, altering the cost-benefit calculation of enlargement by adding preferences for more versus fewer common policies and for delegating more (or less) power to the supranational institutions.

From an international politics perspective, the big questions about enlargement and the deepening of integration refer to the optimality of the process, whether it is amenable to theory, whether it is continuous, consistent and necessary, or whether it is the product of push-pull dynamics. If we are trying to evaluate enlargement from a comparative politics perspective, the question should examine the contribution of enlargement to the coherence of the polity, its resilience and legitimacy. In this sense, the deepening/widening dichotomy replicates key debates in integration theory: about the relationship between economics and politics, and about the place of the EU institutions relative to the member states.

References

Alesina, A., I. Angeloni and F. Etro. 2001. "The political economy of international unions." *Discussion paper 1939*. Cambridge: Harvard Institute of Economic Research. http://www.economics.harvard.edu/pub/hier/2001/HIER1939.pdf (20 June 2012).

Alesina, A., I. Angeloni and F. Etro. 2005. "International unions." *American Economic Review* 95 (June): 602-15.

Bindi, F. and I. Angelescu. 2011a. *The Frontiers of Europe: A Transatlantic Problem?* Scuola Superiore della Pubblica Amministrazione (SSPA). Washington, DC: Rome and Brookings Institution Press.

Bindi, F. and I. Angelescu. 2011b. "Conclusion: The European Union Should Again Be 'Open for Business'." In *The Frontiers of Europe: A Transatlantic Problem?*, eds. F. Bindi and I. Angelescu. Scuola Superiore della Pubblica Amministrazione (SSPA). Washington, DC: Rome and Brookings Institution Press, 272-80.

Browne, A. 2005. "Eleventh-hour call for EU to halt its talks with Turkey." *Times Online*, 28 June. http://www.armenian.ch/forum/phpBB2/viewarticle.php?t=1466&sid=046403ca538baab56858fce5720fb001 (4 November 2012).

Council of the European Union. 2005. *Enlargement: Turkey. Declaration by the European Community and Its Member States*. Document 1254/05 (Presse 243), 21 September.

European Commission. 1993. "Commission opinion on the application by the Republic of Cyprus for membership." COM (93) 313 final, 30 June. *Bulletin of the European Communities*, Supplement 5/93.

European Commission. 2005a. *Eurobarometer* 63. http://ec.europa.eu/public_opinion/archives/eb/eb63/eb63_en.htm (5 November 2012).

European Commission. 2005b. "The European Constitution: post-referendum survey in France." *Eurobarometer* 171. http://ec.europa.eu/public_opinion/flash/fl171_en.pdf (5 November 2012).

European Commission. 2005c. "The European Constitution: post-referendum survey in The Netherlands." *Eurobarometer* 172. http://ec.europa.eu/public_opinion/flash/fl172_en.pdf (5 November 2012).

European Commission. 2005d. "Declaration of the President of the European Commission, José Manuel Barroso, on the opening of accession negotiations with Turkey." Press Release IP 05/1219. October 3. http://europa.eu/rapid/press-release_IP-05-1219_en.htm (4 November 2012).

European Council. 1993. *Conclusions of the Presidency*. Copenhagen, 21-22 June. SN 180/1/93.

European Council. 1995. *General Affairs Council, Conclusions*. 6 March. Brussels: General Secretariat of the Council.

European Council. 1999. *Presidency Conclusions*. Helsinki, 10-11 December. http://www.europarl.europa.eu/summits/hel1_en.htm (22 November 2012).

European Council. 2001. *Presidency Conclusions*. Brussels, 15 December. Annex 1, SN 300/1/01/REV1.

European Council. 2006. *Presidency Conclusions*. Brussels, 14-15 December. 16879/1/06.

European Parliament. 2005. *Debates*. 6 July. http://europa.eu/rapid/press-release_IP-05-1219_en.htm (4 November 2012).

European Union. 2007. "Treaty of Lisbon amending the Treaty on European Union and the Treaty establishing the European Community, signed at Lisbon, 13 December 2007." *Official Journal of the European Union* C 306 (50).

Gouillaud, P. 2005. "Chirac met en question la poursuite de l'élargissement. Un virage de la politique française." *Le Figaro*, 4.

Hillion, C. 2010. "The creeping nationalisation of the EU's enlargement policy." Report No. 6. Stockholm: Swedish Institute for European Policy Studies.

Hurrell, A. 1995. "Theoretical Approaches to Regionalism." In *Regionalism in World Politics: Regional Organization and International Order*, eds. L. Fawcett and A. Hurrell, 37-73. Oxford and New York: Oxford University Press.

Jacoby, W. 1999. "Priest and penitent: The European Union as a force in the domestic politics of Eastern Europe." *East European Constitutional Review* 8(1-2): 62-7.

Jupille, J., J.A. Caporaso, and J.T. Checkel. 2003. "Integrating institutions: rationalism, constructivism, and the study of the European Union." *Comparative Political Studies* 36(1-2): 7-41.

Katzenstein, P. 1997. *Tamed Power: Germany in Europe*. Ithaca and London: Cornell University Press.

Moravscik, A. 1997. "Taking preferences seriously: A liberal theory of international politics." *International Organization* 51(4), 513-53.

Moravscik, A. 1998. *The Choice for Europe: Social Purpose and State Power from Messina to Maastricht*. Ithaca, NY: Cornell University Press.

Moravcsik, A. and M.A. Vachudova. 2002. "National interests, state power, and EU enlargement." http://www.princeton.edu/~amoravcs/library/vachudova.pdf (1 November 2012).

Nugent, N. 2006. *The Government and Politics of the European Union*. Basingstoke: Palgrave.

Olmi, G. 1978. "Aspects institutionnels et juridiques de l'élargissement. L'impact sur les institutions et le droit des Communautés européennes." In *A Community of Twelve? The Impact of Further Enlargement on the European Communities*, eds. W. Wallace and I. Herreman. Bruges: De Tempel, Tempelhof.

Parsons, C. 2003. *A Certain Idea of Europe*. Ithaca: Cornell University Press.

Preston, C. 1997. *Enlargement and Integration in the European Union*. London: Rout ledge.

Rosamond, B. 2000. *Theories of European Integration*. New York: St. Martin's Press.

Sandler, T. and K. Hartley. 1999. *The Political Economy of NATO: Past, Present, and into the 21st Century*. Cambridge: Cambridge University Press.

Schimmelfennig, F. and U. Sedelmeier. 2002. "Theorizing EU enlargement: research focus, hypotheses, and the state of research." *Journal of European Public Policy* 9(4), 500-28.

Schmitter, P. 1969. "Three neofunctional hypotheses about international integration." *International Organization* 23, 161-66.

Schneider, C. 2009. *Conflict, Negotiation and European Union Enlargement*. New York: Cambridge University Press.

Stefanova, B. 2006. "The 'No' vote in the French and Dutch referenda on the EU Constitution: a spillover of consequences for the wider Europe." *PS: Political Science and Politics* XXXIX: 2 (April), 251-55.

Stefanova, B. 2011. *The Europeanization of Conflict Resolution: Integration and Conflicts in Europe from the 1950s to the 21st Century*. Manchester: Manchester University Press.

List of Contributors

Irina Angelescu is a Research Fellow with the European Center of Excellence of the University of Rome Tor Vergata, a Consultant with the Center on the United States and Europe (CUSE) of the Brookings Institutions in Washington, DC and a PhD Candidate in International History and Politics at the Graduate Institute of Geneva. She has published articles and chapters in edited volumes on European policies of migration, European foreign policy, EU enlargement and neighborhood policies and Romanian contemporary history and politics. Her books include two co-edited volumes with Federiga Bindi, *The Foreign Policy of the European Union: Assessing Europe's Role in the World* (second updated edition; Washington, DC: Brookings Institution Press, 2012) and *The Frontiers of Europe: A Transatlantic Problem?* (Washington, DC: Brookings Institution Press, 2011), as well as a co-edited volume with Sergiu Gherghina and Paul Flather entitled *Facets of Migration in Contemporary Europe: Interdisciplinary Approaches to Specific Challenges* (Stuttgart: Ibidem-Verlag 2010).

Federiga Bindi is a tenured Professor at the University of Rome Tor Vergata, where she also serves as the Director and Jean Monnet Professor at the European Center of Excellence, and a Senior Fellow at the Center for Transatlantic Relations at the School of Advanced International Studies (SAIS)-Johns Hopkins University in Washington, DC. Federiga Bindi is currently on academic leave to serve as the Director of the Italian Cultural Institute in Brussels. She holds a PhD from the European University Institute (EUI) in Florence. She has published extensively on Italian foreign policy, European affairs, lobbying in the European Union and transatlantic affairs. Her most recent publications include *The Foreign Policy of the European Union: Assessing Europe's Role in the World* (co-edited, with Irina Angelescu; second updated edition; Washington, DC: Brookings Institution Press, 2012); *Analyzing European Politics* (co-edited, with Kjell Eliassen; Bologna: Il Mulino, 2012); *Italy and the European Union* (Washington, DC: Brookings Institution Press, 2011) and *The Frontiers of Europe: A Transatlantic Problem?* (co-edited, with Irina Angelescu; Washington, DC: Brookings Institution Press, 2010).

Faton Tony Bislimi was born and raised in Kosovo and educated in the United States and Canada. He holds an MA in Political Science from Dalhousie University (2010), a MS in International Development and Public Administration from the Kennedy School of Government, Harvard University (2007), and honors BS and BA in Computer Science and Mathematics, respectively, from Texas Lutheran University (2005). He is a PhD student in Political Science at Dalhousie University and a Doctoral Fellow at the EU Centre of Excellence and the Centre for Foreign Policy Studies. His research interests focus on state-building, international intervention, and international development and his area of expertise is the Balkans and especially Kosovo. He has held positions with RTI International, OSCE, and UNDP, and has taught at a couple of universities in Kosovo. He is the founder and president of the Bislimi Group Foundation, a non-profit educational organization based in Prishtina. He also serves as Senior Fellow and Managing Director of the Kosovo Public Policy Center. While at Dalhousie, he has been teaching undergraduate courses in economics both at Dalhousie University and Mount Saint Vincent University.

Shirley Cloyes DioGuardi has served since 1995 as Balkan Affairs Adviser to the Albanian American Civic League, the only registered volunteer lobby in Washington, DC, representing the concerns and interests of the Albanian people. An independent scholar and human rights activist, Cloyes DioGuardi has lectured widely and written more than 75 articles about the Balkan conflict. She is a contributor to *The EU, Security and Transatlantic Relations* (P.I.E. Peter Lang, 2012). She has made more than thirty trips to Southeast Europe, including fifteen to Kosova since the end of the war in 1999. She has assisted foreign policy leaders in the US Congress in preparing legislation on the Balkans. On five occasions, she has testified before the House Committee on Foreign Affairs about the role of US foreign policy in bringing lasting peace and stability to the Balkans.

Graeme Crouch is a PhD Student at the Department of Political Science, University of Victoria. He completed his B.A. in History Education at Eastern Kentucky University. After teaching secondary education for two years he obtained his M.A. from the University of Victoria, where he is currently working on his PhD under the supervision of Dr. Amy Verdun. His research interests include interest intermediation, Europeanization, multilevel governance, EU enlargement, public opinion, and public policy.

Svet Derderyan is a PhD candidate at the University of North Carolina at Chapel Hill. He graduated Summa Cum Laude and Phi Beta Kappa from Hamilton College in New York with degrees in Economics and International Relations in 2006. Prior to joining UNC in 2008, he worked as an Investment Banking Analyst at Merrill Lynch in New York and as a Legislative Assistant at the US Senate Finance Committee. Currently working on his dissertation focusing on political corruption, he is also co-authoring a book with Prof. Gary Marks and Prof. Liesbet Hooghe on the authority and change of 72 international organizations since the 1950s. His research interests lay in the fields of political corruption, democratization, multi-level governance, Europeanization and post-communist studies.

Gentian Elezi is a PhD Candidate in Politics and European Studies, at the University of Sussex, UK. He also holds a Masters Degree in European Politics from this University. He was awarded his degree in Political Science/Economics in 2005 from the University of Milan, Italy. His current research focuses on the relation between democratization, policy implementation and institutional change in post-communist countries. His doctoral thesis is about the influence of the EU in policy implementation and institutional building process in Albania. His previous research interests and publications were focused on post-communist democratization and rule of law, EU enlargement, political and economic reform, Southeast European politics and specific areas of institutional reform.

Eli Gateva a member of the Centre for Comparative Politics at the University of Manchester. She holds an MA and PhD from the University of Manchester. She has published articles on the evolution of EU enlargement policy and the effectiveness of the EU's post-accession conditionality towards Bulgaria and Romania. Her main research interests cover EU Enlargement policy, Europeanisation, transition and regional development in Central and South-Eastern Europe.

Seçkin Bariş Gülmez is a PhD candidate and teaching assistant at Royal Holloway University of London. He holds a BSc and MSc degrees at Middle East Technical University, Ankara, Turkey. His research focuses on EU enlargement, accession countries, political parties and euroscepticism. He published on euroscepticism of Turkish political parties in *Turkish Studies* and *Acta Politica.*

Tanel Kerikmäe is a Jean Monnet professor in European Law and Director of Tallinn Law School at Tallinn University of Technology, Estonia. Dr Kerikmäe, is a an author of numerous articles and publications published by Ashgate, Martinus Nijhoff, Kluwer, Cambridge University Press, Springer, Lexis Nexis, EJLR, etc. He has been active as an expert for public and private institutions, international organizations e.g. working as EU expert in Central Asia as a head of the component of constitutional law. Prof. Kerikmäe has been teaching and supervising at several universities (as permanent and ad hoc instructor and Erasmus exchange professor) e.g. in the United Kingdom, Latvia, Switzerland and Kyrgyzstan.

Finn Laursen, PhD from the University of Pennsylvania (1980), currently Canada Research Chair in EU Studies at Dalhousie University, Halifax. He also holds an *ad personam* Jean Monnet Chair. Previously he has been a professor at the European Institute of Public Administration (EIPA), Maastricht, 1988-1995, and Professor of International Politics at the University of Southern Denmark, Odense, 1999-2006. Recent edited books include: *Comparative Regional Integration* (Ashgate, 2010), *The EU and Federalism* (Ashgate, 2011), *The Making of the Lisbon Treaty* (P.I.E. Peter Lang, 2012), *The EU's Lisbon Treaty: Institutional Choices and Implementation* (Ashgate, 2012), and *The EU, Security and Transatlantic Relations* (P.I.E. Peter Lang, 2012).

Heather A. D. Mbaye is an Associate Professor of Political Science and Planning, Research interests include policy implementation in the European Union, regional activities and offices in Brussels, and European political parties. Published works have appeared in *The American Sociological Review*, *European Union Politics*, and *Regional and Federal Studies*, among others. Dr. Mbaye is also interested in research on best practices in teaching the European Union and is an active member of the Georgia Political Science Association and the European Union Studies Association. She is currently the Director of the European Union Studies Program of the University System of Georgia and Associate Dean of the College of Social Sciences.

Marko Milenković is a junior research fellow at the Institute of Social sciences in Belgrade. He has graduated from the University of Belgrade and obtained LLM degree from the University of Cambridge. Mr. Milenković is pursuing a PhD at the University of Belgrade where he teaches seminars in Environmental and Spatial Planning Law. He has published articles in the field of Administrative Law, Environmental Law, process of European integration, European Union Law and Economic Law.

Milos Milenković is an Associate professor at the University of Belgrade, Faculty of Philosophy where he has served as a Vice Dean for Academic affairs (2009-2012). He teaches history, theory and methodology courses at the Department of Ethnology and Anthropology. Dr Milenković published five books and articles on anthropology, history of ideas, and philosophy of social science. During the last years his research has focused on authority of science in social policy and social ontology of legal discourses. He is currently leading two research projects: "Identity politics of EU: Customization and application in the Republic of Serbia" and "Social sciences and humanities as intangible cultural heritage and public good".

Nanette Neuwahl holds a bachelor's and master's degrees in public law and administration from the University of Leiden and a PhD in Law of the European University Institute. She is a Jean Monnet Professor of European Law and member of the Centre de Recherche en droit public at the Faculty of law of the University of Montreal. She is also a regular visiting professor at the faculty of law of Yeditepe University in Istanbul. She has published widely on subjects such as EU constitutional law, EU enlargement, and EU external relations law. Together with Joerg Monar she is co-director of the *European Foreign Affairs Review*.

Demetrios Nicolaides is an alumnus of the University of Calgary where he received his Bachelor of Arts in International Relations and Military/Diplomatic History. He was then accepted to study Peace & Conflict Studies at the European University Centre for Peace Studies in Austria and enjoyed the honour and privilege of studying with internationally known academics such as Johan Galtung, Jan Oberg, James Calleja and Hossain Danesh. His MA thesis focused on the application of conflict transformation theory with regard to the Cyprus Problem. He is also founder of the Forum for Youth Advocacy (FOYA) Cyprus and is working through the organization to create an online introduction to Peace Studies course and fund a Peace Scholarship for Cypriot students. Apart from his work with FOYA Cyprus, Demetrios is currently a PhD Candidate at the University of Cyprus. His PhD research will focus on the role of Peace Education in creating unity-based worldviews and their effectiveness in ethno-nationalist conflicts such as Cyprus. Other areas of research interest include EU Integration, Nonviolence, Conflict Transformation the Cyprus issue and reconciliation.

Lehte Roots is Head of the Chair of Public Law in Tallinn Law School, Tallinn University of Technology. She obtained her PhD in law at the European University Institute in Florence where she also worked as a researcher for the EUCITAC project at the Robert Schuman Centre for Advanced Studies. She has published articles about the changes of EU law after Lisbon, (The Impact of the Lisbon Treaty on the Development of EU Immigration Legislation, CYELP, Vol. 5. 2009), also articles about citizenship and rights of third country nationals (European Union Citizenship or Status of Long Term Resident: A Dilemma for Third Country Nationals in Estonia, BJES. Vol. 2, No. 1 (11)). She has worked as project manager, researcher and country expert in various projects funded by the EU Commission and EU Parliament. She is also acting Estonian expert for the European Citizens Action Service and ICMPD. Vice president of ECSA Estonia. Her research interests include EU law, migration law, citizenship, enlargement, equality law and sustainable development.

Alan Siaroff is Professor of Political Science at the University of Lethbridge, Alberta, Canada. He is the author of *Comparative European Party Systems: An Analysis of Parliamentary Elections Since 1945*

(2000) and *Comparing Political Regimes: A Thematic Introduction to Comparative Politics* (third edition forthcoming 2013), as well as articles and book chapters on democratization, political institutions, party politics, electoral systems, women's representation, and voter turnout in various European and North American journals.

Boyka Stefanova is an associate professor in the Department of Political Science and Geography at the University of Texas, San Antonio. She holds a Doctorate in Economics from the University of National and World Economy, Sofia (Bulgaria) and a PhD in Political Science from the University of Delaware (USA). Her teaching and research specialization is in European Union studies and regional perspectives on European security. Her published work covers the evolution of European integration and processes of institutional expansion, as well as the democratization of Eastern Europe through the politics and membership in regional institutions. She has published two books: *The Europeanization of Conflict Resolution: Integration and Conflicts in Europe from the 1950s to the 21st Century* (Manchester University Press, 2011) and *The War on Terror in Comparative Perspective: US National Security and Foreign Policy after 9/11* (Palgrave Macmillan, 2007). Her recent publications include also articles on the European security institutions and electoral politics in Eastern Europe.

Marko Stojic is a doctorate candidate and an associate tutor at the Sussex European Institute, University of Sussex. He has a BA in International Relations from the Faculty of Political Science, University of Belgrade, and an MA in International Relations and European Studies from the Central European University. His research interests focus on the study of political parties and party systems in the Western Balkans, and include the domestic politics of European integration, the attitudes of political parties towards the EU and party-based Euroscepticicm in former Yugoslavia.

Index

'Multiple Europes'

The series 'Multiple Europes' is multiple in two ways: it understands Europe in an interdisciplinary manner with a strong historical perspective, and it understands Europe as being inserted in transnational and global contexts. On both levels, the perspectives on Europe and the very role and understanding of Europe is multiple. The special emphasis of the series thus lies in understanding the pasts of Europe as well as its complex present.

The history of Europe and the history of European integration have influenced each other in the past and will continue to do so in the future. There is an inbuilt tension in the relation between European history and the history of European integration. Europe signifies a space and semantics much broader and more complex than the EU. The relations between ideas of Europe, European history, global history and European integration need to be faced more openly. In order to do this, an open dialogue between academic disciplines is just as necessary as critical self-reflection within each discipline. Furthermore, European history was preoccupied with looking at itself and needs to be connected to global relations.

Series Editor: **Hagen Schulz-Forberg**,
Associate Professor for Global and European History

Series Titles

EU Enlargement. Current Challenges and Strategic Choices, Finn LAURSEN (ed.), No.50, 2013

Cosmopolitanisms in Enlightenment Europe and Beyond, Mónica GARCÍA-SALMONES & Pamela SLOTTE (eds.), No.49, 2013

The European Public Sphere. From Critical Thinking to Responsible Action, Luciano MORGANTI & Léonce BEKEMANS (eds.), No.48, 2012

Intercultural Dialogue and Multi-level Governance in Europe. A Human Rights Based Approach, Léonce BEKEMANS (ed.), No.47, 2012

Imagining Europe as a Global Player. The Ideological Construction of a New European Identity within the EU, Christoffer KØLVRAA, No.46, 2012

Capital City Cultures. Reconstructing Contemporary Europe in Vienna and Berlin, Monika DE FRANTZ, No.45, 2011

Building a European Public Sphere. From the 1950s to the Present / Un espace public européen en construction. Des années 1950 à nos jours, Robert FRANK, Hartmut KAELBLE, Marie-Françoise LÉVY & Luisa PASSERINI (eds./dir.), No.44, 2010

'We belong to them'. Narratives of Belonging, Homeland and Nationhood in Territorial and Non-territorial Minority Settings, Tünde PUSKÁS, No.43, 2008

Imagining Europe. Europe and European Civilisation as Seen from its Margins and by the Rest of the World, in the Nineteenth and Twentieth Centuries, Michael WINTLE (ed.), No.42, 2008

Figures of Authority. Contributions towards a Cultural History of Governance from the Seventeenth to the Twentieth Century, Peter BECKER & Rüdiger VON KROSIGK (eds.), No.41, 2008

Europe and the Historical Legacies in the Balkans, Raymond DETREZ & Barbara SEGAERT (eds.), No.40, 2008

Histoire économique et sociale de la construction européenne, René LEBOUTTE, n° 39, 2008

Collective Traumas. Memories of War and Conflict in 20th-Century Europe, Conny MITHANDER, John SUNDHOLM & Maria HOLMGREN TROY (eds.), No.38, 2007

Reflections on Europe. Defining a Political Order in Time and Space, Hans-Åke PERSSON & Bo STRÅTH (eds.), No.37, 2007

London – Berlin. Authenticity, Modernity, and the Metropolis in Urban Travel Writing from 1851 to 1939, Hagen SCHULZ-FORBERG, No.36, 2006

(Un)Doing Europe. Discourses and Practices of Negotiating the EU Constitution, Michał KRZYŻANOWSKI & Florian OBERHUBER, No.35, 2007

Developing Cultural Identity in the Balkans. Convergence vs. Divergence, Raymond DETREZ & Pieter PLAS (eds.), No.34, 2005

Statehood Before and Beyond Ethnicity. Minor States in Northern and Eastern Europe, 1600-2000, Linas ERIKSONAS & Leos MÜLLER (eds.), No.33, 2005

Berlin en musée. Changements sociopolitiques et usages du patrimoine, Véronique CHARLÉTY, n° 32, 2005

Democratisation in Turkey. The Role of Political Parties, Huri TÜRSAN, No.31, 2004

Unravelling Civilisation. European Travel and Travel Writing, Hagen SCHULZ-FORBERG, No.30, 2005

Nation States and Minority Rights. A Constitutional Law Analysis (provisional title), Christina JOHNSSON, No.29, forthcoming

Living Boundaries. Frontiers and Identity in the Basque Country, Zoe BRAY, No.28, 2004